MW01244348

the Spiritual Discernment Guide

How to Detect and Correct False Teachings,
Scripture Twisting, and New Age Counterfeits

Ronald T. Tyler, Ph.D.

A Division of WINEPRESS PUBLISHING

ISBN 1-4141-0127-9
Library of Congress Catalog Card Number: 2004100726

Dedication

To my wife, Virginia, for her steadfast love, incredible patience, continuous support, wise counsel, and amazing postponement of an enormous honey-do list.

Table of Contents

Part III: Discerning Deception in the Church—The New Age Invasion 221

Appendices 555

Now the serpent was more crafty than any of the wild animals the Lord God had made. He said to the woman, "Did God really say, 'You must not eat from any tree in the Garden'?"

The woman said to the serpent, "We may eat fruit from the trees in the garden, but God did say, 'You must not eat fruit from the tree that is in the middle of the garden, and you must not touch it, or you will die.'"

"You will not surely die," the serpent said to the woman. "For God knows that when you eat of it your eyes will be opened, and you will be like God, knowing good and evil" (Genesis 3:1–5).

Preface

For ten years (1963 to 1973), I was a member of a cult called the Gurdjieff Foundation. They taught and practiced a mixture of Hinduism, Buddhism, Sufism, Theosophy, Gnosticism, and what they called "esoteric Christianity." Prior to that, I had been involved in transcendentalism, Christian Science, Rosicrucianism, astrology, numerology, the use of a Ouija board, and a variety of New Age-type activities—before anybody had even heard of the New Age Movement. I had out-of-body experiences, "past life" visions, "cosmic" vibrations, and moments of extra-sensory perception—all of which were spiritual dead-ends.

I even tried "Christianity"—a deeply disappointing experience in a very liberal, humanistic church which spent more time talking about current trends in psychology and the poetry of T.S. Eliot than about the Bible. When I asked about spiritual matters, such as how Jesus' death on the cross could pay for my sins, they looked at me as though I were weird. So I gave up on "Christianity" because it obviously (it seemed) didn't have what I was looking for.

When I finally did come to the Lord, through a series of miraculous interventions, it was at the height of the "Charismatic Renewal," in which I was given direct experience of the power of the Holy Spirit (something I had never heard of before). And my life and my self were radically changed for the better.

Shortly thereafter and totally unexpectedly, I got a teaching job at a Bible college which was in reality a "Christian" cult. It was founded by a woman who controlled everything and everyone in her church/ college and who was worshipped more than Jesus by her followers.

Later, I attended a charismatic church with many cult-like characteristics, such as a leader who was accountable to nobody, had a direct pipeline to God, considered himself an "apostle" and "the anointed of the Lord," and demanded absolute loyalty from his "followers." I also attended a fellowship which was part of the Word of Faith Movement, also known as the Name-It-and-Claim-It or Positive Confession school. They believed that no Christian should ever suffer or have adversity and, if you did, it was because your faith was not strong enough or your "confession" was wrong.

I am now a member of a solid, biblically based evangelical church which is steadily and responsibly seeking the power and guidance of the Holy Spirit.

In the following chapters, I will go into more detail about many of these things as they pertain to spiritual deception and discernment.

Why did God allow me to experience all these ungodly things—eastern religions, false doctrines, cults, occultism, New Age philosophy, etc.? For two reasons, I believe: (1) I was searching on my own, according to my self-will, for meaning and purpose and I needed to come to the end of myself and my own ideas about truth, and (2) God, for reasons I do not understand, wanted to use me to help warn His church about the dangers of demonic deception and Satan's strategies for luring Christians away from their faith and into apostasy. In other words, all this spiritual wandering along wrong paths was for a purpose. God used these experiences with the deceitful ways of Satan to prepare me so I could tell the body of Christ about the reality of such things and what to do about them.

In addition, I believe God has enabled me to acquire specialized knowledge and skills for this task—gained during my career as a teacher of English literature, language, and composition. I believe this background has enabled me to recognize and point out Satan's deceptive use of language—especially in the areas of semantics and logical reasoning. These are, I believe, the primary weapons in his campaign to confuse, divide, and lead astray the church.

He also prepared me to help counteract a growing divisiveness within the church. By polarizing Christians over "charismatic Christianity," Satan is, I believe, successfully splitting large segments of the church between charismatics and non-charismatics. By deceiving many non-charismatic evangelicals into rejecting—as of the devil—everything associated with the charismatic movement (such as the supernatural gifts of the Spirit), Satan is robbing the church of much of its potential power at the very time when it needs it most. In other words, he is causing them *to throw out the baby with the bathwater,* not discerning the difference between genuine manifestations of Holy Spirit power and counterfeit ones. And, by convincing a large number of charismatic Christians to accept any kind of bizarre, self-indulgent, and unscriptural manifestation of the "Spirit" as from God, Satan is effectively injecting his own perverted brand of supernaturalism and spiritual deception into the church. In other words, he is causing them *to swallow everything whole,* without discerning what is truly of God and what is not.

This book, then, is the result of a lifetime of preparation, mostly without my being aware of it. Its basic thesis is that most Christians (both those who are new and those who are more mature in the faith) are largely naive and uninformed regarding how Satan operates in his campaign to draw them away from God, the Bible, and true faith; that they need discernment to be able to recognize how Satan is infiltrating the church for these purposes; and that they need to know how to defend themselves against such deception.

But most importantly, they need to know the fullness we have in Christ, that we don't need any of the "helps" Satan offers in such appealing and seemingly innocent forms—such as "angelic" guides, self-enhancing meditation and psychological teachings, "creative" visualization, "new" extra-biblical revelation, and special mental techniques for developing spiritual power. In essence, what the church needs to know—and practice—is that the Father, the Son, the Holy Spirit, and the Bible are truly sufficient for all our spiritual needs.

The ideas and conclusions presented in the following pages are based not only on my personal experience but also on many years of Bible study, research, and prayer. A number of them are controversial. I know there will be those who disagree with at least some of what I have written. (My wife tells me that I have included so many red flags that there is bound to be something to offend everybody!) All I ask is that you consider what is said and take it for what it is worth (or, as my friend Walt would say, read it the way you eat fried chicken: chew the meat and spit out the bones). The Lord didn't say we had to agree on everything. But He did say we *must* love one another—unconditionally. I have written this book because I love you—as my fellow Christian and member of the body of Christ—because I want what is best for you, and because I believe the Lord has directed me to do so.

For reasons only He understands, I believe God has brought me to the place where I can, in some measure, help the church understand and apply the principles of spiritual discernment. That is the purpose of this book, and it is my prayer for all who read it.

Acknowledgments

I wish to thank the following people for generously reading all or part of the manuscript and giving me much-needed encouragement, honest commentary, and helpful feedback: Tim Brock, Glenn Elliott, Laverne Foltz, Sandy Horton, Judie Patterson, Dee Ruelas, Walt Tatham, Virginia Tyler, and Chet Weld.

Scripture References

Scriptural quotations are from the New International Version (NIV) unless otherwise noted. KJV indicates the King James Version.

Author's Note

In this book, many specific examples of false teachings are given to illustrate Satan's strategies and techniques of deception. This has been done partly as a warning to help Christians avoid the harmful influence of such teachings. Therefore, many of the particular teachers involved have been identified by name. However, this does not mean that the entire ministries of these teachers are being condemned or considered invalid. I believe all of them have beneficial aspects which are scripturally sound. Their redeeming qualities and spiritual fruitfulness should not be overlooked. People are helped through all of them and saved, healed, delivered, and/or discipled through many of them. Thus, although the focus of this book is on false teachings and their dangers, the baby should not be thrown out with the bathwater.

Also, in this book, I have given many examples from my own personal experience of spiritual deception and faulty discernment. I have done this, not to set myself up as a judge over others. (Indeed, many of the examples involve my own undiscerning vulnerability.) But I have included them because the Lord has enabled me, I believe, to observe and identify them in order to show very clearly how *real* people—like you and me—can be deluded by *real* demonic deception.

The Threat of Spiritual Deception

A TRAGIC DELUSION

There was an eerie quietness in the isolated compound. Even the jungle birds and other tree dwellers were subdued. By all appearances, it was a typical October day in equatorial South America—hot, humid, listless.

Nearly a thousand searching, deluded souls had gathered, crowding the vegetable gardens and central pavilion. All felt a nervous excitement—and kept a taut control. Mothers, fathers, children, grandparents, and single adults stood obediently in line—as they had been trained to do. Each was given a styrofoam cup half-filled with strawberry Kool-Aid and laced with cyanide.

On this bright, sunny afternoon in 1978, surrounded by lush tropical beauty, nine hundred and

fourteen "Christian" followers of Jim Jones committed suicide in Guyana. According to Walter Martin,
who is perhaps the foremost authority on cults and
spiritual deception in our time, the Jonestown mas-
sacre was a "tragedy of cultic deception and
murder . . . traced unerringly to the New Age doctrines of man's divinity and the relativistic world view
of the New Age Cult."[1]

How could, Jones, at one time an apparently
dedicated, fundamentally sound minister of the gospel in the Methodist church and later in the Disciples of Christ denomination, have become so
confused and deviant in his doctrine and practice?
To understand how this could have happened, we
need to go back to the early influence of a man whom
Jones admired and imitated: George Baker, more
commonly known as Father Divine.

Baker, the son of a former slave, declared himself to be God and "believed quite literally in 1
Corinthians 3:16, which refers to believers as the
'temple of God'; so he reasoned that since God dwelt
in him, he *was* God and entitled to divine authority.
Baker became known as 'the messenger,' bearing the
exalted title 'God and the Sonship Degree.'"[2]

Baker's reasoning illustrates the kind of faulty
logic and semantic leaps involved in the misuse of
scripture that characterize the thinking of people
who are deluded by deceiving spirits. In this case,
Baker failed to make a distinction between being
indwelt by God and *being* God. In terms of formal
logic, this is a non sequitur, a phrase meaning "it

does not follow because there is no logical connection." Here, it is equating two completely different things simply because they happen to share a common element, the word "God." It is the logical equivalent of saying: This glass is *filled with* water; therefore, this glass *is* water. In semantic terms, this is also an example of redefinition ("indwelt" = "being").

Baker also believed that he was the reincarnation of Jesus Christ, "the Holy Ghost personified," and God the Father, all rolled into one. His mission, he said, was to free people from the effects of racial prejudice and from "living in poverty, debauchery, lacks, wants and limitations."[3]

Baker pursued these goals with notable success in his "Peace Mission Movement," which Jones greatly admired, with good reason, because of its positive humanitarian effects. At the same time, unfortunately, Baker set forth this unbiblical and obviously demonically inspired goal: to "lift humanity from all superstition and cause them to forget all about the imaginary God I am now eradicating and dispelling from the consciousness of the people." The "imaginary God" he was referring to was the one, true God of the Bible.[4]

In these statements, Baker not only espouses the unscriptural doctrine of reincarnation but also directly attacks the God of the Bible and sets himself up as God, committing the ultimate sin of pride—to attempt to "be like God," which caused Satan to be expelled from heaven and Adam and Eve to fall from innocence in the Garden of Eden (Genesis 3:5).

The sources of Baker's teachings were found in the Unity School of Christianity, a pre-New Age mind-sciences cult which "was heavily influenced by Hinduism and Theosophy [a mystical religious/philosophical system combining elements from spiritism and eastern religions], teaching the New Age concept that man is essentially deity and needs only to recognize that fact in order to be freed from the limitations of this existence. 'Father Divine' believed and taught the same thing, combining this with a genuine effort to feed, clothe, and shelter people during the Great Depression of the 1930s."[5]

Jones was not only greatly influenced by Baker's ideas and example, but he was also strongly attracted by the communal lifestyle of the movement, taking bus loads of his people to observe it in action.[6]

Thereafter, Jones copied the methods he had observed:

> Eyewitness accounts tell of how Jones would begin by quoting from the Bible in his hand. Later, as he shifted emphasis from the Bible to himself as the messenger of God, he would throw the Bible on the ground and kick it because he considered his authority as the representative of deity to be superior to the written Word of God. . . . Jones would use pseudo-Pentecostal fervor, expressions, and illustrations to inflame his audience until . . . he became God's substitute to them.[7]

Jones, like Baker, then, under the influence of false doctrines and satanic deception, set himself up as an authority higher than the Word of God and, in his delusion of godhood, led his equally deluded followers into mass suicide.

THE ROOT OF SPIRITUAL DECEPTION—THE SERPENT'S LIE

This desire to be like God (or to be one's own god) was the original sin of Satan and of Adam and Eve. When Satan led the rebellion against God in heaven, he said, "I will make myself like the Most High" (Isaiah 14:14). And when he tempted Eve, he said, ". . . you will be like God" (Genesis:3:5). This same sin of spiritual pride—to exalt oneself to the level of deity—is at the root of all spiritual deception and rebellion against God.

Jones was not an isolated case—although he was a highly visible and dramatic one. Much less obviously, this same deception is present in the church today, taking on a wide variety of subtle forms, but in essence boiling down to "doing your own thing" spiritually. In every case, these are self-directed activities which are contrary to God's Word and are, in fact, substitutes for reliance on God as the all-sufficient, almighty provider who meets our needs, answers our questions, and enables us to solve our problems.

David Wilkerson explains how materialism has become such a substitute for many Christians:

> . . . that is the sin of covetousness. It is a damning sin. A love for the things of this world and

> lust for more and better material possessions has enslaved the hearts of many Christians. People can't seem to get enough and their debt is piling up. They think our nation's prosperity will never end. Americans have gone mad with acquisitiveness.[8]

He cites examples of churches which have blatantly "compromised the true gospel of Christ" by doing their own thing: "Divorce is rampant in their congregations. And many of their young singles lead permissive, sexually active lives."[9]

I can personally attest to the truth of this in my own church and even my own family—as you probably can, as well.

A less obvious example of the church doing its own thing can be found in the church growth movement. "I'm amazed and perplexed," says Wilkerson,

> by the scores of ministers, both young and old, who run all over the world looking for strategies to produce growth in their churches. Today, many preachers attend seminars, conventions and "think tanks," where young ministry professionals use charts and polls to show them how to build larger churches. Other ministers flock to "revivals," hoping to learn new methods of how to have the Holy Ghost fall on their congregations.[10]

However, what is needed are churches with "a testimony of intimacy with Christ and a holy walk." In one such church where the focus is on actually living the gospel, "the Spirit of God is moving mightily . . . People are flocking to the Lord, getting their lives straightened—because they're hearing a gospel with a testimony behind it!"[10]

A LACK OF SPIRITUAL FULFILLMENT

All such cases of running after substitutes for God, His power, and His Word are happening partly because the church is failing to provide the spiritual fulfillment that people need. As Dave Hunt and T. A. McMahon, two other well-known defenders of the faith, put it,

> The question is why it should be necessary to develop and pursue techniques for making Christianity "work" that were unknown to earlier generations of victorious Christians and are not found in the Bible. It is obvious that there would be no takers for these methods unless multitudes of Christians were failing to find the joy and fulfillment they seek. This can only mean that Christianity is deficient and needs outside help, or else that biblical Christianity is not being taught and lived in many of our churches.[11]

Because of this failure to provide seekers with the reality of a loving, holy God and His power to change their lives for the better, many novice Christians and would-be Christians are turning to New Age philosophy because it presents a convincing illusion of providing what they are looking for. In many cases, their withdrawal from the church has resulted from guilt trips laid on them by misguided ministers preaching a gospel which lacks forgiveness and genuine caring.

Where such an extremely negative spirit has not driven them away, others in the church are finding an absence of positive change in their lives that leaves them feeling they are without control, empowerment, success, prosperity, happiness, or satisfaction—all of which the New Age Movement purports to supply.

Often there is also an undefined sense that meaningful spirituality is lacking—that they don't really know God, are not getting fed on the Word of God, and are therefore being spiritually starved. This was my experience, when, as a young seeker, I tried "Christianity," and I, like many today, was forced to turn elsewhere to try to find what I was seeking—since obviously (it seemed) it could not be found in the church.

The growing popularity of a New Age teaching based on the book, *A Course in Miracles*, is a case in point. In the 1970s, this book came into the world through a channeller (i.e., medium) named Helen Schucman, who claimed Jesus was the spirit entity who dictated it to her.

This course is described by one of its teachers, a young man raised in the Catholic church but driven away by the guilt placed on him by the nuns who were his teachers:

The Course in Miracles is about the experience of love. We are here to tell you how to be free of guilt and practice forgiveness. . . . That Adam and Eve ate of the tree of guilt is insane. The God of the Old Testament is completely insane. Guilt is bred into us, but the Course in Miracles is a radically new thought system that says everything we have been taught was wrong. . . . God didn't make the world, and God didn't make your body, but He can use your body. We are a part of the world we made, and we can change that world . . . In the new priesthood, we are all ministers. Coffee shops are the new confessionals . . . we're all forgiving each other . . . The purpose of the Course in Miracles . . . is to know that it is God's will to make you happy.[12]

Almost all the people who attend the Course in Miracles belonged to a church at one time, but they became sick of the guilt trip or lack of caring.[13] David Jeremiah sums up the situation well:

As secularism invades our churches, the sovereign God of the Bible has been dethroned and replaced by self-directed religion, do-it-yourself rituals, and morality based on feelings. The people attending A Course in Miracles are like many who are spiritually hungry and seeking to find the power that only Jesus can [supply] . . . when He said, 'I have come that they may have life and that they may have it more abundantly' (John 10:10).[14]

DECEPTION AMONG THE DEVOUT

Such deception and drift into false doctrine is not limited to extreme cases like that of Jim Jones, who established his own cultic version of Christianity, or like those who study *A Course in Miracles* and have renounced the church entirely. Those who are more mature in the faith may imagine they are immune, but no one is "bulletproof" when it comes to deception. In fact, there are many supposedly devout, solid Christians who have unknowingly bought into various forms of occultism, demonic deception, and eastern religion, including unscriptural visions of and communications with "angels" (i.e., demons), shamanistic visualization, animism, pantheism, and reincarnation.

Here are some examples I have personally encountered. (These and other persons from my personal experience are real, but their names are fictitious.)

- A local pastor, Rev. Smith, was excited by his participation in the so-called "Toronto Blessing," which took place at the Vineyard Fellowship of Toronto, Canada, from 1994 to 1996. In these meetings, supposed manifestations of the Holy Spirit produced extremely bizarre behavior and dramatic "spiritual" experiences among those attending its "charismatic" services. Rev. Smith shared some of these phenomena with our prayer group. He said he and others saw angels of light flying about above the heads of the worshippers, pouring out the Holy Spirit in sparkling streams from large golden jars. When this "spirit" substance fell upon the people, they burst forth in "holy laughter," various animal sounds (barking, roaring, crowing, etc.), and grotesque physical movements (writhing, jerking, rolling, bowing, etc.).

This would certainly have been an impressive sight, but, unfortunately, his interpretation of it was totally unscriptural.

First, the Holy Spirit is not some kind of liquid that can be divided up in jars and poured out on people. He is a person. In fact, He is God—one of three members of the Trinity.

Second, the Holy Spirit is not something angels carry around and dispense to believers as they see fit. This is getting it backwards. The Holy Spirit is God, and God is not used by angels. Angels are used by God!

Third, the purpose of the manifestations of the Holy Spirit is not to cause people to behave in bizarre ways—no matter how "ecstatic" the accompanying sensations may be. Rather, it is to strengthen, encourage, comfort, and edify the members of the body of Christ—the church—for their common good. (See 1 Corinthians 12:7; 14:3–4, 36.) So, if this is not what angels do, then who were these shining beings who were apparently using the "Holy Spirit" in this exciting way? Obviously, they were masquerading demons intent on deceiving those in the "Toronto Blessing," not only about their supposed identity as angels but also about the nature and purpose of the Holy Spirit. And what was this sparkling liquid they were using to counterfeit the Holy Spirit? Perhaps it was a mass hallucination, but, obviously, it was a demonic deception designed to confuse the recipients about the character of the Holy Spirit. Rather than a divine person who guides, empowers, and ministers to help the body of Christ, He was depicted as a kind of energy or "force" that can be accessed indiscriminately for the personal gratification of the user.

- Rev. Smith, at the same prayer meeting, also introduced us to a technique for obtaining, as he put it, "more of the Father's love." He said this is what they had been seeking and learning how to do in the meetings in Toronto. He asked us if we would like to receive more of the Father's love. Of course, we said yes. So he proceeded to teach us the technique.

It consisted of visualizing God as a father-figure and oneself as a child sitting on His lap, encircled by His arms, and experiencing the love coming from Him. Each of us had a different image of this father. Mine was like an elderly Charlton Heston; another was more like Santa Claus; a third like a favorite grandfather, and so on. Obviously, none of them was in reality a true likeness of our heavenly Father.

It was a pleasant, comforting experience. But, again, as I realized later when I had time to think about it, it was a totally unreal, unscriptural, and, ultimately, demonic activity.

First, God is not a human being whose image we can conjure up in our minds. He is a Spirit (John 4:24) whom no one can see:

> No one has ever seen God; but if we love one another, God lives in us and his love is made complete in us (1 John 4:12).   .

Second, as this verse indicates, we do not receive God's love by means of a visualization exercise. Rather, it exists in us as a result of our loving one another. And we do not receive more of His love by mentally climbing into His lap. Rather, again, it grows to completion as we love one another.

Third, we cannot manipulate God by exercising the power of our minds. He is not a force or an entity that we can control in this or any other way. He is sovereign, and we are at His mercy, not vice versa. We are His creations—His creatures—totally dependent on Him for our very being:

> . . . the Lord God formed the man from the dust of the ground and breathed into his nostrils the breath of life, and the man became a living being (Genesis 2:7).

Like the potter who holds the clay in his hand (Jeremiah 18:6), God can manipulate *us*. Not vice versa! He can make of us whatever He wants and use us for whatever purposes He desires. And, although we can exercise our free will and refuse to cooperate in His plan, we cannot change that plan or remake ourselves:

> But who are you, O man, to talk back to God? "Shall what is formed say to him who formed it, 'Why did you make me like this?'" Does not the potter have the right to make out of the lump of clay some pottery for noble purposes and some for common use? (Romans 9:20–21; see also Isaiah 45:9).

How arrogant—what spiritual pride and presumption of god-like power—to imagine that we can get from God what we desire by manipulating an image of Him that we have manufactured in our minds—as though the clay could control the potter! No, it is God who is sovereign over us, not vice versa!

Fourth, the kind of visualization that we were being taught by this Christian minister is an occult technique commonly practiced by

witches, witch doctors, sorcerers (or shamans), and others involved in the occult. In
fact, a basic definition of sorcery is the manipulation of reality through the power of
the mind, especially by means of visualization. (I knew this but was seduced by his
apparent sincerity, good intentions, and
gentle, benign manner, as well as by the pros-
pect of my own spiritual benefit.)

As Hunt and McMahon (hereafter referred
to as Hunt) put it, "the whole idea of visualizing a vivid image in the mind in order to
produce an effect in the physical world is not
just missing from the Bible but is present in
all occult literature as far back as we can go
[and is in fact one of the most basic shamanistic devices]."[15] Visualization, then, is a basic technique of sorcery, and sorcery is
explicitly condemned in the Bible, along with
other occult practices:

> Let no one be found among you who sac-
> rifices his son or daughter in the fire, who
> practices divination *or sorcery*, interprets
> omens, engages in witchcraft, or casts
> spells, or who is a medium or spiritist or
> who consults the dead. Any one who does
> these things is detestable to the Lord . . .
> (Deuteronomy 18:10–12, emphasis
> added).

Finally, visualizing God as a father-figure is a form of idolatry because it is creating an image of God that takes the place of the true God and thus serves as a substitute for Him. Not only is this idolatry, but it is *self*-idolatry—that is, a form of self-deification, because it is placing trust in the power of one's own imagination rather than in God.

Scripture, of course, is very clear about the importance of avoiding idolatry. In fact, God considers it so important that He made it the subject of the first two of His Ten Commandments: (1) "You shall have no other gods before me." And (2) "You shall not make yourself an idol in the form of anything in heaven above or on the earth beneath or in the waters below. You shall not bow down to them or worship them . . ." (Exodus 20:3–5). (See also Leviticus 26:1; Isaiah 44:9–20; and 1 Corinthians 10:14.)

Committing idolatry through visualization is a more widespread and critical issue in the church than you might think. In fact, I have reason to believe from my personal experience that many Christians routinely visualize God or Jesus when they pray. They claim that this is necessary as an "aid to more effective prayer." For example, when I taught an adult Sunday school lesson on this subject, several members of the class raised objections about what I was saying, and one woman stopped me afterwards and complained that such visualization was essential to her prayer life. Without it, she said, she was unable to focus on praying and keep her mind from wandering. She added that she knew a number of other Christians who felt the same way.

This is not to say that all visualization is wrong. There are many legitimate uses of visualization, but the magical manipulation of God is certainly not one of them. (This issue is discussed more fully at various points in the following pages. See especially chapter seventeen.) It may be that there is a scripturally acceptable form of mental imagery by which we can represent God to ourselves. But, as Selwyn Hughes shows, the practice of idolatry through visualization is one of the most crucial issues of Christian living:

> [We must see] God as He is, not as we would like Him to be. Unless we have an understanding of God as He is, not as we wish Him to be, then our lives will lack spiritual force and power. This is because our lives will never rise higher spiritually than our vision of God. Among the sins which are hateful to God is the sin of idolatry, for idolatry, at its heart, is libel on His character. Yet consider how many of us in the church may be committing the sin of idolatry without realizing it. The idolatrous heart assumes that God is other than he is, and

substitutes for the true God one made after its own imagining. But a god who is created out of the darkness of our hearts is not the true God. The greatest affront we can give the Almighty is to view Him other than He really is.

God has gone to great lengths in the Scriptures to give us a clear picture of Himself, but when we continue to hold wrong ideas of Him, preferring to see Him the way we think He should be rather than the way He is, we demean Him. If we try to worship the god of our own imagining, we then commit idolatry, for we are worshipping our idea of Him drawn from the darkness of our minds. . . . if, in the secret chamber of our soul, we have an image of God which differs from the one we profess with our lips, then it is that core image which will have the greatest influence on our lives.[16]

Let me give you a few more examples from my personal experience of deceptions among Christians which contain the seeds of apostasy.

- For several months, I discipled a young man, Bill. He had a background in the occult with several points in common with my own. Because of some type of "mystical" experience he had had before becoming a Christian, he believed that everything in the universe was spiritually alive—in other words, that every rock, clod, bush, tree, planet, or star was in-habited by an individual spirit and by one great universal spirit.

This is a form both of animism (the belief that spirits inhabit all things) and of pan-theism (the belief that God is in everything or is everything). Both of these beliefs are basic to the religions of many primitive peoples, who also believe in witch doctors, evil spirits that must be placated, and su-pernatural abilities (or magical powers) which may be obtained through the agen-cies of demons (or nature gods).

Pantheism is also the core belief of Hindu-ism and Buddhism. I explained this to Bill and tried on numerous occasions to show him from the Bible that such beliefs were not compatible with Christianity. But to no avail. Bill persisted in his animistic-pantheistic beliefs and in trying to reconcile them with what he understood of Christianity. He had had a "realization," a "spiritual experience" of the reality of what he believed. And no amount of scriptural evidence was going to dissuade him. In other words, he had set his own subjective experience above the Word of God as the standard of truth. He had put his own personal idea about the nature of God above that which is revealed in the Bible. Bill was another example of a Christian prac-ticing a form of idolatry by serving his own false concept of God. I believe he, like Rev. Smith, was a sincere, born-again believer. How then could they have been so misguided? It was, I believe, because Satan had deceived them by manipulating their subjective perceptions, their personal experiences of what appeared to be reality. And so "real" were these illusions that they outweighed scripture as the basis for truth.

In a later chapter, we will discuss in detail the specific means by which Satan succeeds in his campaign of deception. Suffice it to say for now that scripture makes it abundantly clear that Satan has the power to deceive Christians, even to the degree that he can appear to them as an angel of light (2 Corinthians 11:14). The Bible also states that such deception will lead to apostasy:

> The Spirit clearly says that in later times *some will abandon the faith* and follow deceiving spirits and things taught by demons (1 Timothy 4:1, emphasis added).

So convincing are Satan's deceptions that they can include the truly bizarre, as in the case of another Christian friend:

- Janet, like the others, was deluded through a personal experience of the "supernatural." In seeking the guidance of the Holy Spirit, Janet apparently became fixated on the idea that He would speak to her directly by physical means. Somehow, in her imagination, this became "angels" giving her the answers she was seeking from God. Satan was quick to take advantage of this confusion in her mind. The eventual result was that this otherwise sensible woman firmly believed that her houseplants (of which she was very fond) were used by angels to speak to her when she sought their guidance.

- Then, there is Rita, who believes unquestioningly in reincarnation. Why? Like the others, she had a "spiritual experience" which convinced her of its truth. When Rita was a child, she had a "vision" of herself in a "previous life." This experience carried such emotional impact that she still believes it was absolutely true—in spite of the fact that scripture clearly teaches the opposite.

  Both my wife and I have tried, unsuccessfully, to explain to her that reincarnation is a belief of Hinduism, Buddhism, and New Age philosophy and that it contradicts the Christian doctrines of resurrection, judgment, salvation by faith, heaven, hell, and grace.

  Reincarnation is the belief that one is automatically reborn into another body (whether animal or human) when one dies. Then there is a continuing repetition of this cycle until one has suffered and learned sufficiently from one's karma (cause and effect) to earn righteousness, experience enlightenment, and become one with the universe ("the void"). Unfortunately, there appears to be little hope offered that any but a very few will ever attain to this state of "nirvana." If this belief were true, then there would be no possibility for the resurrection of the dead and the following scripture would be totally false:

> For the Lord himself will come down from heaven with a loud command, with the voice of the archangel and with the trumpet call of God, and *the dead in Christ will rise first.* After that, we who are still alive and are left will be caught up together with them in the clouds to meet the Lord in the air. And so we will be with the Lord forever (1 Thessalonians 4:16–17, emphasis added).

There is no room here for endless cycles of rebirth because *all* the dead in Christ— meaning all those who have previously died in all ages—rise together and then *all* the living in Christ rise together with no possibility for additional lives in new bodies with new identities.

In addition, the Bible says we will each be judged for what we have done in *the body* (singular) (2 Corinthians 5:10). This raises the question, at what point would the reincarnation process be broken in order for judgment to take place? As we have seen, there is no concept of judgment in the doctrine of reincarnation. Consequently, there is no room for heaven or hell. For, if there is no judgment, there are no eternal rewards or punishments. And there is no need for the places where these things would be experienced. It is, instead, a process of "spiritual evolution" in which, if he is lucky, one eventually attains freedom from the wheel of death and rebirth.

On the contrary, the Bible says, "Just as man is destined to die *once*, and after that to face judgment, so Christ was sacrificed once to take away the sins of many people . . ." (Hebrews 9:27–28, emphasis added).

As this verse states, man dies *once*. This is *not* followed by rebirth, but by God's judgment.

Also, as this verse shows, reincarnation eliminates the need for and the possibility of salvation by Christ's sacrificial death on the cross. For, if we can work off our karma by being reincarnated time after time, there is no need for Christ to take our sins upon Himself and pay for them by dying on the cross. Likewise, there is no need for God's grace because karma *means* paying the price in this life for past-life sins.

Thus, Christ's death becomes pointless, the gospel of Christ becomes meaningless, and the whole reason for Christianity is done away with. What a stupendous victory for Satan—all because of a deceptive personal experience cleverly orchestrated by the devil!

Indeed, so convincing is it, that a Christian such as Rita continues to believe in it even though it directly contradicts basic biblical doctrines and the very gospel of Jesus Christ—all of which she professes to believe!

• Here is a final example of deception, this time involving the secret practice of satanism in the church, as described to me by Ann. She said that satanists frequently pose successfully as Christians. Yes, it sounded unbelievable to me, too, when I first heard it. But I became convinced it was true partly because there is documented evidence of the reality of such satanic activity. For example, in her book, *He Came to Set the Captives Free*, Dr. Rebecca Brown quotes Elaine, a former witch and high priestess in a satanic cult who is now a born-again Christian:

> These Satanists infest every level of society—the poor and the rich. The very well educated, the police force, government officials, business men and women, and even some so-called Christian ministers. Most of them attend local Christian churches and are considered "good citizens" because of their involvement in local civic activities. This is all done as a cover-up. They lead double lives and are expert at it; masters of deception.[17]

Even more convincing was the story Ann told. She was desperately seeking prayer and counseling about such satanism for her son, Jim, her daughter-in-law, Peggy, and her daughter-in-law's family. Here is the story in brief, as told to Ann by Peggy.

Peggy's grandfather was a satanist, posing as a Christian. He was a highly regarded elder in his church. Such infiltration by satanists, Ann said, exists in nearly every church in the land, although it is almost totally unsuspected by Christians in general. The purpose of these satanists is to create division and discouragement among Christians and thereby weaken the body of Christ.

(Judging by the frequency of splits in congregations and the large number of denominations and factions within denominations, this strategy of Satan has been highly successful.)

Both Peggy and her mother, Helen, were used by satanists as "breeders." That is, they were given fertility drugs starting when they were seven or eight years old. Then, when they were about nine or ten, they were taken to a breeding facility and put in a room with a "stud," or male satanist whose function was to impregnate such girls. The resulting babies would normally be taken before term and the fetuses used either for human sacrifices or to supply blood to be drunk during satanic rituals.

In addition to such breeding facilities, satanists also control certain hospitals, staffed, at least partially, with their own doctors.

When Helen was "bred" in this way, the result was female triplets. Labor was induced and her babies taken prematurely. Fortunately, the attending nurse was a Christian who knew what was going on. When the first of the triplets was born, it was immediately taken away by the attending physician, a satanist. The second triplet was born dead and the doctor thought there were no other babies in Helen's womb. After he left, Helen continued to have contractions and the nurse realized there was still another baby to be born. She whispered to Helen not to push, in order to delay delivery. Then, when it was safe, the nurse assisted with the birth of the baby—who was Peggy.

The nurse helped Helen to escape with Peggy because she feared the satanists would destroy them. Helen and Peggy managed to survive, and Helen eventually married and had another child.

When Peggy was nine or ten, she was abducted by satanists, who probably knew her whereabouts all along. She was given fertility drugs and bred, as her mother had been. She had Siamese twin boys who were removed from her womb prematurely. One died during the operation to separate them.

The other was somehow rescued by Christians. This baby was raised by Peggy's sister, Polly, the other surviving triplet, who is still alive. Polly, likewise, had been rescued as a baby and raised by Christians.

Polly's whereabouts remain a secret to this day, and Peggy's only contacts with her are cards she receives at Christmas and on birthdays.

An incredible story, yes. And Ann was understandably skeptical. However, her doubts were removed when she became acquainted with Ed, a dedicated Christian active in missionary work and ministry to the homeless. Ed, it turns out, had been involved in the occult before his conversion to Christianity and had, in fact, been a warlock, the male counterpart of a witch.

When Ann told him Peggy's story, he verified that it was an accurate account of how satanists operate. He explained that satanists are able to function clandestinely in this way because they have their own underground society. They are able to do this, he said, by being born and raised outside of normal society, with no documentation of their existence, such as birth certificates, driver's licenses, social security numbers, public school records, etc. Ed also recommended to her the book, *He Came to Set the Captives Free,* as an accurate account of such satanic activity and infiltration.

These stories illustrate just a few of the ways the devil deceives many in the church in his effort to confuse and discourage us and lure us away from the faith. They all involve apostasy in some form. In some ways, they all reject the hope we have in Jesus Christ. In each, there is the temptation to believe that we can handle the situation and solve the problems ourselves; that God, the Bible, the church, and prayer are not sufficient; that, on the contrary, spiritual additives or substitutes are necessary.

A Real and Present Danger

The apostle Paul predicted this drift into error and deception. He said it would lead to a "falling away"—a great apostasy, or abandoning of the faith—in the church prior to Jesus' second coming (2 Thessalonians 2:1–3 (KJV)).

Jesus Himself spoke of this in Matthew 24, where it says His disciples came to him privately and asked, ". . . what will be the sign of your coming and the end of the age?" Jesus answered, "Watch out that no one deceives you. For many will come in my name, claiming, 'I am the Christ,' and will deceive many." At that time, He said, there will be reports of wars with nation rising against nation. Famines and earthquakes, He said, will happen in various places. Christians will be persecuted and put to death and hated by all nations.

At that time many will *turn away from the faith* and will betray and hate each other, and many false prophets will appear and deceive many people. . . . At that time, if anyone says to you, 'Look, here is the Christ!' or, 'There he is!' do not believe it. For false Christs and false prophets will appear and perform great signs and miracles to deceive even the elect—if that were possible. See, I have told you ahead of time (Matthew 24:3–27, emphasis added).

As these verses indicate, it will be a time of spiritual deception, frequent wars, economic upheaval, natural disasters, and persecution, betrayal and hatred of Christians—in other words, *the world as it is today*. This, I believe, is the age of the great end times apostasy predicted in many scriptures in addition to those quoted above (e.g., 1 Timothy 4:1–8; 2 Timothy 4:3–4; 2 Peter 3:17).

This apostasy has already begun and is in fact well under way. All of these conditions are presently being fulfilled. Christians are being persecuted and even executed in China, Africa, the Middle East, and elsewhere. Natural disasters are increasing in frequency and intensity. Earthquakes, especially, are much more common today than in previous periods of history, having increased exponentially in frequency within the past one hundred years. Economies of third world countries are in chaos, wars and reports of wars have become more and more frequent throughout the world.

In addition, spiritual deception has been on the rise for a number of years with widespread activity in cults, witchcraft, satanism, the occult, and manifold expressions of New Age philosophy, many of which have infiltrated the church in subtle and appealing ways. These strategies of Satan are often successful in luring Christians away from their faith. Unbiblical teachings are replacing sound doctrine for many immature and poorly trained Christians, and reliance on humanistic and occult ideas and practices for the solution to life's problems is replacing reliance on the Bible and on the Father, the Son, and the Holy Spirit.

One of the major strategies of the enemy in all this is to convince Christians that the New Age Movement is really no threat and that Satan himself doesn't really have any power to deceive or destroy the church. In fact, this tendency to underestimate the enemy and his New Age campaign is a common attitude among many Christians, including even scholars and researchers in these areas. Douglas Groothius, for example, minimizes the possibility of a New Age conspiracy, saying he doubts that it exists at all.[18] While he acknowledges Satan's influence on nonbelievers, he believes that Satan has little or no influence on believers, supporting his view by referring to the following scriptures taken out of context and without regard to related scriptures which contradict this view:

> Christ, not Satan, has been given all authority in heaven and on earth (Matthew 28:18–20; Colossians 1:15–20); God owns the earth (Psalm 24:1–2); and Christ has destroyed the works of the devil (1 John 3:8).[19]

However, Matthew 28:18–20 is about Jesus conferring the great commission on His disciples and announcing His authority to do so. It is *not* about the idea that Satan has little or no power over Christians or the world in general. Colossians 1:15–20 is about Jesus' Godhood and His identity as Creator, Sustainer, and Savior, *not* about Satan's lack of power. The purpose of Psalm 24:1–2, also, is to proclaim the Lord's identity (according to the NIV Study Bible) as

> . . . The Creator, Sustainer and possessor of the whole world, and therefore worthy of worship and reverent loyalty as "the King of glory" . . . .[20]

These verses have nothing to do with limitations on Satan's power over Christians or anyone else.

First John 3:8 does *not* say that "Christ *has destroyed* the works of the devil" but that the reason He came "was *to destroy* the devil's work"(emphasis added). That is, to free us from sin and its effects and to protect us from the devil's deceptions (verses 6–9). In other words, the verse says that, through Christ, we *overcome* the devil's power, *not* that he has no power.

On the contrary, Peter warns Christians that "the devil prowls around like a roaring lion looking for someone to devour" and that we must resist him by "standing firm in the faith" (1 Peter 5:8–9). And Paul (who was tormented by a "messenger of Satan" (2 Corinthians 12:7)) cautions Christians that "Satan himself masquerades as an angel of light" (2 Corinthians 11:14).

There are, of course, many other scriptures which speak of the power of Satan or his demons. Many of these verses warn Christians to guard themselves against his power (for example, Acts 10:38; Ephesians 4:27; 2 Thessalonians 2:9–11; 2 Timothy 2:26). Many such scriptures will be discussed in the following pages.

In *The New Age Cult*, Walter Martin has provided abundant documentation that a New Age conspiracy does exist, that it threatens Christianity, and that it is being directed by Satan. Martin sounds this warning:

> In dealing with the New Age Cult, we are in reality dealing with spiritual warfare against the forces of darkness, and we are told by God to put on the whole armor of heaven so that we will be able to withstand the forces of Satan (Ephesians 6:11).[21]

Indeed, Satan's New Age strategies to destroy the church pose a real and present danger! And we shall examine these strategies in many different contexts as we proceed. (The New Age conspiracy is described in detail in chapter eight.)

In view of these facts, then, it is clear that all of the conditions Jesus said would exist before His return are being fulfilled before our eyes. And Satan is busy within the church promoting a great falling away from the faith. For example, thousands of Christians have been leaving mainline Protestant churches. Since the early 1900s, their numbers have declined drastically. In 1920, such denominations as the Presbyterian, Episcopal, Methodist, and Lutheran made up 76 percent of Protestant America. By the mid-1980s, they were down to 50 percent, and in the 1990s, these denominations were still experiencing declines.[22]

Some have turned to more conservative evangelical or charismatic churches where they find fundamental Bible truths taught and practiced. But many others have left the church entirely to follow New Age teachings, or, perhaps worse, have remained in the church while adopting New Age attitudes and practices which directly contradict scripture or are subtle substitutes for it.

This fact is a direct fulfillment of 1 Timothy 4:1, which says, "The Spirit clearly says that in later times some will abandon the faith and follow deceiving spirits and things taught by demons." How this is happening and what forms it is taking will be discussed in detail in later chapters.

But first, we must look at the various types of temptations which call for spiritual additives or substitutes. These are discussed in detail in Part I (chapters one through five). They are the primary seeds of apostasy.

PART I:

"You Will Be Like God"— The Seeds of Apostasy

The basic temptation with which we ended the Introduction, to think that something more is needed, something of my own ability and effort or some special knowledge that I can obtain apart from God's revelation by His Holy Spirit and through His Holy Word—this is the basic cause of apostasy. This master temptation is based on the idea that I can become my own god in some manner, putting myself on the throne of my life and usurping the power and position of God in providing for my own needs and determining my own destiny.

This temptation to exalt self is the master seed of apostasy. I believe it can be broken down into at least five subordinate temptations :

The temptation of power
The temptation of wealth

The temptation of status
The temptation of happiness
The temptation of health

None of these things is wrong in itself. It is when they are acquired by self-centered or ungodly means and for selfish purposes that they may become substitutes for reliance on the Holy Spirit, scripture, and prayer. Then they become seeds of apostasy because they put self in the place of God.

All of Satan's deceptions are aimed at leading us into one or another of these temptations and thereby into apostasy. His technique in each case is to diminish or eliminate discernment of right and wrong, good and evil, as revealed in the scriptures by getting our focus off of God and the things of His kingdom and onto ourselves and things of this world. His appeal is always to the self—what the Bible calls the sinful nature, the flesh, or the old man.

Satan's successes in this campaign can be attributed in part to the failure of the church to deal decisively with two main obstacles to spiritual growth: self-will and worldliness. In recent years, the church has been ineffective in helping Christians struggle against self-will because it has not instilled in them a deep appreciation of the need for truth, righteousness, holiness, and obedience in their Christian walk. Likewise, the church has been weak in helping Christians to overcome worldliness because it has neither clearly taught nor powerfully modeled the idea that willingness to compromise for the sake of a perceived worldly or spiritual benefit is wrong.

Satan's orchestration of these temptations has been rightly called "the seduction of Christianity." This seduction does not appear as a "frontal assault or oppression of our religious beliefs. Instead, it [comes] as the latest 'fashionable philosophies' offering to make us happier, healthier, better educated, even more spiritual."[1] In other words, it is not an outright attack but rather a subtle and unrecognized infiltration of the church.

In *The Screwtape Letters*, C.S. Lewis has defined the essence of these subtle temptations to apostasy— the falling away from God, the Bible, and the church—and the substitution or addition of something "other" or "more." The demon, Screwtape, is instructing his subordinate, Wormwood, on the technique for luring Christians into apostasy:

My Dear Wormwood,

The real trouble about the set your patient is living in is that it is *merely* Christianity. They all have individual interests, of course, but the bond remains mere Christianity. What we want, if men become Christians at all, is to keep them in the state of mind I call "Christianity And." You know—Christianity and the Crisis, Christianity and the New Psychology, Christianity and the New Order, Christianity and Faith Healing [not faith in the power of God to heal but in a special healing technique], Christianity and Psychical Research, Christianity and Vegetarianism, Christianity and Spelling Reform. If they must be Christians, let them at least be Christians with a difference. Substitute for the faith itself some Fashion with a Christian colouring. Work on their horror of the Same Old Thing.[2]

What are some of these "Christianity And" items that have taken root in the church today? Here are just a few among many others, which we will discuss in detail as we proceed:

"Christian" psychology with its emphasis on self-esteem.

Ecumenicalism with its emphasis on tolerance of divergent, unscriptural doctrines for the sake of unity.

"Holistic" health care with its alternative treatments based on eastern religious traditions and occultism. (Occultism is the pursuit of "secret" or "hidden" knowledge related to supernatural phenomena and magic arts. Occultism is discussed more fully in chapters sixteen, seventeen, and eighteen.)

Positive thinking and positive confession with their mind-over-matter techniques.

Self-help philosophies with their New Age "success" and "inner peace" concepts.

Extra-biblical revelation which claims to supercede or correct the scripture.

Material wealth and a comfortable lifestyle without suffering—as valid purposes of prayer and signs of spiritual advancement.

Social and political action as primary purposes of the church and tests of valid Christianity.

Consumer marketing techniques as valid and necessary means of evangelism and fund raising.

Why *are* Christians looking elsewhere or for something more? Because major portions of the church have lost touch with the power of the gospel and have deteriorated into ritual, tradition, legalism, and compromise with and tolerance of the worldly. The bottom line is that these Christians are not finding a transforming purpose or fulfilling experience in the church. They are, instead, tacitly and probably unconsciously accepting the idea that Christianity is deficient and needs outside help. This deception is, I believe, where Satan is having his greatest success in the church today.

We shall look at Satan's techniques—the specific strategies and tricks by which he carries out this campaign—in Part II of this book. For now, let's look at the basic characteristics of the seeds of apostasy.

CHAPTER ONE

Seed One: The Temptation of Power

This temptation involves the notion of "power" in the sense of one's ability to manipulate reality. It includes two basic ideas: (1) that through self-effort we can expand our control over ourselves, others, the environment, and events, for our own purposes and (2) that by obtaining special "knowledge," we can solve all our problems whether on a personal or global level.

Satan uses every means at his disposal to promote these ideas, but primarily he uses concepts from the following sources:

1. **Psychology**—self-esteem, positive thinking (i.e., we are inherently good and capable and all we have to do is realize it and think properly). But the Bible says we are all naturally

sinners who must be transformed by the renewing of our minds (Galatians 2:17; Romans 12:2).

2. **Humanism**—self-development, self-realization, human intelligence and ability (i.e., we have all the potential we need within ourselves). But the Bible says we can do nothing of any real value without Christ (John 15:5).

3. **New Age philosophy**—expanded selfhood through "spiritual" experiences (i.e., we can tap into supernormal sources of energy and information through special physical and mental techniques, finding all the truth and power we need within ourselves). But the Bible says spiritual transformation comes by God working in us (Philippians 2:13; 2 Corinthians 3:18).

A major means by which Satan has conveyed these ideas into our culture and, through our culture into the church, is his influence on our minds through ideas about power, control, and knowledge as they relate to technology. With the enormous advances in computer, space, and communications technology, has come a parallel development in science fiction. And it is through this form of mass entertainment in movies, TV series, books, games, and toys that these ideas have taken on graphic reality in our imaginations. *Star Wars* and *Star Trek*, for example, have, almost by themselves, set the stage for accepting the "truth" of such ideas.

THE STAR WARS PATTERN

Self-improvement through supernormal means is, in fact, the basic theme of the movie, *Star Wars*. As a disciple of his guru, Yoda, Luke Skywalker learns to control and use The Force for levitation, mental telepathy, clairvoyance, and kinesthesis (mental manipulation of matter and energy), among other mind-over-matter phenomena. This is not only a demonstration of what the Bible calls sorcery (in modern parlance, shamanism), it is also a form of self-deification, for Luke exercises god-like, supernatural powers in battling Darth Vader, the personification of the dark side of The Force. All of this is a direct depiction of New Age occultism.

According to Hunt, these ideas have invaded the church in the form of "mind-science and PMA [positive mental attitude] techniques (from visualization to positive self-talk and other forms of self-hypnosis and self-image psychology)."[3] This is happening largely because of a lack of accountability on the part of church leaders, especially TV evangelists and teachers, and operators of Christian TV networks:

> After becoming Christians, many who have been involved in the New Age Movement and know it from the inside inquire why they find much of the same occultism in the church and on Christian TV, and why very few pastors seem willing or able to confront this issue. There is a growing grassroots concern that most Christian television is controlled by a handful of people who have a

final say on all programming. They wield great power and influence, yet are insulated from any correction from the financially supporting body of Christ and are accountable to no one but themselves. The same thing applies to the spreading Christian satellite networks.[4]

According to Hunt, this kind of shamanism is often promoted in the church. For example, he quotes from a letter about such a case written by a Christian bookstore owner:

... our United Methodist pastor led the congregation in an imaging exercise ("Close your eyes...") I recognized it and did not participate.

Recently he attended a seminar in California and is teaching it during Sunday school . . . a visualization technique that helped his son control pain after surgery.[5]

Hunt believes such activities are part of "a growing pattern of seduction pointing in a particular direction prophesied in the scriptures, and none of us is immune from being deceived and deceiving others."[6]

In the mind-science cults (such as Christian Science, Religious Science, New Thought, and Unity), as well as in the Word of Faith movement (also known as Positive Confession, Name-It-and-Claim-It, and Prosperity Gospel), this type of mind-over-matter control extends even to the manipulation of God Himself to get Him to do what one wants Him to do.

Magical Use of Prayer

In this process, visualization is combined with positive affirmation as an aid to prayer, a practice which can accurately be called magical prayer. In other words, first you form a mental picture of God or Jesus. Then you create an image of the thing you desire (let's say a new car, visualized in exact detail—make, model, color, accessories). Then you pray to this visualized "God," "claiming" this desired image as a reality in your life—something you have already received—based on promises taken from the Bible (out of context). For example,

> So I say to you: ask and it will be given to you; seek and you will find; knock and the door will be opened to you. For everyone who asks receives; he who seeks finds; and to him who knocks, the door will be opened (Luke 11:9–10) .

> If you believe, you will receive whatever you ask for in prayer (Matthew. 21:22).

> . . . whatever you ask for in prayer, believe that you have received it, and it will be yours (Mark 11:24).

The "proper" technique for using such scriptures, which I was taught in the Word of Faith church I attended, is to remind God of what He said in His Word and then believe that God *must* honor His Word by responding accordingly.

For example, you say, "God, You said in Your Word that everyone who asks receives and if I believe, I will receive whatever I ask for. So I'm asking for that new car and I'm believing Your Word and that You must honor Your Word. Therefore, I'm claiming that new car, according to Your Word, and I'm confessing that it is mine."

Then, if you receive it, it proves that your technique was correct and your faith was strong enough. Conversely, if you don't receive it, there must have been something lacking in your technique or your faith or both.

The problem with this approach, of course, is that it leaves out God's sovereignty, which includes the facts that we must *ask according to His will* (Matt. 6:10; 1 John 5:14) and *obey His commandments* (1 John 3:21–22) as two conditions for answered prayer, among others. In addition, it is not really prayer at all. In essence, it is no different than a magical incantation spoken to bring about a desired result by supernatural means. True prayer, on the other hand, as the scripture explains, is simply speaking to God and *asking* Him to meet your needs, with a thankful heart, regardless of the outcome. And the outcome, in any case, will be spiritual peace:

> Do not be anxious about anything, but in everything, by prayer and petition, with thanksgiving, present your requests to God. And the peace of God, which transcends all understanding, will guard your hearts and your minds in Christ Jesus (Philippians 4:6–7).

John and Paula Sandford explain the difference:

. . . there is a fine line between prayer and magic. When we discover the laws of God's universe and hear the promises of God, we can claim those promises and activate those principles by prayer with such a wrong heart that we have actually merged into magic rather than prayer. Magic would take hold of God's Word and so claim His promises as to try to manipulate or force God to do what we want. True prayer is petition, humbly respecting the free will of a Father who may in wisdom say "No." Authority in prayer to accomplish something can and ought to be expressed, but only after carefully listening to God so that it is the Holy Spirit who acts in and with us as we express what is also the Father's will. But when we grasp His promises and insist that He do what we want because He promised, "And, Lord, your Word is true, so we know you have to," we are actually trying to manipulate God. Our prayer has become magic. We are operating His principles to obtain what we want. . . .

I used to listen to a well-known teacher of healing and would occasionally hear the Lord saying in my spirit, "This teacher is teaching magic." The teacher was urgently insisting that, if we apply faith, God *must* heal. Please, dear Body of Christ, never try to get a handle on God! God doesn't *have* to do anything. To try to make Him do anything is magic; magic is the operation of principles or laws of God to accomplish our own selfish ends. . . . Magic interferes by the will of the magician, forcing a thing to happen by occult or hidden principles.

In this regard, the teachers of the recent faith movement unwittingly have led many who are sincere Christians into the operation of magic. [For further discussion of the Word of Faith movement and the wrong use of prayer, see chapter twelve.]

The Sandfords wisely add this plea for discernment, unity, and love in the church:

We plead with the Body of Christ to repent, to pray for all who have stumbled into this kind of magic, and above all, not to condemn people or fracture the unity of the Body by rejection. We all pioneer, in frontiers of faith, stumbling by trial and error into maturity. Let us love one another, be reconciled and healed.[7]

Other forms of occultism which have been embraced by many Christians to enhance their personal power include eastern forms of meditation and exercise (e.g., yoga and tai chi), martial arts, and astrology (all of which are discussed in later sections).

Astrology in the Church

Not only are daily horoscopes consulted by many Christians, but astrology, in a cleverly disguised form, has taken firm root in many evangelical churches. This is the study of "temperaments" as an aid to identifying one's ministry calling. There is well-documented evidence that the concept of the four temperaments (sanguine, choleric, phlegmatic, and melancholy) comes directly out of ancient belief in the "four humors" (blood, yellow bile, phlegm, and black bile) which are related to the "four elements" (air, fire, water, and earth), which in turn are found in the four zodiacal groups of elemental signs: air (Gemini, Libra, Sagittarius), fire (Aries, Leo, Scorpio), water (Aquarius, Pisces, Cancer) and earth (Capricorn, Taurus, Virgo).[8]

According to Shirley Ann Miller, a former professional astrologer who became a born-again Christian,

> The temperaments were the ancient philosopher's mystical interpretation of the function of the human body based upon the worship of the heavens. . . .
>
> The elemental deities of *fire, air, earth,* and *water* were the gods ruling over the personality and temperaments. The temperaments were believed to be the nature of the personality which is governed by the movements of the planets in heaven (astrology) . . . The temperament classifications of strengths and weaknesses evolved from Empedocles' views on astrology.[9]

If the study and use of the four temperaments is a form of astrology, what then should our response be to this practice in the church? I believe it should be one of total rejection, for, as Miller points out, when "Christians practice the temperaments, they are in essence practicing the ancient philosopher's worship of the elemental deities and astrology. When Christians study the strengths and weaknesses of each temperament type, they are studying Empedocles' doctrine on reincarnation of the soul. This is definitely not a part of Christian theology."[10]

Rather, it is, I believe, a foothold for Satan that can lead to other more serious forms of heresy and ultimately into apostasy.

Once more, I can speak from personal experience. In one of the churches I have attended, there is a well-established ministry of helping believers to identify their individual callings within the body and to move into these areas of ministry. An important part of this process is the identification of one's temperament. When I discovered the astrological basis of this practice, I reported this to the associate pastor in charge of this ministry.

Unfortunately, so deep was his commitment and so extensive was the church's involvement in this form of occultism, that he refused to seriously consider what I had told him. When I gave him a copy of Miller's book, he took it but never got around to reading it. Today, the practice of identifying temperaments continues unabated in that church, the justification being that it is useful, it has been strongly promoted by well-known Christian leaders, and it is widely practiced by other churches. Here, I believe, is a case of pragmatic expediency which sets aside God's specific injunction against involvement in the occult (Deuteronomy 18:10; Revelation 22:15) for the sake of a perceived pastoral benefit.

Some who are involved in such ministry have argued that the identification of temperaments is merely a study of "human makeup" and "genetic tendencies" which is helpful in identifying one's ministry potential. Therefore, they maintain, it is a legitimate activity for Christians, and to exclude such information from consideration is to "throw out the baby with the bathwater."

However, this is to miss the point. I am not saying we should not use helpful information about one's personality tendencies. I am saying that the *source* of this particular view of human behavior (the four temperaments) is occult and, therefore, is "forbidden fruit" which the Bible says we should have nothing to do with because it is "detestable" to God (Deuteronomy 18:9–13).

Just as Adam and Eve were forbidden to eat a certain fruit in the Garden of Eden, even though it was "good for food, pleasing to the eye, and also desirable for gaining wisdom," (Genesis 3:6), so we are forbidden to use anything associated with occultism. Rather, we are to "be blameless before the Lord [our] God" (Deuteronomy 18:13).

The issue is not whether the knowledge is "useful" but whether it is *forbidden*. Other sources of information about one's natural tendencies or personality makeup are available. We don't have to obtain such information from an occult system derived from astrology and the worship of pagan gods.

And we should not do so, no matter how pleasing to the eye or desirable for gaining wisdom it may appear to be.

Thus, to reject the four temperaments as an aid to Christian ministry is *not* to throw out the precious baby with the unholy bathwater—because the baby in this case is also unholy. On the contrary, to keep both the unholy baby and the unholy bathwater would be indeed to swallow everything (unholy) whole!

Therefore, I continue to pray that that church and others so involved with the occult will receive clarification on this matter and be delivered from any defilement or demonic inroads which may have resulted from this involvement.

All of these occult practices and beliefs are embraced by the New Age philosophy, which, according to Peter and Paul Lalonde, are being bought into by a large number of Christians:

> One of the most alarming trends that we're seeing today is the increasing tendency of Christians to combine faith with an assortment of New Age beliefs. A recent Gallup poll examined the trend and found that nearly 50 percent of all American Christians believe in psychic healing, and more than 25 percent believed in astrology.[11]

This, then, is the Star Wars pattern: personal enhancement, power, and control through shamanistic mind-over-matter and other occult techniques.

THE STAR TREK PATTERN

Star Trek, on the other hand, gives us an image of humanity at the height of its humanistic evolution, able to solve all of its social and environmental problems through the enlightened application of technology and scientific knowledge.

Here, the world has indeed become a global village with war, economic problems, poverty, disease, and widespread crime things of the past. Hunger and want are gone because food and consumer goods can simply be replicated as the need arises. Consequently, there is no need for money. Thus, greed for financial wealth and things is no longer the motivating force behind most human endeavors. Man is free to focus his enlightened mind on self-improvement, self-fulfillment, and the exploration of the universe. There is no need, as well, for God, except as an aspect of each person's inner self, since man has everything he needs and can do everything he wants. The worldview is New Age and the "theology" is eastern.

Vishal Mangalwadi, a Christian theologian at the Himalayan L'Abri Resource Center, points out how the Star Trek spin-off series, Deep Space Nine, routinely promotes eastern religious ideas. "It seems like the gurus are making the film," he says. In addition, he finds that the Star Trek films consistently promote an eastern perspective. For example:

- We are the Creator: In one movie, Capt. James T. Kirk and crew go looking for God and find a projection of themselves.

- The cosmos is merely a creation of human consciousness. Over and over, "Star Trek" episodes seem to suggest that perception may be reality and that life is merely the product of consciousness rather than the creation of a transcendent God.
- Time is cyclical. In Eastern religions, you are always repeating your life over and over.
- Karma, the energy generated by a person's actions, is a recurrent theme in the series and films.[12]

In each of these themes, all power and control reside in man, and, in fact, reality itself is created and controlled by the mind of man. In other words, these ideas provide an alternative belief system which is a combination of materialistic humanism and New Age shamanism. As the Lalondes explain, this is in essence, a counterfeit gospel:

> That's right. In the continuing adventures aboard the good ship *Enterprise*, there is an entire belief system, so complete, and so powerful that it literally represents the greatest alternative to the gospel that has ever been offered to mankind. And given the sense of expectancy and anticipation that exists in our world today, it is a counterfeit tailored perfectly for this exact moment in history.[13]

In this alternative gospel, there is "no need for repentance, no need to deal with sin, just peace and happiness on our own terms . . . human worldly problems have been solved . . . Members of the human race . . . are now working toward the common goal of 'seeking out new life and new civilizations . . .'"[14]

Surely, this seems like a noble and desirable outcome, and it suggests to the viewer that there is hope for humankind after all. But most importantly, this picture gives the non-Christian world something to hang on to and something to believe in.

Here, man has no need for the gospel, which

> . . . human beings do not like . . . because we cannot control our own destiny. But in the world of *Star Trek*, we are the masters of our fate; we can decide what is right and wrong, what is true and false. There is truly nothing else that can give us such an illusion of control.[15]

Reconstructionism/Dominion Theology

The temptation to buy into this illusion of power and control through human effort has taken over a significant segment of the church in the Reconstructionism movement with its Dominion Theology, also known as Kingdom Now. Their doctrine states that the church must reform the world and establish God's kingdom on earth, politically, socially, and in every other way before Jesus returns. In other words, it is up to the church to solve all of mankind's problems, and then the Lord will come back to earth to take over the kingdom which *they* have established.

I can attest from personal experience that this false doctrine is alive and well in the church. The senior pastor of one of the churches I have attended was a strong proponent of Reconstructionism. He was so convinced of this view that he expected his associate pastors to accept it. When they did not, a conflict resulted which contributed to a split in the church. This was related to me by two of the associate pastors involved in the split.

This "Kingdom Now" concept is, of course, directly contrary to the scripture, which states that, before Jesus returns, things will get progressively worse spiritually, economically, politically, environmentally, etc., ending in the Great Tribulation and the Battle of Armageddon. (See Matthew 24 and Revelation 6, 8, 9, 11, 14, 16 and 18.)

Moral decay will also be accelerated and pervasive:

> But mark this: There will be terrible times in the last days. People will be lovers of themselves, lovers of money, boastful, proud, abusive, disobedient to their parents, ungrateful, unholy, without love, unforgiving, slanderous, without self-control, brutal, not lovers of the good, treacherous, rash, conceited, lovers of pleasure rather than lovers of God—having a form of godliness but denying its power (2 Timothy 3:1–5).

Contrary to the Reconstructionists' view that human effort through the agency of the church will save the world, the Bible says the only hope for the world to be saved from destruction will be the supernatural intervention of Jesus at the end of the age. He will come with the armies of heaven to wipe out this corruption and destroy the antichrist and his followers:

> I saw heaven standing open and there before me was a white horse, whose rider is called Faithful and True. With justice he judges and makes war. His eyes are like blazing fire, and on his head are many crowns. He has a name written on him that no one knows but he himself. He is dressed in a robe dipped in blood, and his name is the Word of God. The armies of heaven were following, riding on white horses and dressed in fine linen, white and clean. Out of his mouth comes a sharp sword with which to strike down the nations. "He will rule them with an iron scepter." He treads the winepress of the fury of the wrath of God Almighty. On his robe and on his thigh he has this name written:
>
> KING OF KINGS AND
LORD OF LORDS.
(Revelation 19:11–16)

Hunt sums up these divergent views about the role of the church in history:

> Two factions are now emerging within the church. One side adheres to the belief that an apostasy is coming for the church in the last days, and with it a great tribulation and God's judgment for the

world. We are to rescue as many as we can before it is too late, calling them to citizenship in heaven. On the other side are those, equally sincere, who see the primary call of the church as solving social, economic, and political problems. Although they are also concerned to see souls saved, the conversion of the masses provides the means for taking over the world for Christ, taking dominion back from Satan, and thereby establishing the kingdom in order that Christ might return as king to reign at last. Within the latter group are two divergent factions whose goals are beginning to sound more and more alike. Christian socialists hope for a redistribution that will share what the wealthy have with the poor, while the success-oriented Christians of the Positive Confession or Faith Movement hope to make everyone wealthy. From their increasingly isolated corner, the fundamentalists warn that neither will succeed because the world is heading for a great tribulation climaxing in the Battle of Armageddon, which will involve the return of Christ to rescue Israel, to stop the destruction, and to set up His kingdom. There is a growing rejection within the church of this fundamentalist scenario as negative, "gloom-and-doom" eschatology.[16]

To think that *we* can save the world by reforming it *for* Christ, is to set ourselves in His place and to assume a power and control which is not ours to possess and which the Bible declares is God's alone. It is a seed of apostasy, for it substitutes reliance on human effort and ability for reliance on God and His Word and the power of the Holy Spirit.

The gospel of Reconstructionism is primarily about the historical changing of society and culture. The gospel of Jesus, on the other hand, is about the transformation of the human heart and the development of the body of Christ. He is coming for His bride, the church, *not* for a reformed social order.

According to Gary North, perhaps the foremost spokesman of Reconstructionism, the "gospel" is "God's historic means for making the world better," "a program leading to the victory of Christ's people in history" and "a New World Order."[17]

The apostle Paul, however, says that the reason Jesus Christ came to earth and gave Himself for us was "to redeem us from all wickedness and to purify for himself a people that are his very own, eager to do what is good" (Titus 2:14).

Jesus Himself said He came to fulfill the Law and the Prophets by enabling us to practice and teach the commandments so that we may not only enter the kingdom of heaven but even "be called great in the kingdom of heaven" (Matthew 5:17–20). He said we are to "seek first his kingdom and his righteousness" (Matthew 6:33).

At the beginning of His ministry, He announced in the synagogue in Nazareth that the Holy Spirit had anointed Him "to preach good news to the poor, . . . to proclaim freedom for the prisoners and recovery of sight to the blind, to release the oppressed, to proclaim the year of the Lord's favor" (Luke 4:16–19). He sent His disciples out to preach this message: "the kingdom of heaven is near" and to "Heal the sick, raise the dead, cleanse those who have leprosy, drive out demons" (Matthew 10:7–8). After His resurrection, He told His apostles that His purpose for them after He was gone was to witness for Him in power:

> . . . you will receive power when the Holy Spirit comes on you; and you will be my witnesses in Jerusalem, and in all Judea and Samaria, and to the ends of the earth (Acts 1:8).

This is all about the kingdom of heaven being established in the hearts of believers, first to save, deliver, and purify them and then to enable them to minister in like manner to other individuals. There is absolutely nothing here about setting up an earthly kingdom or the church triumphing over the humanistic world system in history. In fact, I believe the Bible says just the opposite—that Satan will exercise power over the earth during the Tribulation period after the church has been removed in the Rapture and that only when Jesus returns to rescue Israel and the Tribulation saints will God's victory (*not* the church's) over Satan be completed. Then *Jesus* (*not* the church) will set up His millennial kingdom on earth.

Jesus said that Satan is "the prince of this world (John 12:31; 14:30); Paul called him "the god of this world" (2 Corinthians. 4:4, KJV). But Gary North says that Dominion Theology affirms not only Christ's victory over Satan at Calvary but also His *"progressive victory over Satan in history through His church."* North also says that, if one "denies victory in history for the church of Jesus Christ," he "affirms that Christ's chosen people are losers in history."[18] [Emphasis in original.]

Therefore, according to North, if we say that Satan is the god of this world (i.e., that the world system is under his control), then we are saying that he has defeated the church in this world ("in history"). However, I believe this is a total misunderstanding of what the church is and what its role is in history. And the fact that the kingdom of darkness continues to exist does not mean that the church has been defeated.

The church is those who have been called out of the world system ("church": Greek *ekklesia*, called out ones [Matthew 16:18]), who are the body of Christ (Romans 12:5) and His representatives (the ambassadors of His kingdom) on the earth (2 Corinthians 5:20). (See also 1 Corinthians 12:27; Ephesians 1:23, 4:12; Colossians 1:24, 2:19.) *His kingdom is not of this world* during the time prior to His return, as Jesus Himself declared (John 18:36). When He returns, He will destroy Satan's kingdom (i.e., his rule over the world system) and abolish that system in the earth (Revelation 19:11–16). Then He will establish His kingdom over this world, and His church will rule and reign with Him in this world (2 Timothy 2:12; Revelation 20:6).

In the meantime, Christ's kingdom is a spiritual kingdom based in heaven where He rules at the right hand of the Father, and it is also in the hearts of believers in this world (Luke 17:21; 1 Corinthians 15:50), who are His kingdom subjects and His spiritual body. These terms are metaphorical. His "kingdom" and His "body" in this world refer to the same thing: the believers who express, and witness to, His power by the Holy Spirit.

The term "church" does not refer to an institution. It describes the spiritual condition of believers—the "called out ones" who have been separated from the world system and the kingdom of Satan and set apart ("saints" is a translation of the Greek *hagioi*, meaning separated or set apart) to be His instruments in this world. They are members of the kingdom of light who are in the midst of the kingdom of darkness but not part of it,

> "joyfully giving thanks to the Father, who has qualified [them] to share in the inheritance of the saints in the kingdom of light. For he has rescued us from the dominion of darkness and brought us into the kingdom of the Son he loves . . . (Colossians 1:12–13).

You who are in the church are to become ". . . children of God without fault in a crooked and depraved generation in which you shine like stars in the universe as you hold out the word of life . . ." (Philippians 2:15–16).

The purpose of the church (those in the kingdom of light), then, is to hold out the word of life to those caught in the kingdom of darkness so that they too might escape and be translated into the kingdom of light.

By attempting to shift the church's proper focus from this spiritual rescue operation (which includes evangelism and sanctification) to social reform, Reconstructionism has planted a major seed of apostasy. For they have misinterpreted Jesus' purpose for the church and obscured the proper role of Christians in this world as they await His return.

Moreover, in the long run and in a broad sense, Reconstructionism is a fruitless effort doomed to failure, and all that it is trying to accomplish will be accomplished by Jesus when He comes again and establishes His earthly kingdom.

God's purpose in allowing the Tribulation and the reign of the antichrist is not to see who will rule in history (the church or Satan's world system) but to give the world one last chance to choose which side it will serve. The purpose of the Rapture is to preserve the church from the destruction which will result when the wrath of God is poured out on the earth. When the church (and with it the Holy Spirit) is removed, there will be nothing to restrain Satan (2 Thessalonians 2:7–8). The reign of the antichrist will reveal the true nature of Satan's program and its fruit. Those who choose it will do so knowing they are opposing God and cursing Him (Revelation 16:9, 11, 21).

Then the earth will be cleansed and healed. Like a disease which has been allowed to fester and erupt in a painful abscess, its poison will be released and all traces of the infection removed by the power of Jesus Christ and His heavenly host. Then the curse will have been cancelled, the elect will be fully redeemed, unregenerate man cast into outer darkness, and Satan and His demons bound in the bottomless pit (Revelation 20:2–3).

In summary, then, I believe Reconstructionism contradicts the clear meaning of scripture regarding the role of the church and the events of the end times, causing doctrinal confusion and division within Christ's body. By teaching that the Rapture is not imminent and that there will be no future Tribulation, Reconstructionism removes the need for urgency and preparation for Jesus' return.

The temptation of power and control, then, exists within the church as disguised occultism and humanism among those who would take control away from God by seeking to accomplish His work through their own efforts. The Bible, however, says just the opposite, that power and control are His and become available to us only if we ask for it according to His will:

> This is the confidence we have in approaching God: that if we ask anything *according to his will*, he hears us. And if we know that he hears us—whatever we ask—we know that we have what we asked of him (1 John 5:14–15, emphasis added).

CHAPTER TWO

Seed Two: The Temptation of Wealth

The second seed of apostasy is similar to the first in that it has a basis in shamanism. Those who see Christianity as a means to material wealth believe such prosperity comes through mental control or the power of one's thinking. This heresy was first introduced in America in the early Nineteenth Century through Transcendentalism and then into the church through New Thought. It has since become

> the basis for such mind science cults as Christian Science, Religious Science, and Unity. Today's church is being swept by a revival of New Thought, now called Positive Thinking, Possibility Thinking, Positive Confession, [or] Positive Mental Attitude. . . . One of the most basic New Thought techniques is visualization, which is now firmly entrenched within the church.[1]

The Positive Confession Movement (PCM)

Hunt shows that the techniques of success/motivation seminars have been introduced into the church by such Positive Confession leaders as Dennis Waitly, a Christian psychologist, and pastor/author C.S. Lovett. In these seminars, "imagination" (i.e., visualization) is considered to be the key that unlocks infinite human potential and leads to business, professional, and financial success. "Waitly declares: 'As you see yourself in the heart of your thought, in your mind's eye, so you do become.'" Lovett says,

> Imagination is the key to creation. Everything God is doing He first sees in His mind. And so it is with men made in His image. . . .
>
> While our faith allows us to accept what we can't see . . . imagination takes us a step beyond, allowing us to PICTURE what we cannot see.[2] [Emphasis in original.]

The power to acquire wealth, or to accomplish any other purpose, then, is supposedly in the mind and in the words spoken to claim what is visualized. This basic technique of the PCM is the same as that of shamanism. "The metaphysical philosophy underlying Positive Thinking and Possibility Thinking as well as major aspects of the Positive Confession movement is founded upon the alleged power inherent within thoughts and words."[3]

Those in the PCM believe that, by thinking in a certain way and speaking certain words, they compel God to respond as they wish. As Hunt says, anyone doing this "has slipped into sorcery, and, if not playing God, is at the very least attempting to manipulate God. PCM teacher Charles Capps . . . says, 'This is not theory. It is a fact. It is spiritual law. It works every time it is applied correctly. . . . You set them [spiritual laws] in motion by the words of your mouth . . . everything you say—will come to pass.'"[4]

Again, Christians who use such techniques are not relying on God or honoring His sovereignty. They are usurping God's authority and substituting the power of their own minds and words for the power and authority of God. They are putting themselves in the place of God and thereby saying God is not necessary. They are also demonstrating that all they are really interested in is results on a humanistic level and not in a proper relationship with their heavenly Father.

All of these characteristics of the PCM are, in fact, parts of the New Age model for success and prosperity (which we shall examine in detail in Parts III and IV). The biblical model, on the other hand, is to rely on God as our provider, petitioning Him *to meet our needs (not give us wealth)*, obeying His Word, denying ourselves, walking in His Spirit, and being good stewards and content with what we have.

In fact, so contrary to the scripture is such preoccupation with wealth that the Bible warns Christians repeatedly about its dangers. For example,

> No one can serve two masters. Either he will hate
> the one and love the other, or he will be devoted
> to the one and despise the other. You cannot serve
> both God and Money (Matthew 6:24).

> But godliness with contentment is great gain. For
> we brought nothing into the world, and we can
> take nothing out of it. But if we have food and
> clothing, we will be content with that. People
> who want to get rich fall into temptation and a
> trap and into many foolish and harmful desires
> that plunge men into ruin and destruction. For
> the love of money is a root of all kinds of evil.
> Some people, eager for money, have wandered
> from the faith and pierced themselves with many
> griefs (1 Timothy 6:6–10).

Thus, the temptation of wealth and materialism
has infiltrated the church through the PCM and New
Age visualization and mind-over-matter techniques.

But the Bible says there should be no hint of greed
among God's people (Ephesians 5:3). You should not
worry about your material needs, "but in everything,
by prayer and petition, with thanksgiving, present
your requests to God" (Philippians 4:6). We are to
live by faith—not by mental manipulation—knowing that godliness with contentment is great gain and
that our God will meet all our *needs* (*not* our wants)
"according to his glorious riches in Christ Jesus"
(Philippians 4:19). Our focus should not be on the
things of this world, which are temporary and ultimately unsatisfying, but on the things of heaven,
which are eternal and permanently satisfying:

Do not love the world or anything in the world. If anyone loves the world, the love of the Father is not in him. For everything in the world—the cravings of sinful man, the lust of his eyes and the boasting of what he has and does—comes not from the Father but from the world. The world and its desires pass away, but the man who does the will of God lives forever (1 John 2:15–17).

CHAPTER THREE

Seed Three: The Temptation of Status

The third seed of apostasy, like the previous temptations, is based on a desire for superiority. In this case, it is not the godlike self-image of power and control nor the prestige and influence that comes with wealth, but rather the superiority of spiritual elitism and its accompanying sense of status.

Here, the lust of the eyes and pride of life associated with power and wealth have been transferred to one's sense of his own superior spirituality.

There are four basic areas where this deception can be found in the church:

Experiential religion
Extra-biblical revelation
Denominationalism
Racism

EXPERIENTIAL RELIGION

In experiential religion, one's personal, subjective "spiritual" experiences take precedence over scripture or logic or common sense as the basis of truth. It gives those who practice it a heightened sense of status and elitism because they believe they have attained special, exclusive knowledge as a result of their superior spirituality.

As we saw earlier, Christians who have experienced certain supernatural phenomena (such as angels pouring out the Holy Spirit from golden jars) may believe such experiences are from God, even though they clearly contradict the teachings of the Bible. However, they persist in this belief because such experiences give them a sense of heightened spiritual status. Thus they believe a lie, come under demonic deception, and may be led step by step into apostasy.

A number of abuses in the charismatic movement fall into this category. For example, in seeking the supernatural gifts and manifestations of the Holy Spirit (such as the gifts of prophecy, word of wisdom, and interpretation of tongues, as described in 1 Corinthians 12 and 14), many Christians have fallen into the trap of seeking after the gifts rather than the Giver. Their focus is on experiencing sensational phenomena, with its accompanying sense of spiritual superiority, rather than on growing in their relationship to Christ and their obedience and humility in service to Him. The result can be a lack of discernment in accepting any "prophetic word" as coming from God—no matter how unscriptural or hurtful the message may be.

Similarly, such bizarre experiences as those we observed earlier in the Toronto Blessing are accepted by large numbers of otherwise rational Christians as being genuine manifestations of the Holy Spirit. Since only those elite Christians who are on a higher spiritual level, supposedly, can have such experiences, they carry with them a sense of heightened spiritual status. (This subject is discussed in more detail with specific examples in chapter twelve.)

EXTRA-BIBLICAL REVELATION

An inevitable result of experiential religion is extra-biblical revelation. It means that "prophets" and "prophecies" become the source of "new truth" which adds to and frequently contradicts that found in scripture. The sense of spiritual superiority in this comes from the belief that one has a direct pipeline to God. In its extreme forms, this spiritual elitism produces cults which believe they have exclusive access to divine truth and that their leaders are infallible in their teachings because they are directly inspired by "God" or at least His ministering "angels."

Again, abuses in this area abound in the charismatic church, sometimes with disastrous results, as in the case of Jonestown.

The flip side of these charismatic abuses is the rejection of most (if not all) supernatural experiences and manifestations as "of the devil" by many Christians in the evangelical church.

This throwing-out-the-baby-with-the-bathwater mentality gives Satan a double victory, for, not only has he duped the charismatics into swallowing whole everything labeled "supernatural," but he has also robbed the evangelicals of those genuine supernatural gifts of power and knowledge which God wants them to have.

This closed-mindedness to the manifestations of the Holy Spirit often carries with it its own brand of spiritual superiority and status. If we set ourselves up as the judges of what God can or cannot do in supernatural matters, then we must have better knowledge and higher truth and sounder doctrine than others. So we are right back into spiritual elitism.

DENOMINATIONALISM

This attitude of doctrinal superiority and exclusiveness is, unfortunately, the basis for much of the denominationalism in the church. And this may automatically give a sense of spiritual status and approval to anyone who belongs to any particular denomination. As John Hagee says,

> Denominationalism is to approve of a person because he belongs to your brand of church. Denominationalism is idolatry. It's love for who you are, not what you are. . . . The devil's crowd can come together in absolute unity over anything. God's crowd looks for a reason to reject anything

spiritual not born of our respective denominations. The concept seems to be, "If we didn't
think of it, neither has God."[1]

Thus, it is the doctrinal *tradition* of the denomination, handed down and passed on unquestioningly and without discernment over the generations,
that excludes any truth but theirs. Only their interpretation is the right one, and all other possible interpretations are excluded.

Legalism and Asceticism

Closely associated with this attitude of doctrinal elitism are those of legalism and asceticism. Legalism says, "Since we have the truth, our way is
the right way. And our rules are what God requires.
Therefore, if you don't follow these rules, you can't
be a good Christian or please God. However, if you
do follow them, then you are spiritually superior to
all those in other denominations who don't agree
with us."

Asceticism is a type of legalism which says,
"There are certain kinds of pleasures (food, drink,
entertainment, etc.) which you must deny yourself in order to be spiritually pure and acceptable
to God. If you exercise the self-discipline required
to do this, then you will be spiritually superior to
those who don't."

This kind of submission to human rules and authority in the church can lead to cultism. The cult
mentality is essentially one of spiritual elitism car-

ried to the extreme. The cult member not only believes his group has special, exclusive knowledge and truth, but also that the leader is infallible, accountable only to God, and has absolute authority and control over his followers, who must submit to his direction without question.

In one of the charismatic churches I attended, this kind of cult mentality had not yet become quite so extreme. But the senior pastor believed himself to be an apostle and "the anointed of the Lord" with direct authority from God over his congregation. Those who did not agree with him or carry out his directives, he considered disloyal. When he required his staff to sign a statement saying they were in submission to him, several associate pastors refused and left the church, causing a split in the congregation. I believe they were probably fired since this was the senior pastor's pattern—to get rid of those who disagreed with him or who he felt posed a threat to his total control.

It so happened that my wife was the secretary to these associate pastors. The senior pastor called her into his office and told her that her loyalty must not be to them but to him. She replied that her loyalty was not to any man but to Jesus Christ. Needless to say, she did not keep her job, and we left the church.

From what I have since read and heard, similar experiences are not too uncommon in churches throughout America.

Behind all these forms of elitism, then, is spiritual pride, the desire of believers (including pastors) to compare themselves with other Christians in order to feel spiritually superior. The result in all such cases is to see less of a need for God's grace, guidance, and discipline and to move closer to apostasy. But the Bible says,

> All of you clothe yourselves with humility toward one another, because "God opposes the proud but gives grace to the humble."
>
> Humble yourselves, therefore, under God's mighty hand, that he may lift you up in due time (1 Peter 5:5–6).

RACISM

The fourth deception involved in the temptation of status is racism within the church. It is based on the delusion that physical and cultural differences make one group of Christians superior to another, not only on a natural level but also, perhaps, on a spiritual level. This belief is, of course, very divisive and has been one of Satan's major strategies for disrupting and weakening the church. For this reason, its elimination has been a major focus of some corrective movements in the church, including Promise Keepers.

The Bible says that among Christians who have taken off the old self and put on the new self, "which is being renewed in knowledge in the image of its Creator, . . . there is no Greek or Jew, circumcised or uncircumcised, barbarian, Scythian, slave or free, but Christ is all and in all" (Colossians 3:9–11).

It also says, "Do nothing out of selfish ambition or vain conceit, but in humility consider others better than yourselves. Each of you should look not only to your own interests, but also to the interests of others" (Philippians 2:3–4).

And Jesus prayed to the Father for *all* believers

> . . . that all of them may be one. Father, just as you are in me and I am in you, may they also be in us so that the world may believe that you have sent me. I have given them the glory that you gave me, that they may be one as we are one: I in them and you in me. May they be brought to complete unity to let the world know that you sent me and have loved them even as you have loved me (John 17:20–23).

Thus, the scriptures declare that spiritually there are no distinctions among Christians based on race, nationality, socio-economic status, or anything else, but that we are all one in Christ. Therefore, if we make such distinctions, we are not only guilty of the sin of pride, by setting ourselves above others, but we are also directly contradicting the teaching of scripture and the will of Christ. We are also damaging the church's credibility and witness to the world and hindering Jesus' message to the lost: that God loves them.

The temptation of status, then, is essentially the sin of pride. It is a sense of spiritual superiority derived from special supernatural experiences, supposed new revelations of truth, identification with the elitism of a certain denomination, or an imagined elevation based on one's race. Not only is each of these deceptions a source of division in the body of Christ, it is also a potential seed of apostasy, for it places subjective experience and self-glorification above scriptural truth and unconditional love.

CHAPTER FOUR

Seed Four: The Temptation of Happiness

In the fourth seed of apostasy, there is no desire for superiority, but only for self-gratification through physical and psychological pleasure. This temptation, which could also be called hedonism or worldliness, takes a number of forms in the following categories: sensation, ease, and peace.

Essentially it means living after the flesh (i.e., doing your own thing according to the old, unregenerate, carnal, or sinful nature). This is defined in Romans 8:5–8:

> Those who live according to the sinful nature ["after the flesh" (KJV)] have their minds set on what that nature desires; but those who live in accordance with the Spirit have their minds set on what the Spirit desires. The mind of the sinful man is death, but the mind controlled by the

Spirit is life and peace; the sinful mind is hostile
to God. It does not submit to God's law, nor can
it do so. Those controlled by the sinful nature
cannot please God.

This way of living—separate from, hostile toward, and displeasing to God—can also be thought
of as love of, or friendship with, the world and living according to the ways of the world:

You adulterous people, don't you know that
friendship with the world is hatred towards God?
Anyone who chooses to be a friend of the world
becomes an enemy of God (James 4:4).

This lust after the world's "happiness" not only
separates us from God (because it is in fact hostility
toward God and His ways), but it also can lead to
total apostasy and spiritual death.

Unfortunately, as we have already seen, a large
percentage of Christians have bought into a worldly
lifestyle, dedicated primarily to achieving "happiness" according to the world's standards. They prefer entertainment and physical gratification to
righteousness and truth. And other forms of hedonism, including comfort and luxury, are high on
their priority list.

At best, such Christians, like those in the church
at Laodicea, are lukewarm. This is the final church
described in the Book of Revelation, and I believe it
applies directly to the church in our day, especially
in America:

I know your deeds, that you are neither cold nor hot. I wish you were either one or the other! So, because you are lukewarm—neither hot nor cold—I am about to spit you out of my mouth. You say 'I am rich; I have acquired wealth and do not need a thing.' But you do not realize that you are wretched, pitiful, poor, blind and naked (Revelation 3:15–17).

In the Laodicean church of our day, there is a focus on self rather than God. "What's in it for me?" has become more important than "What is the truth?" or "What does God want for me and from me?" The Laodiceans trusted in their wealth rather than in God, and so it became their god. Thus, it is our attitude toward riches and not the wealth itself which is the problem.

The consumer marketing mentality among many pastors says packaging is more important than content and numbers are more essential than righteousness. Entertainment and gimmicks are used to attract the worldly into the church, but what they find there is not much different than what they had in the world.

Is it any wonder, then, that many churches are experiencing the revolving door syndrome with potential converts leaving as fast as they are coming in? The problem, as Wilkerson says, is that these churches lack a godly testimony.

The goal is wrong. It should be conviction of sin and not fun and games. It should be the need for God to be in charge, for spiritual rebirth, and for transformed lives and not comfortable surroundings, a better lifestyle, and more "happiness." These things are not wrong in themselves, but they become seeds of apostasy when they become more important than serving God and ministering to others.

SENSATION

Thrills, excitement, and pleasure are the basic appeals of the entertainment gospel. In using these enticements, the church is displaying a pragmatic attitude of expediency which says, "Whatever works is okay."

For example, in-church concerts featuring loud, hard rock music are geared to get young people in the doors. This music is barely distinguishable from the worldly sounds and beats found at a rock concert. It certainly is not worshipful in the sense of promoting an attitude of awe and adoration for a holy and majestic God. And there is nothing about it likely to bring one to a conviction of sin or the need for repentance. At one of the churches I have attended, this type of music, along with flashing psychedelic lights and billowing clouds of colored smoke, is a major element of their "evangelistic outreach." (For a fuller discussion of rock music in the church and its satanic origins, see chapter sixteen.)

While it is apparently true that people do get saved at such events, is it really by means of the music and entertainment, or is it that God uses the occasion anyway—in spite of the means—to bring sinners to salvation by the amazing convicting power of the Holy Spirit? It is a controversial issue, but one which I believe needs to be raised and considered with careful discernment.

This same desire for sensation is also the driving force behind many of the charismatic abuses which we have already noted. Spiritual goose bumps are more important than spiritual discernment. We need to test the spirits to see if supernatural experiences are based on truth rather than deception and if they lead to righteousness and holiness rather than apostasy.

EASE

The temptation to find happiness through ease takes two basic forms: the desire for comfort and the inclination toward apathy.

Comfort is a predominant theme of the New Age philosophy which focuses on such things as the resolution of conflict, the promotion of harmony, the reduction of stress, the enhancement of self-image and self-esteem, and the relaxed, passive flow along the lines of least resistance. These objectives are calculated to satisfy our natural desire for comfort, and many Christians have accepted them as worthwhile goals without concern for whether they are achieved through biblical, godly means or not.

Rejection of Suffering

A perfect example is the false doctrine which holds that Christians should not suffer, either from lack of resources, from poor health, or from adversity. The Word of Faith church that I attended taught that it was a sign of spiritual weakness and lack of faith if one experienced suffering and that God wanted to remove all suffering from the Christian's life because of His desire to bless His children. When I told the pastor I had found a scripture that said there is a kind of suffering that is according to God's will, he couldn't believe it. I had to show it to Him in his Bible. He was literally dumbfounded because it contradicted the denominational doctrine that he was totally committed to. When I naively taught on the subject of godly suffering at our Wednesday night service, it aroused a storm of protest within the congregation.

However, this anti-suffering teaching is totally unscriptural. The apostle Peter says to the church,

> Dear friends, do not be surprised at the painful trial you are suffering, as though something strange were happening to you. But rejoice that you participate in the sufferings of Christ, so that you may be overjoyed when his glory is revealed. . . . So then, those who *suffer according to God's will* should commit themselves to the faithful Creator and continue to do good (1 Peter 5:12–13, 19, emphasis added).

This says that, if we participate in the sufferings of Christ, it is according to God's will. This means that we should suffer for the same reasons He did: to deny ourselves in order to do the Father's will, to speak the truth without compromise, to share the gospel as directed by the Holy Spirit, to endure mistreatment without complaint or retaliation, to undergo physical hardship and emotional stress in order to serve God.

For these reasons, Paul spent time in prison, was flogged, stoned, and shipwrecked, faced dangers and threats of many other kinds, went without sleep, food, and water, and endured cold, nakedness, and emotional trials (2 Corinthians 11:23–29). In all these situations, he learned to be content and to rely on the Lord to give him the strength to come through them (Philippians 4:12–13). Were they a sign that his faith was weak, that he was not walking in the Spirit, or that there was hidden, unconfessed sin in his life? Obviously not.

Moreover, thousands of mature, totally committed Christians are suffering and/or being martyred for their faith around the world—in Sudan, China, Russia, the Middle East, and elsewhere. Only in Western countries, especially America, it seems, is suffering considered something to be avoided, based on the belief that we are protected *because* we are Christians.

However, Peter tells us that suffering is a necessary part of our Christian walk and our sanctification, enabling us to grow spiritually and become all that God wants us to be:

> In this you greatly rejoice, though for a little while you may have had to suffer grief in all kinds of trials. These have come so that your faith—of greater worth than gold, which perishes even

though refined by fire—may be proved genuine
and may result in praise, glory and honor when
Jesus Christ is revealed (1 Peter l:6–7).

Adherence to Tradition

Our natural desire for comfort may also lead
us to cling to our religious traditions at the expense of truth (as did the Pharisees). In our natural walk, we continue in the old ways and beliefs
without examining them to see if they are scriptural because it is more comfortable to feel that we
have all the answers. We like the "security" of believing that we are right, and we avoid the fright-
ening feeling of being unsure or the threat to our
pride of admitting that we don't know or—horror
of horrors—that we are wrong.

Self-righteous pride and fear of the unfamiliar
may cause Christians to adhere blindly to their doctrinal tradition—in the face of clear scriptural evidence to the contrary. An example of this, I believe,
is the belief that the baptism in the Holy Spirit with
its manifestations of supernatural gifts is not for today. This rejection of what God wants His church to
have "for the common good" and for our strengthening, encouragement, comfort, and edification (1
Corinthians 12:7; 14:3–4) is based on two assumptions: (1) that all the supernatural gifts of the Spirit
(except, oddly, the gift of healing) ceased in the first
century after the New Testament scriptures were
written and/or (2) that we receive everything we are
going to get in the way of gifting (supernatural or
otherwise) at the moment of conversion.

These beliefs are currently widespread in the body of Christ. Many evangelical Christians believe the former, and a surprising number also believe the latter. In one church I have attended, several members of the pastoral staff and eldership believe the latter—that the baptism in the Holy Spirit happens when you are saved and whatever gifts you are to have are received only at that time.

Those with this view believe that the baptism in the Holy Spirit is synonymous with the "infilling" or "quickening" of the Holy Spirit that one receives at the moment of salvation. However, some with this view also believe that the gifts of the Spirit may be given to any believer at any time as the Spirit sees fit.

I agree with the latter view because my own experience and several passages in scripture (cited below) contradict the former view. In my experience, the spiritual *infilling* and *baptism* were two distinct events. About three months after I was saved, the pastor prayed for a group of believers (of which I was a part) to receive the baptism in the Holy Spirit. I (and several others) immediately began to speak in tongues. My pentecostal pastor defined this as the baptism in the Holy Spirit.

Later, I found that occasionally I was moved by the Spirit to speak in tongues and interpret or to minister words of prophecy and knowledge for the encouragement and strengthening of others. These "manifestation" gifts have remained with me throughout my Christian walk.

More rarely, the Holy Spirit operates through me to minister in faith, healing, and other gifts as the need arises, but I do not feel that these have been given as my permanent or continuing gifts—as have the others. Therefore, I believe there are two categories of such gifts: those that are given as one's personal gifts at the time of the Spirit baptism and those which are occasional gifts, activated only for special purposes at special times.

"SUPERNATURAL GIFTS HAVE CEASED"

Tradition number one, the assumption that supernatural gifts are not for today, implies, first, that we don't need direct revelation and guidance from God today. In other words, the prophetic gifts— prophecy, word of wisdom, word of knowledge, and interpretation of tongues—are no longer needed as they were in the early church. Second, it implies that the Bible contains all the guidance we need for every situation we may ever face. In other words, God no longer speaks directly or individually to His people by means of gifted individuals who communicate His will regarding specific situations or needs in their lives. In addition, according to this view, He no longer directly provides supernatural power or knowledge through gifting to help them in times of physical or spiritual need.

This, of course, effectively cuts off those who hold to this tradition from much of the help that the Bible plainly says is available from God and that He wants us to have. Paul states that

> . . . *in the church* God has appointed first of all apostles, second prophets, third teachers, then workers of miracles, also those having gifts of healing, those able to help others, those with gifts of administrations, and those speaking in different kinds of tongues (1 Corinthians 12:28, emphasis added).

Here, Paul mixes supernatural gifts (prophecy, miracles, healing, and speaking in tongues) with commonly recognized ministry gifts (apostleship (i.e., missionary activities), teaching, helps, and administration). There is no distinction drawn between these two categories nor any indication that some of them are to cease and others are not. They are all equally appointed in the church by God. And, if they were *all* needed in the church in Paul's day, they are certainly all needed just as much if not more in our day—in view of widespread persecution, demonic attack, deception, immorality, and ungodliness. (This controversial issue and its implications for the church today are discussed more fully in chapters twelve and thirteen.)

"BAPTISM IN THE HOLY SPIRIT HAPPENS ONLY AT CONVERSION"

Tradition number two assumes that there is no possibility of receiving spiritual gifts or the baptism in the Holy Spirit after the moment of salvation. In other words, if you didn't get it when you were saved, you're never going to get it. This totally cuts you (and the church) off from receiving what God wants you to have—*if*, in fact, you didn't receive any clear gifting at salvation. But Paul, speaking to born-again Christians, says, we are to "eagerly desire spiritual gifts" (1 Corinthians 14:1) and that we should "try to excel in the gifts that build up the church" (i.e., prophecy, tongues and interpretation, word of instruction (word of wisdom), and revelation (word of knowledge)), and, finally, that "All of these *must* be done for the strengthening of the church" (1 Corinthians 14:26, emphasis added).

Let me ask: what is the point of desiring spiritual gifts if there is no possibility of receiving them, and how can we try to excel in something that there is no possibility of having? The above scriptures clearly indicate that, when these Christians were saved, they *did not* receive all of their gifting, for they are told to eagerly desire them, and we only desire that which we do not have.

Let me also ask: by declaring these things obsolete, eliminating them from the church, and/or making them unavailable after conversion, who wins? Certainly not the church! On the contrary, it is obviously Satan and those in his camp, who thereby achieve their goals of weakening and robbing the church.

Spiritual Apathy

Closely allied with blind adherence to tradition is spiritual apathy, the feeling that all is well and there is no need for concern about our spiritual condition, individually or corporately. This lack of a sense of urgency stems from the desire to maintain the feeling of comfort and security found in the status quo. Therefore, those in this state feel there is no need to exercise discernment regarding possible deception by false teachers or ungodly influences in the church. Often, there may even be no sense of a need to be on guard against demonic attacks or to take part in spiritual warfare. "After all," such thinking goes, "Satan has already been defeated, so we don't need to worry about him."

Again, let me ask: who wins with such an attitude? Obviously, the enemy that we think doesn't exist or that we think doesn't pose any real threat.

The Bible, however, says that "Your enemy the devil prowls around like a roaring lion looking for someone to devour (1 Peter 5:8). And Jesus warned that Satan "comes only to steal and kill and destroy" (John 10:10).

PEACE

The temptation to find happiness through peace (or harmony) takes two main forms: (1) the desire for *unity among people* and (2) the desire to be in harmony with nature or the whole earth; that is, *environmentalism.*

Unity Among People

The desire for unity is certainly not wrong in itself—unless it comes at the expense of truth. This, unfortunately, is becoming increasingly the case among Christians. It can be seen in the tolerance of "christian" cults (such as Mormonism, Jehovah's

Witnesses, and Christian Science) and of the paganizing of traditional Christian holy days such as Christmas, Easter, and Halloween.

This attitude of tolerance toward unscriptural and ungodly beliefs and practices is a reflection of the New Age idea that there must be no "negativity" but only a positive acceptance of "diversity." Thus, truth and righteousness are compromised for the sake of unity and harmony.

This kind of compromising at the expense of scriptural truth can also be seen in the acceptance of homosexual clergy and same-sex marriages, which clearly are condemned according to the following scriptures:

> . . . God gave them over to shameful lusts. Even their women exchanged natural relations for unnatural ones. In the same way the men also abandoned natural relations with women and were inflamed with lust for one another. Men committed indecent acts with other men and received in themselves the due penalty for their perversion (Romans 1:27).

> Neither the sexually immoral nor idolaters nor adulterers nor male prostitutes nor homosexual offenders nor thieves nor the greedy nor drunkards nor slanderers nor swindlers will inherit the kingdom of God (1 Corinthians 6:9–10).

> . . . Sodom and Gomorrah and the surrounding towns gave themselves up to sexual immorality and perversion. They serve as an

example of those who suffer the punishment of eternal fire (Jude 7).

Ecumenicalism

But it is in the ecumenical movement, the purpose of which is to bring all of the world's religions together, that such compromise perhaps becomes most extreme in its disregard for the teachings of the Bible.

The birth of the ecumenical movement may have taken place at the first World Parliament of Religions in 1893. One of its objectives was

> . . . "to bring the nations of the earth into a more friendly fellowship, in the hope of securing permanent international peace." One hundred years later, the goal was the same.

> [From] August 28 to September 5, 1993, the second World Parliament of Religions. . . representing 50 world religions and quasi-religions gathered for the centennial celebration. There were representatives from the Buddhist; Orthodox; Roman Catholic; Anglican and other Protestant denominations; Hindu; Jewish; Confucian; Native American; Jain; various Muslim groups; Taoist; Wiccan; Unitarian Universalists; The Fellowship of Isis; The Covenant of the Goddess; The Center for Women, the Earth, and the Divine; The Temple of Understanding; The Theosophical Society; The Earth-Spirit Community; and many, many more faiths. . . . Equal voice and footing was given to each of the

religions represented. And together these representatives put together a document titled *Towards
a Global Ethic (An Initial Declaration)*.

The *Global Ethic* document . . . replaces intolerant and exclusionary teachings, such as
those of Biblical Christianity, with ethical principles found in each of the world's religions,
even secular humanism. . . . The purpose behind them is to provide an earth-based salvation for humanity, rather than the spiritual
salvation offered through Jesus Christ, man's
only true hope.[1]

As expressed in the World Parliament of Religions, then, the ecumenical movement subscribes
to the following principles:

1. All religions are valid and worthy of honor
    and respect.
2. Biblical Christianity is intolerant and exclu-
    sionary and therefore not as valid or worthy
    as other religions.
3. The ethical principles common to all reli-
    gions are what is really important, imply-
    ing that salvation is through works rather
    than through God's grace as provided for
    by Jesus Christ.

These basic principles have not been repudi-
ated by Christians who support the ecumenical
movement in its various forms today because such
believers apparently place unity and harmony

above the truth of the gospel. Sadly, even a number of prominent Christian leaders have been identified by Hunt as supporting and promoting such ecumenical groups because they too apparently value tolerance over truth.[2]

Does this mean that I think these men are not good Christians or are heading straight for apostasy? Not at all. But it does mean that I think, no matter how learned, eminent, successful, or revered they may be in their ministries, they may still be deceived in certain areas because of a lack of proper caution and spiritual discernment.

Some liberal churches have carried the ecumenical spirit to the point where they even openly promote certain teachings of the New Age Movement and eastern religions. These churches, according to Hal Lindsey, are "ever concerned about being 'pluralistic' and 'open-minded'" and "have embraced some of the teachings of Buddhism, yoga, and other New Age spiritualities with open arms."[3]

Environmentalism

The desire to be at one with nature and to revere the earth is another aspect of the quest for peace. This is, once again, to be achieved through unity and harmony at the expense of truth.

Mikhail Gorbachev, a strong advocate of environmentalism and ecological globalism, expresses well this point of view: "Ecological education implies, above all, respect and love for every living thing. It is here that ecological culture interferes with religion. . . . Honoring diversity and honoring the earth creates the basis for genuine unity."[4]

Indeed, environmentalism has become a new religion with the earth as its deity. Unfortunately, many of its principles have taken on doctrinal status within the church. The Lalondes note that, by 1990, many pastors and church leaders had already been encouraging Christians to view salvation from sociological and ecological perspectives. For example, Richard Land, executive director of the Southern Baptist Convention's Christian Life Commission, told ministers gathered in Nashville for the promotion of Earth Day 1990, to "embrace a broader sense of salvation: 'salvation of humankind and redemptive creation.'"

Others were blaming Christianity and biblical teaching for the environmental degradation facing mankind. This comment was found in the *St. Petersburg Times*:

> It's going to take a rethinking of Western society's interpretation of those bible passages, particularly the one that gives humans dominion over all living things. "Be fruitful and multiply," God said: "fill the earth and subdue it."
>
> Another contributing factor to the Earth's demise is the salvation-oriented view that many Christian groups maintain. Why bother with taking care of this world when a much better one is waiting just around the corner.

The Lalondes note that many Christians have joined the environmentalists, wanting to become good stewards of the earth. Unfortunately, many were at the same time being swept up in a worldview contrary to the Word of God. . . .the movement was telling us that the "Earth"—Mother Earth, Gaia, the Earth Goddess—is sacred. . . .

Even former Vice President Al Gore, a practicing Southern Baptist, suggested that perhaps the time had come to consider some of the wisdom of the ancient religions based on respect for the planet.

In his book, *Earth in the Balance*, Gore called for

. . . a renewed *investigation of the wisdom distilled by all faiths*. This panreligious perspective may prove especially important where our global civilization's responsibility for the earth is concerned.

Native American religions, for instance, offer a rich tapestry of ideas about our relationship to the earth.[5] [Emphasis added.]

In these quotes, we see a direct, unbiblical connection in the church between ecumenicalism and environmentalism/globalism. In the name of "stewardship," the church's message of salvation is negated, and in its place are put ideas and values from other religions including the worship of "Mother Earth."

The temptation to happiness, then, is the desire for an emotional state that finds pleasure in sensations and comfort in ease and peace. While these things are not wrong in themselves, they can be seeds of apostasy when they become more important than adherence to the teachings of the Bible. The result can be compromising with truth and righteousness and substituting a temporary feeling of satisfaction for the abiding joy which comes from an intimate relationship with Jesus Christ.

Joy, unlike happiness, is not based on circumstances or emotional or physical gratification. It is the result of our dependence on and obedience to God. It is, in fact, an attribute of Christ Himself that we receive directly from Him when we choose to remain in His love and therefore to obey His commands:

> As the Father has loved me, so have I loved you. Now remain in my love. If you obey my commands, you will remain in my love, just as I have obeyed my Father's commands and remain in his love. I have told you this so that *my joy* may be in you and that *your joy* may be complete (John 15:9–11, emphasis added).

CHAPTER FIVE

Seed Five: The Temptation of Health (Holistic Medicine)

The fifth seed of apostasy, the temptation of health, applies specifically to the quest for health through holistic medicine. It is related to the temptation of happiness in that it too involves the desire for ease, comfort, a sense of well-being, and avoidance of suffering. It is termed "holistic" because it views health as the harmonious condition of the *whole* person—physically, mentally, emotionally, and spiritually.

The entire field of holistic health contains numerous seeds of apostasy because many of its beliefs and practices involve occult principles, and, unless one is extremely cautious and discerning, it can lead one gradually into deeper and deeper involvement in the occult. In this process, reliance on eastern medical practices (and their underlying religious beliefs) can become a substitute for reliance on the healing power of God. Similarly, reliance on psycho-spiritual techniques can become a substitute for reliance on prayer and the guidance and power of the Holy Spirit.

At the same time, it is important to remember that all holistic medicine is not based on the occult or necessarily spiritually dangerous in itself, especially those aspects which rely on natural remedies (e.g., herbs, diet, and exercise). But, again, there is the tendency among many Christians to throw the baby out with the bathwater—to reject *all* aspects of holistic medicine because *some* are associated with occult principles or practices.

In fact, this is another area in which Satan robs the church. God has provided many safe, effective natural remedies for man's benefit. But Satan, by putting his stamp upon them through New Age, eastern, or shamanistic practitioners, has denied their benefits to those Christians who fail to exercise discernment, not separating what is natural and God-given from what is demonic.

My own experience is, once again, a case in point. In 1982, the arthritis in my wrists was so severe that writing a sentence was an extremely laborious, painful process. If I stood for more than ten minutes, my knees hurt so much I had to sit. The pain in my joints kept me from sleeping unless I took several aspirin during the night and rubbed in pain-killing ointment. Even then, the pain didn't leave completely and my sleep (what little I got) was restless and shallow. Consequently,

I was tired all the time. I was also becoming stiff and slow and discouraged.

The day eventually came when I realized that I was not functioning effectively in my job and other areas of my life and things were going downhill rapidly. I knew I had to do something about it—and fast.

So, of course, I went to the doctor. He said take aspirin and vitamin E and see the physical therapist. I was already taking far too much aspirin, but I started immediately on the vitamin E and physical therapy. The vitamin E seemed to help a little and the physical therapy felt great while it lasted. Then, as soon as the treatment was over, the pain and stiffness returned. My symptoms might be a little better one day and much worse the next.

I followed this routine for several months with no real improvement. So I decided that, if this was all orthodox medicine had to offer for my arthritis, I had better start looking elsewhere. I went to the library and read everything I could find on the subject. I went to health food stores and asked what they had for arthritis. I went to a naturopathic physician, who prescribed a variety of natural remedies. At the same time, I began trying the other things I had read or heard about.

Today, some twenty years later—after experimenting with literally dozens of diet changes, food supplements, vitamins, minerals, herbs, and exercise—I am free of nearly all arthritis symptoms, and have been so for approximately the last ten years.

I have recounted this experience in some detail because it illustrates so clearly the limitations of standard medical treatment, in certain cases, and the necessity of finding alternative (i.e., holistic) therapies and the tremendous benefits that can be obtained from them.

On the other hand, we must not fall into uncritically swallowing everything whole where holistic medicine is concerned. Everything labeled "natural" or "holistic" is not from the same source or necessarily good. Again, discernment is needed to separate the ungodly from the God-given. As one pair of notable researchers have found,

> occultism and spiritistic influence are frequently the source of power behind the origin and/or treatments of numerous specific holistic health practices . . . holistic health methods are frequently found to depend upon some form of energy channeling. . . . These energies are frequently associated with the mystical energies of occultic religion; e.g., the Hindu *prana*, Taoist *chi*, shamanistic *mana*, etc.[1]

These energies are psychic in nature and therefore subject to demonic manipulation and/or transference for purposes which are ultimately unholy and spiritually damaging. They may, in fact, "lead a person into occult involvement and therefore bring the same kinds of physical, psychological, and spiritual dangers associated with occult practices." Ankerberg and Weldon find that "not only are holistic health methods increasingly employed by Christians, but . . . many don't seem to care about the spiritual issues involved—as long as a practice 'works.'"[2]

TREATMENT OF PHYSICAL CONDITIONS

(In this and the following sections, there are literally dozens of possible treatments. However, in the interest of relevance and brevity, only a few of the most common will be discussed.)

Holistic practices related primarily to the treatment of physical ailments include the following examples, all of which may be wholly or partially based on occult principles:

Traditional Chinese Medicine

A system based on the yin and yang principle of Taoism. Its purpose is to restore harmony and balance to the energy flow in the body. This involves the manipulation of *chi* (also known as *qi* or *ki*), the "vital life energy" which supposedly follows pathways in the body called meridians. Traditional Chinese medicine encompasses herbal medicine, acupuncture, acupressure, dietary therapy, and massage, and incorporates meditative relaxation, calisthenics, internal energy exercises, and laying on of hands.[3] Its followers recommend the regular practice of tai chi which is also based on Taoist philosophy and is said to "help balance the body's energy and prevent health problems."[4] (See chapter fifteen for a detailed discussion of tai chi.)

Since traditional Chinese medicine is based on an eastern religion incorporating occult practices and altered states of consciousness, it poses the danger of bringing one under occult bondage and demonic influence. Other dangers of the system as it relates to herbal medicine are discussed below under that heading.

Hatha Yoga

Physical postures and breathing exercises based on Hinduism and designed to manipulate prana.

My experience with yoga mainly involved breath control and manipulation of *prana*. I practiced this for a number of years in the cult I belonged to, along with other psychic exercises. Eventually this produced altered states of consciousness and a variety of psychic phenomena, including out-of-body experiences, which were exciting at the time but led to a spiritual dead-end. I believe the major danger involved was that it opened me up in a limited way to demonic influence and led to fascination with the experiences for their own sake. This tended to convince me that occultism was the means to spiritual development.

Other physical and psychic exercises involved in various forms of yoga (for which hatha yoga is the preparation) can be very dangerous, exposing one to powerful occult forces that can result in severe pain, mysterious physical ailments, mental illness, and even demon possession. These conditions are the direct result of arousing the *kundalini* energy, which, according to Hindu mythology, arises from the serpent goddess Kundalini who "rests" at the base of the spine. "She is aroused," Ankerberg and Weldon explain, "by yoga practice." She then

> travels up the spine regulating *prana*, opens the body's alleged *chakras* (psychic centers), unleashes psychic powers, and finally reaches the top or crown *chakra* permitting occult enlightenment. Symptoms of kundalini arousal—which frequently constitutes spirit possession—include indescribable mental and physical pain, undiagnosable medical conditions (some severe), and/or temporary and sometimes permanent insanity. . . . Widespread claims to the contrary, it [yoga] is *not* a health practice. The person who engages in yoga for health purposes may find himself converted to an occultic way of life. In spite of its perception as a safe and valuable technique, true yoga involves occultic meditation and the development of psychic powers which may result in spirit contact or spirit possession.
>
> Although the public falsely perceives yoga as a safe or neutral practice, even authoritative yoga literature is replete with warnings of serious physical consequences, mental derangement, and harmful spiritual effects. Paralysis, insanity, and death are frequently mentioned. Allegedly such consequences arise from *wrong* yoga practice, but, in fact, they really arise because yoga is an *occult* practice. Those who care about their overall health should not practice yoga.[5]

(See chapter fifteen for a more detailed discussion of yoga.)

Naturopathy

A system using natural substances and methods to eliminate toxins from the body and stimulate the immune system. May include eastern meditation, yoga, and other occult practices.

Fortunately, my experience with a naturopathic physician was very positive and involved no occult elements that I am aware of. This particular practitioner was also an M.D., and he utilized this medical knowledge as appropriate. I believe he represented holistic medicine at its best. Through him, I received help for several conditions which regular medicine was unable to improve (including an enlarged prostate and arthritis). This, I believe, is an example of the benefit of not throwing the baby out with the bathwater. This naturopathic physician used herbs and other natural remedies in the way that God intended—to promote health without the admixture of occultism.

Herbal Medicine

The use of herbs and other plant products to treat a wide variety of physical ailments. May include the use of "spiritually potentized" herbs and plants "for physical or psychic healing and/or other occult pursuits."[6] It is the basis for the Bach Flower Remedies, Vita Florum, aromatherapy, and similar practices. Herbal medicine may also produce "altered states of consciousness and spirit contact through the use of hallucinogenic plants (as in many forms of shamanism)." It may also involve "psychic healing through regulating a supposed occult power latent within plants and herbs."[7]

As noted above, I had a very positive experience with herbal medicine through the prescriptions of a naturopathic physician. Again, this shows that herbs in themselves are not occult or demonic, but are a useful means that God has provided through His creation in nature that we may legitimately use for healing according to His will.

TREATMENT OF MENTAL AND EMOTIONAL CONDITIONS

Holistic treatments intended primarily for mental and emotional conditions are more directly psychological in nature. They are all unbiblical forms of psychology involving the manipulation of attention and psychic energy (which are basic to all occult techniques). Their ultimate purpose, in most cases, is to produce an altered state of consciousness. Here are some examples:

Hypnosis

The "*deliberately induced condition of heightened suggestibility and trance, producing a highly flexible state of consciousness capable of dramatic manipulation.*"[8] Many promoters of self-help psychology, some of whom are Christian practitioners, claim that hypnosis has applications to "personal growth, human potentialism, and self-transformation." They believe that it can cure a wide variety of ailments and personal problems—"from allergies, obesity, and cancer to low self-esteem, smoking, and guilt."[9]

Unfortunately, the altered states of consciousness produced by hypnosis can be used for a wide variety of occult purposes, "including psychic development, spirit contact, astral travel, automatic writing, past-life (reincarnation) regression," and others.

According to Ankerberg and Weldon, hypnosis may be a form of "the biblically forbidden practice of 'charming' and/or 'enchanting.'"[10] I know a Christian psychologist who uses hypnosis for the treatment of neurotic symptoms and harmful behavior patterns. While I have no reason to believe he uses it for occult purposes, I do believe it is probably contrary to the teachings of scripture. Also, since an hypnotic state is in fact an altered state of consciousness and a condition of high suggestibility, it can open one up to possible occult and/or demonic influences. In any case, it certainly constitutes a substitute for reliance on the transforming power of prayer and the Holy Spirit.

Biofeedback

A method of using special electronic equipment in conjunction with mental exercises in order to gain control over physical functions normally regulated subconsciously. These biological functions include such things as muscle tension, brain waves, and pulse rate. In this way, the patient may find relief from high blood pressure, headaches, irritability, etc. While there is nothing directly occult in these practices, they are identical (except for the use of electronic equipment) to many of those involved in yoga, and they can be used to "develop altered states of consciousness, psychic abilities, and spirit contact."[11] Thus, as Ankerberg and Weldon warn, "Those people who choose to use biofeedback should avoid any occultic methods or applications and be certain of their practitioner's orientation and qualifications."[12]

In my own experience with biofeedback (administered by the same Christian psychologist mentioned above), I found it helpful in reducing my feelings of stress, which were contributing to a condition of muscle tension and irritability, and in helping me to attain a more relaxed state in my daily life. Thus, when used appropriately, it proved a valuable treatment, and, to reject it because of possible misuse for occult purposes would be, I believe, another case of throwing out the baby with the bathwater.

Subliminal Programming

A system of influencing the subconscious mind through the use of messages transmitted below the threshold of consciousness on audio and audio-visual tapes for the purpose of improving thinking patterns and behavior. Again, while not necessarily occult, this system poses the danger of being used for occult purposes without the patient's knowledge since its messages are not consciously perceived. Also, many tapes encourage visualization to produce altered states of consciousness or out-of-body experiences.[13]

A similar system, although not subliminal, is neurolinguistic programming. As espoused by Anthony Robbins, for example, its purpose is to influence the subconscious mind through "self-talk" in order to promote success in one's life. Like subliminal programming, it relies on the power of one's own mind as a substitute for prayer, the Bible, and the Holy Spirit. (Robbins' system is spelled out in his book, *Awaken the Giant Within: How to take immediate control of your mental, emotional, physical & financial destiny!*) I have several Christian friends who have used this system and through them have become aware that many other Christians have bought into its spiritually dangerous New Age practices.

Meditation

As used in New Age practice, a method of controlling the mind to acquire physical, mental, and spiritual benefits. New Age meditation uses occult techniques to achieve "spiritistically induced states of consciousness . . . wrongly interpreted as 'higher' or 'divine' states of consciousness."[14]

The danger for Christians is that they may mistakenly practice a form of meditation involving either "emptying" the mind or using visualization in order to still the mind and open it to what they believe are godly spiritual influences. What they don't realize is that this form of meditation is occult and may open the mind to demonic influences, including "divine messages" from spirit beings, who may appear as angels, Jesus, or God the Father, among other disguises. Mistaking these demonic counterfeits for the real thing, they may be led into demonic deception and occult bondage.

True Christian meditation, on the other hand, involves mental activity focusing on the meaning and application of scripture or other spiritual concerns (such as the reality of God's power, majesty, goodness, and love), resulting in spiritual edification and a closer relationship with God. (See chapter seventeen for further discussion of meditation.)

TREATMENT OF SPIRITUAL AND PSYCHIC CONDITIONS

Holistic practices intended primarily for the treatment of spiritual and psychic conditions all directly involve altered states of consciousness and are therefore overtly occult. The following are examples:

Guided Imagery (Creative Visualization)

The use of the mind to produce and direct imagery for the purpose of attaining physical, mental, or spiritual goals, such as optimum health, wealth, or psychic abilities; channeling spirit guides; and contacting one's higher self. This type of so-called creative visualization is said to enhance the body's immune system and healing processes. However, since this is essentially the use of "mind over matter" and relies on psychic energies, it is a form of shamanism and therefore highly suspect and potentially dangerous.

Visualization for medical purposes is usually referred to as guided imagery. As taught by New Age practitioners such as Andrew Weil and Depak Chopra (both of whom are popular among large numbers of Christians), this involves creating a mental scenario in which one "sees" the disease being destroyed by the immune system in some highly graphic form. For example, the patient might imagine white blood cells that look like piranhas devouring cancer cells which look like evil octopi.

By expecting this type of mental activity to produce a cure, one is, in fact, practicing sorcery. When Christians put their faith in such a technique, they have made it a substitute for prayer and the healing power of God.

Of course, the fact that visualization may be misused in this way does not mean that it has no valid uses. God gave us imaginations because He intended for us to use them—for useful, beneficial purposes such as planning, designing, artistically creating, memorizing, vicariously sharing the experiences of others (real or fictional), and meditating on and contemplating the reality of the Word of God, among other possibilities.

Shamanistic Medicine

The application of ancient witchcraft and other occult techniques to health care. Its ostensible purpose is to promote healing by bringing the patient into harmony with nature. This is accomplished through the application of a variety of occult techniques, including visualization, altered states of consciousness, dream work, and the use of "power animals" (spirit guides in the form of animals). Ankerberg and Weldon explain that this form of healing involves the direct influence of or possession by demons: "Achieving true health according to shamanism demands that the practitioner be 'energized' by his/her 'power animal' or spirit guide. Thus, healing and possession by spirits are one and the same."[15]

The dangers of shamanistic medicine include "temporary insanity, demon possession, extreme physical suffering from shaman initiation, and conversion to occultism as a result of being treated with shamanistic techniques."[16]

Here again, I can speak from personal experience regarding shamanistic medicine, for, several years ago, God brought into my path a native-American medicine man, who claimed to be a Christian. This man, a one-quarter Cherokee Indian, was a distant relative of my wife. He advised us regarding a number of health issues, including arthritis, pain relief, and weight control. Although I am sure he was knowledgeable in occult practices, he never used any with us. Instead, he recommended various vitamins, supplements, herbs, natural foods, dietary practices, and exercises, which we found beneficial.

This example illustrates the fact that holistic health practitioners come in all shapes and sizes. And, once more, it points up the need for discernment. The medicine man was undoubtedly misguided in some of his beliefs and practices, but he was right on in his acknowledgement of Jesus Christ as his Lord and Savior and in his knowledge and application of natural means to promote health.

Medical Channeling

The practice of contacting spirit entities to obtain psychic healing, psychic diagnosis, or health advice. These supposedly helpful spirits are, of course, demons in disguise. As Ankerberg and Weldon explain, they "claim to be wise and loving entities sent from God to help people" but are "really lying spirits that the Bible identifies as demons . . . The hidden purpose of the spirits is to gain the trust of men so they can exert influence and control over them in order to bring about their eventual ruin."[17]

As in all occultism, the dangers of channeling include "spiritual deception, occult bondage, demon possession, mental breakdown, physical harm, and other consequences . . . ."[18]

Dream Work

A technique, which is involved in a number of other holistic practices, used ostensibly for the purpose of identifying unhealthy physical, emotional, and spiritual conditions and assisting in their healing. It may involve occult revelation, spirit contact, psychic development, astral travel, and altered states of consciousness. As employed by numerous Christians, the exploration of dreams may become a substitute for the study of the Bible because "dreams are seen as signs or even personal messages or revelations from God; therefore, for some, exploring dreams is equivalent to studying 'God's Word.'"[19]

On the other hand, I believe God can and does use dreams today, as He did in the Old and New Testaments, to give spiritual guidance and insight. So, again, discernment is needed to ascertain whether such dreams are from God or another source.

These are but a few of the many practices and treatments of holistic medicine that may involve occultism and demon activity. They are given here to illustrate the dangers of uncritical acceptance of unorthodox treatments simply because somebody recommended them and said they worked.

OTHER TREATMENTS INVOLVING OCCULTISM

Other holistic practices, which you may have heard about, also involve occult elements. These include the following: anthroposophical medicine, antogenic training, attitudinal healing, ayurvedic medicine, bioenergetics (Reichian therapy and neo-Reichian body work), breath awareness, chromotherapy/color therapy, crystal healing/crystal work, Edgar Cayce methods, New Age intuition, iridology, Kirlian photography, medical psychometry (radionics), polar therapy, psychic anatomies, psychic diagnosis, psychic healing, psychic surgery, psychosynthesis, reflexology, Reiki, self-help therapy, and therapeutic touch (Touch for Health).[20]

Other methods, which I believe are basically legitimate and beneficial but which can be combined with occult elements are homeopathy, muscle testing, and osteopathy. Again, discernment is called for to separate the good from the bad.

As we have seen, without the proper discernment, Christians may swallow holistic medical practices whole, exposing themselves to spiritual deception, demonic influences, harmful psychic energies, hallucinations, and mental illness—any one of which can lead to apostasy.

On the other hand, with proper discernment, one can benefit from the legitimate and God-given treatments and remedies available outside of the orthodox medical establishment. These may be holistic in approach but not contaminated by occult or demonic elements. Once more, we should not allow Satan to rob us of the healing benefits God intends for us to have because we have allowed ourselves to be deceived into throwing out the legitimate and helpful baby with the occult and harmful bathwater.

PERSONAL TRANSCENDENCE (SUMMARY OF PART I)

All of these seeds of apostasy—the temptations to power, wealth, status, happiness, and health—by ungodly means and for unchristian purposes—are, in one way or another, the result of man's natural desire for personal transcendence. Satan plays on our longing to be more powerful, knowledgeable, prosperous, significant, spiritually advanced, happy, and healthy to entice us into accepting appealing substitutes for the sufficiency of God, the Bible, the church, and prayer. Thereby, he would rob us of what God has for us, weaken or destroy our relationship with the Father, Son, and Holy Spirit, and ultimately enslave us through spiritual deception, occult bondage, and/or demon possession.

By contrast, true personal transcendence comes through the process of Christian sanctification. As one matures spiritually, he or she is gradually transformed, becoming more like Jesus in the character qualities the Bible calls the fruit of the Spirit: "love, joy, peace, patience, kindness, goodness, faithfulness, gentleness, and self-control" (Galatians 5:22–23). These qualities are the result of the Holy Spirit working in our hearts, transforming each of us into "a new creation" (2 Corinthians 5:17). In this way, we transcend our old nature and become more than we could ever be through our own efforts and resources.

PART II:

Preparation and Defense Against Spiritual Deception and Apostasy

Satan's plan, as we have seen, is to deceive us into accepting appealing alternatives to the Christian faith and, in the process, to rob us of the blessings and gifts God wants us to have. The devil's primary strategy is to lead us astray by luring us into temptations that exalt self and offer substitutes for the power of God and the truth of the Bible. By these means, he hopes, ultimately, to cause our fall into apostasy and thereby to destroy the church.

However, God has a plan to counter Satan's assault. It is designed to make us immune to temptations that exalt self and deceptions that distort truth. Basically, His method is to help us become spiritually mature and discerning. Then we will be able to recognize and reject Satan's cunning strategies and devious tricks.

CHAPTER SIX

God's Plan

In Matthew 24, as we saw earlier, Jesus warned His disciples—and by extension the church—that we must not allow ourselves to be deceived:

> Watch out that no one deceives you. For many will come in my name claiming "I am the Christ," and will deceive many. . . . And many false proph ets will appear and deceive many people (Matthew 24:4–5, 11).

Likewise, Paul charges Timothy—and by extension the church—to correct and rebuke error and provide careful instruction in scriptural truth because there will be Christians who will no longer hold fast to the truth but will believe in myths:

> I give you this charge: Preach the word; be prepared in season and out of season; correct, rebuke and encourage—with great patience and careful instruction. For the time will come when men will not put up with sound doctrine. Instead, to suit their own desires, they will gather around them a great number of teachers to say what their itching ears want to hear. They will turn their ears away from the truth and turn aside to myths (2 Timothy 4:1–4).

In view of these and many similar warnings in the Bible, it is essential that we prepare ourselves so that we will not be deceived. From these scriptures, one thing is certain: deceivers will come. In fact, they are already among us, as we have seen, busily leading thousands of Christians into error and ultimately into apostasy.

Fortunately, God's plan provides for our protection and defense. It consists of two basic types of preparation: *training in godliness* and *training in discernment.*

TRAINING IN GODLINESS

The first requirement for resisting deception is to become more mature spiritually. For it is those who are immature in their faith, understanding, righteousness, and obedience who are most vulnerable to the temptations which are the seeds of apostasy and to the errors by which Satan entices us into these temptations.

In other words, the key to protection against the enemy's wiles is godliness. Paul admonishes us to "have nothing to do with godless myths and old wives' tales; rather train yourself to be godly" (1 Timothy 4:7).

God's goal of godliness for the church is spelled out in 2 Peter and Ephesians:

> You ought to live *holy* and *godly* lives as you look forward to the day of God and speed its coming . . . we are looking forward to a new heaven and a new earth, the home of *righteousness*.
>
> So then, dear friends, since you are looking forward to this, make every effort to be found *spotless, blameless* and *at peace* with him (2 Peter 3:11–14, emphasis added).
>
> Live as children of light (for the fruit of the light consists in all *goodness, righteousness* and *truth)* and find out *what pleases the Lord* (Ephesians 5:8–10, emphasis added).
>
> . . . Christ loved the church and gave himself up to her to make her *holy, cleansing* her by the washing with water through the word, and to present her to himself as a radiant church, *without stain or wrinkle or any other blemish* but *holy* and *blameless* (Ephesians 5:25–27, emphasis added).

Holiness, righteousness, spotlessness, blamelessness, goodness, peace, truth—these are the qualities God has set for His church. We are to be cleansed—unstained, unwrinkled, unblemished—all as preparation for His return. Then we will not be led astray nor left unprotected by the light of the Holy Spirit, for we shall be trained in godliness.

Wise and Foolish Christians

By seriously pursuing this training, we shall become like the five wise virgins in the parable of the ten virgins in Matthew 25:1–13. Like them, with the oil of the Spirit in our lamps, we will be impervious to any deceptions and errors of darkness which may come against us.

I believe that the five foolish virgins, by contrast, refer to the spiritually immature in the church who have not developed the godliness which truly following Jesus requires. Let's look at the parable more closely with this idea in mind:

> At that time, the kingdom of heaven will be like ten virgins who took their lamps and went out to meet the bridegroom. Five of them were foolish and five were wise. The foolish ones took their lamps but did not take any oil for them. The wise, however, took oil in jars along with their lamps (Matthew 25:1–4).

Here is my interpretation from the perspective of deception and apostasy:

This parable as a whole refers to the church's preparation for the return of Jesus. "At that time" refers to the time of Jesus' rapture of the church. The ten virgins refer to all members of the church. The lamps refer to the light of the Holy Spirit (2 Samuel 22:29

and Revelation 4:5), providing spiritual awareness and understanding, thereby increasing the Christian's capacity to see truth in the light of discernment.

The oil speaks of the power of the Holy Spirit indwelling, sanctifying, and anointing the individual believer, producing the inner spiritual qualities known as the fruit of the Spirit: love, joy, peace, patience, kindness, goodness, faithfulness, gentleness [meekness (KJV)] and self-control (Galatians 5:22–23). Christians need these qualities to be ready for Christ's return and to be counted worthy to meet Him in the air and go with Him to heaven for the wedding supper of the Lamb (Revelation 19:6–8). The Bible says this anointing with the oil of Holy Spirit power was given to Christ at the outset of His ministry (Luke 4:19–20) as well as to all who are in Christ (2 Corinthians 1:21).

The absence of light and oil among the five foolish virgins speaks of the lack of understanding, power, and holiness among professing Christians who are in danger of falling away. They are the spiritually unready.

At the wedding of the Lamb, the church is described as "his bride [who] *has made herself ready*." She is wearing "fine linen, bright and clean . . . [which] stands for the *righteous acts* of the saints" (Revelation 19:7–8, emphasis added).

In Matthew 24, Jesus warns us that He will return at a time when we do not expect Him and that, therefore, we must keep watch (verse 42) and be ready (verse 44). Being ready involves being a "faithful and wise servant," doing good, and remaining responsible in the circumstances in which God has placed us (verses 45–46).

Thus, it is the five wise virgins—those who are righteous, holy, pure, and made ready—who will go with Him when He comes for His church:

> "At midnight the cry rang out: 'Here's the bridegroom! Come out to meet him!'

> "Then all the virgins woke up and trimmed their lamps. The foolish ones said to the wise, 'Give us some of your oil; our lamps are going out.'

> "'No,' they replied, 'there may not be enough for both us and you. Instead, go to those who sell oil and buy some for yourselves.'

> "But while they were on their way to buy the oil, the bridegroom arrived. The virgins *who were ready* went with him to the wedding banquet. And the door was shut" (Matthew 25:6–11, emphasis added).

Thus, we see that the preparation of godliness cannot be transferred from one Christian to another but must be obtained for oneself. Those who "sell" the oil are the pastors and teachers who can train the spiritually immature, if they are willing to pay the price to "buy some" for themselves. But this cannot be done when the Bridegroom arrives, for then it is too late. It must be done while the time is still available, which means *right now*. For "No one knows about the day or hour, not even the angels in heaven nor the Son, but only the Father" (Matthew 24:36).

If we prepare now, we will be like the wise virgins, fully ready, with "oil in jars" to supply our lamps.

I believe that today much of the church is in the situation of the five foolish virgins—and their number is growing. The foolish virgins were deceived. They believed they could slumber comfortably, without seriously seeking the power and light of the Holy Spirit or making significant effort to grow spiritually—through Bible study, prayer, worship, and service. Their complacency was a direct result not only of their own failure as disciples but also of the church's failure to disciple them.

In too many church groups, the emphasis is on numbers rather than on righteousness, holiness, and spiritual growth. Evangelistic programs are packaged as entertainment to attract the worldly into church. And, once there, they are kept comfortable with pleasant messages, rock-n-roll worship, and tolerance of sin. (Sex outside of marriage, for instance, is rampant among Christians, as we have noted previously.)

The need is for the Holy Spirit to strengthen and sanctify the church—*not* for sensational "spiritual experiences" and a better lifestyle. The truth is, we need the gifts of the Spirit today, as never before, for the strengthening and edification (building up) of the church.

"Ye have not because ye ask not" (James 4:2, KJV). We need to "eagerly desire spiritual gifts," as Paul instructed the Corinthians (1 Corinthians 14:1). And that need has not diminished. Rather, it has grown. When the church is truly following God, walking in the Spirit, and bearing the fruit of the Spirit, then God will add to the church as He did in the first century (Acts 2:47). And there will be no reason to think we need slickly packaged, entertaining evangelistic programs and fund-raising campaigns.

The Model of the Early Church

So what is to be done? I believe we need to take the First Century church as our model. We need to return to the kind of dynamic faith, love, and commitment, as well as knowledge and application of the scripture, found in the early church. Though they had the same problems then, the church leaders (Paul, Peter, James, etc.) did not tolerate unrighteousness or compromise with it. They attacked it directly and preached against it powerfully and explicitly—calling sin sin and calling for confession and repentance.

For example, Peter directly confronted Ananias and Sapphira about their lie regarding the money they held back from the sale of their property. He did not temper his words to spare their feelings or minimize their sin. Rather, he spoke the unvarnished truth like a prophet of old—that they had lied to the Holy Spirit—and they both dropped dead at his feet! As a result, the people were filled with a holy fear of God: "Great fear seized the whole church and all who heard about these events" (Acts 5:1–11).

Why was the early church filled with awe and joy and love and zeal and power? Because they were not comfortable in the world; they were on the spiritual cutting edge, living as God's agents and instruments, welcoming His power and guidance and supernatural manifestations in their lives. They were not afraid to operate in the gifts of the Spirit or to be guided directly and empowered step-by-step in their daily lives by God Himself.

I believe, those who are not accounted worthy, which is to say, not sufficiently righteous and holy, are like the five foolish virgins—*fifty percent* of professing Christians! Just as the foolish virgins did not go with the bridegroom, so these Christians are *not* going to be included in the Rapture because they are not among those who were ready (Matthew 25:11). Jesus warns the church about this in Luke 21:36 (kjv):

> Watch ye therefore, and pray always, *that ye may be accounted worthy to escape all these things* that shall come to pass [in the end times, especially the Tribulation], and to stand before the Son of man (emphasis added).

Otherwise, the door will be shut on us, as on the foolish virgins, and we will be forced to go through the Tribulation in order to become what God wants us to be. We will have been deceived because we will not have been prepared against deception by having been trained in godliness.

Becoming Spiritually Mature

To help us in this purpose, God has provided apostles, prophets, evangelists, pastors, and teachers

> to prepare God's people for works of service, so that the body of Christ may be built up until we all reach *unity in the faith and in the knowledge of the Son of God and become mature, attaining to the whole measure of the fullness of Christ* (Ephesians 4:11–14, emphasis added).

If the whole body of Christ is unified in the faith and the knowledge of the Son of God, then there will be no room for error and deception because we will all be as one in the truth. And if we all become mature, growing up spiritually until we have attained the full knowledge and character that is ours in Christ, then false doctrines, substitutes, and counterfeits will not be able to deceive us, for we will know the real thing and will be fully committed to living according to that reality.

Then, indeed, "we will no longer be infants, tossed back and forth by the waves, and blown here and there by every wind of teaching and *by the cunning craftiness of men and their deceitful scheming*" (Ephesians 4:14, emphasis added).

Likewise, we are admonished in Hebrews 5:13–14 to exchange spiritual milk for solid spiritual food, for

> Anyone who lives on milk being still an infant, is not acquainted with the teaching about righteousness. But solid food is for *the mature, who*

*by constant use have **trained** themselves to distinguish good from evil* (emphasis added).

This says, in effect, that by regularly receiving and consistently applying the teaching of righteousness, we develop discernment, the ability "to distinguish good from evil."

In this process of becoming spiritually mature, a key element is the study and application of the Holy Scriptures,

which are *able to make you wise for salvation through faith in Christ Jesus.* All Scripture is God-breathed and is useful for teaching, rebuking, correcting and **training** *in righteousness,* so that the man of God may be *thoroughly equipped* for every good work (2 Timothy 3:15–16, emphasis added).

If we are wise for salvation through faith in Christ Jesus, then we are prepared to recognize anything which could confuse our understanding of, or faith in, Christ as the source of our salvation. If we are *trained* in righteousness and thoroughly equipped as men and women of God, then no new teaching or technique will have any appeal or validity in our minds as the means of our becoming more spiritual or of acquiring what we need as Christians.

Spiritual Armor

Ephesians 6:10–13 beautifully summarizes this process of preparing (i.e., training) ourselves to stand firm in our faith, no matter what temptations the enemy may bring against us to make us doubt or waver or be misled:

> Finally, *be strong in the Lord and in His mighty power.* Put on the full armor of God so that you can take your stand *against the devil's schemes.* For our struggle is *not against flesh and blood,* but against the rulers, against the authorities, against the powers of this dark world and *against the spiritual forces of evil* in the heavenly realms. Therefore, *put on the full armor of God* so that when the day of evil comes, you may be able to stand your ground and after you have done everything, to stand. [Emphasis added.]

These verses remind us that our strength is in the Lord and His power and not in ourselves. This is why training in godliness is so vital—because godliness comes through knowing Jesus and following Him and studying His Word. Then we are able to surrender our natural desire to be in charge and instead to rely on Him.

We are also reminded of who the enemy really is—the devil—not men, not false teachers nor misguided prophets, but the power behind them, using them against us.

We also see that our part is to put on our spiritual armor and stand in faith. The armor, which is described in Ephesians 6:14–17, is the strength of character that we acquire through our training in godliness: our adherence to truth, our righteousness, our readiness, our faith, our certainty of salvation, and our reliance on the power and guidance of the Word of God:

> Stand firm then, with the belt of *truth* buckled around your waist, with the breastplate of *righteousness* in place, and with your feet fitted with the *readiness* that comes with the gospel of peace. In addition to all this, take up the shield of *faith*, with which you can extinguish all the flaming arrows of the evil one. Take the helmet of *salvation* and the sword of the Spirit which is *the word of God.* [Emphasis added.]

All of these qualities constitute the protection of a godly character. But it is *faith* and *salvation* that are most directly involved in defending against satanic attack. Faith as a *shield* against fiery arrows suggests protection from painful physical or emotional trials, circumstances, or afflictions. The *helmet* of salvation, on the other hand, suggests mental protection against deception and error.

What does it mean to "take up the shield of faith" and "take the helmet of salvation"? I believe we take up our faith by calling on God in prayer to be our protector and then making a decision to believe that He does, and will continue to, shield us from the temptations and doubts that Satan brings against us.

On the other hand, we take our salvation by reminding ourselves of the truths of the gospel— that Jesus is God the Son, that He died for our salvation, that He rose from the dead and is interceding for us at the right hand of the Father in heaven, and that we are saved, not by our own works or merit, but by God's free gift of forgiveness and cleansing. Then we place that protective helmet of truth over our minds by consciously rejecting any teachings, doctrines, or practices which contradict those truths.

Note that the *sword* of the Spirit is the only piece of armor which is not purely protective. Note also that it is not *our* sword but the *Spirit's*. It is with the Word of God, the truths of the Holy Scripture, that we are to take the offensive, through the Holy Spirit's power, against Satan's lies and illusions—as Jesus did during His temptation in the wilderness (Matthew 4:1–11).

In Ephesians 6:18, we are admonished to "pray in the Spirit on all occasions." Prayer is not presented as part of the armor of God—because it is not a godly character quality. However, it is given special significance as a separate defensive measure—one which should be used on *all* occasions. It is, therefore, probably intended to be our primary means of protection against demonic deception and the most important element in our armory of godliness.

But what does it mean to pray in the Spirit? I believe we do this by first asking the Father to fill us with His Holy Spirit. Then we ask the Holy Spirit (or the Father by His Holy Spirit) to bring to our minds those things about which we need to pray, to show us how we are to pray, and to empower our prayers as they come forth under His direction. Some in the charismatic church believe praying in the Spirit simply means praying in tongues. However, I believe this is a very limited view, and—while tongues may be part of the prayer—it is the guidance and empowerment of the Holy Spirit which is the truly important part.

John Hagee adds the following four recommendations to the church for taking godly actions to combat spiritual deception:

1. Read the Bible every day. Underline passages that you fear are neglected or violated in your life.
2. If your church does not teach biblical truth, make an appointment with your pastor and share with him the verses you have read. If he and the elders don't listen, leave that church. Your commitment is to God, not that church. The apostle Paul commands, "From such turn away."
3. Pay your tithes and offerings. This is obedience to God's Word. If good teaching is supported, it will prosper and grow. If it is not, it will wither and die.
4. If you are a member of a denomination where biblical values are being questioned, voice your opinions at national conventions. If you are not heard, then you must leave that denomination.[1]

Training in Discernment

The development of discernment requires three basic spiritual capabilities: *alertness, watchfulness,* and *scrutiny.* They are defined here as general principles, without going into great detail because many specific examples illustrating the use of discernment skills are included in the following chapters.

Alertness

Alertness means being spiritually awake and therefore sensitive to the guidance and revelation of the Holy Spirit. We have the light of God, but we must remember that fact, keep ourselves from spiritual sleep, and be in control of our faculties:

> You are all sons of the light and sons of the day. We do not belong to the night, or to the darkness. So then, let us not be like others who are asleep, but let us *be alert* and self-controlled (1 Thessalonians 5:5–6, emphasis added).

A special form of spiritual alertness is the gift of discerning (or distinguishing) between good and evil spirits (1 Corinthians 12:10). Paul tells us we should eagerly desire such spiritual gifts (1 Corinthians 14:1). I believe this means we should put such desire into action by asking God in prayer for all of the gifts, including the gift of discerning of spirits.

Watchfulness

Watchfulness means being on guard, consciously observing what is going on—what messages are being preached, what new insights or techniques are being taught—so that we will notice when something seems out of line and not be sucked into accepting what is false simply because it looks good or seems beneficial. Peter says it this way: ". . . *be on your guard* so that you may not be carried away by the errors of lawless men and fall from your secure position" (2 Peter 3:17, emphasis added). But, Peter continues, to permanently secure our position in the truth, we need to focus on our spiritual growth and godly knowledge: "But grow in the grace and knowledge of our Lord and Savior Jesus Christ" (2 Peter 3:18).

Being on our guard applies not only to what *others* are saying or doing but also to what *we* are doing and believing. Paul warns us to observe ourselves in this regard: "*Watch* your life and doctrine closely" (1 Timothy 4:16, emphasis added).

Scrutiny

Scrutiny means looking closely at what is said or done to test it and see if it is true and good or false and evil. This involves four basic aspects of testing: *examining, suspending judgment, checking scripture*, and *watching and waiting*.

EXAMINING

Examining is the most basic aspect of testing. It means simply paying close attention to new or different teachings to see if you can recognize what there is in them that may be true or false and good or bad.

This is where the gift of discerning of spirits can be most helpful, for it is by the enlightenment of the Holy Spirit that, ultimately, we are able to distinguish good from evil. It is for this reason, I believe, that Paul says, "Do not put out the Spirit's fire; do not treat prophecies with contempt. *Test* everything. Hold on to the good. Avoid every kind of evil" (1 Thessalonians 5:19–22, emphasis added).

We should examine prophetic messages (as well as every other message that is claimed to be from God) under the illumination of the Holy Spirit. Then we can retain what we find to be good and reject what is evil.

SUSPENDING JUDGMENT

Suspending judgment means not swallowing everything whole nor throwing out the baby with the bathwater but first getting all the necessary facts: Who is the speaker? What are his credentials? What is his record? What is the source of his message? What does he believe about Jesus? The latter is the most critical test, for it reveals whether he is speaking by the Spirit of God or some other spirit. John admonishes us accordingly:

> Dear friends, do not believe every spirit, but *test* the spirits to see whether they are from God, because many false prophets have gone out into the world. This is how you can recognize the

Spirit of God: Every spirit that acknowledges
that Jesus Christ has come in the flesh is from
God, but every spirit that does not acknowledge Jesus, is not of God. This is the spirit of
antichrist, which you have heard is coming and
even now is already in the world (1 John 4:1–
3, emphasis added).

Thus, it is vital to find out if the messenger acknowledges that Jesus is the incarnation of God the
Son. Here "acknowledge" means more than to know
intellectually. It also means to confess one's belief
publicly and follow it as a governing principle of
one's life. It is instructive, in this regard, to note that
a primary characteristic of every cult which falsely
claims to be Christian is that it does *not* acknowledge Jesus Christ as the incarnation of God the Son.
(This includes Mormons, Jehovah's Witnesses,
Christian Scientists, and others.)

CHECKING SCRIPTURE
Checking scripture means searching it to see if
the message agrees logically and factually with what
the Bible says. This is what the Bereans did and why
Paul considered them to be of noble character:

Now the Bereans were of more noble character
than the Thessalonians, for they received the
message [of the gospel] with great eagerness and
examined the Scriptures every day to see if what
Paul said was true (Acts 17:11, emphasis added).

This verse indicates that we should take the Bible as our final authority in determining what is of God—and *not* "prophetic inspiration," an angelic being, a beloved pastor, a popular evangelist, or any other source of "truth."

Two indispensable tools which will assist greatly in this process are a good study Bible (such as the NIV) and a good Bible commentary (such as *Nelson's*). In my own Bible study, I have also found three other aids to be most helpful: *Vine's Complete Expository Dictionary, The Interlinear Literal Translation of the Greek New Testament,* and *Strong's Exhaustive Concordance.*

WATCHING AND WAITING

Watching and waiting is similar to suspending judgment because it involves not jumping to conclusions. But it also means taking the long view—having a patient willingness to see what happens. It means *seeing what fruit is produced* as a result of the message or teaching. Jesus gave this as the primary means of discerning the falsity and deception of those who pretend to be members of the body of Christ but are not.

> Watch out for false prophets. They come to you in sheep's clothing, but inwardly they are ferocious wolves. *By their fruit you will recognize them.* Do people pick grapes from thornbushes, or figs from thistles? Likewise every good tree bears good fruit, but a bad tree bears bad fruit. A good tree cannot bear bad fruit, and a bad tree

cannot bear good fruit. Every tree that does not bear good fruit is cut down and thrown into the fire. *Thus by their fruit you will recognize them* (Matthew 7:15–20, emphasis added).

I believe the "fruit" of which the Lord is speaking is, first and foremost, the qualities of godliness, noted earlier, that are the signs of lives transformed by the working of the Holy Spirit. In other words, *does it tend to bring you closer to God and help you to become more like Jesus, or does it lead you farther away and pull you back toward your old, self-centered, carnal nature?* This is the key question in the exercise of spiritual discernment.

Where you see these spiritually fruitful qualities active and developing as a result of a particular message, teaching, or ministry, you will know that it is of God. But where you detect their absence or opposite, you will know it is of the devil.

The Criteria of Discernment

As the required capabilities (alertness, watchfulness, and scrutiny) discussed above imply, there are two basic criteria for discernment: *truth* and *logic*. Although some of the points which follow (as well as some in the above discussion) may seem obvious, I have spelled them out to make sure no one misses them. I don't mean to insult anyone's intelligence or bore them with unnecessary details, but I have found that it is often the obvious which gets overlooked when one is exposed to clever and appealing deceptions.

It should have been obvious to Eve that Satan was lying and misusing logic when he contradicted what God had told her. But she ignored the obvious and believed the lie because it promised her what she wanted—with disastrous results. Since we are all heirs of Eve's fallibility, I will assume we all need reminders and will try to be absolutely clear about the fundamental principles of discernment. Then, it is my hope, you will be able to recognize the obvious (as well as the expertly disguised) and actually practice the skills involved in the discernment process.

Truth

1. To determine the truth of a message, we must check it to see that there are *no factual inaccuracies* as determined by our own experience and knowledge. In other words, we must be satisfied that the presenter is not lying or misrepresenting reality.

2. In addition, there must be *no semantic manipulation*. That is, we must check to see that words are not being used in such a way as to obscure the truth or mislead us into accepting as true something that is false.

3. Finally, we must check to see that there are *no contradictions of scripture*, according to the principles discussed above.

Logic

There are numerous ways to misuse logic, and we must check to see that arguments are not being cleverly presented so as to appear valid when, in fact they are not.

We will examine the specific means of discerning the truth and logic of a teaching or message in the next chapter.

STEPS IN DISCERNING DECEPTION

With all of the above points in mind, let me suggest a basic procedure for practicing discernment:

1. Realize that deception is real and dangerous and that you can be deceived if you are not careful.
2. Pray for ability to discern and for guidance from the Holy Spirit, including the gift of discerning of spirits.
3. Recognize deception by exercising alertness, watchfulness, and scrutiny.
4. Check it out for scriptural agreement, fruit, truth (factual and semantic), and logic. ·

BASIC DISCERNMENT SKILLS

Finally, then, putting it all together, here are the basic skills I believe we must practice in our training in discernment:

1. Don't throw the baby out with the bathwater. (Just because one thing is wrong, doesn't mean everything is wrong.)
2. Don't swallow everything whole. (Guard against uncritical acceptance of everything that a given teacher presents. Just because it

looks good at first sight or is good in part, it doesn't necessarily mean it is all good.)

3. See whether it brings you closer to God or leads you farther away. (Is its focus on God and our relationship with Him or on something else that is in fact a substitute for God—and therefore an idol?)

4. Recognize Satan's primary strategies (i.e., counterfeiting, substituting, perverting, and distorting scriptural truth and spiritual reality—all covered in the next chapter) by practicing alertness, watchfulness, and scrutiny.

5. Recognize Satan's tricks: logical fallacies, semantic manipulation, and lies. (See the next chapter.)

6. Use common sense. (What does your experience and observation of the real world tell you?)

CHAPTER SEVEN

Satan's Strategies and Tricks

In his campaign of deception, Satan has only a few basic methods and a small bag of tricks which he uses over and over in a variety of guises. Basically, he has two strategies: counterfeiting and perverting.

The first involves two kinds of tricks by which he carries out this strategy: lies and logical fallacies. The second consists of several kinds of tricks involving semantic manipulation. We will look closely at each of these as we proceed.

But first, let's review what the scripture says about these things. Most importantly, it says their purpose is to cause believers to abandon the faith and that they come directly from deceiving spirits and things taught by demons:

> The Spirit clearly says that in later times [the last days (KJV)], *some will abandon the faith and*

follow deceiving spirits and things taught by demons.
Such things come through *hypocritical liars,*
whose consciences have been seared as with a hot
iron. They forbid people to marry and order them
to abstain from certain foods which God created
to be received with thanksgiving by those who
believe and know the truth. . . . If you *point these
thing out to the brothers,* you will be a good minister of Jesus Christ, brought up in the truths of
the faith and of the good teaching that you have
followed. *Have nothing to do with godless myths
and old wives' tales, rather train yourself to be godly*
(1 Timothy 4:1–7, emphasis added).

Who are these hypocritical liars through whom
these deceptions come? They are obviously people
in the church, supposedly our fellow Christians, for
it is "to the brothers" that these things are being
taught and to whom Timothy is instructed to point
them out. These hypocritical liars are without consciences, pretending to be Christians but in fact acting as Satan's instruments of deception. Their lies
are false doctrines, rules they have made up and
imposed on those in Timothy's fellowship, controlling how they should live and what they can and
cannot do. In these verses, Paul also says we are to
avoid godless myths and old wives' tales. That is,
we are to discern what is not of God and has no
biblical basis—no matter how popular, attractive,
and seemingly innocent and beneficial they may
be—or we will be seduced by them to the point of
abandoning our faith and following the devil.

How are we to combat such false teachings? First, by discerning and then by pointing out to those who are being deceived, or who might be susceptible, how such teachings depart from "the truths of the faith and of the good teaching that [they] have followed."

An example of such false teachers as described above is found in Acts 13:9–10:

> Then Saul, who was also called Paul, filled with the Holy Spirit, looked straight at Elymas and said, "You are a child of the devil and an enemy of everything that is right! You are full of all kinds of *deceit and trickery*. Will you never stop *perverting* the right ways of the Lord? [Emphasis added.]

Notice that it is by the Holy Spirit that we (like Paul) are warned of such deception and by which we are able to recognize and confront it. False teachers need to be confronted directly in order to be exposed to other believers and also to be corrected. However, this confrontation should come only under the direction and power of the Holy Spirit, not according to our own ideas or in our own strength.

As we invoke the Holy Spirit's help and are led and empowered by Him, we shall be able to recognize Satan's strategies and tricks and prevent him from weakening the church and even destroying parts of it by *robbing, confusing*, and *dividing* us. He robs us, as we have seen, by deceiving us, for example, about the gifts of the Spirit, inner healing, and natural medicine. He confuses us, for example, about prayer by injecting the occult technique of visualization, about faith by making it a force controlled by positive confession, and about the authority of scripture by introducing extra-biblical revelation which contradicts or supposedly supercedes the Bible.

He divides us with false doctrines and unbiblical traditions. For example, here are a few of the better known ones that have been the bases for denominational division and/or polarization within the church:

Spiritual gifts are not for today.

If you haven't received the baptism in the Holy Spirit and don't speak in tongues, you are spiritually inferior.

Speaking in tongues is of the devil.

Musical instruments should not be used in worship.

Christians should not eat meat and should observe the Sabbath on Saturday.

If you're not baptized, you're not saved.

Now let's look more closely at Satan's strategies and the tricks involved in each.

COUNTERFEITING

Satan uses counterfeiting to divert us from relying on the truth to relying on a substitute for the truth. A counterfeit is a fake that resembles the real thing so well that it fools us into accepting it as the real thing. The most common trick Satan uses for this strategy is lying.

Lies

There are two basic types of lies which Satan uses to deceive the church:

False ideas and assumptions
False teachings and doctrines

FALSE IDEAS AND ASSUMPTIONS

C. S. Lewis's concept of "Christianity And," as we saw earlier, is a general category of this kind of lying. Unscriptural use of visualization as an aid to prayer is another good example. If we visualize God the Father as an old man with a long white beard and flowing robe, we are creating a counterfeit of the true God. In fact, as we have seen, we are creating an idol and *all* idols are substitutes for God. In other words, Satan is feeding us a false idea or assumption—in this case, that praying to our own mental picture of God is useful to our prayer life and therefore something valid and good. If we swallow this without realizing that it is in fact a lie, he has won by moving us away from a close personal relationship with the true God.

FALSE TEACHINGS AND DOCTRINES

I believe that introducing teachings and doctrines which are untrue is the most important of Satan's spiritual tricks. We are given warnings against this in numerous places in scripture (e.g., Isaiah 32:6; Matthew 7:15, 24:11; Mark 13:22; Ephesians 4:14; Colossians 2:8; 1 Timothy 4:1–2, 6:3–5; 2 Timothy 4:3; Titus 1:11; Hebrews 13:9; 2 Peter 2:1). And it was the first trick the devil used against mankind, as recorded in Genesis 3:1–6:

> Now the serpent was more crafty than any of the wild animals the Lord God had made. He said to the woman, *"Did God really say,* 'You must not eat from any tree in the garden'?"

> The woman said to the serpent, "We may eat fruit from the trees of the garden, but God did say, 'You must not eat fruit from the tree that is in the middle of the garden, and you must not touch it, or you will die.'"

> *"You will not surely die,"* the serpent said to the woman. "For God knows that when you eat of it, your eyes will be opened and *you will be like God,* knowing good and evil."

> When the woman saw that the fruit of the tree was *good for food* and *pleasing to the eye*, and also *desirable for gaining wisdom*, she took some and ate it. [Emphasis added.]

Here Satan not only suggests the false idea that it's okay to question God's commandments ("Did God really say. . .?"), but he also blatantly lies by smoothly introducing two false doctrines: (1) that we will not die (spiritually) if we reject His sovereignty and disobey His commandments and (2) that, by acquiring special knowledge on our own (by eating of the tree of the knowledge of good and evil), again in disobedience, we will become godlike.

In this deception, Satan uses the three fundamental temptations which the apostle John identifies as "the love of the world" in 1 John 2:15–16:

> Do not love the world or anything in the world. If anyone loves the world, the love of the Father is not in him. For everything in the world—*the cravings of sinful man, the lust of the eyes and the boasting of what he has and does*—comes not from the Father but from the world [emphasis added].

The three basic appeals, then, that Satan used in the Garden of Eden are

1. "The cravings of sinful man"; also called the lust of the flesh (KJV)
2. "The lust of the eyes"
3. "The boasting of what he has and does"; also called the pride of life (KJV)

Eve saw that the fruit "*was good for food*" (the cravings of sinful man), "*pleasing to the eye*" (the lust of the eyes), and *"desirable for gaining wisdom"* (the boasting of what man has and does).

These are the primary inducements Satan still uses in peddling his lying counterfeits, and the same kind of love of the world is found in the church today (as we saw earlier).

A WORD OF FAITH TEACHING

As an illustration of doctrinal counterfeits in the present-day church, let's look at one major example: the Word of Faith teaching that faith is a force and it is this force in which our faith should be placed. In this discussion, I don't mean to imply that the ministries of all Word of Faith teachers are totally invalid or should be written off as completely worthless. I know from personal experience that people are saved, healed, and discipled in these ministries. Therefore, we need to be careful not to throw out the baby with the bathwater where such ministries are concerned.

In the words of Kenneth Copeland, perhaps the foremost teacher of this false doctrine,

> Faith is a power force. It is a tangible force. It is a conductive force. . . . it is this force of faith which makes the laws of the spirit world function. . . . faith is God's source of power.[1]

This faith-force is very similar to The Force of the Star Wars movies, which, as noted earlier, is the essence of sorcery, a power that can be used and manipulated through special mental (or "spiritual") techniques. Like The Force, faith-force has a dark side.

This "source of God's power," according to Copeland, is like a coin with a positive and negative side:

> The positive side, or "heads," represents faith. Faith activates God. The negative side, or "tails," represents fear. Fear activates Satan. Copeland puts it like this: "Fear activates Satan the way faith activates God!"[2]

The positive side is activated or deactivated through a person's words. Hank Hanegraaff explains:

> Words are the containers that carry the substance of faith. In Faith theology, if you speak words of faith, you activate the positive side of the force; if you speak words of fear, you activate the negative side of the force. In Faith vernacular this is called "making positive or negative confessions." . . . according to the proponents of the prosperity message, everything is controlled by words filled with the substance of faith.[3]

This substance that is also a force is the stuff out of which the universe is made, according to Copeland.

The idea that faith is a substance is based on a misinterpretation of one scripture, Hebrews 11:1, which in the KJV says, "Now faith is the substance of things hoped for, the evidence of things not seen." Unfortunately, the Faith teachers attach to "substance" the modern meaning of the word: the basic stuff or raw material out of which things are made. They either choose to ignore or are unaware of the fact that "substance" in the Elizabethan English of

King James meant "assurance" or "confidence," equivalent to the Greek *hupostasis*[4], and it is translated in this sense in the NIV: "being sure of." (Similarly, the word translated as "evidence" in the King James is the Greek *eleghos*, meaning "conviction.")

Hupostasis (assurance, confidence), according to Vine, was translated as "substance" in the sense of something foundational. Literally it means

> a standing under (*hypo*, under, *stasis*, standing), that which stands, or is set, under, a foundation, beginning; hence the quality of confidence which leads one to stand under, endure, or undertake anything.[5]

Likewise, a little word study would have shown the Faith teachers that the word "faith" itself could not have the meaning of either "a force" or "a substance." It is a translation of the Greek *pistis* which means "firm persuasion, a conviction based upon hearing." In the biblical context, it has three elements:

> (1) a firm conviction producing a full acknowledgement of God's revelation of truth . . . ; (2) a personal surrender to Him . . . ; (3) a conduct inspired by such surrender.[6]

Had the Faith teachers honestly considered only the context of Hebrews 11:1, they would have known that the writer of Hebrews was not talking about a force or a metaphysical substance but about an assurance or confidence in God's revealed truth (His Word and His Son), which enables men to surrender totally to Him and to act with utmost courage and in total accordance with that conviction and submission. The context (Hebrews 11:4–40) is about men and women like Noah, Abraham, Joseph, Moses, Rahab, Gideon, Samson, David, and many others, "whose weakness was turned to strength" and who were willing to endure torture, imprisonment, persecution, and death for the sake of God's true word and their commitment to their true God.

It is *not* about "activating" or manipulating God by the words you speak in order to acquire wealth or to gain whatever you want! Not only does this false definition of faith *not* fit its immediate scriptural context, it does *not* even fit the context of the Bible as a whole. As Hanegraaff points out,

> . . . *Scripture must always be interpreted in light of Scripture.* That being the case, faith cannot be rightly understood to mean 'the building block of the universe,' since it is never used in that sense in the book of Hebrews, much less the entire Bible.[7]

The importance of being able to discern such inaccurate and dishonest use of scripture is dramatically and tragically illustrated by the case of one young couple.

> Larry and Lucky Parker . . . had listened to the Faith message for years. They knew the Faith formulas practically by heart. But this time when

a Faith peddler rode through town, they swallowed more of his spiritual cyanide than they could safely digest. They charged in the wrong direction down a one-way street of faith.

Their tragic tale was courageously published in 1980 by Harvest House. Their book, *We Let Our Son Die*, recounts the tragic details of a misguided trip of faith. In painful and painstaking detail, Larry and his wife paint the picture of how they withheld insulin from their diabetic son. Predictably, Wesley lapsed into a diabetic coma.

The Parkers, warned about the impropriety of making a "negative confession," continued to "positively confess" Wesley's healing until the time of his death. Even after Wesley's demise, the Parkers, undaunted in their "faith," conducted a resurrection service rather than a funeral. In fact, for more than a year following his death, they refused to abandon their firmly held faith that Wesley, like Jesus, would rise from the dead. Eventually, both Larry and Lucky were tried and convicted of manslaughter and child abuse.

A tragic tale? Yes. But even more tragic is that countless other stories like this could be painfully retold. In each case the moral is always the same: A flawed concept of faith inevitably leads to shipwreck—sometimes spiritually, in other cases physically, and in still other scenarios, both.[8]

What then are the tools of discernment to be used in such cases of deception? How could Larry and

Lucky Parker have discerned that "faith as a force or substance to be manipulated" is a false doctrine?

1. *By analyzing the accuracy of its use of scripture*—in this case, noticing that it is based on a shifting of meaning from an obsolete usage to a modern usage to produce a new definition of "substance," and by noticing that it redefines the word "faith" to give it a meaning totally absent in the original language.

2. *By considering the context of its proof text*—in this case, showing that its intended meaning has nothing to do with the manipulation of a force or substance, but rather with conviction and confidence in the reality, power, and truth of God that changes *our* behavior, not *God's*.

3. *By considering its implications about the nature of God and our relationship to Him and comparing this with what the Bible says*—in this case, revealing that this false doctrine says we can control, manipulate, or "activate" God for our purposes, thereby denying His sovereignty, elevating ourselves to the level of godhood, and directly contradicting the most basic teachings of scripture.

Logical Fallacies

The second basic trick that Satan uses for counterfeiting is faulty logic, that is, statements that sound good on the surface, that seem to be based on truth, and that make an enticing emotional appeal but, when examined more closely, turn out to be illogical and, therefore, untrue.

When Satan told Eve, "You will not surely die . . . you will be like God" (Genesis 3:4–5), he was committing the logical fallacy known *as begging the question* (assuming the truth of the proposition that needs to be proved). As in this case, this fallacy usually consists of telling people what they want to hear without giving any proof or evidence or logical reasons to show that it is in fact true. In other words, it is an appeal to our emotions in order to bypass our faculty of logical reasoning without that fact being noticed.

With Eve, it worked beautifully; she never questioned it because she was thinking only of herself and what she wanted. For this reason, she was totally lacking in discernment—as are many Christians today who buy into false teachings and false doctrines because they make promises which are attractive to the natural desires of our old, carnal nature (the lust of the flesh, the lust of the eyes, and the pride of life).

If we have developed the qualities associated with godliness, we will be on our guard against such things, and, if we are familiar with logical fallacies, we shall be able to recognize them when we see them.

Essentially, logical fallacies are weaknesses in thinking that lead to false conclusions. To be logical, one's thinking must both be based on *truth* and be *valid.* That is, its basic premises (statements about what is taken to be true) must be factually accurate based on real evidence and not merely opinions. In addition, our thinking must follow a reasonable line of development. Fallacies are faults in the premises (truth) or in the reasoning process (validity) or both. In other words, they are false propositions or distorted issues.

Satan, in his campaign of deception, uses the following fallacies, which are those involved in the false teachings identified in this book:

- *Begging the question*—Stating as true the proposition that needs to be proved.
- *Hasty generalization*—Inadequate evidence, using only one or a few instances to prove something about a whole group.
- *Non sequitur*—A conclusion that does not follow logically from the reason(s) given; there is no logical connection.
- *Argument by popularity (Bandwagon)*—Saying, in effect, everyone's doing or saying it, so it must be good or true.
- *Appeal to authority*—Because an expert or person of high status says it, it must be true.
- *False cause* (sometimes called *post hoc ergo propter hoc:* "after this therefore because of this")—Assuming that, because one event follows another, the first event must have caused the second.
- *Either, or*—Falsely stating that there are only two alternatives.
- *False analogy*—Assuming that, because things are alike in some ways, they must be alike in other ways.
- *Over simplification*—Leaving out relevant considerations.

As we proceed through the remaining chapters, we will consider many important examples of the faulty logic used by false teachers. But for now, we will simply look at three to illustrate their technique.

DECEPTION BY BEGGING THE QUESTION

We have already noted two examples of begging the question: when Satan told Eve, "You will not surely die" and "you will be like God."

Let's look more closely at that last lie, which begs the question, Can we in fact become like God and, if so, how? And beyond that, is it in fact a valid goal of spiritual growth? These are significant questions for the church today because, as we have seen, this is exactly what we are being told by Word of Faith teachers and others.

One of these others is author, M. Scott Peck, "a psychiatrist who purportedly became a Christian in writing two best-selling books, *People of the Lie* and *The Road Less Traveled.* . . . Both of these books appeared in a leading evangelical magazine's Book of the Year list. . . . Both books contain the new psychologized spirituality . . . which is being widely accepted in the church."[9]

Essentially, Peck's New Age teaching goes something like this: We can become gods and have the responsibility as Christians to do so. If we don't believe we can or should be gods, then there is no point in trying to grow spiritually because *godhood is the only valid goal of spiritual growth.* Therefore, if we don't accept that idea, then we are spiritually irresponsible and the whole idea of sanctification (growing up spiritually) becomes meaningless.

But let's let Peck explain this in his own words:

> . . . no matter how much we may like to pussy-foot around it, all of us who postulate a loving God and really think about it eventually come to a single terrifying idea: *God wants us to become Himself (or Herself or Itself).*

> We are growing toward godhood. God is the goal of evolution. It is God who is the source of evolutionary force and God who is the destination. . . .

> Were we to believe it possible for man to become God, this belief by its very nature would place upon us an obligation to attempt to attain the possible. But we do not want . . . God's responsibility. . . .

> *As long as we can believe that godhood is an impossible attainment for ourselves, we don't have to worry about our spiritual growth,* we don't have to push ourselves to higher and higher levels of consciousness and loving activity . . . [10] [emphasis added].

Hunt notes that

> The humanists have been saying this for years, but now they are being joined by a number of evangelical Christian leaders who are saying much the same thing and are working toward the same goal of creating a new world of peace, love, and brotherhood.[11]

No proof is given by Peck that "we are growing toward godhood" or that this is "the goal of evolution" or that evolution is true. All of these points are unscriptural and all of them are false. They are all classic examples of begging the question.

When Peck says that, as long as we believe that godhood is impossible, we don't have to worry about spiritual growth or about pushing ourselves to higher levels of consciousness, he is assuming that godhood is possible, that it is a valid goal for Christians, that it is irresponsible not to pursue it, that it is something that we can accomplish by our own efforts, and that spiritual growth is basically about attaining a higher level of consciousness. Again, all of these assumptions are examples of begging the question and they are all doctrines of demons straight out of New Age philosophy.

DECEPTION BY HASTY GENERALIZATION

An episode of the TV series "Touched By an Angel" provides a striking example of how Satan attempts to rob the church by the use of hasty generalization. Remember that hasty generalization means drawing a conclusion about a whole group based on only one or a few examples. This is also known as "guilt by association" or what I call "throwing out the baby with the bathwater." By pointing out one thing that is wrong with a group, Satan all too often gets us to assume that everything about the group is wrong. In other words, he is substituting a part for the whole and counting on our failure to notice the difference.

In the "Touched By an Angel" episode, a family is led to the conclusion that they should abandon the Internet (the whole) because it can be used for access to pornographic material (the part). Here Satan is using something useful and good in many ways (the Internet) for his own purposes. His goal in this case is not only to pervert the minds of those lured into viewing pornography but also to brand the entire Internet as corrupt because it is used by some for immoral purposes. This is a classic case of hasty generalization, of judging the whole by a part and consequently throwing out the baby with the bathwater.

In the TV program, the father and mother, who were Christians, were ready to throw away their computer because their daughter had been affected by pornography and was threatened by a sexual stalker on the Internet. The angel, Monica, said they needed to ask God to protect them and give them discernment when they used the Internet, which, she pointed out, has the potential for great good.[12]

This same kind of logical fallacy, as indicated earlier, is involved in the rejection of the baptism in the Holy Spirit, the manifestations of the Spirit in supernatural gifts, the validity of inner healing (healing of spiritual wounds), and the use of natural medicine— in each case, simply because they have been associated with something unscriptural (such as bizarre behavior, deviant teachings, mind-over-matter techniques, or other occult or demonic elements). In each case, there is a substitution of a part for the whole and guilt by association based on the fallacy that, if one part is bad, then the whole thing must be bad.

Now let's look at one more common type of deception by means of a logical fallacy.

DECEPTION BY ARGUMENT BY POPULARITY (BANDWAGON)

In this fallacy, the majority rules. If everybody or many people say so or are doing it, then it must be true or okay. This kind of thinking says, for example, "Everyone else is cheating on their income tax, so why shouldn't I?"

Some Christians adopt New Age practices and beliefs because they are so prevalent in our culture. Let's take two examples that we discussed earlier: If "everybody" is using visualization as an aid to prayer, or using the study of the four astrological temperaments and related psychological tests as a means of finding their calling (instead of being led by the Holy Spirit), then it must be all right to do these things. If the pastors think it's okay, then, of course, it *must* be okay, right? Here we also have deception by appeal to authority.

Incidentally, the advocacy of four temperaments is also an example of begging the question, based on the assumption that, if it works it must be good and therefore of God. The question is, Is the use of temperaments something that can be defended scripturally in Christian ministry? Is it a godly practice or not?

Ignoring the ungodly source of a practice for the sake of apparently good results is blatant pragmatism, the abandoning or ignoring of truth and righteousness for the sake of expediency. Swallowing a clearly unscriptural practice whole without the exercise of any discernment whatsoever is not something that is justified by a seemingly desirable result. It is, in fact, based on the belief that the ends justify the means. But the means *are* important. They must be those prescribed by God in His Word or at least not forbidden therein. Otherwise, they may become seeds of apostasy that can lead us away from God.

Perverting

To carry out his second major strategy of deception, perverting or distorting the truth, Satan uses two basic tricks: *stereotyping* and *semantic manipulation*.

Stereotyping

The assumption that all members of a given category are exactly alike is a semantic fallacy called stereotyping (or labeling). It is a wrong idea that distorts the truth by causing confusion between words used as labels and the things they represent.

For example, if you categorize all charismatics as "spiritual weirdos," then, if you meet one, you will automatically apply this label to him and, consequently not be able to see him as he really is—a unique individual—but only as somebody strange. Thus, stereotyping is the essence of prejudice.

Stereotyping can also be called *black and white thinking* because it is based on the failure to make distinctions or see gradations or variations. It is an all-or-nothing mind set that leaves out individual differences and often sees things as either totally good or totally bad.

For example, in black and white thinking, there is no recognition that a valid ministry can be imperfect, containing some errors of doctrine or practice. But, if we must all be totally *perfect* in our doctrinal understanding and practice in order to have a valid ministry, then who will be left to minister?

Inner healing is an example of a valid ministry which has been discredited by being stereotyped. In this case, the label applied is "shamanistic." Some Christians believe that *all* inner healing relies on occult visualization and meditation and/or what Hunt calls "psychospiritual pseudoChristian techniques."[13] This excludes the possibility that some inner healing could be based on purely biblical principles. They also reject *all* inner healing as "unscriptural" since "there is no clear teaching in the Bible to support it."[14]

It's not that they believe hurtful experiences in our past don't have an effect on our present attitudes and behavior and that these things need to be dealt with by making changes in the present. But those who oppose inner healing believe that it is a "common delusion that . . . healing comes through uprooting memories and 'hurts' . . . ."[15] In this belief, they are rejecting inner healing per se because they are saying that the original hurts that are the root of the problem should *not* be dealt with.

This is neither logical nor effective. It is like saying that physical healing should deal only with outward symptoms and not the underlying causes (such as a weakened immune system or inadequate removal of toxic wastes) because these things are not specified in the Bible as valid objects of healing. Obviously, however, without dealing with the root causes, no real healing nor lasting freedom from symptoms can take place.

Once more, I can speak from personal experience. My wife and I both suffered from spiritual wounding in our early lives, the harmful effects of which were brought into our marriage. Hers were related to underlying fear and mine to pervasive anger.

We received instruction about such problems in a small group. This was based primarily on the teachings of John and Paula Sandford, which we found not only very helpful but also soundly scriptural. We were taught to pray that the Holy Spirit would bring to our remembrance those experiences which had wounded us spiritually. As these memories came to us, we forgave those who had inflicted them, asked for forgiveness for harboring bitterness and resentment towards these people, confessed our resulting unhealthy attitudes and behavior as sin, prayed that these hurts and their effects would be removed from us, and asked for our deliverance from them through the blood of Jesus and the sacrifice that He made for us on the cross.

There were no shamanistic visualization or meditation techniques and no "psychospiritual pseudoChristian" elements involved.

Thus, it is clear that all inner healing is not the same, and to label it all shamanistic and therefore invalid without considering the possibility that some inner healing practices may be godly and therefore valid is to be guilty of the worst type of stereotyping. For it throws out an important form of healing on the assumption that it is all unscriptural, unholy bathwater—and thereby, once more, robs the church of what it needs and what God wants it to have.

(The subject of inner healing is discussed more fully in chapter eleven.)

Semantic Manipulation

The misuse of language in ways that obscure or distort truth can be called semantic manipulation. For example, if you take the phrase "Christ *lives in me*" (Galatians 2:20; 4:19) and make it mean "Christ *is me*," as New Agers and some Christians do as the basis for their doctrine of the divinity of man, then you are using the semantic manipulation known as *redefinition*. You are tacitly changing the meaning of one word (or phrase) to make it the same as that of another ("lives in" = "is"). Thereby, you are causing the undiscerning to assume that the two things are the same when in fact they are not.

I believe semantic manipulation is the most common trick Satan uses to pervert scripture and confuse the body of Christ about the basic doctrines of the faith. In addition to *redefining*, here are the other forms that are involved in the false teachings covered in this book: *ignoring the context, ignoring related scripture, rewriting scripture, mistranslating, slanting, shifting terms, shifting the meaning, taking metaphors literally,* and *taking literal statements metaphorically.*

We will define and illustrate each of these here and then discuss them more fully as we encounter additional examples in the following chapters.

REDEFINING

Again, redefining is changing the meaning of a word to make it the same as another so that two different things can be equated. It can therefore also be called *false equivalency.* Let's look at a couple more examples of how this works.

A major false doctrine that is flourishing in the church today is based on such an equivalency. This is the idea that we are gods because the Bible says God made man in His image.

According to Hunt, until fairly recently, this was considered the most blatant kind of heresy, but now it is being preached from many pulpits and is widely accepted by Christians:

> Only a few years ago it was extremely difficult to convince Christians that Mormons hoped to become gods. Anyone who said that was likely to be accused of having it in for Mormons and speaking lies about them. Today many Christians themselves believe not that they are going to *become* gods like the Mormons, but that they *already are gods* like the Hindus, and just need to "realize" it.[16]

This delusion is based on the teaching, as expounded, for instance, by pastor Casey Treat, that, when God said "Let us make man in our *image*," He was saying, "Let us make man *an exact duplicate of us.*"[17] Thus, the word "image" has been redefined to mean "exact duplicate." Or, put another way, if one thing is the *image of* another thing, then it is *identical to* that other thing.

This is obviously not true. An image is a picture or representation of something. And a picture is not the thing itself. In effect, this is the same as saying that my photograph is me.

As we have seen, the idea that we are gods (potentially) was the basic lie of Satan in the Garden of Eden and is the basic delusion of the New Age Movement.

As Hunt points out, this belief

> is foundational to the teachings of the Positive Confession movement. The reason they can allegedly "speak the creative word" and "call those things which are not as though they were" just as God does is because we *are* gods.[18]

In addition to Treat, some of the others in this movement who are teaching this heresay include Norman Grubb, Bill Volkman, Yongii Cho, Charles Capps, Frederick K.C. Price, Kenneth Copeland, and Robert Tilton.[19]

This false doctrine is also supported by another trick of redefining: changing the meaning of *dominion* from "power to rule"[20] to ultimate sovereignty or control that is the same as God's. Thus, when God gave man "dominion" over all members of the animal kingdom (Genesis 1:28, [KJV]) according to the Word of Faith teachers, He gave His dominion to man, so man is now in the driver's seat and is in control of every-thing on the earth, including God Himself.

As Hanegraaff says, this means that "God is a puppet whose strings are controlled by humanity." Frederick Price puts it this way:

> . . . God has to be given *permission* to work in this earth realm on behalf of man.

> . . . Yes! *You are in control!* So, if man has con-trol, who no longer has it? God.

> . . . When God gave Adam dominion, that meant God no longer had dominion. So, God cannot do anything in this earth unless *we let* Him. And the way we let Him or give Him permission is through prayer.[21]

Not only is this redefining "dominion," but it is also redefining "God." God is no longer sovereign. He is more like a genie in a bottle. This also does away with the authentic worship of God because He is no longer truly God. (Incidentally, it also involves a redefinition of the very nature of prayer. For, if prayer now means "giving permission" to God to do what *we* want Him to do, it no longer means "petitioning Him to do what is according to *His* will.")

This redefinition of "dominion" also ignores the fact that there are different levels of rulership. God didn't surrender His total dominion to Adam. He gave him *partial* dominion—over the animals only—to use them, control them, and care for them as part of his stewardship. This doesn't mean that God isn't still ultimately in charge but only that He delegated some of His authority to man, as the NIV says, to "Rule over the fish of the sea and the birds of the air and over every living creature that moves on the ground" (Genesis 1:28).

IGNORING THE CONTEXT

The false doctrine regarding man's dominion is also an example of an interpretation that ignores the context, for the passage referred to above is about God's creation, man's position in that creation, and man's subsequent fall, *not* about man's exaltation to godhood. It shows how false teachers attach meanings to scripture that were clearly not intended in order to support their own preconceptions.

A clear-cut example of how this works is the *new* interpretation, based on the notion of self-esteem from modern psychology, of Matthew 19:19 to "love your neighbor as yourself." Hunt explains:

> . . . through the influence of Fromm and other psychologists, the church has now accepted the idea that when Jesus said, "Love your neighbor as yourself," He was teaching that we must "learn to love ourselves first of all" before we can love God or our neighbor.[22]

This idea was first promoted by Robert Schuller and kindred church leaders and more recently by James Dobson. (See chapter eleven for a fuller discussion of Dobson's views on self-love/self-esteem.)

"Many others followed suit, until today this is the generally accepted interpretation heard from many evangelical pulpits." However, for nearly 2000 years, the church "has taught that we are innately self-centered beings who do not need to *learn* to love ourselves. What we are urged to do is to love God and others."[23]

In the context, Jesus is talking about obeying God's commandments ("Do not murder, do not commit adultery, do not steal," etc.). Included in this list, is the commandment to "love your neighbor as yourself." It is put there as an example of what a Jew must do to "get eternal life" (Matthew 19:16). He must love his neighbor. And how is he to do that? Just as he naturally loves himself. That is, by taking care of him, feeding him, protecting him, looking out for his welfare, etc., as illustrated so clearly in the parable of the good Samaritan (Luke 10:30–36).

Incidentally, although I believe Schuller is mistaken and unscriptural in his teaching in a number of areas (as we shall see), I believe Dobson's teaching and ministry have been a source of great good for the body of Christ. But he is a fallible human being, like the rest of us. And in this particular area, I believe he is mistaken and unknowingly promoting a false teaching derived from the New Age Movement through secular psychology.

IGNORING RELATED SCRIPTURE

This semantic fallacy is a form of ignoring the context because it fails to consider the context of the Bible as a whole in which other scriptures may provide clarification of the passage in question. For example, the verse above (Matthew 19:19) about loving your neighbor as yourself is based on Leviticus 19:18. It says, "Do not seek revenge or bear a grudge against one of your people, but love your neighbor as yourself." This in turn is in the context of Moses' prophetic word from the Lord to the Israelites to "Be holy because I, the Lord your God, am holy" (Leviticus 19:2).

God is saying that we are to behave in a way that reflects God's purity and goodness, not doing harm to another by seeking revenge and not having a negative attitude toward him by bearing a grudge, but just the opposite. That is, by doing good and seeking his welfare, just as we do for ourselves. I believe "as yourself" can also, in the context, legitimately mean "putting yourself in your neighbor's place" and, therefore, treating him as you would want to be treated.

There is absolutely nothing here about learning to love yourself first before you can be capable of loving another. Obviously, this new interpretation can only be arrived at by superimposing the modern psychological concept of self-love/self-esteem onto this scripture in total isolation from its context and without regard for the intended meaning.

Thus, in this case, ignoring the context involves not only ignoring the immediate context and the related scriptures but also ignoring the historical and cultural contexts as well. The teaching of concepts now promoted in secular psychology was not part of what God was doing with the Jewish people under Moses' leadership, and such concepts were obviously not part of the intellectual background of the time.

REWRITING SCRIPTURE

The trick known as *rewriting* consists simply of changing the wording of scripture to make it say what you want it to say. The Bible says this is a form of lying: "Do not add to his [God's] words, or he will rebuke you and prove you a liar" (Proverbs 30:6). Word of Faith teachers are guilty of just such lying, for example, in their interpretation of Job's suffering. Because they believe suffering results either from secret sin or lack of faith (expressed in a negative confession), they *must* account for Job's suffering in these terms. They therefore claim that his troubles came because he lacked faith and spoke words of fear. It was this confession of fear ("What I feared has come upon me" (Job 3:25)), they say, that caused his terrible problems.

In order to support this view, they must deal with such scriptures as Job 1:21 (KJV): "The Lord giveth and the Lord taketh away." Benny Hinn, speaking for the Faith group, says this was a wrong confession on Job's part. By confessing that the Lord takes away His blessings, he caused them to be taken away from himself. This confession, Hinn says, is "not even scriptural. . . I have news for you: that is not Bible, that's not Bible. The Lord giveth and *never* taketh away."[24]

In adding the word "never" Hinn *reverses* what the Bible (in the next verse) says was a *correct* confession: "In all this, Job did not sin by charging God with wrongdoing" (Job 1:22).

Hanegraaff notes that such rewriting of scripture is far from uncommon:

> Long before Hinn bludgeoned Job, men like Copeland, Capps, Savelle, Crouch and a host of others had done the same thing.
>
> Not only do these Faith teachers alter the passage to read precisely the opposite of what is recorded in the Bible, they ignore the fact that the very next verse in Scripture commends Job . . . .[25]

Thus, they not only rewrite scripture to support their false doctrine, they also blatantly ignore the immediate context, which clearly shows that what they are saying is false. In addition, they ignore the general context in stating that Job's negative confession here (and later regarding his fear, in 3:25), *caused* his suffering to come upon him. In 1:21, Job had *already* lost all his cattle, his servants, and his children (1:13–19). And *before* his statement in 3:25—which is a lament over his situation, *not* an expression of fear—Job had *already* been afflicted with painful sores over his entire body. Therefore, the general context shows (1) that what the Faith teachers call "negative confessions" were really not *wrong* confessions and (2) that it is impossible for these so-called confessions (either right or wrong) to have caused Job's losses and suffering since these things happened before the "confessions" were made.

As this example demonstrates, Satan uses semantic manipulation to discredit *real* faith (which Job abundantly exemplifies). He thereby creates confusion about what faith is by putting *faith in one's confession* (or faith in faith) in place of *faith in God*.

On the contrary, as Hanegraaff eloquently explains,

> The book of Job builds an airtight defense for Job's faith. Who can forget Job's unwavering utterance of faith, "though he slay me, yet will I hope in him" (13:15)? This singular statement proves the depth of his reliance on God. He cherished his faith above even his life. His eternal perspective is enshrined forever in his words "I know that my Redeemer lives, and that in the end he will stand upon the earth" (19:25).

> Indeed, the greatest demonstration of faith is trusting God even when you do not understand. How is it possible for Hinn to miss the central theme of the book of Job? . . . Faith, far from being a magical force conjured up through pat formulas, is the sort of confidence in God exemplified by Job as he persevered in the midst of affliction, trusting God despite the whirlwind which blew his life into oblivion. True faith is perseverance in the midst of the storm. True faith is the trait most demonstrated in the life of the apostle Paul,

who not only fought the good fight but finished the race and kept his faith. Paul's faith, like that of Job, was fixed not on the temporary circumstances of life but on the Author and Finisher of faith, on Christ Himself (Hebrews 12 :2).[26]

Finally, by rewriting the passage in Job to say that God *never* takes His blessing away (i.e., it is only lost as a result of negative confession), Word of Faith proponents *ignore the general context and related scriptures* in the book of Job that say that God allowed Satan to take away all the blessings of Job's life. They also deny the value of suffering, which, as we have seen, is necessary to our spiritual development and therefore according to God's will.

Thus, Satan robs the church doubly in this case: (1) by perverting the meaning of faith and substituting an occult technique for it and (2) by denying the value of godly suffering, the very thing which will enable us to fulfill God's ultimate goal for us as His maturing children.

The purpose of faith is not to make all our problems go away, but to enable us to go through them and turn them into something good—as did both Paul and Job. This is not to say that God never honors our faith by delivering us from danger, death, or difficulties. But He does so, I believe, only when it is necessary in specific situations and for His special purposes.

MISTRANSLATION

Closely associated with rewriting scripture is mistranslation—by deleting essential words, adding others that were not present in the original, or using words which do not have the same meaning as those in the original. As in rewriting, the purpose is again to provide scriptural support for false teaching through deception.

Reincarnationists, for example, use this trick to "prove" that the Bible teaches the doctrine of cyclical rebirth. In John 3:3, Jesus says to Nicademus, ". . . no one can see the kingdom of God unless he is *born again*" (emphasis added). Those who believe in reincarnation translate "born again" as "reborn," referring, according to Walter Martin, "to the preexistence of the soul and, therefore, an obvious allusion to preincarnate souls awaiting rebirth."[27]

In this case, the trick is to attach an alternate meaning to "born again"—that is, "reincarnated"—rather than the original and intended meaning "born *from above*" (Greek *anothen*: "from above, or anew"[28] ; which is to say, "born *of the Spirit*" (Greek *pneumatos*) (John 3:5).

This meaning is clearly indicated in the context when Jesus explains His statement:

> I tell you the truth, no one can enter the kingdom of God unless he is born of water and of the Spirit. Flesh gives birth to flesh, but Spirit gives birth to spirit (John 3:5–6).

The subject of the passage, then, is *spiritual birth* (a "second" or *new* kind of birth by the regenerating power of the Holy Spirit), *not* the physical rebirth of reincarnation. Martin explains further:

> Implicit in this statement is the biblical doctrine of regeneration or conversion, an event that takes place only once and has nothing to do with cyclic rebirth. Peter states the same thought when he wrote; "being born again, not of corruptible seed, but of incorruptible, by the word of God, which liveth and abideth for ever" (1 Peter 1:23).[29]

In this case, then, we have not only *a mistranslation* as a result of disregarding the meaning of the original Greek, but also *ignoring the immediate context and related scripture.*

SLANTING

When "loaded" words are used for the sake of their positive or negative connotations (emotional associations) to evoke a favorable or unfavorable response, it is called slanting. You are probably most familiar with this as it is used in political campaigning and commercial advertising. For example, liberal candidates may characterize their conservative opponents as "lackeys" or "puppets" of big business. Conversely, conservative candidates may accuse their liberal counterparts of being "bleeding hearts" who are "soft on crime" or "socialistic" promoters of "welfarism." TV commercials, of course, are notorious for using language and images associating shaving lotion with sexual "attractiveness" and enhanced "masculinity" or suggesting that hair coloring/conditioning products promote "romance," "self-assurance," and "success."

Similarly, any message that has such words as *God, Christ, Jesus, Spirit, the Bible,* etc. is likely to get a favorable response from Christians even if what is being said or sold has nothing to do with real Christianity. This is the case, for example, in the TV ads produced by the Mormon church.

On the other hand, name calling (a negative form of slanting) is designed to create an unfavorable attitude. For example, those who call the Sandfords "psychospiritual pseudoChristian" in their teaching on the healing of spiritual wounds, are guilty of this form of slanting.

SHIFTING TERMS

This trick consists simply of transferring the meaning of one word to another (often with a similar sound). The purpose, as always, is to slip in a false teaching in such a way that it will not be identified as such. For example, some Christian writers who promote *visualization* use the scripture "Where there is no *vision* the people perish; but he that keepeth the law, happy is he" (Proverbs 29:18, KJV, emphasis added) to support their view. Thus, they say, the Bible says that if you do not use *visualization* when you pray, you will perish.

Of course, *vision* and *visualization* are two completely different things. Literally, the word translated "vision" means "a *sight* (mentally), i.e. a . . . *revelation*,"[30] and it is so translated in the NIV.

Also, unfortunately, the King James translation is somewhat misleading. The word translated "perish" comes from a root meaning "to *loosen*."[31] In the NIV, this is translated "cast off restraint." In *Nelson's Commentary*, it is translated "flounder."[32]

In the light of these facts, the NIV translates the entire passage like this:

> Where there is no revelation, the people cast off restraint [or *flounder* morally]; but blessed is he who keeps the law.

Thus, in context and in the light of the original Hebrew, it is clear that the passage is speaking of a prophetic revelation from God which keeps the people obedient to the law and on the course God wants them to follow. It is *not* about creating a mental picture (visualization) which will somehow magically keep the people from perishing.

The verse in question is also used to support the false teachings that anyone can conjure up his or her own visualized "vision" and that God must honor it. In Jeremiah 23:16, God warns against this very perversion:

> Do not listen to the words of the prophets prophesying to you.
>
> They are leading you into futility.

They speak *a vision of their own imagination*, not from the mouth of the Lord. [Emphasis added.]

In this case, then, we see how *shifting terms* is used to equate words with related but significantly different meanings to create the impression that they are the same. The result is a totally new meaning for the scripture with no relation to the intended meaning as revealed by the original language and the context.

SHIFTING THE MEANING

Rather than shifting from one word to another, this trick involves using the same word or phrase in two different senses to change the meaning. For example, take the Word of Faith teaching that Jesus was "born again" in hell where He was dragged by Satan following His resurrection. This idea is supported by shifting the meaning of the word "firstborn" from "primary" to "born again spiritually."

They use Colossians 1:18 as their prooftext: ". . . he is the beginning and the firstborn from among the dead . . . ." They reason that, since He was the firstborn from among the dead, His resurrection refers to spiritual and not physical rebirth. This, says Kenneth Copland, took place in hell:

He was literally being reborn before the devil's very eyes. He began to flex His spiritual muscles. . . . Jesus was born again—the firstborn from the dead.[33]

The trouble with this interpretation, of course, is that "firstborn" does *not* mean "born again spiritually." Literally, it refers to the preeminent position of the elder son, the firstborn in a family. It is a translation of the Greek *prototokos* which denotes "primary," "headship," and "preeminence."[34] Moreover, the context makes this perfectly clear. The full verse in question reads as follows:

> And he is *the head* of the body, the church; he is *the beginning* and the firstborn from among the dead, so that in everything he might have the *supremacy* [emphasis added].

It is about Jesus' *headship, position as initiator,* and *supremacy* over the church (the body), not about His spiritual rebirth. The passage as a whole is about Christ's identity as God, for it speaks of Him as Creator and Sustainer of all things in whom all of the Father's fullness dwells (Colossians 1:16–19).

But the false teaching of Copeland and his group diminishes Christ to the level of men who are spiritually dead and must be born again to inherit the kingdom of Heaven. Simultaneously, it elevates man to the position of God, for it implies that we are just like Christ because He, too, had to be born again. Thus, they use this twisted scripture to lend support to their false doctrine that we are gods.

But Christ is God the Son: sinless, perfect, eternal and omnipotent! He was not a victim of Satan who had to suffer in hell as a sinner and then be rescued like a spiritually dead man by His heavenly Father!

TAKING METAPHORS LITERALLY

A metaphor is a figure of speech in which one thing is compared to another by speaking of it as though it were the other. The purpose of this is to transfer the connotations of the second thing onto the first thing. For example, if I say my wife "is an angel," I don't really mean she is an incorporeal, incredibly powerful, eternal being who is a messenger of God. What I am doing is applying the *connotations* of "angel" (pure, beautiful, good, etc.) to her without having to explain all that.

Such figurative use of language can be misinterpreted by taking it literally, thereby creating a completely different meaning than what was intended. This is the case, for example, when Word of Faith writer Bill Volkman takes the metaphorical use of the word "gods" literally.

Speaking as a proponent of the false doctrine that human beings are all gods and just need to realize it, he asks the question, "But why did Jesus say that they [the Pharisees] were gods? Because all of us are gods. *All humans are incarnations of deity*." [Emphasis added.][35] He was speaking of Jesus' response when accused of blasphemy for claiming to be the Son of God (John 10:33–34). However, Volkman's answer to his own question betrays a total lack of understanding of what Jesus was saying because he takes Jesus' metaphorical statement as a literal one.

Jesus was not saying that all men (including the Pharisees) are literally gods. He was quoting from Psalm 82 in which God was speaking to rulers of ancient Israel, whom He called "gods" because they were acting as judges. In this psalm God says,

> "I said, 'You are "gods"; you are all sons of the Most High.' But you will die like mere men; you will fall like every other ruler" (verse 6).

Jesus makes it clear in the context that (l) He is *not* calling the Pharisees gods and (2) that He is referring to persons in the Old Testament to whom God the Father was speaking:

> Jesus answered them, "Is it not written in your Law, 'I have said you are gods'? If he called *them* 'gods,' *to whom the word of God came*—and the Scripture cannot be broken—what about the one whom the Father set apart as his very own and sent into the world. Why then do you accuse me of blasphemy because I said, 'I am God's Son'?" (John 10:34–36, emphasis added.)

In other words, Jesus is saying, if God could call the rulers gods and sons of the Most High, what is so terrible about my calling myself God's Son? He was, in fact, showing the Pharisees that they didn't understand their own scriptures and at the same time making the point that, if God could call men "gods" because the word of God came to them, then certainly it couldn't be wrong to call the one whom God sent into the world as His very own the Son of God.

Thus, Volkman misses the clear literal meaning of what Jesus is saying and makes out of it something which it does not say at all. He fails to realize that, in calling the ancient rulers "gods," God was speaking metaphorically, not literally. He had called them gods because the word of God had come to them and they were acting in God's stead as His representatives. They were therefore *like* gods in the sense that they had knowledge from a supernatural source and could rule over and sit in judgment of men.

That they were not literal gods is quite clear from the context in Psalm 82. Recall that verse 7 says, "But you will die like men; you will fall like every other ruler." Gods do not die like men nor fall like all rulers do. In other words, God was condemning them as corrupt rulers who had failed to carry out their divinely delegated mandate to judge fairly and righteously and was, in effect, saying that they were certainly not "gods" at all in the sense of God's true representatives.

Incidentally, the use of quotation marks around "gods" in verse 6 shows that the word is to be taken in a metaphorical sense and suggests that it is also an ironical (or even sarcastic) usage. But again Volkman fails to notice or understand this point.

If Volkman had checked the explanatory notes in a good annotated Bible, like the NIV *Study Bible*, he would have found that it was common practice in ancient times to refer to rulers and judges as "gods":

> In the language of the OT—and in accordance with the conceptual world of the ancient Near East—rulers and judges, as deputies of the

heavenly King, could be given the honorific title "god" . . . or be called "son of God" . . . Those who rule (or judge) do so by God's appointment . . . and thus they are his representatives—whether they acknowledge him or not . . . .[36]

Thus, this Word of Faith writer not only changes the metaphorical meaning, by taking it literally, but he also misinterprets the actual literal meaning and *ignores the literary, historical, and cultural contexts* as well—all in order to twist the scripture to make it appear to support a preconceived false doctrine.

TAKING LITERAL STATEMENTS METAPHORICALLY

Much less common than taking metaphors literally is its opposite—denying the literal truth of a statement by saying it is only a figure of speech, a metaphor. Evolutionists and "scientific" Christians do this, for example, when they interpret the Genesis account of creation as "all just a metaphor." (See chapter ten for a fuller discussion of this semantic deception.)

All this discussion of Satan's strategies and tricks may seem overly technical, and I do not expect everyone who reads this chapter to go through such a thorough analysis every time he or she encounters an unfamiliar teaching or an unusual interpretation of scripture. However, I have presented these examples of Satan's deceitful ways in some detail because I hope this will increase your awareness of the lengths to which the devil will go to confuse and deceive the church by means of *lies, specious arguments,* and *manipulation of language.* Armed with this increased awareness of and familiarity with Satan's strategies and tricks, you should be in a better position to recognize them when you see them.

To help you in your application of these principles for discerning seeds of apostasy in the teachings and doctrines you are exposed to—and even in your own thinking and beliefs—we will now examine how they apply to the major source of deception impacting the church today. This is the New Age Movement, which has infiltrated the church with false doctrines based on such beliefs as evolution, personal transcendence, the relativity of truth, magical prayer, secular psychology, humanism, Eastern religions, and occultism.

PART III:

Discerning Deception in the church—The New Age Invasion

In this part, we shall look at the direct attack on the church which Satan has orchestrated through the New Age Movement. This is being done through the implementation of an anti-Christian plan which, on the one hand, is subverting and perverting Christianity through false teachings and, on the other, is simultaneously setting up a counterfeit christianity in its place. This whole scheme is based ultimately on the theory of evolution. Thus, to understand Satan's master strategy, it is essential to understand how evolution underlies New Age thinking and how it contradicts the basic doctrines of Christianity, replacing the authority of scripture with the authority of science.

CHAPTER EIGHT

The New Age, Anti-Christian Conspiracy

The world, and with it the church, is in the midst of a full-scale invasion by demonic spirits. It is called the New Age Movement. It has taken place so subtly, cleverly, and smoothly during the past three to four decades that most people are hardly aware of it and uncritically accept it as just a normal part of modern society and contemporary culture.

Evidence of this invasion is seen everywhere—in occult jewelry, art objects, and music; in movies, on television, and throughout the print media. But it is through books that it has perhaps had its greatest influence. Demonic spirits, working through human agents, have produced hundreds of texts of which there are now millions of copies in print. These "spirit-written" books have been widely accepted and praised by all types of people throughout our society—including those in the church. According to Ankerberg and Weldon,

> Two modern mediums in particular may be considered important catalysts for the current revival of "spirit-written" books. In the 1960's and 1970's both Jane Roberts and Ruth Montgomery crossed over to the large publishing houses. Between them, their two spirit guides, "Seth" and "Lilly" respectively, have penned almost thirty texts for several major publishers. They not only broke the mold, they set a trend. When Richard Bach's *Jonathan Livingston Seagull* (also dictated by an entity) broke all publishing records since *Gone With the Wind* and made the best-seller list for over two years, the die was cast. Over 25 million copies of the book have been sold worldwide. Today, the sheer number of titles of "spirit-written" books in print is unprecedented.[1]

Incidentally, when I was teaching at the Bible college that was also a "christian" cult, *Jonathan Livingston Seagull* was strongly promoted by the cult leader. She declared that it was one of her favorite books and recommended that all the students, faculty, and staff should read it because of its "spiritual" value. Before I became aware of this, I had warned the students in my classes against it because I had recognized its themes taken from eastern religions and its occult nature. In doing so, I had unknowingly directly contradicted the leader's words to her followers. This, of course, did not enhance my approval rating with her or the others. But it did provide a shock which helped me to realize what kind of organization I was involved in. This, combined with other realizations, led to my eventual resignation.

Such "channeled" books have not only infiltrated our churches, they have also invaded our schools, business organizations, and government offices. They have established a worldview and philosophy that a great many people believe in.

Basically, it tells people that they are gods or potential gods. That they can, through their own efforts and by looking inward, find the resources within themselves which will bring them self-improvement, self-fulfillment, and, ultimately, self-deification—if they wish to pursue the quest to its logical conclusion. This New Age philosophy is very much in the humanistic tradition. However, what many of its followers don't realize is that these humanistic benefits are attained through shamanistic and occult means. Likewise, relatively few are aware that the New Age Movement is in fact an occult religion:

> . . . New Agers hold to pantheism, a belief that everything is a part of God. That is, God is all, and all is God. They believe that every man is part of God. . . .

> Through mystical experiences, or while participating in techniques which alter one's state of consciousness, people are powerfully persuaded that the religious world view of the New Age is truth.[2]

Thus, the New Age religion is a mixture of eastern religious beliefs and occultism.

To give it maximum appeal to the greatest number, these elements are typically combined with both traditional and contemporary ideas of success, prosperity, and the good life. In its most undiluted form, however, it appeals directly to the desire for supernormal experience and self-transcendence through supernatural means. This may take the form of channeling (or spirit possession—what used to be called seances conducted by mediums), out-of-body experiences, extra-sensory perception, and other mind trips given by masquerading demons during altered states of consciousness. These altered states may be induced through yoga exercises, meditation, chanting, ecstatic dancing, or drugs, among other means. The resulting "transcendent" experiences can seem wonderful and completely genuine, but they are all designed to fool the victims into believing in a false religious world view.

This false world view is the basic doctrine of demons who are operating in the guise of benevolent spirit guides bringing enlightenment and progress to humanity. It can be summarized in four basic beliefs:

> 1) that all true reality is divine ("God is all, all is God"); 2) that personal "enlightenment" is important (since men exist in a state of ignorance as to their divine nature; 3) that altered consciousness, psychic powers, and spirit contact are the means of such enlightenment; and 4) that in many quarters social

and political activism is needed to help "net-work" (organize) people of like mind to pro-duce a united world—socially, economically, religiously, and politically.[3]

So stated, these doctrines represent a new ver-sion of ancient eastern mystical and occult teach-ings. They are restated in practical, goal-oriented terms to appeal to the prevailing western mind set in order to penetrate our culture most effectively. They have been put forward largely by various cults which present themselves as superior alternatives or correctives to Christianity, including

Transcendental Meditation, the Rajneesh cult, Eckankar, The Church Universal and Trium-phant, the Divine Light Mission, and many oth-ers. The followers of various gurus, such as the late swami Muktananda, Sri Baba, Baba Ram Dass, Maharishi Mahesh Yogi, and Guru Maharijih, personify the essence of modern New Age leadership. Other groups, such as the "Human Potential Movement" exemplified in Est (or The Forum), Lifespring, Silva Mind Control, Summit Workshops, etc., and many (though not all) of the advocates of the various approaches to holistic health, accurately rep-resent the spirit of the New Age.[4]

Who are the people who have bought into some or all of the varied elements in this movement? Ac-cording to Walter Martin, they are members of a loose organization . . ., many of them "Yuppies," who believe the world has entered the Aquarian Age when peace on earth and one-world government will rule. They see themselves as advanced in consciousness, rejecting Judeo-Christian values and the Bible in favor of Oriental philosophy and religion. Among them may be found environmentalists, nuclear freeze proponents, Marxist-socialist utopians, mind-control advocates, ESP cultists, spiritists, witchcraft practitioners, and others using magical arts.[5]

In my experience as a college professor, I found also that many of them were my colleagues in the educational establishment. During these years, I was exposed to numerous "teacher training" sessions which were devoted to the promotion of New Age practices and ideas, including meditation, visualization, breathing and relaxation exercises, the need for tolerance of all points of view (except the Christian), the basic goodness and self-sufficiency of human beings, and the valuing of good feelings over truth and morality.

EVOLUTIONARY BASIS OF THE NEW AGE MOVEMENT

Underlying all these ideas and practices is the belief in evolution, which has been a part of eastern religions and occult teachings since ancient times. It is in fact

the core belief of Hinduism and witchcraft, and is at least as old as the theories of reincarna-

> tion and karma, in which it is a key element . . .
> Occult literature, ancient and modern, contains
> repeated references to evolution, as do commu-
> nications through past mediums and present-
> day channellers.[6]

It is no accident that during the last century, this ancient belief has been revived and given the status of a "science." The educational system and mass media have in turn so promoted and popularized this *theory* that the average person as well as the "intelligentsia" accept if as fact.

The widespread belief in biological evolution has prepared the minds of millions of people to accept New Age ideas about spiritual, historical, and social evolution as well. Accordingly, many are open to the idea that the next step in human evo-lution is a higher level of consciousness and psy-chic power and that the human race has, in fact, developed to the point where it can guide its own further evolution into higher and higher states until it attains god-like characteristics.

Essential to this process is the Darwinian con-cept of "the survival of the fittest"—applied now on a spiritual level. That is, only those who are ready, willing, and able to move into the new conscious-ness of the Age of Aquarius will do so. Those who do not show such preparedness and resist "the inevitable flow of history" will be eliminated. This applies pri-marily to Christians, who, because their faith is in a Creator rather than an impersonal cosmic force, are considered a negative influence that is interfering with the process and, therefore, will be removed—unless, of course, they repudiate the gospel and embrace the New Age world view. Then, as the "master race" emerges, they will remake the world as a global village of peace, harmony, and prosperity.

I believe all of this is now being orchestrated by Satan as a direct preparation for the New Age messiah, whom Christians know as the antichrist. He will attempt to fulfill the New Age vision of a one-world government, economy, and religion, accounting for the disappearance of Christians in the Rapture as the evolutionary removal of those unfit for his new world order.

As usual, however, Satan has got it backwards, reversing the facts and turning upside down what God has revealed in His holy Word. The Bible says that what the New Age calls evolution is actually rebellion and the Rapture is really God's rescue operation for the church prior to the devastation to be wrought during the Great Tribulation. The appearance of the antichrist will not be the signal for the next step in human evolution, but rather for the defeat of Satan's New Age plan. The temporary domination of the world by the antichrist will be the result of God's removal of His restraining influence—the church indwelt by the Holy Spirit:

> Don't let anyone deceive you in any way, for that day will not come until the rebellion occurs and the man of lawlessness is revealed, the man doomed to destruction. He will oppose and will exalt himself over everything that is called God

or is worshiped, so that he sets himself up in God's temple, proclaiming himself to be god.

. . . And now you know what is holding him back, so that he may be revealed at the proper time. For the secret power of lawlessness is already at work; but the one who now holds it back will continue to do so till he is taken out of the way. And then the lawless one will be revealed, whom the Lord Jesus will overthrow with the breath of his mouth and destroy by the splendor of his coming (2 Thessalonians: 2:6–8).

The Bible also says that the coming of the antichrist will be in the context of great deception and delusion among the people of the world and that—rather than evolving into more conscious, god-like beings—they will perish because they will prefer a lie to the truth:

The coming of the lawless one will be in accordance with the work of Satan displayed in all kinds of counterfeit miracles, signs and wonders, and in every sort of evil that deceives those who are perishing. They perish because they refused to love the truth and so be saved. For this reason God sends them a powerful delusion so that they will believe the lie and so that all will be condemned who have not believed the truth but have delighted in wickedness (2 Thessalonians 2:9–12).

The Lie of Personal Transcendence

This lie that much of the world has bought into and that has infected many in the church is, as we have seen, that the solution to all of life's problems lies within each individual. By applying the special techniques for attaining personal transcendence, they believe, mankind can find the solution to social, economic, political, and spiritual chaos. In practical terms, this means *personal empowerment for happiness and success*, which is *the primary message of New Age philosophy*. In other words, the solution to all our problems and the means to spiritual fulfillment are all found within our individual selves and through the wisdom of man.

But the Bible says that our transcendence over the influence of the world and the limitations of our selves comes through the wisdom of God and the power of the Holy Spirit, *not* through human understanding and self effort:

> It is because of him [God] that you are in Christ Jesus, who has become for us wisdom from God—that is our righteousness, holiness and redemption . . . .

> . . . My message and my preaching [i.e., Paul's] were not with wise and persuasive words, but with a demonstration of the Spirit's power, so that your faith might not rest on men's wisdom, but on God's power (1 Corinthians 1:30, 2:4–5)

Moreover, Jesus said that He is the source of the abundant life: "I have come that they may have life, and have it to the full (John 10:10). And it is only through Him that we have real direction, truth, and life: "I am the way, the truth, and the life" (John 14:6).

The idea of personal transcendence is promoted everywhere. For example, a booklet I picked up from a rack in the checkout line at Wal-Mart is entitled *Think Yourself Well: The Amazing Power of Your Mind.* It contains such information as "why prayer really does work, how relaxation can boost your immune system, why laughter is such good medicine, how music can help you live longer, dream messages, . . . past life secrets, and the power of meditation.[7]

Listed in the table of contents are such topics as visualization, hypnosis, inner guides, and biofeedback—all directed toward releasing "the incredible power of the mind."[8]

These topics incorporate an astonishing collection of occult practices, including step-by-step instructions for yoga breathing exercises, self-observation and self-remembering (two of the primary techniques in the Gurdjieff cult to which I belonged), mental focusing (or "centering"), repetition of a selected word (or "mantra"), mental emptying (or "quieting"), manipulation of prana, tapping "the source of energy and creativity which resides at the center of our innermost being,"[9] healing through positive mental affirmations, self-hypnosis, releasing the power of the subconscious mind through prayer, adopting a pantheistic world view, contacting your own inner guide, applying past life (reincarnation) therapy, and inducing altered states of consciousness through biofeedback.

These practices are presented as simply the application of the "scientific principles" by which our minds operate. For its supporting authorities, the booklet cites such organizations as The Mind/Body Medical Institute of the Harvard Medical School and the Office of the Study of Unconventional Medical Practices at the National Institutes of Health. As further support, it quotes the director of The Mind/Body Clinic, who declares, "We are entering a new level in the scientific understanding of mechanisms by which faith, belief and imagination can actually unlock the mysteries of healing."[10]

The booklet goes on to explain that this concept of "mental healing" is the basis for major medical and scientific research programs:

> Major hospitals that once scoffed at such a view are now routinely including programs that employ mind-body techniques to help patients get well; medical centers offer classes in guided imagery techniques; doctors preach the value of meditation, prayer and faith; psychiatrists are studying past-life regression to root out the causes of present-day illnesses; and scientific researchers are proving that mind powers are real and can help people suffering from everything from migraine headaches to heart disease and life-threatening cancer.[11]

Since such practices apparently *can* promote physical healing, they hold an often irresistible appeal and provide convincing "proof" that they are "good." This conviction strengthens the people's willingness (including that of many Christians) to accept the idea that these practices also have positive spiritual value. This belief is strongly reinforced by the experiences which accompany them. The people who practice channeling provide a good example. Time and again in the autobiographies of such persons, we discover that they believe the process of spirit possession is an essentially positive, pleasurable, life-changing, and power-inducing experience.

In her spiritual autobiography, *The Beautiful Side of Evil,* Johanna Michaelson, now a born-again Christian, describes such an inner experience:

> As my [visualized] door came down, the room was filled with a radiant light that emanated from the figure standing behind it. Slowly, an inch at a time, the figure emerged. Shimmering brown hair parted in the middle, a high forehead, dark skin; eyes brown, deep and gentle. There! It was Jesus! The door went down now of its own accord, revealing the rest of the figure which was robed in a long white garment. He was glowing with a holy radiance and smiling softly. I stood, then fell at his feet.[12]

Her story of how she was delivered from such deception is a powerful testimony to the working of the Holy Spirit and how He brings spiritual discernment to those sincerely seeking the truth.

Not only does the New Age Movement provide such inherent appeals as those described above, it also offers the external attraction of many celebrities, such as Shirley MacLaine, Merv Griffin, Linda Evans, the late John Denver, Phelicia Rashad, and Sharon Gless. Shirley MacLaine has been especially influential. She promotes New Age ideas in her books and sponsors seminars that, by 1989, had raised three million dollars to build her New Age center in Colorado. In addition, many talk shows—radio or TV—feature New Age psychics, astrologers, or gurus.[13]

Other influential leaders who strongly support the New Age world religion include former astronaut Edgar Mitchell, former University of Notre Dame head Theodore Hesburgh, former chancellor of the Federal Republic of Germany Willy Brandt, science fiction writer Isaac Asimov, physicist Fritjof Capra, and *Megatrends* author John Naisbitt.[14]

NEW AGE GOALS
The ultimate purposes behind these powerful appeals can be reduced to three basic goals:

1. Discredit, diminish, and destroy Christianity.
2. Set up a counterfeit of Christianity.
3. Establish a new world order.

The Anti-Christian Plan
The process by which New Age proponents intend to discredit, diminish, destroy, and ultimately replace Christianity involves a thirteen point master

plan, as identified by Texe Marrs, president of Living Truth Ministries (a Christian research organization devoted to gathering and disseminating information about Bible prophecy, the New Age Movement, cults, the occult challenge to Christianity, and related topics):

Point #1

The principal aim of The Plan is to establish a One World, New Age Religion and a one world political and social order.

Point #2

The New Age World Religion will be a revival of the idolatrous religion of ancient Babylon in which mystery cults, sorcery and occultism, and immorality flourished.

Point #3

The Plan is to come to fullness when the New Age Messiah, the Antichrist with the number 666, comes in the flesh to lead the unified New Age World Religion and oversee the new one world order.

Point #4

Spirit guides (demons) will help man inaugurate the New Age and will pave the way for the Antichrist, the New Age man-god, to be acclaimed by humanity as the Great World Teacher.

Point #5

"World Peace!," "Love!," and "Unity!" will be the rallying cries of the New Age World Religion.

Point #6

New Age teachings are to be taught and propagated in every sphere of society around the globe.

Point #7

New Age leaders and believers will spread the [heresy] that Jesus is neither God nor the Christ.

Point #8

Christianity and all other religions are to become integral parts of the New Age World Religion.

Point #9

Christian principles must be discredited and abandoned.

Point #10

Children will be spiritually seduced and indoctrinated and the classroom used to promote New Age dogma.

Point #11

Flattery will be employed to entice the world into believing that man is a divine god.

Point # 12

Science and the New Age World Religion will become one.

Point #13

Christians who resist The Plan will be dealt with. If necessary, they will be exterminated and the world "purified."[15]

According to New Age writer Alice Bailey—perhaps the first person to set forth a clear statement of "The Plan" in her book *The Aquarian Conspiracy*—the preparations for the new world order and the New Age Christ "are to be carried out by the 'Masters of the Hierarchy,' a group of exalted beings who supposedly guide the spiritual evolution of people on earth."[16]

These "highly evolved" beings, who are in fact demonic entities, are orchestrating the attack on Christianity in three basic modes: *infiltration, subversion,* and *perversion.*

INFILTRATION

According to Marrs, New Age teachings are infiltrating the church primarily through Christian pastors and lay leaders

who teach Christian converts that the Bible is flawed and that New Age doctrine and the Bible are compatible. . . . New Age leaders now often advise their followers *not to leave* their churches, but instead to work for changes from *within*. The New Age plans to seed the churches with. . . "Cosmic Christians"—people who pretend to be Christians, but are in fact disciples of Satan sent to disrupt and destroy. . . . Calling themselves "spiritual," some support social welfare goals and pacifism but deny the power of Jesus. Others profess a belief in the New Age prosperity gospel.[17]

SUBVERSION

In addition to the above-mentioned subversive teachings which are infiltrating Christianity, persons sympathetic to, or directly promoting, New Age goals are encouraging the following heretical or antisocial activities in the church: witchcraft, satanism, other forms of occultism, homosexual ministries, same-sex marriages, pacifism (i.e., opposition to U.S. military preparedness), opposition to missionary activity, the oneness of all religions, support of Marxist and terrorist groups, and human love that excludes Jesus.[18]

In addition to accepting or tolerating these forms of subversion, many Christians, as we have seen, are also dabbling in various forms of occultism. These include yoga, tai chi, various martial arts, eastern meditation, parapsychology, visualization, positive thinking (i.e., mind-over-matter techniques), psychic healing, automatic writing, and channeling.[19]

Others are intrigued by New Age books that teach techniques for personal success, prosperity, and happiness. Many Christians who read such books do not realize they are based on occult principles and are convinced they are "beneficial" because they give "results." Thus, these Christians incorporate these practices into what they consider their Christian walk and promote them among their friends. I have several Christian friends who have enthusiastically recommended such books to me.

A good example is Napoleon Hill's *Grow Rich With Peace of Mind*, which has influenced many Christians, according to Ankeberg and Weldon. What many Christians apparently either don't understand or don't care about is that Hill's book was channeled by "ascended masters":

> Hill said that unseen spirits hovered about him and . . . gave him the materials in the chapters of his book. Hill joined Clement Stone and co-authored a book using the same philosophy to develop the idea of a positive mental attitude known as PMA. Norman Vincent Peale picked up parts of New Age philosophy (which can be seen in some of his books) and, through evangelical "positive thinkers," these ideas have come into the church.

> It is interesting that even positive thinker Robert Schuller advocates a form of Eastern meditation which brings a person into the "alpha state." He also discusses the benefits of Eastern mantras.[20]

PERVERSION

To pervert means to "corrupt," "misuse," "distort," or "turn from what is considered good or true."[21] This is exactly what is being done to Christianity at the present time by the New Age advocates and false teachers within the church. They are denying the validity of the basic doctrines of Christianity and saying that they are either (1) not true or (2) mean something other than what the church has always believed them to mean. They thereby *diminish Jesus, discredit the Bible,* and *denounce the church.*

DIMINISHING JESUS

About Jesus, they say, for example, that He was just a man who spent His early adulthood studying under the gurus of Tibet, India, Persia, and/or Egypt. Kevin Ryerson, the channeller who works with Shirley MacLaine and other celebrities says his spirit guides revealed that Jesus spent eighteen years in India studying the teachings of Buddha and becoming an adept yogi before beginning His ministry in Israel.[22]

Cult leader Elizabeth Clare Prophet says she discovered documents in the Himalayas that record Jesus' experiences in India, Nepal, and Tibet. In her book, *The Lost Years of Jesus*, she "reveals" that as a youth Jesus traveled to the East, where He studied Hinduism and Buddhism.[23]

The "sleeping prophet," Edgar Cayce, whom New Agers rely on heavily for their esoteric knowledge, channeled other revelations from his spirit guides about this period in Jesus' life.

These guides, said Jesus

> traveled extensively in Egypt, India, and Persia. In Persia, . . . Jesus learned from Mystery Religion teachers about the truth of Zu and Ra, two Babylonian gods. In Egypt, as an initiate of the Mysteries, He was tested at the Great Pyramid, earning membership into the exalted White Brotherhood of Masters.[24]

Other New Agers teach that Jesus' death on the cross did not provide for salvation; that Jesus was a political activist who, as a member of the Essene sect, sought the overthrow of Roman rule and His own installation as king; that Jesus was not the Christ but that the true Christ, Lord Maitreya, brought about His resurrection; that Christians should not pray to Jesus because He is not God; that there will be no second coming of the Lord; that Jesus came specifically to teach people to meditate and communicate with spirit guides; and that Christ has incarnated in many men and will be incarnated in all those who are ready to receive Him.[25]

The latter heresy is set forth clearly by Emmett Fox, a former Christian minister whose writings are popular among New Agers:

> The Christ is not Jesus. The Christ is the active presence of God—the incarnation of God—in living men and women. . . . In the history of all

races the Cosmic Christ has incarnated in man—Buddha, Moses, Elijah, and many other leaders. . . . However, in this New Age, the Cosmic Christ will come into millions of men and women who are ready to receive it. This will be the second coming of Christ for them.[26]

DISCREDITING THE BIBLE

New Agers (as well as liberal "christian" theologians and their adherents) discredit the Bible in many ways, saying, for example, that it has been abridged, that it is full of errors and inconsistencies, that it presents a New Age world view, that much of it is simply mythology similar to that of Eastern religions, and that the Gospels of Matthew, Mark, Luke, and John are in reality veiled mystery writings dictated by disembodied spirit "masters."[27]

One pair of New Age writers even claims that, in the Sixth Century, the information about Jesus' eighteen years of studying eastern religions and occultism, as well as the doctrine of reincarnation, was removed from the Bible because it was an embarrassment to the church and threatened the exclusiveness of Christianity and its control over people.[28]

Another New Age author explains the "true" nature of the gospels. They were compiled by different esoteric schools, each entrusted with a different task:

. . . St. Luke's gospel was written to connect Christianity with the Great Mother tradition through the Virgin Mary . . . St. John's gospel is

an interpretation based on the Gnostic tradition
. . . St. Matthew's is preeminently the gospel of
the Masters of Wisdom.[29]

DENOUNCING THE CHURCH

The anti-Christian environment developing in
America and other democratic nations is being encouraged, if not directly caused, by the New Age
propaganda campaign against the church. The results of this trend are seen perhaps most clearly in
the attacks by the media and certain liberal politi-
cians on Christian leaders in government who are
committed to actually practicing their religion.
These leaders are treated as religious bigots who
want to force their moral and religious doctrines on
everybody and who cannot be trusted to deal fairly
with those who disagree with them.

This hostility toward Christian leaders has been
partially abated in the case of President George W.
Bush (at least temporarily, as I write). As a result of
the terrorist attacks of September 11, 2001, the nation has overwhelmingly supported President Bush
in his outspoken declarations of Christian values
and his campaign against terror. The people have
also responded to these acts of evil with a resur-
gence of religious faith. Therefore, the anti-Christian media and liberal political elements have backed
off in their open hostility toward Christianity and
Christian leaders. However, I believe the hostility is
still there and may find its expression in more subtle
forms, at least in the immediate future.

As we have seen, Christians, and by extension the church as a whole, are seen by those in the New Age Movement to be hindrances to world unity because they do not accept all religions or spiritual approaches as equally valid paths to truth and enlightenment. Because the church does not view the Bible as only one among many sacred books, it is branded negative, exclusive, and separatist. Christians who believe in Jesus as the Savior of the world are stereotyped with such labels as "anti-unity," "intolerant," and "narrow-minded." Because the church rejects the "oneness" of all religions, it is viewed as a stumbling block to the next step in the world's spiritual evolution. Because the church opposes the pantheistic concept that "all is one" and "nothing is separate," it is considered a threat to world peace and brotherhood.

So deep is this New Age hostility toward the church that some of the most outspoken followers of this movement are advocating the killing of Christians "as a humanitarian and creative act of love."[30] Not only, they say, will this accelerate the process of working off bad karma among the misguided and spiritually inferior, it will also accelerate the spiritual evolution of the world, which the New Age defines as the ultimate good.

Marrs points out that The Plan includes taking over

> every Christian church and every Jewish temple in the world and [turning] these great and small architectural structures into centers for the New Age World Religion . . . . New Age leaders are

convinced that they will vanquish and destroy the Christian churches of America and the West *without so much as a whisper of protest* from the tens of millions of Christians in their churches. What's more, they believe that their takeover of Christianity *will be welcomed by most Christian ministers and laymen.* Their victory, these New Age leaders say, will come as Christians abandon their current outmoded doctrines en masse and enthusiastically adopt those of the New Age![31] [Emphasis in original.]

Counterfeit Christianity

The one-world religion that the New Age foresees will be a new form of Christianity which substitutes satanic counterfeits for every major doctrine and concept of the church. These include New Age versions of God, Christ (the Messiah), salvation, new birth, sin, the Second Coming, the Rapture, the new heaven and new earth, heaven, angels, hell, Satan, the antichrist, and Pentecost, among others.

NEW AGE REDEFINITIONS

This grand scheme of substitution is to be accomplished by the simple trick of redefinition. New Agers take what the Bible says about these things and redefine them in terms derived directly from eastern religions and occultism. Here, for example, are the New Age redefinitions (paraphrased) of the Christian concepts listed above:

- *God*—An all-pervading energy, which reveals itself in such nature gods as Mother Earth, the sun, the moon, and the stars.
- *Christ (the Messiah)*—One avatar (incarnated god) among many or a "spirit guide" or a superhuman world leader called Lord Maitreya, who is coming soon. The latter is an incarnation of the Hindu god Vishnu. Also, anyone who attains a higher state of consciousness and thus achieves godhood. Marrs identifies an additional, more occult application of the term:

  > New Agers readily admit their "Christ" is the serpent or dragon. He is . . . Sanet, the reincarnation of Lucifer and the inventor of sorcery and witchcraft. But, they quickly add, he most certainly is *not* Satan, who is alleged to exist only in the warped minds of fundamentalist Christians.[32]

- *Salvation*—A lengthy process of developing psychic powers, higher consciousness, and awareness of personal divinity through personal effort and works. Or, alternatively, working off bad karma.
- *New Birth (Being Born Again)*—Any of the following: reincarnation, psychic birth (realizing godhood, oneness with the universe, cosmic consciousness, or Christ consciousness), the point at which one allows his higher self or inner guide to di-

rect his life, or a moment of higher consciousness and spiritual awareness. Additionally, the Christian experience of being "born again" has been equated to "satori," "samadhi," or "nirvana." These are altered states of consciousness achieved through Eastern occult techniques.[33]

- *Sin*—Ignorance of one's own divinity. Sin as such doesn't exist. It is an erroneous biblical concept. In its place the New Age Movement substitutes karma, which is worked off through reincarnation, thus eliminating the need for Jesus' death on the cross.

- *The Second Coming*—Modern man's realization that he is Christ.

- *The Rapture*—As we have already noted, New Agers will explain the Rapture as the evolutionary cleansing of the hindering element. According to New Age writer David Spangler, Christians and others who are not in tune with the new world order which is about to unfold will be sent to "the inner worlds," where "they can be contained and ministered to until such time as they can be released safely into physical embodiment again."[34]

- *The New Heaven and New Earth*—The New Age under the leadership of the New Age messiah. Spangler's spirit guide revealed to him that, after the cleansing process, there will be a rebuilding:

> This is the message of Revelation: we are
> now the builders of a New Age. We are
> called upon to embark on a creative
> project . . . in order to reveal the new
> heaven and build the new earth.[35]

- *Heaven*—A good state of consciousness in this life. Alternatively, the Buddhist state of nirvana, in which the souls of all mankind will eventually become part of the great "world soul." It is also used to refer to a spiritually purified earth in which the human race has achieved "Christ consciousness."
- *Angels*—Highly evolved beings known variously as ascended masters of wisdom, ancient masters, spirit guides, inner guides, spirit counselors, superbeings, aeons, muses, or walk-ins. Alternatively, the term can refer to one's higher self.
- *Hell*—A bad state of consciousness in this life. That is, one's bad karma or suffering for errors committed in past lives. Martin notes that this "is as close as the New Age Movement gets to the concept of divine judgment."[36] In other words, New Agers deny the existence of hell as well as judgment, just as they deny the existence of sin and evil, as understood in Christianity.
- *Satan*—Man in his state of normal consciousness or unrealized potential. According to Spangler, Satan does not exist as a living be-

ing, but the term is "a human creation" that can represent "the collective thought-form of all those negative energies which man has built up and created . . . Man is his own Satan just as man is his own salvation."[37]

• *The Antichrist*—According to New Ager John Randolph Price, "any individual or group who denies the divinity of man as exemplified by Jesus Christ; i.e., to be in opposition to 'Christ in you'—the indwelling Christ or Higher Self of each individual."[38] This means that, for New Agers, all true Christians are the antichrist because they would never confess that each man is his own Christ.

• *Pentecost*—The awakening of all people on earth to a higher level of consciousness. In the words of Brad Steiger, a New Age leader and practicing occultist,

> . . . there is some kind of new Pentecost going on at this time, some kind of spiritual awakening process at work . . . this growing mystical consciousness may have something to do with the Last Days.[39]

Here, the term "Last Days" has been tacitly redefined to mean the final period of evolution before mankind moves into a higher level of being. Ironically, this idea is in fact an example of the very spiritual deception which Jesus said would be the principal evidence of the arrival of the "last days" ("the end of the age" and of the satanic world system) prior to His return. In Matthew 24, Jesus says that the first sign of His coming will be widespread deception: "Watch out that no one deceives you . . . Many false prophets will appear and deceive many people" (Matthew 24:3–4, 11). And He also declares that, rather than evolutionary advancement, it will be a time of spiritual degeneration:"Because of the increase of wickedness, the love of most will grow cold . . ." (Matthew 24:12).

Establishing a New World Order

New Agers believe that globalism is the solution to all the world's problems. This means throughout the entire earth there would be established a new world order consisting of a single, unified religious, political, economic, and social/cultural system, all under the authority of a single world leader. Then mankind will be able to control all aspects of human life on this planet and thus eliminate the causes of rebellion, war, poverty, crime, etc. Of course, in the process they will also eliminate human freedom and the possibility of true individual creativity and spiritual fulfillment.

The Bible describes this process in the book of Revelation, where Satan is called "the dragon" and the world leader is known as "the beast":

The dragon gave the beast his power and his throne and great authority. . . . Men worshiped the dragon because he had given authority to the beast, and they also worshiped the beast . . . . And he was given authority over every tribe, people, language and nation. All inhabitants of the earth will worship the beast—all those whose names have not been written in the book of life belonging to the Lamb that was slain from the creation of the world . . . Then I saw another beast . . . He exercised all the authority of the first beast on his behalf, and made the earth and its inhabitants worship the first beast . . . He also forced everyone, small and great, rich and poor, free and slave, to receive a mark on his right hand or on his forehead, so that no one could buy or sell unless he had the mark . . . (Revelation 13:2, 4, 7, 11–12, 16–17).

As we have seen, the New Age Plan has already outlined the steps which will result in the above one-world scenario. A number of groups are actively promoting this process. For example, one group which has publicly endorsed The Plan is called The New Group of World Servers. It is totally committed to the formation of a one-world government and a one-world religion. Its official statement of purpose includes these objectives:

1. Bring about world peace, guide world destiny and usher in the New Age.

2. Form the vanguard for the Reappearance of the Christ, and his Great Disciples (the Masters of Wisdom).
3. Recognize and change those aspects of religion and government which delay the full manifestation of planetary unity and love.
4. Provide a center of light within humanity and hold the vision of the *Divine Plan* before mankind.[40]

According to Marrs, the blueprint for the new world order embodies four foundational points which include the counterfeit of everything prophesied in the Bible about the future Kingdom of God:

> . . . *First*, the one world system must be formed upon the premise that is "found at the roots of all the great world religions": that man is destined "to progress toward a state of *Godhood* translated into terms of a living human civilization."

> *Second*, the framework of the one world design must include *unity*, the concept that "Both man and his planet are living organisms and that the love of man must include an understanding and *love for our planet as a living being*, and of all the kingdoms of nature."

> *Third*, the planet earth (including all animal and plant life) and man will make up a *World Body* to be governed by an elite group of twelve wise men. Collectively known as *The World Mind*, this

body will constitute a *World Government* which will act for the good of all humanity.

Finally, The Plan will confer to this World Mind of elite rulers sufficient power and authority so it can *synthesize or unify all aspects of life including religion, art and science*[41] [emphasis added].

In addition to the godhood of each person and the worship of the planet earth as a living being, the counterfeit Christianity will incorporate the following New Age heresies, all of which are already being taught in various forms within the church (as will be shown in later chapters):

1. You are not sinful, but full of goodness and perfection.
2. By believing in and exploring yourself, you can awaken your Christ-consciousness.
3. To prepare yourself for self-realization, you must build your self-esteem and love yourself.
4. God is an impersonal energy source which is available to you because you are part of God.
5. The messiah (world leader) is an evolved man.
6. All religions teach the same core of truth and therefore can and must be unified so that mankind can be unified.

In the one-world government of the New Age, there will no longer be any separation of church and state. On the contrary, the two will be merged into a system in which one man will be both the religious and the political leader.

THE UNITED NATIONS AND THE NEW AGE

Many New Agers believe the United Nations is the first step toward such a theocratic government. In fact, as early as 1975, the push for this began. In that year, a group of spiritual leaders read the following statement to the United Nations General Assembly:

> The crises of our time are challenging the world religions to release a new spiritual force transcending religious, cultural, and national boundaries into a new consciousness of the oneness of the human community and so putting into effect a spiritual dynamic toward the solutions of the world's problems. . . . We affirm a new spirituality divested of isolarity and directed toward planetary consciousness.[42]

This challenge was taken up by the UN's former assistant secretary general, Robert Mueller. He advocated "a One World Religion using the UN as a model" and proposing that "the UN flag be displayed in every church throughout the world. . . ."[43]

As Marrs points out,

> . . . The Plan is to create a world order in which not only churches and religions but all society will be controlled by Lord Maitreya—the Antichrist—and his demonic spirit guides. Benjamin Creme and his group, Tara Center, have proclaimed that Maitreya will establish both a world religion and a world Socialist government that will bring peace to the planet and finally solve our economic and hunger problems.[44]

A major step toward giving the UN such world-wide control was the establishment of the International Criminal Court (ICC) under the provisions of the Treaty of Rome in 1998. This document

> creates an international star chamber under the auspices of the UN that claims criminal jurisdiction over every person in the world, regardless of whether their nation has ratified the treaty. . . .
>
> Under the treaty, a U.S. soldier serving in Bosnia could be apprehended by local authorities for an offense, real or imagined, turned over to the ICC and flown to the Hague where he could rot for months, or await trial—without the benefit of what we consider due process. No speedy trial; no confronting accusers; no protection from double jeopardy; not even a unanimous verdict of a jury is required for conviction. The ICC metes out justice by majority vote of the foreign judges presiding at a trial. . . . the treaty grant[s] the ICC prosecutor global authority to bring charges anywhere, against anyone. The prosecutor can collect secret evidence that is never revealed to the defendant. . . .[45]

Ex-President Bill Clinton, with only twenty-one days left in office, ordered that the United States be made a signatory to the treaty. Fortunately, President George W. Bush has declared that the signing of the document by the Clinton administration is no longer valid. White House officials said this means the United States "will not recognize the court's jurisdiction and will not submit to any of its orders."[46]

Many of the ideas set forth in the New Age Plan have crept into the church in subtle ways and some of them are being taught overtly from the pulpit. These include *evolution, personal transcendence (self-deification), tolerance of non-biblical views (including humanism and ecumenicalism), elements of eastern religions,* and *occultism.* The most important aspects of these subjects will be discussed, as they affect the church, in the remaining chapters.

CHAPTER NINE

The Master New Age Delusion—How Evolution Undermines the Christian Faith

The lie of evolution is at the heart of New Age philosophy, for that movement has adapted the principles of biological evolution to the psychic and spiritual realms. Biological evolution says that all living things are the result of natural processes operating according to blind, amoral chance to produce ever higher, more complex forms of life. Therefore, say the New Agers, we, as the end-products of that process, have risen to a level of self-conscious awareness that enables us to participate consciously in our own further psychic and spiritual evolution. It is this deliberate participation, the ultimate goal of which is the realization of our own personal godhood, that the New Age Movement is basically all about.

The belief in evolution originated in ancient Babylon, not in the writings of Charles Darwin—

although Satan has certainly used Darwin's theories of natural selection and survival of the fittest to further his own program. He has been using the lie of evolution throughout human history. It is found in all the ancient origin myths (for example those of Babylon, Egypt, India, and Greece). These declare that the universe was not created out of nothing by an act of God as the Bible maintains, but that non-living matter always existed. In fact, this belief

> . . . in spontaneous generation of life from the non-living and in transformations of the species was quite common among the ancients. Among the early Greeks, for instance, Anaximander taught that men had evolved from fish and Empedocles that animals had been derived from plants.[1]

Thus, there is nothing new about the idea of evolution—except the "scientific" refinements. But when the story of special creation was set forth in Genesis, it was a completely new idea in the ancient world.

Moreover, the ancients also believed in an extremely old universe, which is a necessary part of the theory of evolution. Indeed,

> . . . many ancient astronomers and philosophers dated the universe almost infinitely old. Thus, the Biblical revelation of origins was unique in the ancient world, and was in fact almost universally resisted and rejected until the supposed triumph

of Christianity in Europe. And even this apparent triumph was short-lived, as evolutionary speculations continued to thrive even within the church, preparing the way finally for the emergence of modern Darwinism in the 19th Century.[2]

EVOLUTION IN THE CHURCH (THEISTIC EVOLUTION)

Hank Hanegraaff insightfully sums up the impact of the theory of evolution on the church:

> Under the banner of "theistic evolution," a growing number of Christians maintain that God used evolution as His method for creation. This, in my estimation, is the worst of all possibilities. It is one thing to believe in evolution, it is quite another to blame God for it. Not only is theistic evolution a contradiction in terms—like the phrase *flaming snowflakes*—but . . . it is also the cruelest, most inefficient system for creation imaginable. . . .
>
> An omnipotent, omniscient God does not have to painfully plod through millions of mistakes, misfits, and mutations in order to have fellowship with humans. Rather He can create humans in a microsecond. If theistic evolution is true, Genesis is at best an allegory and at worst a farce. And if Genesis is an allegory or a farce, the rest of the Bible becomes irrelevant. If Adam did not eat the forbidden fruit and fall into a life of constant sin terminated by death, there is no need for redemption.[3]

Science Versus Scripture

Christians who accept evolution because it is "scientific fact" are believing a lie. It is probably Satan's all-time, number one success since it is so widely believed and so basic to his campaign of deception. Unfortunately, these Christian evolutionists include many of notable influence in the church, among them well-known writers, teachers, and others in positions of leadership, including James Dobson and Billy Graham, according to Dave Hunt.[4] Even such a world-renowned Christian apologist as C.S. Lewis, I regret to say, was taken in by this masterful delusion.

He makes this clear in *Mere Christianity*, where he indicates that his reason for so believing is that "scientists say so." In speaking of how the new life in Christ is spread in the world, he says, "It is not merely the spreading of an idea; it is more like *evolution—a biological or superbiological fact.*"[5] [Emphasis added.] He notes that human authority is a sufficient basis for many of our beliefs and indicates that his belief in evolution is like his confidence that there is such a place as New York:

> I have not seen it myself. I could not prove by abstract reasoning that there must be such a place. I believe it because reliable people have told me so. The ordinary man believes in the Solar System, atoms, *evolution* and the circulation of the blood on authority—because scientists say so . . . a man who jibbed [i.e., balked] at authority in other things as some people do in

religion would have to be content to know nothing all his life[6] [emphasis added].

In this passage we see that the authority of man
and especially the authority of science take precedence
over the revelation of God's Word as the basis of truth.
Lewis, of course, knew that the Bible says God made
all living things during the six days of creation, "according to their various kinds" (Genesis 1:11, etc.), as
distinct, fully-developed plants and animals. Yet he sets
aside this divine revelation in favor of a human theory.

The well-known scientist and Christian writer,
Hugh Ross, is another case in point. I believe Ross is
a sincere, born-again Christian who has done much
good in reconciling the findings of science with the
revelations of the Bible. But as a scientist, he is committed to the authority of scientific research and the
conclusions of his fellow scientists. Thus, he totally
believes in and vigorously defends the concepts of
theistic evolution and the "big bang theory." The latter holds that the universe came into being some eighteen billion years ago as the result of an immense
explosion. This explosion, by which God initiated
His "creation," introduced a chaos of swirling matter
and energy into space where it has been expanding
in all directions ever since and has somehow (under
God's direction) been forming itself into more and
more complex and highly organized forms.

Some may object that Ross never says explicitly
that he believes in theistic evolution. But, if we take
the fundamental principle of evolution to be the

emergence of order out of disorder, then any view of creation which begins with an explosion of matter must be evolutionary in essence. In his book, *The Fingerprint of God,* Ross says he believes the scientific evidence shows that God "designed, initiated, shaped, and sustained" the universe "exactly as the Bible describes."[7] But, as we shall see, Ross's evolutionary version of creation is far different from what the Bible actually says.

Furthermore, the order of God's activities in the above quote gives away Ross's real belief. He says God first *designed* the universe. That is, He *planned* it. Then He *initiated* it. That is, He started it with the big bang. Then He *shaped* it. That is, He brought order into it according to His plan over a period of eighteen or so billion years. Then He *sustained* the creation He had developed by this process. The process so described by Ross *is* theistic evolution!

Occasionally Ross makes his belief in theistic evolution (also known as "progressive creationism") explicit. For example, at one point, he says,

> The basic definition of evolution is change taking place through time. As such *the universe clearly has evolved.* Evolutionism, however, attributes all change in the universe, both organic and inorganic, to natural processes alone, i.e., without *input from a divine designer*[8] [emphasis added].

In other words, God gave His input as the divine designer into the process of evolution. Elsewhere, he says that the change taking place through time that constitutes evolution "may be . . . supernatural."[9]

Ross's book, *The Fingerprint of God*, is an explication of this evolutionary version of creation based on the authority of science. In other words, his view is that, if enough scientists say so, it must be true—even though one scientist is continually contradicting another and today's scientific truth corrects yesterday's scientific error. Ironically, his explication of modern scientific theories about the origin of the universe is full of examples of just such changes in the "truth" of science. He completely ignores the fact that many scientists, both Christian and non-christian—do *not* believe in either evolution or the big bang.

Such argument by authority is also prevalent among Christians in general, both professional clergymen and ordinary laymen. For example, two of my friends, who are pastors, both believe in the big bang theory and therefore some form of the theistic evolution which must logically accompany that theory. One of them told me he does not believe in evolution even though he does believe in the big bang. He sees no logical contradiction in simultaneously holding these two beliefs (presumably in totally separate mental compartments). I have been unable to convince him that there is any contradiction.

He says the big bang was a "special" kind of explosion which produced order rather than chaos. Thus, one must conclude, it wasn't really an explosion at all and therefore not really a big bang. Rather, it was simply a starting point out of which the universe expanded and order emerged (or *developed*). But, if order has developed, then things must have previously been less ordered. So they must have originally been in a state of at least relative disorder. But this is the definition of evolution: order developing out of disorder. Therefore, the big bang (whatever kind it was) cannot be separated from evolution. It is the *origin* (starting point) of evolution!

These two pastors believe these things, apparently, because Christian scientists, such as Ross, say they are so. Unfortunately, they are either ignoring or are unaware of the other scientists who say they are not so. For example, researcher Paul S. Taylor cites over 800 notable scientists (past and present) who believe in creationism rather than evolution. The list includes such names as Agassiz, Babbage, Bacon, Boyle, Cuvier, Davy, Faraday, Fleming, Herschel, Joule, Kepler, Linnaeus, Lister, Maxwell, Mendel, Newton, Pascal, Pasteur, Kelvin, and da Vinci. Taylor also lists over twenty eminent contemporary scientists who deny evolution. However, he refrains from listing others with this ominous note:

> A more thorough list of current Creationist scientists is not provided due to fears of job discrimination and persecution in today's atmosphere of limited academic freedom in Evolutionist-controlled institutions.[10]

Apparently, my two pastor friends, along with other dedicated Christians with similar views, are ignoring the abundant scientific evidence (see appendix C) against any form of evolution—theistic or otherwise—and discounting the clear teaching of scripture which contradicts both the big bang origin of the universe and the evolutionary creation of the species. I cannot judge the motives of my friends for persisting in such beliefs, but I believe there are many well-educated Christians who consider themselves members of the Christian "intelligentsia" and, therefore, feel compelled to adopt the beliefs of their peers in that elitist group.

However, to believe in theistic evolution and/or the big bang because scientists say so is to put God in a box called "scientific theory." But some things are simply beyond the limited understanding of man's finite mind. To insist on squeezing the infinite Creator into such a narrow mental space is to reject not only the ultimate mystery of God and His creation but also the need for simple faith in such matters.

The Emperor Has No Clothes

In other words, some Christians who go along with the science-based view of Hugh Ross are, I believe, denying the fact that the emperor is wearing no clothes. Rather than face the ridicule of their scientifically minded peers and the possibility of being branded as shallow or uninformed, they bow to the intellectual and theological powers that be—regardless of the plain truth. Instead, they accept the heretical conclusions of science because of the authority it carries. And they refuse to acknowledge the unpopular fact that there is no real scientific evidence for evolution or its corollary, the big bang;

that it is an illogical and impossible explanation of things; and that it contradicts the Bible, the revealed Word of God. It is, therefore, I believe, a major deception by the enemy, a profound heresy, and an exceedingly dangerous seed of apostasy.

The Bible says that "the great dragon . . . that ancient serpent called the devil, or Satan, . . . leads the whole world astray" (Revelation 12:9). Rather than believing his lie, we should listen to the angel sent by God who "had the eternal gospel to proclaim to those who live on the earth—to every nation, tribe, language and people":

> He said in a loud voice, "Fear God and give him glory, because the hour of his judgment has come. Worship him who *made the heavens, the earth, the sea and the springs of water* (Revelation 14:7, emphasis added).

Yes, God *made* all things, just as we see them and just as it says He did in the first chapter of His Word.

NEO-ORTHODOXY: HUMANISTIC, EVOLUTIONARY CHRISTIANITY

Unfortunately, a large number of the "intellectually elite" in the church do not believe this. These are the proponents of "neo-orthodoxy," which rejects much of the Bible as historical fact. They include modern theologians who

> would eliminate the first eleven chapters of Genesis from the realm of true history . . . removing

the foundation from all future history. They, in effect, reject the teachings of Peter and Paul and all the other Biblical writers, as naive superstition and the teachings of the infallible Christ as deceptive accommodationism. The "framework hypothesis" of Genesis, in any of its diverse forms is nothing but neo-orthodox sophistry and inevitably leads eventually to complete apostasy.[11]

The framework hypothesis (mentioned above by the eminent scientist and former director of the Institute for Creation Research, Dr. Henry M. Morris) views Genesis chapters 1–11 as merely a literary device, or "rhetorical framework" used as a means of developing the theological themes of creation, the fall, and reconciliation.[12] Those who accept this hypothesis speak of Genesis as "allegorical," "liturgical," "poetic," or "supra-historical."[13]

As Charles Ryrie (Dean of the Graduate School of Dallas Theological Seminary) puts it, by rejecting the Genesis account of creation and the fall as history, "Science has [these theologians say] delivered us from having to believe the Genesis stories, and through this scientific deliverance, we are supposed to be able to see the real meaning of the accounts."[14] These neo-orthodox theologians believe the evolving human race is at least a million years old and, therefore, conclude that Genesis 1–11 is purely mythological and has no historical content at all.

According to Morris, "Even in those religious circles still regarded as theologically conservative, the Bible record is increasingly being interpreted as 'allegorical' or 'liturgical' rather than historical and scientific."[15]

This kind of humanistic Christianity, in rejecting the truth of biblical creationism, is extremely dangerous spiritually, for it is turning many churches into essentially secular organizations. In such churches, the scriptural account of creation

> . . . *must somehow be accommodated to the latest scientific theories* of origins (which are always evolutionary). This accommodation inevitably and necessarily leads to a softening of the doctrine of Biblical inspiration and infallibility. Other creative acts of God (that is, the recorded miracles) begin to be questioned, and a view of Biblical inspiration which allows for cultural limitations and even outright contradictions, becomes adopted. The authority of the Gospels and even of Jesus Christ then must necessarily be questioned. Soon the entire Bible becomes merely a record of man's religious evolution, an outgrowth of biological evolution. The proper activity for modern Christians therefore eventually becomes merely *"social action,"* striving to help in the future evolution of the social order into a more advanced and enlightened humanistic society*[16] [emphasis added].

Such theological "modernism" has had a profound influence on the church as a whole, in large measure causing it to accept the doctrine of evolution. According to Morris, this is true among mainline denominations such as the Methodist, Presbyterian, Episcopalian, and Baptist, and also among more conservative groups such as Roman Catholics and evangelicals.[17]

Morris notes that the rise of such religious modernism in the Nineteenth Century

> followed the scientific propaganda of Darwinism,. and was in large measure based on it. Theologians were persuaded that science required acceptance of the geological ages and the evolutionary origin of the various species, including man.

> . . . the necessary outcome was final and complete rejection of the records of Genesis as nothing but myth and legends.[18]

Not only did this neo-orthodox thinking result in the rejection of such basic Christian doctrines as the fall of man, the curse of sin on the world, and the substitutionary atonement of Christ, it was also the basis for Reconstructionism. This heretical doctrine, as we saw earlier, is the belief that it is the church's function to establish the physical kingdom of God on earth before Jesus returns. This idea is supported by the humanistic attitude of modernism, which puts emphasis on human effort and knowledge as the means of man's religious evolution. It thereby promotes the illusion that the kingdom of God can be fulfilled in history through the work of man.

Exchanging the Truth of Scripture for a Lie

Thus, again, we see that evolution is a major seed of apostasy in its promotion of Christian modernism, neo-orthodoxy, and Reconstructionism. And in these ways, "scientific knowledge" and the "wisdom" of men has replaced the truth of scripture.

But the Bible says God "will destroy the wisdom of the wise" and the "intelligence of the intelligent he will frustrate" (1 Corinthians 1:19). Moreover, the wisdom of the world—and along with it the "scientific" understanding of evolution and creation—is foolishness to God:

> Where is the wise man? Where is the scholar? Where is the philosopher of this age? Has not God made foolish the wisdom of the world . . . For the foolishness of God is wiser than man's wisdom. . . .

> Do not deceive yourselves. If any one of you thinks he is wise by the standards of this age, he should become a "fool" so that he may become wise. For the wisdom of this world is foolishness in God's sight (1 Corinthians 1:20, 25, 3:18–19).

Christians who believe in evolution are not merely foolish; they are (in this regard) "futile" in their thinking, and their hearts (regarding this subject) are "darkened" (Romans 1:21). In fact, I believe they are, without realizing it, practicing a form of idolatry. For they have denied God as the biblical

Creator and have put their trust in a supposedly natural process and the living things of nature. Or, as the scripture says, they have

> exchanged the glory of the immortal God for images made to look like mortal man and birds and animals and reptiles. . . . They exchanged the truth of God for a lie, and worshiped and served created things rather than the Creator . . . (Romans 1:23, 25).

EVOLUTION VERSUS CREATIONISM

Evolution and creationism are mutually exclusive even though many Christians have tried to combine them.

The Essence of Evolution

Evolution teaches that present-day life forms gradually came into existence and developed over billions of years through natural processes and that all present life came from a single original form. It says that the material of the universe has always existed but is slowly growing more organized. Based on the findings of modern astronomy and astrophysics, it now says the universe began with an explosion and order has been forming out of that chaos.

The Essence of Creationism

In contrast, creationism teaches that all the elements of the universe and all living things were made by a Creator for His purposes. It says that, out of nothing, He created a complete, fully-functioning cosmos. It says that all basic kinds of living things were created independently of each other. It says that God created all things and that, as the omnipotent and omniscient supreme being, there is no reason He could not have done it in six literal days. It therefore suggests that He could have completed all this only a few thousand years ago.

In essence, creationism says all things were created in the beginning, basically just as we know them today, that this did not begin with an explosion or happen by random natural processes, that it did not require an immense period of time, and that order and complexity did not somehow emerge out of chaos.

There is abundant evidence which shows the falsity of evolution and the truth of creationism. However, it is not within the scope of this book to present such evidence fully. Many excellent works are available which do this very well. Nevertheless, it is important for the church to understand these facts. Therefore, for those who wish to pursue the subject, I have provided a summary of the evidence and a list of recommended books in appendix C.

How Evolution Contradicts the Bible

Evolution is a major seed of apostasy, for it contradicts the Bible in many ways. Among the most important of these are the following:

- It contradicts the chronology of the six-day creation process.

- It contradicts the biblical account of the worldwide Flood.
- It contradicts other biblical statements about how God created everything.
- It contradicts the character of God as revealed in the Bible.

Biblical Chronology

The immense periods of time involved in the geological dating of the rock strata and the fossil record cannot be correlated with the six days of creation. Therefore, if the Bible is true, then geological dating—and thus a fundamental premise of evolution—must be false. (See appendix C for a discussion of geological dating.)

According to Genesis 1:1–26, God created everything in six days, and it followed this chronological sequence:

Day 1—God created the heavens, the earth, and light.

Day 2—God created the atmosphere or sky (including the water vapor envelope surrounding the earth above the expanse of sky).

Day 3—God separated the oceans from the dry land and created the vegetation on the land.

Day 4—God created the sun, moon, and stars.

Day 5—God created fish, other water animals, and birds.

Day 6—God created land animals (including livestock, insects, and wild animals) and human beings.

This sequence of events obviously contradicts that assumed by evolution, which goes something like this:

1. Matter and space always existed.
2. Matter (which had *somehow* become highly compressed) exploded.
3. From the swirling chaos of this exploding matter, galaxies (beginning as gaseous clouds) were *somehow* formed.
4. Stars (including our sun) *somehow* condensed out of these gaseous clouds and produced light.
5. Planets (including the earth) were also *somehow* produced out of this gaseous matter orbiting the stars.
6. Primitive forms of plant and animal life were *somehow* spontaneously generated on the earth.
7. Simple plants and animals *somehow* evolved over billions of years into complex plants and animals, including man.

This is not the way God did it, according to the Bible. In the scriptural account, there is no big bang producing galaxies, stars, light, and planets and their moons, in that order. Instead, God created space and one planet (earth) first. Then He created light (before there were any stars). Then He worked on the earth some more, creating the atmosphere, oceans, land, and vegetation on the land, in that order. Only at this point, did He create the sun, moon, and stars, in that order. Next, He created all the fully formed species of water animals and birds. Finally, He created all the fully formed species of land animals, including man.

There is no evolution here nor condensation from gaseous clouds in some kind of universal progression from simple to complex structures. Rather, *God focused on His primary concern first—the creation of the earth* (covered with water). *Then, He added the other elements which would be necessary to maintain life* (light, atmosphere, dry land, vegetation, and the sun). *Finally, He created animal life*—but not in the order or way that evolutionists require. (For example, birds could not have evolved from fish, for they were created at the same time. And man could not have evolved from apes (or ape-like creatures) because they were both created on the same day.

Thus, for a Christian to believe in evolution, he not only has to ignore the mass of scientific evidence against evolution, but he also has to either ignore the biblical account of creation or else change scripture by twisting and reinterpreting it in various ways to make it mean something other than what it clearly says. (We shall discuss these tricks in the next chapter.)

The Biblical Account of the Flood

Evolution contradicts the account of the worldwide Flood given in scripture because it says that there was no such flood. Rather, it says geological strata and the fossils they contain were laid down over billions of years. This is a lie not only because it contradicts the Bible but because there is abundant evidence that such a flood did in fact take place. As you are probably aware, huge numbers of marine fossils (seashells, etc.) are found throughout the world at high elevations far inland from oceans.

Only by inventing complex hypotheses about numerous continental uplifts and downshifts, and receding and returning oceans, can evolutionists account for the geological strata and its "fossil record." The sedimentary beds and the geological and fossil record can all be explained much more simply and reasonably by the Flood.

Legends and mythologies of many tribes and nations in all parts of the world lend compelling support to the fact of a biblical flood. They all tell of a time when the entire earth was devastated by water. For example, anthropologists have collected at least fifty-nine flood legends from the aborigines of North America alone and another thirt-seven from the South Sea Islands and Australia. They all agree on at least three things:

- A worldwide flood destroyed both man and animals.
- There was a vessel of safety provided.
- An extremely small remnant of people thus survived.[19]

These points, of course, correspond precisely with the account given of Noah and the ark in Genesis 6–8.

Incidentally, the Grand Canyon in Arizona is a striking example of the problems geologists and evolutionists face in explaining how things got the way they are, if one rejects the possibility of the Flood (or catastrophic drainage of trapped "lake" water following the Flood). Few people realize that the north rim of the Canyon is approximately a thousand feet higher than the south rim. However, the north rim shows the same type of erosion as the south rim. How could this be so if this erosion were caused primarily by the Colorado River? How did it get a thousand feet above the opposite canyon wall?

I asked this question of a knowledgeable Ph.D. who was a believer in evolution (and also a Christian) and who had a scientific background. His answer was "uplift." (Only the north rim was uplifted a thousand feet, while the south rim remained in place.) In other words, "Don't bother me with the facts. My mind's made up." As I gazed at the immense breadth and depth of the canyon, I could see the meandering Colorado a mile below, and it struck me: there is no way that tiny stream plus wind and rain could have eroded that gaping chasm with its huge walls of mostly solid rock. It had to be a gigantic volume of rushing water, as deep as an ocean, to have accomplished that by covering the north rim as well as the south rim. (See Steven

A. Austin, Ph.D., *Grand Canyon: Monument to Catastrophe* (Institute for Creation Research, 1994), for a scientific explanation of this phenomenon by a creation scientist.)

Biblical Statements About How God Created Everything

The Bible says three basic things about how God created all things:

> He *made* them instantaneously.
> He *made* them as separate, distinct kinds.
> He *made* them as fully functioning, mature entities.

Regarding the first point, recall that Revelation 14:7 says, "Worship him who *made* the heavens, the earth, the sea and the springs of water" [emphasis added]. God *made* all these things (i.e., He produced finished products). He didn't just allow them to develop by evolution over aeons of time. The word "made" here is the translation of the Greek *poiesanti* which means "produce by workmanship." It is closely related to the Greek *poieme* (a thing which is made) from which we get our word "poem."

Thus, from this point of view, God's creation is a thing which He made as a poet creates a poem—something produced out of His mind and heart as a completed expression of Himself. Unlike a human poet, however, He did not have to work and struggle and refine and polish it to bring it to completion. He produced it instantaneously by speaking it into exist-

ence. On the first day, He said, "'Let there be light,'
and there was light." He continued in this manner
through the five remaining days of creation, bringing
each new thing immediately into existence as He
spoke forth His creative Word (Genesis 1:1–26).

Regarding the second point, the Bible says that,
as God made the plants and animals in this way, He
made each "after his [its] *kind*" (Genesis 1:11–12,
21, 24–25 [KJV]). The Hebrew word for "kind" here
is *miyn*, which means "a sort, i.e. *species*."[20] At least
ten major categories of "kinds" are mentioned in
Genesis 1: grass, herbs, fruit trees, whales, other sea
creatures, birds, cattle, crawling animals, beasts of
the earth, and human beings. 1 Corinthians 15:39
reinforces this idea of distinct, separate kinds:

> All flesh is not the same: Men have one *kind* of
> flesh, animals have *another*, birds *another* and
> fish *another* [emphasis added].

There is no indication here of an evolutionary
continuity of life forms, but rather an unambiguous
identification of different kinds that were created in
the beginning.

"Scientific" Christians who read evolution into
the Bible can do so only by either ignoring these
scriptural statements or twisting them, perhaps by
redefining the word "kind" to make it mean something like this: "the product of change from one form
into another at any given moment in the evolutionary process."[21] In other words, the "kinds" we see
today, evolutionists would say, are the intermediate

products of this process, which is still going on but is undetectable to human observation.

Regarding the third point, the scriptures say that God created all things as mature, fully functioning entities—whether they be galaxies, stars, planets, plants, animals, or man. Most explicit in this regard is the story of Adam. This story, of course, clearly contradicts evolution because it says that at one time there was a single human being on earth. According to evolution, this could not have been because that theory says *populations* evolve, not single individuals.[22] After creating Adam out of the dust of the ground, the Bible says, God created Eve by using a portion of Adam's side (Genesis 2:7, 21–22).

Obviously, evolution contradicts this account of how man and woman came into being. They did not evolve gradually or even by a sudden synchronization of separate parts into integrated systems. Evolutionists call this refinement on Darwinism "punctuated equilibrium." (See appendix C.) Adam and Eve appeared in the beginning as fully-grown, adult people, ready to "Be fruitful and increase in number" (Genesis 1:28).

God formed "the *man* from the dust . . . and the *man* became a living creature" (Genesis 2:7). Then He "took the *man* and put him in the Garden of Eden to work and take care of it" (Genesis 2:15). (Emphasis added in both verses.) Adam was not created as a boy or an infant or a fetus or the descendant of a "monkey," but as a *man*, ready and able to

work and care for the Garden and produce offspring
with his fully grown wife, Eve.

The Character of God

Finally, evolution is also a lie from the biblical
point of view because it contradicts the character
of God and the nature of His creation. The God of
the Bible is one of goodness and life—not of evil
and death. The Bible says that, when God finished
His creation, it was *all very good* (Genesis 1:31).
And there was no suffering or death for humans,
for these entered the world as a result of Adam and
Eve's sin (Genesis 3:17–19).

But evolution says that life developed to its
present state by a long, slow, inefficient, cruel process, emerging from disorder and involving suffering, aging, decay, and death. This contradicts
the nature of God, as described in the Bible, as
orderly, kind, and loving.

As Jacques Monod puts it, natural selection is

> the blindest, and most cruel way of evolving new
> species. . . . The struggle for life and elimination
> of the weakest is a horrible process against which
> our whole modern ethic revolts. . . . I am sur-
> prised that a Christian would defend the idea
> that it is the whole process which God more or
> less set up in order to have evolution.[23]

Evolution contradicts the character of God, not
only because it rejects His love, but also because it

denies His omnipotence, omniscience, purposive-
ness, graciousness, and desire for fellowship:

- *God is loving*—Why would a God of love have
  created such a brutal, violent method as survival of the fittest with its five-billion-year history of struggle, suffering, disease, and death?
- *God is omnipotent*—Why would God stretch
  out His creation over billions of years when
  He had the power to do it in an instant?
- *God is omniscient*—Why would a God who
  knows everything, including the end from
  the beginning, use random mutation—with
  its resulting "fossil record" of extinctions and
  supposed evolutionary dead ends—as His
  chosen method of creating? Did He have to
  keep tinkering with it to get it right?
- *God is purposive*—Why would He "waste
  billions of years in aimless evolutionary
  meandering before getting to the point?
  What semblance of purpose could there
  have been in the hundred-million-year
  reign and eventual extinction of the dino-
  saurs, for example?"
- *God is gracious*—Why would a gracious
  God—who provides salvation on the basis
  of faith in His sacrifice of Himself for the unfit
  and unworthy—choose a method which
  eliminates the unfit and unworthy by violent and cruel means?

- *God wanted fellowship with man*—Why
  would He have waited billions of years to
  get around to creating man if His ultimate
  goal was to have fellowship with him?[24].

To believe in evolution, then, is to disbelieve in
the God of the Bible and to believe that the biblical
accounts of creation and the Flood are myths. In
other words, evolution is a lie of the enemy, for it
contradicts the character of God and His revelation
of how all things came to be.

Since these two models for the origin of things
are totally contradictory, how is it that many Christians attempt to combine them in the various versions of theistic evolution? And how do they
manipulate scripture so that it will appear to accommodate both models? These are the basic questions
answered in chapter ten.

Evolution and Satan's Tricks (Lies, Logical Fallacies, and Semantic Manipulation)

In their efforts to combine evolution with biblical creation, Christians who have unknowingly bought into Satan's lie have also bought into the lie that scientific theory supercedes the Bible as the source of truth. But the Bible says

> "For my thoughts are not your thoughts, neither are your ways my ways," declares the Lord.

> "As the heavens are higher than the earth, So are my ways higher than your ways and my thoughts than your thoughts . . ." (Isaiah 55:8–9).

This says, in effect, that God is the ultimate source of truth and His truth is far above that of mere men, no matter how philosophically or scientifically advanced they may be.

REDEFINING CREATION AS EVOLUTION

It is a sad fact that a growing number of Christians do not believe that God's truth is superior to man's. They reject or distort what the Bible says about creation in favor of some form of theistic evolution, which, as we have seen, is the belief that God used evolution as His method of creation. Some of these people believe that occasionally God interrupted the process to create new types of creatures or to redirect the evolutionary process. This variation is called "progressive" or "continuous" creation.

"Continuous creation" is an attempt, on a cosmic scale, to neutralize the second law of thermodynamics, which says that the universe is running down and becoming more disordered. Rather, "continuous creation" teaches continuous *evolution* and says that matter is, under God's supervision, becoming more ordered.

Thus, the first major trick the enemy uses to promote this lie is the semantic manipulation called redefinition. The continuous creationists have redefined creation, (the appearance of ordered matter out of nothing) as evolution. To say that it is continuous is also to ignore related scripture, for it contradicts the passages which say that creation is no longer taking place. For example, Genesis 2:1–2 says, "Thus the heavens and the earth were *completed* in all their vast array," and Hebrews 4:3 declares, ". . . his work has been *finished* since the creation of the world" [emphasis added].

Reinterpreting Biblical Chronology

The second way in which evolution is made to
fit into scripture is to reinterpret biblical chronology. This is accomplished in six major ways:

1. Uniformitarianism
2. The day-age theory
3. The gap theory
4. The genealogical gaps theory
5. The local flood theory
6. The big bang theory

Uniformitarianism

Uniformitarianism is the theory that, since the
beginning, conditions have always been the same and
that the great worldwide Flood of Genesis 6 through
8 never happened.[1] Thus, biblical chronology is re-
vised to fit the evolutionary model that life has been
steadily evolving, that fossils and geological strata
were laid down prior to Adam and Eve, and that there
was no flood. The Bible prophesied that this is exactly what would happen in the last days:

> First of all, you must understand that in the
> last days scoffers will come, scoffing and fol-
> lowing their own evil desires. They will say,
> "Where is this 'coming' he promised? *Ever
> since our fathers died, everything goes on as it
> has since the beginning of creation.*" But they
> deliberately forget that long ago by God's word
> the heavens existed and the earth was formed
> out of water and by water. *By these waters also*

the world of that time was deluged and destroyed
(2 Peter 3:3–6, emphasis added).

We see, then, that uniformitarians ignore the scriptures in Genesis and 2 Peter which contradict their view. What is more interesting, the theory of uniformitarianism itself is a fulfillment of Peter's prophecy. As Gish points out,

> For 1,800 years after Peter had written his epistles, the flood of Noah was generally accepted, and up until about A.D. 1800 the interpretation of geology that was taught in the great universities, such as Cambridge, Oxford, Harvard, and Yale, was based on flood geology . . . today any such worldwide catastrophe as the Noachian Flood is completely discounted in the teaching of geology in all of the world's major universities."[2]

The Day-Age Theory

This theory is, once again, the result of humanistic brainwashing which says that scientific theory takes precedence over scriptural revelation as the source of truth. As a result, many Christian Bible scholars have become convinced that the so-called geological ages have been proven by science. Therefore, it would be folly to question them, and a means of reconciling modern geology to Genesis must be found. The logical choice is a theory in which the ages of geology can be made to correspond to the record of Genesis. Therefore, each *day* of creation is made to signify an *age* of geological time. Presto! The day-age theory is born!

The day-age theory reinterprets biblical chronology, once again, by means of redefinition. This time, the literal meaning of "day" (a 24-hour period consisting of daylight followed by darkness) is made to mean "an immense period of time (or 'age') lasting for millions of years."

Morris points out that ". . . the Hebrew word for 'day' (*yom*) is *never* used for a definite delimited, or circumscribed time period except that of a solar day, and . . . the plural 'days' (*yomim*) is *never* used at all for anything but solar days"[3] [emphasis added]. Thus to redefine it as "age" is, at the same time, to commit a gross mistranslation of scripture.

Those guilty of such mistranslation try to justify it by saying that *yom* is sometimes used to mean "time" in an indefinite sense, for example, as in "the *day* of the Lord"[4] [emphasis in original]. However, this usage does not mean an "age," but the point in time when the Lord will return and pour out His judgment on the satanic world system. It does not denote an extended period of time, and certainly not one covering millions or billions of years. Therefore, those who use this argument are also ignoring the context.

They also ignore the context in the first chapter of Genesis. There *yom* is clearly defined the first time it is used: "God called the light *yom*, and the evening and the morning were the first *yom*" (Genesis 1:5). Morris explains further:

Thus the "day" is defined as the "light" period in the succession of periods of "light" and "darkness." . . . On the fourth day, the meaning is obviously literal, since the very purpose of the sun and moon is said to be to rule the "day" and "night." . . . When the word "days" appears in the plural . . ., as it does over 700 times in the Old Testament it always refers to literal days. Thus in Exodus 20:11, when the Scripture says that "in six days the Lord made heaven and earth, the sea, and all that in them is," there can be no doubt whatever that six literal days are meant. This passage also clearly equated the week of God's creative work with the week of man's work. . . . If the intent of the writer had been to write of long ages of creation, he could certainly have done so. For example, the Hebrew word *olam* (meaning "long indefinite time") should have been used instead of *yom*. . . . But, if his intent were to tell of a literal creation in six solar days, it would be impossible to express this concept any more clearly than in the account as we actually have it.[5]

Therefore, not only are the day-age proponents guilty of redefinition in all this, but also of mistranslation, ignoring the specific and general biblical context, and ignoring related scriptures.

Thus, we see that there is no possibility of harmonizing geological chronology with biblical chronology by means of the day-age theory.

The Gap Theory

The gap theory is an attempt to "have your cake and eat it, too." It allows for the five billion years of evolution and at the same time retains the six literal days of creation. But it does so only by taking truly bizarre liberties with the Genesis account.

Essentially, this theory says that the entire history of evolution took place *before* the six days of creation in a "gap" between Genesis 1:1 and 1:2. In other words, in the first verse, God "created the heavens and the earth" as scripture states, and then He populated the earth during five billion years of evolution, thereby allowing for the geological and fossil record. Then He destroyed it all, thus rendering it "formless and empty," as described in verse 2. At this point, He again created all the things He had destroyed (for some unknown reason), this time without evolution and therefore was able to finish it in only six days instead of five billion years as before. Now, I ask you, isn't it amazing the lengths to which Satan will go to pervert scripture and foist his lies on Christians? And isn't it even more amazing what otherwise sensible, intelligent people will believe, given the right appeals to their carnal natures and natural minds?

Obviously, this theory contradicts scripture (and is therefore a lie of Satan) because there is *no gap* between Genesis 1:1 and 1:2! The transitional "Now" ("And" in the KJV) makes this perfectly clear. Verse 2 follows directly from verse 1 and is part of the same idea—that on the first day of creation, when the heavens (space) and earth (the first object in space) appeared, the planet was initially formless and empty.

Verse 1 of chapter 2 reinforces the fact that the heavens and the earth were initially made as part of the six days of creation with no gap involved: "Thus the heavens and the earth were completed in all their vast array." Verses 2 and 3 of chapter 2 reinforce this fact further by repeating the idea that God rested "from *all* his work." It was not the *second* phase of His work that He rested from but *all* of His work. He did not create/evolve everything for five billion years, rest, destroy everything, recreate everything, and rest again.

Exodus 20:11 confirms this reading, for it says the Lord made the heavens and the earth in six days. Again, *no gap* and *no re-creation* of the earth. (And, incidentally, there is no reference to such a gap anywhere in the Bible.) Once more, we have an example of grossly ignoring the context and related scripture.

Such flagrant abuse of scripture is bad enough, but the gap theory also abuses the very geological theory on which it is based. It says that there was a pre-Adamic cataclysm which destroyed all life and all traces of life on earth. But the geological record does not indicate any such thing—to either non-christian geologists or evolutionists. They see no indication of any kind of worldwide catastrophe or destruction of all life on earth. And such an event is not permitted in their theory, for it is based on *uniformitarianism, not catastrophism.*

Not only that, the gap theory also contradicts it-self! For, if there had been a cataclysm that left the earth without form and void, there would be no geological or fossil record because it would have been destroyed along with everything else. Therefore, the gap theory is based on a logical contradiction or non sequitur, for it says a cataclysm destroyed everything, *and* the cataclysm left the geological record intact.

Finally, the gap theory is also a lie of Satan be-cause, once again, it contradicts the character of God. God is not capricious or incompetent. So why would He create all life forms by evolution and then de-stroy them and then create them all over again with-out evolution? Did He decide He didn't like what He had done or hadn't done a good job the first time? If so, He must be a very limited and imperfect God and therefore not really God at all! (It also indicates, once more, that He must be a God of confusion, disorder, and destruction, introducing death before sin and evil before good.)

The explanation commonly offered for God's ap-parent capriciousness is that the pre-Adamic cata-clysm was caused by Satan's rebellion in heaven as described in Isaiah 14:12–15 and Ezekiel 28:11–17. In other words, somehow the devil's rebellious activ-ity brought on the destruction of all life on earth. This makes this part of the argument an outstanding example of begging the question, for no reason is given for such universal destruction and no evidence is provided to show that it actually did happen. It is just stated, like evolution itself, as a "fact."

Furthermore, the fact that Satan's rebellion was in heaven, not on earth, would seem to indicate that any effects of his rebellious activity were limited to heaven. In addition, there is absolutely nothing in scripture connecting Satan's fall with any type of worldwide cataclysm. Therefore, gap theory proponents are once again guilty of making untrue statements by reading into scripture meanings which are not there and, at the same time, of ignoring the context and related scripture. (I will use "untrue statement" instead of "lie" hereafter because "lie" implies intentional deception, which I am sure is not usually the case—especially among Christian theistic evolutionists.)

In addition, to say that Satan's rebellion in heaven caused worldwide destruction on earth is also another non sequitur. The Bible indicates no causal relationship between such events. (In this regard, it is also an example of the false cause [post hoc] fallacy.)

Finally, gap theory advocates also resort to mistranslation, for they say that the "was" of Genesis 1:2 ("Now the earth *was* formless and empty. . ." (emphasis added) should be translated "became." This, they say, implies that there was a gap between Genesis 1:1 and 1:2 because after the earth was created it *became* formless and empty. However, the word in question is *hayah* which is the Hebrew for "was." It is not *haphak* which is the word for "became."[6] Also, as we have seen, the use of *waw* ("and" or "now") between the verses indicates that they are parts of one general event and not two actions separated by five billion years.

Other proof texts used to support the gap theory are equally invalid. The errors in each case involve one or more of three kinds of semantic manipulation: ignoring the context, mistranslation and shifting the meaning of a word .[7]

The most important of these is Isaiah 45:18. In the KJV, this says, speaking of the earth, "God . . . created it *not in vain*, He formed it to be inhabited." "In vain" is a translation of the Hebrew tohu (literally, "without form").

The argument goes like this: The above verse says that the earth was not created without form. But the earth of Genesis 1:2 was without form. Therefore, the earth in Genesis 1:1 must have been a different earth which already had form and which became without form as a result of the pre-Adamic cataclysm.

However, this ignores the context of Isaiah 45:18 which is about God's purpose for Israel, not about how He created the earth. In verse 17, He says, ". . . Israel shall be saved in the Lord with an everlasting salvation: ye shall not be ashamed nor confounded world without end." This indicates that the subject is God's purpose (or promise) to provide salvation for His people. To support this promise, God then (in verse 18) reminds His people that the creation itself was not without purpose. The world was not created to be empty (or without form)—i.e., *without purpose* or *in vain*—but to be inhabited. And the NIV so translates verse 18: ". . . he did not create it to be empty. . . ."

Thus, the gap proponents ignore the fact that, in context, *tohu* has the meaning of "empty," "without purpose," or "in vain" and refers to God's promise to Israel and *not* to a pre-Adamic cataclysm.

Finally, the gap theory contradicts biblical chronology in many ways similar to those in the day-age theory. For example, Genesis 1:16–17 says God made all the stars on the fourth day, but, if there was a previous creation of the universe, then the stars must have been created at that time (some eighteen billion years ago, according to evolutionists). Therefore, God must have destroyed and recreated, not just life on earth, but also the rest of the universe as well!

But this contradicts the gap theory itself which says the cataclysm in the gap between Genesis 1:1 and 1:2 occurred on the earth, not throughout the whole universe. Therefore, the gap theory as a whole ignores the context of Genesis 1. And we have absurdity piled on absurdity in this futile attempt to reconcile evolution with biblical chronology.

The Genealogical Gaps Theory

Another attempt to harmonize the evolutionary time scale with the Bible is the genealogical gaps theory. This version attempts to integrate the supposed million or so years of human evolution into the genealogical record of Adam's descendants in Genesis 5 through 11. In order to do this, evolutionists must assume an average "gap" of 50,000 years between each of the twenty patriarchs from Adam to Abraham.

This, of course, completely ignores the context of the genealogical list, which indicates *no* gaps. Moreover, if it is a complete list, the ages given for the patriarchs add up to about two thousand years, not the million of evolution.

Theistic evolutionists justify the "necessary" gaps in genealogy by means of a redefinition of the term "begat" (KJV) to mean "was an ancestor of" rather than "procreated."

Morris has shown that there are really only ten possible gaps in the wording of the text.[8] Therefore, the average gap would have to be 100,000 years. Thus, each gap would be twenty-five times longer than all known human history. What conceivable purpose would such a chronology serve?

If the gaps were included in the genealogy, it would read something like this: "When Seth had lived 105 years, he became the father of [a son whose remote descendant, 100,000 years in the future would be] Enosh" (Genesis 5:6). Such a listing means 20,000 or so names were omitted from the genealogical record. Such a record is useless, to say the least.

Such "gaps" make the chronology totally absurd and the genealogical information utterly pointless. As Morris asks,

> What conceivable purpose can there have been
> . . . in carefully recording the age of each father
> at the birth of some unknown son who was then
> to be the ancestor of the next individual named
> in the list some fifty [or one hundred] thousand
> years in the future?[9]

Also, if man has existed for 1,000,000 years, why is there no record or archeological trace of this? Moreover, in 1,000,000 years, the world population would have been enormous. So why is there no indication of this in the fossil record?

Obviously, the genealogical list was intended to provide a complete record of the line from Adam to Abraham. The fact that the same genealogy is recorded in 1 Chronicles 1 (from Adam to Abraham) and Luke 3 (from Jesus back to Adam), clearly indicates that it was intended as a complete record of the patriarchal line from Adam to Abraham and of the messianic line from Adam to Jesus.

The Local Flood Theory

One additional theory is advocated by a number of evangelical writers in order to preserve science's geological record and simultaneously retain the biblical story of the Flood. This theory states that the biblical Flood was not worldwide, but only local. This is necessary because a global deluge is not compatible with either uniformitarianism, the day-age theory, or the gap theory, as we have seen.

This idea ignores a number of related scriptures, including those in Genesis 6 through 9, which say that there was a one-time global deluge that covered the tops of the highest mountains. It must therefore have been at least 17,000 feet deep—the height of Mount Ararat, on which the Ark came to rest (assuming Mount Ararat was not "uplifted" at some

time following the Flood.) Obviously, a *local* flood
of that magnitude is impossible.

Furthermore, this theory ignores the general
scriptural context of verses which say that the ark
was used to preserve plants and animals from anni-
hilation (Genesis 6:19–20), that all other life over
the entire earth was destroyed, and that God would
never again send such a flood (Genesis 9:11; 2 Peter 2:5, 3:6; Hebrews 11:7; and Luke 17:27). Clearly,
all of this was not referring to a local flood.

Finally, even if we were to forget all the rules of
logical and semantic discernment and assume that
it was only a local flood, then we must also assume
that God was a liar when He said there would never
again be such a flood. For He would have broken
His promise many times because there have been
many local floods.

In the local flood theory, then, we again have
ignoring the context and an untrue statement (i.e.,
defaming the character of God by implying that He
doesn't keep His word).

The Big Bang Theory

At last, we come to the cosmological theory that
has probably influenced the contemporary church
more perniciously than any other: the belief of science and evolution that the heavens and the earth
and all that is in them originated in a gigantic explosion which occurred some eighteen billion years
ago—"the big bang."

The basic proposition, as indicated earlier, is that all the matter and energy in the universe were originally concentrated in a spot "no bigger than the head of a pin."[10] Suddenly, this incredibly dense and tiny package exploded, giving rise to the galaxies, stars, planets, and organic life as we know them today.

This would mean that the universe was not created as fully functioning and mature, but as a chaos of mass and energy from which order somehow emerged according to the processes of evolution. This, like the other theories we have examined, contradicts the character of God, for (as we have seen) He is a God of order and not of chaos.

And we know from simple observation that explosions do not produce order. The idea that the incredibly complex, highly organized design of the universe could result from an explosion of matter just does not make sense. No one has ever observed explosions producing ordered complexity. Rather, they *destroy* complexity and produce *disorder.*

Nevertheless, the idea that order can result from disorder is the essence of the theory of evolution. Therefore, the big bang requires a belief in some form of evolution. To say, as the theistic evolutionists do, that God used evolution or some form of "progressive creation," is to defame the character of God and rewrite or ignore scripture—as we observed earlier.

VARIETY OF HEAVENLY BODIES

Perhaps the most telling argument against the evolutionary implications of the big bang is the in-

credible variety of galaxies, stars, and other astronomical phenomena. These include the following,
among others: "planets, comets, meteors, white
dwarfs, red giants, variable stars, star clusters, bi-
nary stars, dark nebulae, interstellar dust, radio stars,
quasars, neutron stars, and black holes." Scientific
data has confirmed that "no two stars, out of the
innumerable host of Heaven are exactly alike."[11]

The Bible agrees with this finding, declaring that
each heavenly body was created with its own dis-
tinctive qualities:

> The sun has one kind of splendor, the moon
> another, and the stars another; and star differs
> from star in splendor (1 Corinthians 15:41).

The question is, How could they have all evolved
from the same source (energy and matter released
in an explosion) and yet be so different? The big
bang doesn't account for this, and evolution doesn't
account for it either. Believers in progressive creation may answer that God intervened at various
stages of the explosive expansion of the universe to
create distinct types of heavenly bodies. But, again,
this contradicts the character of God as well as the
testimony of scripture.

SCIENCE VERSUS THE BIBLE

Whatever version of theistic evolution one may
combine with the big bang, the result is the same: scientific theory is substituted for biblical truth. One may
identify God as the First Cause or Creator behind the

big bang, but this only provides another source of confusion for many Christians who put confidence in the scientific explanation of the way things came to be.

What they are confused about is the omnipotent nature of God. They may believe that God started it, but, since science *assumes* it all had to begin at a single point and expand from there, they also *assume* that there was no other possible method God could have used. This assumption, of course, ignores the possibility that God could have created the universe as a fully functioning, completely organized whole—just as He did with Adam and each kind of plant and animal, according to the Bible.

Thus, Christian scientists, like Hugh Ross, and their followers, limit God by declaring that He could create the universe only by means that scientific measurements indicate He might have used. What they forget or choose to ignore is that *God is not limited by the findings of scientific measurements and the "wisdom" of men.* They are putting God in a box of their own design labeled "scientific measurements"—as though God and His ways *could* be measured. But God is not limited by the ideas of mere human beings, no matter how "scientifically brilliant" they may be. The bottom line, then, is really their human pride and arrogance which sets the intellect of man above the revealed Word of God and feels impelled to manipulate that revealed Word to make it somehow conform to their conclusions about the behavior of God and the nature of His creation.

In this way, Satan uses sincere Christians who are also scientists, such as Ross, to foist the big bang lie on the church. They do this by holding science to be the ultimate source of truth regarding such matters. For example, citing scientific authorities regarding the "primeval atom" as the basis for the big bang, Ross says this:

> Picking up on Eddington's presumption that the universe might begin with a specific non-zero radius, Lemaitre conjectured that the present universe came from the disintegration of a single atom.

> We could conceive the beginning of the universe in the form of a unique atom, the atomic weight of which is the total mass of the universe. This highly unstable atom would divide in smaller and smaller atoms by a kind of super-radioactive process.

> At the origin, all the mass of the universe would exist in the form of a unique atom; the radius of the universe, although not strictly zero, being relatively very small. The whole universe would be produced by the disintegration of this primeval atom.[12]

Clearly, Ross agrees with Lemaitre's conjecture and approves of it as a reasonable scientific explanation of how the universe began.

Of course, this is profoundly unscriptural. In Genesis 1:1, it says, "In the beginning God created the heavens and the earth." It does not say He created a "primeval atom'" which for some reason was unstable, exploded, and over a period of eighteen billion years produced the universe as it exists today.

So the question for the church is, Which version do you believe and where do you put your trust—in the words of Eddington, Lemaitre, Ross, et al—or in God and His Bible?

We now turn to the specific arguments that Ross and the others use to support Satan's big bang lie (not that they do so knowingly or deliberately).

THE RED SHIFT ARGUMENT

The "red shift (or receding nebulae) argument" is based on the change in light coming to earth from stars, supposedly caused by the Doppler effect. This means that, if the star is moving *away*, the light coming from it is stretched out and appears slightly redder. Conversely, the light from a star moving *toward* the viewer is compressed and becomes slightly bluer.

Tracing the history of this "evidence" of the big bang, Ross says,

> Armed with the velocity and distance measurements for many more galaxies . . . Hubble in 1929 announced his famous *law of red shifts*; the more distant a galaxy, the greater, in direct proportion, is its velocity of recession (determined by the shifts of its spectral lines to long, or redder, wavelengths). This observation by Hubble was exactly what the simplest expanding universe model would predict.

Finally, Arthur Eddington and other theoreticians pointed out that the second law of thermodynamics had all along demanded the disintegration of the universe. For the universe as a whole, disorder must continually increase and energy must irreversibly flow from hot to cold bodies. In other words, the universe is running down like a wound up clock. And, if it is running down, then there must have been a time when it was fully wound up.[13]

I find it amazing that Ross uses the very scientific principle (the second law of thermodynamics), which *disproves* evolution, to support his theory of the big bang, which *requires* evolution. The second law of thermodynamics says essentially (in layman's terms) that everything in the universe is running down and falling apart—*not* becoming more complex and better organized, as evolution requires. (See appendix C for a fuller explanation of this law.)

What Ross seems to be saying is that the big bang began winding up the clock, and, once it was fully wound up by an evolutionary process, then the second law of thermodynamics took over and it has been running down ever since. This is not only unscientific, it is also a non sequitur. The second law of thermodynamics proves that the universe could not have been wound up by an evolutionary process set in motion by an explosion. Rather, it proves that some other process must have produced the initial wound-up clockwork (creating order) which has since been running down (being converted into disorder). This process was the biblical six days of creation!

In other words, what the red shift *may* show is that, when God created the fully functioning universe, He designed it as one which is expanding. However, even this possibility is questionable, for some astronomical findings indicate that some galaxies are *not* moving away from each other and some may even be moving toward each other; the same galaxy may have several different red shifts; not all galaxies have red shifts; some have blue shifts; gravity can cause a red shift; and the red shift could indicate that the universe is rotating instead of expanding.[14]

Why then do those who believe in the big bang ignore this contradictory evidence and maintain, as Ross does, that the universe is unquestionably expanding and that all other explanations are invalid? The answer has to be that they have rejected the biblical account of the creation process and have chosen to believe a particular "scientific" view based on a form of theistic evolution.

And why have they made this choice? Because they have placed the speculations and problematic claims of science above the divine revelations of scripture, believing science is a more reliable and authoritative guide to truth than the Bible.

THE APPEARANCE OF AGE ARGUMENT

The second argument that Ross and those Christians who share his view use to support the big bang

theory is that God is not a deceiver, and therefore He
would not have created a universe with a false appearance of age. The idea here is that, since the universe
has the appearance of age, it must have come through
an immensely long aging process beginning with the
big bang. Therefore, when the Bible says God created
the heavens and the earth and all that is in the earth, it
doesn't mean He did it all in only six days. Rather, it
means that the account of creation in Genesis must be
figurative rather than literal. And it must be a mythi-
cal (or at least a metaphorical or allegorical) account
of the creation process.

Therefore, so the argument goes, to say that God
created the universe in its mature form (with the appearance of age) cannot be true. It would mean that
God orchestrated a gigantic hoax—making things look
old when in fact they were brand new. On the other
hand, theistic evolution avoids this negative view of
God by assuming that He created everything with a
big bang and then it developed into its present condition of age.

However, to say that God would be a deceiver if
He created everything with an appearance of age is
very poor logic. It is in fact a non sequitur of the first
order. *Anything* that is created will necessarily and
automatically have an appearance of age. If a sculp-
tor fashions a statue of a man, it will necessarily appear to be a man of a certain age. It would in fact be
impossible for an artist to create an image of any living thing without an appearance of age; that is, without the object having the appearance that it would

naturally have at some given point in its life cycle. The same principle applies to the creations of God. Therefore, it doesn't follow that something created in a mature form involves a deception.

Let's take Adam as an example. The Bible says God created Adam as a full-grown man. He was not created as a fertilized egg or an embryo or a child and then allowed to develop. Thus, he had an appearance of age (perhaps that of a young adult), but he was not a deception. That was just the point in the human life cycle at which God created him.

In like manner, the Bible says everything was created as a fully developed whole. Light from the stars was visible on earth in the same moment it was created. It didn't have to travel for years before it reached the earth. It was created already reaching the earth! Yes, God created the universe and, in some sense, wound it up like a great clock. But, as the Cosmic Clockmaker, He could have set it at any time He chose. It didn't have to start at 12:01 A.M. It could have been set at high noon.

As Morris points out, "to say that God could not create anything with apparent age is tantamount to saying nothing could be created, and, therefore is essentially the same position as . . . atheism. . . . the doctrine of creation of apparent age does not in the remotest degree involve a divine deception, but is rather inherent in the very nature of creation."[15]

Ross adds this additional twist to the argument:

Taken to its logical conclusion, the appearance of
age theory would imply that we could not establish that our past existence actually occurred. For
example, we could have been created just a few
hours ago with the Creator implanting memory,
material possessions, scars, and hardening of the
arteries to make us appear and feel older than we
really are. As such, we could not be held responsible for any of our "past" actions.[16]

Now, there are two fallacies in this argument. First,
it ignores the context of the creation account in Genesis. At each stage of His creation—space, earth, vegetation, aquatic life, birds, animals, and man—He
declared that it was "good" and finally "very good"
(Genesis 1:10, 12, 18, 21, 25, and 31). But memories
of non-existent things, scars, and hardening of the
arteries, are not "good." So God could not have created such conditions at the beginning. Therefore, they
must have come later as the actual aging process pro-
gressed, and they must have been the result of natural causes and not divine deception.

Secondly, it is a non sequitur because it applies
conditions which God created in the beginning to
present day human beings. To say that, if God created
the universe in a mature form, then every appearance
of age thereafter would be false is to claim a logical
connection where none exists. There is no reason that
Adam, although he was created in a mature form, could
not then actually accumulate memories, go through
the natural aging process, or be held accountable for
his actions. Furthermore, Adam was not created with

false memories or fraudulent signs of deterioration. Therefore, it is also false to say that the appearance of age (as an aspect of biblical creation) means that this appearance is a deception. The Bible makes no such assumption, but speaks of people really growing old and accumulating real memories and being responsible for their behavior (ignoring related scripture).

Also, the Bible obviously contradicts the idea that everything could have been created just a few hours ago. According to this line of reasoning, the truth of the whole Bible would have to be brought into question and there would have to be a possibility that all of scripture was nothing but a fabrication foisted on mankind by God Himself—because none of it really happened. Again, Ross demeans the character of God and the validity of the Bible by using such an argument.

THE LIGHT YEARS ARGUMENT

Ross's third argument for the big bang hinges on the speed of light. Essentially, this argument says that, since some galaxies are so far away that it has taken billions of years for their light to reach earth, the universe must be billions of years old.[17]

This assumes that light emitters (stars) must have been created before light itself (or at least at the same time). But the Bible says this is not so. God created light on the first day and the stars on the fourth day. Therefore, once again, Ross contradicts the biblical account and ignores the context of biblical chronology.

The question is, Which came first, the chicken
or the egg? Light or stars? The Bible says the
chicken! Light was shining on the earth on the same
day both were created. It didn't have to travel billions of years to reach earth. As Morris notes,

> It was certainly no more difficult for God to form
> light waves than the "light-bearers" which would
> be established to serve as future generators of
> those waves. . . . the light source for the first
> three days had the same function ("to divide the
> light from the darkness") as did the heavenly
> bodies from the fourth day onward (Genesis 1:4,
> 18). This "division" now resulted from the sun
> and moon and the earth's axial rotation. For prac-
> tical purposes, therefore, the primeval light must
> essentially have come from the same direction
> as it would later when the permanent light
> sources were set in place.[18]

THE RADIOACTIVE DECAY ARGUMENT

Finally, many scientists, including Ross, argue that
scientific evidence proves that the earth is "some 4.5
billion years" old [19] (or 4 or 5 billion, depending on
which scientist's "proof" is involved). Therefore, they
maintain, the biblical account cannot be taken literally and the universe must have begun billions of
years ago with a big bang as science declares. This
is all based on the radio-decay rates of uranium and
thorium.[20]

However, radioactive decay as a measure of age
has proven to be very problematic. As evolutionist
Frederick B. Jueneman explains,

There has been in recent years the horrible realization that radio-decay rates are not as constant
as previously thought, nor are they immune to
environmental influence, and this could mean that
the atomic clocks are reset during some global
disaster, and events which brought the mesozoic
to a close may not be 5 million years [old], but
rather, within the age and memory of man.[21]

ROSS'S INTERPRETATION OF GENESIS CHRONOLOGY

Ross says that it is "unfortunate" that

most people now assume that . . . the Bible directly states that the earth and all its life forms
were created in six consecutive 24-hour days.
Because of the implausibility of such a position,
many reject the Bible out of hand without seriously investigating its message or even reading
for themselves the relevant passages.[22]

This implies that the Bible does *not* say that the
days of Genesis 1 were normal, consecutive earth
days. And it also implies that anyone who believes
that this *is* what the Bible says must be either misin-
formed or at least confused. But we all know that
the Bible *does* in fact say this. Therefore, Ross bases
his interpretation of Genesis on an untrue statement.
Moreover, he is simultaneously begging the question. He gives no proof that a literal reading of Genesis is "implausible." What is implausible about an
omnipotent God doing whatever He wants in what-

ever way He wants to? What *is* implausible is assuming that such a God can only do things in the
way that Hugh Ross says He can.

Although he doesn't say so directly, Ross obviously thinks it is implausible only because it contradicts a scientific theory. And this theory—the
big bang—by the way, is *only* a theory. It has not
been proven by the scientific gathering of empiri-
cal evidence because no one can go back to the
time of creation to see what actually happened or
trace the expansion of the universe by direct observation or directly measure the time which has
passed from the moment of creation until the
present. These are all impossibilities, and, therefore any conclusions about them must remain theo-
retical or speculative inferences.

Ross also declares that a literal reading of Genesis requires an ancient date of creation because early
church fathers and scholars said so:

> Many of the early church fathers and other bib-
> lical scholars interpreted the creation days of
> Genesis 1 as long periods of time. The list in-
> cludes the Jewish historian Josephus (1st cen-
> tury); Irenaeus, bishop of Lyons, apologist,
> and martyr (2nd century); Origen, who rebut-
> ted heathen attacks on christian doctrine (3rd
> century); Basil (4th century); Augustine (5th
> century); and, later, Aquinas (13th century),
> to name a few.[23]

Whether these people actually so interpreted Genesis or not, I don't know, and Ross gives no supporting documentation. However, in any case, the significant point here is that Ross is using the logical fallacy of argument by authority to support his view. The *opinions* of church leaders and scholars do not *prove* anything. But, in Ross's view, they take precedence over what the Bible writers themselves say as the basis for understanding the meaning of Genesis.

Ross commits another logical error, the either-or fallacy, when he says the word "day" in Genesis 1 can only mean *either* "twenty-four hours, *or*, rather, something in the order of millions of years."[24] [Emphasis added.] There is no contextual reason for assuming it doesn't mean 24 hours, but, even if there were, there is no reason to assume that the only alternative is "millions of years." It could, with equal reason (or lack thereof), be interpreted as any period of time longer (or shorter) than 24 hours, and, since the Bible says "With the Lord a day is like a thousand years" (2 Peter 3:8), *"a thousand years"* would seem to be a better choice than "millions of years."

In fact, what the Bible does say is "And there was evening, and there was morning—the first day" (Genesis 1:5). Now, the period of time bounded by evening and morning in our experience is a 24-hour day. And Moses was writing to Israelites whose experience in that regard was the same as ours. However, whether this exact time interval was involved in the days of Creation, we do not know. All we know is that it consisted of a time of darkness which began with evening and a time of daylight which began with morning. Nevertheless, there is no reason for assuming that either a shorter or longer period than a normal day of the present time was intended. And the scripture gives no such indication.

Rather, the actual wording indicates just the opposite, that it is to be taken as a normal day. The only way it could be taken to mean millions of years is to completely disregard the actual wording and apply some kind of metaphorical, allegorical, or symbolic meaning to the word "day" and then assume that this figurative meaning must be "millions of years"—because that is what the scientific establishment has decided.

Therefore, this case involves not only the either-or fallacy, but also ignoring the context and taking literal language metaphorically.

In addition to these arguments, Ross says that there are a "dozen or more different indicators from the Bible that a literal reading of Genesis 1 demands an ancient rather than a recent creation date"[25] and that there are "many reasons for interpreting the creation days of Genesis as long periods of time."[26]

I found thirteen such "reasons" in his book *The Fingerprint of God*. I also found that faulty logic or semantic manipulation was involved in every single one of them. Since it would take far too much space to analyze the logic and semantics involved in each, we will look at just a few of the more interesting ones.

"THE SEVENTH DAY NOT YET ENDED"

The first "reason" contains several of these logical and semantic problems. This is the idea that the seventh day, on which God rested, has never ended but has lasted for "a long time," and, therefore, the other six days must have also lasted for a long time. Ross acknowledges that the wording of Genesis 1 "indicates that each of the first six creation days had a beginning and ending." However, he says,

> for the seventh creation day no such statement appears either in Genesis 1–2 or anywhere else in the Bible. Given the parallel structure for marking the creation days, this distinct change in form for *the seventh day* strongly suggests that this day has (or had) *not yet ended.*

> Further information about the seventh day is given in Hebrews 4 and Psalm 95. Here we learn that *God's day of rest continues even now.* The writer of Hebrews says,

>> On the seventh day God rested from his work. . . . It still remains that some will enter that rest. . . . There remains, then, a Sabbath-rest for the people of God; for anyone who enters God's rest also rests from his own work, just as God did from his. Let us, therefore, make every effort to enter that rest (Hebrews 4:4–10).

> He indicates here that *the seventh day of creation week carries on through the centuries,* from Adam

and Eve, through Israel's development as a nation, through the time of Christ's earthly ministry, through the early days of the church, and on
into future years. King David in Psalm 95:7–11
also refers to *God's seventh day of rest as an ongoing event.* From these passages we gather that
*the seventh day of Genesis 1 and 2 represents a
minimum of several thousand years* and a maximum that is open ended (though finite). It
seems reasonable to conclude then, *given the
parallelism of the creation account, that the first
six days also were very long time periods.*[27] [Em-
phasis added.]

Here are the logical and semantic problems involved in this passage:

1. **Non Sequitur.** Even if the seventh day is still
   continuing, that doesn't prove a period of
   millions of years for creation (as Ross himself recognizes in the passage just quoted).
   It doesn't follow. If I rest for a year after building a shed, it doesn't mean that I must have
   taken a year to build the shed. How long I
   rest after a job has nothing to do with how
   long it took to complete the job. There is no
   direct correlation between the two.
2. **Redefinition.** Hebrews 4:4–10 is *not* talking
   about a "day" but about a spiritual condition, "a Sabbath rest." This is a false equivalency (or redefinition) because "rest" or
   "Sabbath-rest" is equated to the seventh
   "day" of creation week, thereby implying that

the creation week is still continuing. *But the fact that God's rest continues does not mean that the seventh day is still continuing.* Rather, it means that the rest which *began* on the seventh day is continuing.

To say that the seventh day is still continuing is equivalent to saying that, because my vacation began on the seventh day of the week (let's say Saturday), that it is still Saturday even though I've been vacationing for two and a half weeks. Obviously, it isn't still Saturday (the seventh day) just because my vacation began on Saturday. Likewise, *it isn't still the seventh day of creation week just because God's rest began on that day.* (This is also another non sequitur.)

Moreover, it also involves rewriting scripture, for nowhere in Hebrews 4:4–10 does the phrase *day of rest* appear. Rather, it uses the term *rest* by itself. To this, Ross has added the words *day of* to make it say something which is not in the original.

3. **Non Sequitur.** The parallelism of the six days doesn't prove anything for two reasons. (1) Such parallelism is an aspect of Hebrew poetic structure, not a device to show equivalent time periods between the seventh day and the other six days. (2) *The seventh day is not expressed in terms parallel to the first six days* because the "evening" and "morning" phraseology is missing in the verse dealing with the seventh day. Also, the seventh day is not parallel to the first

six days for another reason: it is not a part of
the creation process. Therefore, it does not follow (based on parallelism) that, because the
seventh day is a long period time (assuming it
was), the first six days must be equally long
periods of time. In addition, since Ross's statement is false (that all seven days are parallel),
it is also an untrue statement.

4. **Begging the Question**. There is nothing here
   that proves (or even remotely indicates) that
   the seventh day has lasted for a very long
   period of time. Therefore, this is also an example of assuming the truth of the thing that
   needs to be proven.

5. **Rewriting Scripture**. Psalm 95:7–11 (like Hebrews 4:4–10) doesn't use the word "day" in
   referring to God's rest, as Ross claims. Rather,
   it says, "'They shall never enter my rest.'" Again,
   "rest" is a spiritual condition, not a period of
   time. But Ross makes it read, "They shall never
   enter my *day of* rest." [Emphasis added.] Therefore, this is, once again, a case of changing scripture by inserting two words ("day of") which
   are not present in the original.

6. **Redefinition**. Ross's use of Psalm 95:7–11 is
   also another example of false equivalency
   because it redefines the word "rest" as "day."
   Thus, in this one "reason" why Genesis days
   must be long periods of time, we have the
   following logical and semantic fallacies: three
   non sequiturs, two redefinitions, three re-

writing scriptures, one begging the question, and one untrue statement.

MORE SCRIPTURE TWISTING

There are many additional examples that we could look at of how Ross twists scriptures to make them fit his science-based preconceptions. However, in the interest of brevity, we will focus on only a couple which involve three major problems: rewriting scripture, false analogy, and slanting—among others.

1. Rewriting Scripture
   Ross begins his section on the "advent of modern man" with the statement: "According to Genesis 1, the origin of the universe predates the six days of creation, while the origin of man occurs at the very end of the six days."[28] While this statement of the gap theory is a nicely balanced sentence, the first clause dealing with something prior to the six days and the second clause dealing with something at the end of that period—lending a kind of structural logic and persuasiveness—it is, unfortunately, only half true and contains a blatant example of rewriting scripture.
   Verses 1–5 of Genesis 1 do *not* say that the universe ("the heaven") was created before ("predates") the six days of creation; they say it was the *first step in a series*—all occurring *during* the six-day period:

> In the beginning God created the heaven
> and the earth. *And* the earth was without
> form, and void; *and* darkness was upon
> the face of the deep. *And* the Spirit of God
> moved upon the face of the waters. *And*
> God said, Let there be light: *and* there was
> light. *And* God saw the light, that it was
> good: *and* God divided the light from the
> darkness. *And* God called the light Day,
> *and* the darkness he called Night. *And* the
> evening and the morning were the first
> day. (KJV, emphasis added.)

Notice that this is a series of independent
clauses connected by the conjunction "and"
(repeated ten times). Each clause is, therefore, directly connected to the one preceding it, either commenting upon it or
advancing to the next step in the creation
process. For example, the second clause
("And the earth was without form, and void")
is a descriptive comment on the appearance
of the earth which has just been created in
the previous clause. There is no indication of
any "gap" in time between the two clauses,
just as there is no indication of any gap between any of the other clauses which follow
it. They are all connected in parallel structure
to form a single sequence, ending with the
declaration that it was "the first day." There is
no indication that the first clause ("In the beginning God created the heaven and the

earth") is not part of this seamless sequence and therefore not part of the first day.

Thus, to conclude, as Ross does, that the first clause, referring to the universe as a whole ("the heaven"), was a separate act preceding the six days of creation is to invent and then interject a meaning which simply is not there. That is to say, it is to rewrite scripture to make it say something which, in fact, it does not say. In addition, since no evidence is given to support the statement, it is also another instance of begging the question.

Ross's purpose in doing this, of course, is to accommodate to the scriptural context (the six days of creation) his "scientific" theory that the universe, including the earth, is billions of years old. The implication is that this immense period of time must have predated the six days of creation and therefore that this is what is referred to in the clause, "In the beginning God created the heaven and the earth."

This is also a case of totally ignoring the general as well as the specific context, for the book of Genesis is about "origins" or "beginnings" (the meaning of the word "genesis"). It is *all* about what happened in the *beginning*. Therefore, the words "In the beginning," with which the book starts, are not just about a separate creation (or beginning) of the heaven and the earth (in verse one), which is what it would have to mean if Ross's reading were correct.

For his point is that those things "predated"
the six days of creation by billions of years.
Furthermore, this idea is self-contradictory
because the universe and the earth did not
"begin" at the same time according to Ross's
own "scientific" theory, which holds that the
universe began some eighteen billion years
ago and the earth began a mere four billion
years or so ago. Therefore, both could not have
taken place simultaneously "in the beginning," and these words in verse 1 could not
be referring to such an event.

2. False Analogy
This section of Ross's book also contains a
beautiful example of false analogy. Referring
to God's creation, Ross speaks of it in glow-
ing, poetic terms as a long, drawn out, awe-
inspiring process:

> Observe any skilled sculptor, painter,
> or poet, a craftsman of any kind. Ob-
> serve the painstaking yet joyful labor
> poured into each object of his design.
> Examine the creation on any scale, from
> a massive galaxy to the interior of an
> atom, from a whale to an amoeba. The
> splendor of each item, its beauty of form
> as well as of function, speaks not of in-
> stantaneous mass production, but
> rather of time and attention to detail,
> of infinite care and delight. Such delight
> is expressed throughout Genesis 1 in

326 The Spiritual Discernment Guide

the oft-repeated statement, "And God saw that it was good."[29]

Here, Ross is equating God with a human artist or craftsman, his point apparently being that, because careful creation by human beings takes a long time, therefore, the creation by God on an immensely grander scale must have taken a correspondingly longer time. The obvious fallacy here is that God is not a man, and therefore the way God creates is not the same as the way a man creates, and the amount of time required for human creation in no way determines or corresponds to the time required for divine creation. In fact, to imply such a thing seems to me at least mildly blasphemous, for it places human restrictions on God's creativity and says that He is limited in this regard in the same way man is!

But God is not limited by time or human restrictions. He operates in eternity—outside of time! And He is not restricted by anything—He is omnipotent! And how long it might take God to do something is a concept which does not apply because He exists not in time but in eternity. Neither has it anything to do with the degree of care or delight He takes in His creation. He is beyond all human limitations. He is the almighty Creator of the universe!

3. Slanting

The above case of false logic is at the same time a rather skillful example of the semantic fallacy of slanting. By using such terms as "massive," "splendor," and "infinite," Ross is marshalling positive connotations that suggest great size and beauty. By means of such terms as "painstaking," "joyful," "labor," "attention to detail," "care," and "delight," he is projecting an image of a craftsman or artist with human qualities. The overall impression is one of a human-like "person" who is dedicated, hard working, and oblivious to how much time or effort his project may require. At the same time, he is also highly idealistic, for he would not stoop to the crass values and shoddiness implied in "instantaneous mass production."

In other words, the slanted word choice is designed to produce a favorable impression of God as a human-like artisan who needed immense amounts of time to do His vast amount of work properly as such a praiseworthy, dedicated "person" would naturally be expected to do. Of course, all of this proves nothing, either about the nature of God or the age of the universe, but it does illustrate the tendency toward semantic manipulation and the God-limiting mind set of some theistic evolutionists.

Young Age Evidence

We have seen abundant evidence that an immense time scale is an invalid assumption from the biblical perspective. This is true also from the scientific perspective (see appendix C). But it would be remiss if we neglected the even more abundant evidence for a short time scale. About this fact, astrophysicist/geophysicist and creationist Dr. Harold Slusher has this comment:

> There are a number of indicators that seem to indicate an age of no more than about 15 thousand years, at the most, for the solar system and the earth.[30]

And Taylor lists no less than 110 scientific indicators of the earth's young age.[31] Obviously, we cannot examine all 110 here, but we will look very briefly at eight of the most important:

1. *Magnetic Field*
    The earth's magnetic field is decreasing at a rate which shows that it is only between 6 and 15 thousand years old.[32] This conclusion is based on the fact that the magnetic field has a half life of approximately 1400 years. In other words, 1400 years ago it was twice as strong as it is now, 2800 years ago it was four times as strong and so on. Thus, between only 10 to 15 thousand years ago it would have been as strong as that of a magnetic star, which can generate its tremendous magnetism only by a thermonuclear process. But the earth has never had a thermonuclear process; therefore, its mag-

ńetism must have originated no more than
10 to 15 thousand years ago.

2. *Helium*

There is very little helium in the earth's atmosphere. But helium is constantly entering
the atmosphere through radioactive decay,
emissions from the sun, and leakage from
the earth's core. Very little of this escapes into
space. This small amount of atmospheric helium indicates that the earth is only ten to
fifteen thousand years old.[33]

3. *Population*

The earth's population growth is relatively
small. It has been calculated that

> it would take only 4000 years to produce
> today's population beginning from a single
> original couple. Creationists . . . believe
> Earth's entire population (save 8 people)
> was destroyed about 4,000 years ago due
> to a worldwide flood.
>
> If life on Earth is as ancient as evolution-
> ists claim (with humans here for more than
> a million years), Earth could potentially
> have been overpopulated long ago. If the
> population increased at only 0.5% per year
> for 1 million years, there could conceiv-
> ably be trillions of trillions of people to-
> day (to be more exact 10^{2100}).
>
> Even if the population was assumed to
> have grown at a *drastically* slower, almost
> zero rate, so that it would have taken a
> million years to reach the present level,

there would have been at least 3,000 billion people that have lived on this planet . . . Yet, where is the fossil or cultural evidence for such massive numbers?[34]

Thus, the evolutionists' assumption that the human race is over a million years old is completely absurd in the light of population statistics.

It is clear, then, that the facts of population growth fit biblical chronology perfectly but that they do not fit evolutionary chronology at all.

4. *Comets*

    The rapid breakup of short-period comets indicates a young age of the solar system. Astronomers believe that the lifespan of a short-period comet is about 10 thousand years and that such comets originated at the same time as the solar system. Therefore, the solar system (including earth) could not be more than about 10 thousand years old.[35]

5. *Earth and Moon*

    The increasing distance between the earth and the moon has been much smaller than it should be if the earth and its satellite were billions of years old. This fact is evidence that the moon's age is at least eighty percent lower than that assigned by evolutionists.[36]

6. *The Sun*

    The shrinkage rate of the sun is too small to have permitted more than a relatively young age for the earth. It has been shown that, for 99.8% of the supposed *evolutionary* age of the earth, life could not have existed because of the sun's greater size and closer proximity to the earth. Therefore, life on earth could not have existed before about nine million years ago (0.2% of 4.5 billion). Not only would it have been far too hot on earth prior to that, but only 210 million years ago, the sun would have been so large that it would have touched the earth! Therefore, the earth could not have existed prior to that.

7. *Meteorites*

    Meteorites are not found in geological strata. This supports the creationist view that these strata were formed quickly during a year-long, global flood. Therefore, there was no chance for meteorites to become imbedded in the strata.[37]

8. *Space Dust*

    Relatively little space dust was found on the moon. Based on their measurements of incoming space dust and their estimates of the deposition rate over billions of years, evolutionist scientists expected astronauts to find moon dust to be as much as 180 feet deep. The greatest fear of one astronaut was that he would sink into this dust.

To avoid this possibility, the Lunar Lander was equipped with large, saucer-shaped feet. However, the astronauts actually discovered a loose dust layer of only a few inches or less. This fact indicates that the moon has been accumulating space dust for a relatively short period of time.[38]

The Allegorical Interpretation of Genesis

Finally, theistic evolutionists have attempted to reconcile their view of creation with that of the Bible by taking Genesis 1 through 11 as an extended metaphor or allegory, as we noted earlier. Thereby, they open up the scripture to their own "scientific" view. They do this in two basic ways: (1) by confusing the literal with the metaphorical and (2) by taking the creation story as a "framework" (or literary device) for an allegory.

LITERAL VERSUS METAPHORICAL
Morris reports that

. . . an increasing number of evangelical scholars today . . . are advocating the notion that this section [Genesis 1 through 11] is only a great hymn, or liturgy, or poem, or saga—anything except real history![39]

What does Satan gain by such a misreading of scripture (i.e., taking a literal meaning metaphorically)? Nothing short of undermining all biblical truth and the whole of Christianity! Morris explains:

. . . this type of interpretation inevitably undermines all the rest of Scripture. If the first Adam
is not real, as Paul taught, and if therefore the
Fall did not really take place, then neither is the
second Adam real and there is no need for a Sav-
iour. . . . this allegorical type of interpretation
leads eventually and inevitably to the rejection
of belief in Biblical inspiration and finally the
Gospel itself.[40]

THE FRAMEWORK HYPOTHESIS

By ignoring the scriptural context and related
scriptures, theistic evolutionists can interpret the
first eleven chapters of Genesis as merely a rhetorical framework for the allegorical development
of spiritualized themes of creation, the fall, and reconciliation. Thus, they reject Genesis as an accurate historical record and avoid the "scientific
embarrassment" of contradicting the theories of
evolution and the big bang.[41]

As we have seen, the biblical text contains no
evidence that an allegorical or metaphorical meaning is intended. At the same time, later writers of
scripture—including Moses, Joshua, Hezekiah,
Nehemiah, Job, David, Solomon, Matthew, Mark,
Luke, John, and Paul (as well as Jesus and others)—
took the Genesis account literally, regarding it as
factual history and authoritative doctrine.[42]

A SATANIC DELUSION

We have seen that evolution is a lie of the devil
because *it contradicts the account of creation in the*

Bible, defames the character of God, places the wisdom of men above the truth of scripture, and *is in fact a rival religion.*

It also *removes man's accountability to God.* For, if all things, including man, have evolved by natural, random, amoral processes out of primal, exploding matter, then we have no responsibility to a Creator, man did not fall into sin, and there is no need for repentance and redemption.

Confidence in the wisdom of man is really confidence in Satan since Satan is in control of this world system (1 John 5:19) and is in fact its god (2 Corinthians 4:4, KJV). Therefore, belief in evolution and the big bang are two profoundly important ways in which the minds of many Christians have been deceived, if not corrupted, by Satan.

Thus, evolution is a major delusion which the enemy has brought upon the bulk of mankind, including a large portion of the church. It is, therefore, also *a major seed of apostasy, for it destroys confidence in the Bible* as the supreme source of truth and it *substitutes faith in science for faith in God.*

Morris provides a comprehensive summary of this satanic delusion and its effects on the church, society, and mankind as a whole. Speaking of it as a form of pantheistic humanism, he says,

> This [pantheistic humanism] is the basic framework of all man-centered, as opposed to Creator-centered, religion. It is evolutionary because it rejects creation *ex nihilo* [out of nothing] and always accounts for the world as some-

how developing from pre-existent materials; it is pantheistic because it identifies God with nature in one way or another; and it is humanistic because it exalts man's reason above the revealed Word of God. . . . Modern scientism is evolutionary because it seeks to account for all things in the universe in terms of natural developmental processes from pre-existent materials. It is pantheistic because God is identified with and limited to his "creation." And it is humanistic because it "worships and serves the creature more than the Creator." Man, as the highest stage to which evolution has yet attained, is in essence his own God. . . . the origin of all the evil in the universe must have been coincident with the origin of the idea of evolution, but stemming from Satan's rejection of God's revelation of himself as Creator and Ruler of the universe. This primal act of unbelief and pride led to Satan's fall; the same basic act of unbelief and pride led to the fall of man. Similarly, unbelief in God's Word and man's pride in his own ability to rule his own destiny have yielded the bitter fruits of these thousands of years of human sin and suffering on the earth. And today, this God-rejecting, man-exalting philosophy of evolution spills its evil progeny—materialism, modernism, humanism, socialism, Fascism, communism, and ultimately Satanism—in terrifying profusion all over the world.[43]

The Bible says we have a choice: either to believe God's Word or Satan's lies. We can't have it both ways—as the theistic evolutionists attempt to do:

But I am afraid that just as Eve was deceived by the serpent's cunning, your minds may somehow be led astray from your sincere and pure devotion to Christ. For if someone comes to you and preaches a Jesus other than the Jesus we preached or if you receive a different spirit from the one you received, or a different gospel from the one you accepted, you put up with it easily enough. . . . For such men are false apostles, deceitful workmen, masquerading as apostles of Christ. And no wonder, for Satan himself masquerades as an angel of light. It is not surprising, then, if his servants masquerade as servants of righteousness (2 Corinthians 11:3–4, 13–15).

I do not mean to imply that Ross or my two pastor friends or any other Christian who believes in theistic evolution and/or the big bang are servants of Satan. But I am saying that, in this regard, they are deceived and that, by advocating these unbiblical doctrines, they are unknowingly aiding Satan in his program to lead Christians away from the truth and into apostasy.

PART IV:

The Many Faces of New Age Deception—Discerning Other False Teachings and Beliefs

In Part III, we saw how Satan's tricks apply to false teachings about evolution and cosmology. In a previous chapter, we analyzed examples of how he uses various logical fallacies and types of semantic manipulation. In this part, we will complete our survey of demonic deception and the application of spiritual discernment. We will now look at a number of other especially dangerous false teachings and beliefs which have infiltrated the church, primarily through, or in association with, the New Age Movement. These can be grouped under the following headings:

False Teachings From Secular Psychology
False Charismatic Teachings
False Anti-Charismatic Teachings
False Teachings From Humanism
Infiltration by Eastern Religions
Infiltration by Occultism

CHAPTER ELEVEN

False Teachings from Secular Psychology

Much of what is believed and practiced by secular psychology promotes the New Age goal of personal transcendence and, ultimately, self-deification. It is, therefore, ungodly and unscriptural. Some Christian psychologists have indeed incorporated some of these heretical elements into their practices. However, I believe there is such a thing as valid Christian psychology that provides real help to suffering Christians, in spite of what some critics maintain.

SEPARATING THE BABY FROM THE BATHWATER

Unfortunately, most, if not all, Christian psychology has been written off as worthless, ungodly, and unbiblical by a number of Christian commentators. This deprives Christians of a legitimate source of truth and help simply because it is not specifically identified in the Bible or because parts of it are derived from non-Christian sources. In other words, if it is not in the Bible, it can't be valid. What is needed, once again, is discernment, a middle course between accepting everything uncritically and rejecting everything blindly.

It is true that some practices in Christian psychology do promote the view that the solutions to our problems lie within ourselves. In speaking of Christian psychology, Hunt puts it this way:

> . . . to whatever extent we seek our own will, seek to use God to bring about our will, pander to our self-centered desires, or in any way are afraid or unwilling to surrender wholly to God's will—to that extent we are exalting ourselves to the position of gods . . . Whatever the label on the package, the product inside is the same old satanic ploy: "The answer is within ourselves." We can "do it" if we only learn the "laws" and "principles" that apply and put them into operation by "faith." The goal is always to reward *self* in some way.[1]

He also points out that basic shamanistic practices, such as visualization and other mind-over-matter techniques, are being accepted in the church under such psychological labels as "inner healing," "healing of the memories," "healing at a distance," and "holistic healing."[2] However, to reject *all* forms of healing emotional and spiritual wounds because *some* of them may include occult elements is to exhibit a gross lack of discernment.

Hunt and others have also rightly pointed out that Christian psychology may promote personal transcendence apart from the transforming power of God, through self-love, self-esteem, and personal empowerment for happiness and success. But, again, the fact that some Christian psychologists may be guilty of this kind of humanistic approach does not mean all Christian psychology is invalid. Such a conclusion is a hasty generalization, pure and simple.

Once again, I can speak from experience. I have personally consulted two Christian psychologists, one of whom had a predominantly secular perspective and practiced holistic techniques. The other one had a predominantly biblical perspective and utilized some of the findings of secular psychology as tools to help me accomplish what the Bible says about overcoming spiritual problems.

The approach of the first psychologist was to utilize methods and techniques which he considered appropriate to address symptoms and relieve dysfunction. I found these treatments beneficial and not unscriptural—although his methods and orientation may have been more secular than scriptural.

The second practitioner based all of his counseling on scripture. He utilized psychology as a body of knowledge about behavior patterns from which he drew insights that would be helpful in my particular case. This "Christian integrative approach," as he called it, emphasized prayer and the Word of God and integrated what worked from psychology that either agreed or did not disagree with scripture.

For example, he noted that the Bible says very little of a specific nature about marriage or raising children. Therefore, he used the findings of psychology to supplement the general guidelines on these subjects provided in the Bible.

The purpose of this supplemental knowledge was to help the client understand the reasons for and meaning of dysfunctional behavior. In other words, he used insights and techniques from psychology which helped one apply scriptural principles to specific problems. He acknowledged that secular psychology has an insidious side, for example, in its humanistic belief that man is intrinsically good. He also noted that many Christian psychologists are merely adding a Christian veneer to their psychology without praying with or giving helpful scriptures to clients. All in all, he used psychology as a neutral body of information for fixing dysfunctional behavior while exercising discernment in deciding what pieces of that information to incorporate.

My experience with him was very positive, and I feel I received a great deal of scriptural help from him regarding several problem areas in my life.

I am also acquainted with another Christian psychologist whose approach is similar to that of the one just described. His basic view is that many Christians are unable to resolve their problems on their own and therefore need professional help based on scriptural principles. In other words, these Christians are unable to understand and apply the scripture without additional help. He believes that the

Bible tells us what to do and that appropriate psychology tells us how to do it.

Psychological principles that do not violate scripture, he believes, constitute a legitimate supplement to biblical principles and are much like a set of tools used by a carpenter. The *true* Christian psychologist, then, uses his tools to perform specific repairs while following the blueprint of scripture. He told me that authentic Christian psychologists don't break the biblical teachings and commandments and "have a heart for reconciliation, service, and ministry."

Self-esteem: The Focus on Self

Teachings on self-esteem have been accepted *without question* by large numbers of Christians through the ministries of such people as James Dobson and Robert Schuller. This lack of discernment regarding this subject has created a confusing mixture of scriptural and unscriptural concepts of self-esteem. The unscriptural form is based on the idea that we enhance our effectiveness as persons (and Christians) by building up our self-esteem through self-effort. The scriptural form, on the other hand, is based on the idea of personal transformation through the sanctifying work of the Holy Spirit.

Hunt summarizes the false version while citing David as an example of true self-worth:

> David's Christ-like humility contradicts the teaching of self-esteem promoted by Christian psychologists. David was the total opposite of

the self-assured and self-assertive person that so many Christians are convinced they must become to taste success. David was willing to do the menial tasks no one else wanted and sought no approval from man but only from God, an attitude which today's Christian psychologists would attribute to low self-esteem.[3]

Like David, Moses saw himself, not as the successful, competent, assertive leader of people, but rather as totally dependent on God for his success. In fact, God chose him to lead the Israelites and challenge the mightiest king in the world precisely because of his lack of self-assertive self-esteem—that is, because he was "very humble, more than any man who was on the face of the earth" (Numbers 12:3).

As Hunt reminds us, "Moses shrank from this call, considering himself incapable. Instead of giving him months of psychological counseling to bolster his poor self-image and build up his self-esteem, God promised to be with Moses and to work through him miraculously (Exodus 3)."[4] God chose this man, who considered himself unworthy, because he was usable (i.e., meek and obedient) and because he wanted God, not man to get the glory.

The teaching on self-esteem which says we must first love ourselves so that we can then love others is false, not only because it twists the scripture about loving your neighbor as yourself (as we saw earlier) but also because it has the wrong focus: the self. It is through self-effort, perhaps reinforced by psychological counseling, these teachers say, that one acquires the proper confidence and motivation to become successful and fulfill his god-given potential.

Real self-esteem, however, does not come from some man-made process of jacking up our self-image. It comes from the worth I acquire because God loves me. It does not come because of who I am (my merit) but because of who He is (His grace blessing me in spite of my lack of merit). The Father wants me to become like Jesus so that I will have true merit. But it is not my merit; it is Jesus' merit *given to me.* Therefore, I have worth because He is worthy, and I share in that worth as He lives in me. I have no worth of my own and no worth at all apart from Him. I am the recipient and beneficiary of His worth. Therefore, my self-esteem is based, not on what I have done for myself, but on what Jesus has done for me and my acceptance of that.

The psychology of self-esteem says we are victims of a low self-image, which is the cause of all our problems. But the Bible says that *self* is the *enemy, not* the ruler and the answer. The Old Testament says that we are not innately good but that

> All of us have become like one who is unclean,
> and all our righteous acts are like filthy rags; we
> all shrivel up like a leaf, and like the wind our
> sins sweep us away (Isaiah 64:6).

The New Testament agrees with this assessment: ". . . all have sinned and fall short of the glory of God" (Romans 3:23). We are not innocent victims of a bad self-image. We are sinners, creatures with a naturally fallen nature, in need of redemption through faith in Jesus Christ.

Thus the doctrine of self-esteem is **a lie**, directly contradicting what the Bible says and substituting self-effort for the transforming power of the Holy Spirit:

> And we, who with unveiled faces all reflect the Lord's glory, are being transformed into his likeness with ever-increasing glory, which comes from the Lord, who is the Spirit (2 Corinthians 3:18).

Human Potential: The Journey Within

These ideas about self-esteem and self-effort are behind the thinking of the Human Potential Movement. This teaching, which is the basis of New Age cults[5] "has penetrated the evangelical church and is subtly seducing overwhelming numbers of Christians."[6] According to Hunt,

> Self is the predominant theme of a large percentage of Christian books and sermons. Former Episcopal priest Alan Watts turned Zen Buddhist Master is a good example of where this seduction leads Christians who succumb to it. Watts declared:
>
> > The appeal of Zen, as of other forms of Eastern philosophy, is that it unveils . . . a vast region . . . where at last the self is indistinguishable from God.[7]

This vast region is the area of "inner space" where Christians are being encouraged to tap into their "unlimited human potential," an idea which is being increasingly expressed by numerous Christian leaders. One of these is Rodney R. Romney, senior pastor of Seattle's First Baptist Church.

> Romney has written a book titled *Journey to Inner Space: Finding God-in-Us.* Its message is summarized in bold type on the back cover: "MISSION: to Find God. METHOD: By finding one's self."
>
> Inside the book the message is spelled out: "To understand God is finally to realize one's own godhood"; Jesus was not God but "simply a man who knew the laws of God" and who expected His followers to "realize the Christ within their own consciousness. . . . Romney . . . recommends such forms of Eastern Mysticism as Zen, Yoga, Sufism, and Transcendental Meditation."[8]

As the primary technique for accessing this vast reservoir of inner potential, success/motivation teachers and some Christian psychologists are advocating visualization. This is based on the theory that it is in the "great unconscious" mind, "hidden in the deepest depths of the psyche" where one finds and may tap into the "unlimited power potential. This is the basic idea behind the Human Potential movement."[9]

The Spiritual Discernment Guide

"The Innate Goodness of Man"

Self-esteem psychology is also based on the idea of man's innate goodness. This false, humanistic view of man teaches that traditional Christianity damages self-esteem because of guilt and sin.[10] Unfortunately, as Hunt points out, some influential Christian psychologists, including James Dobson, have bought into this humanistic view of man, which

> ridicules as "worm theology" the [traditional Christian] emphasis upon conviction of sin, repentance, and human unworthiness.
>
> In this new gospel, we must avoid anything that threatens the sinner's fragile self-esteem.[11]

I believe that James Dobson is a sincere, dedicated Christian whose ministry has been a source of great good for the body of Christ. However, I do not believe Dobson is perfect. He is a fallible human being like the rest of us. Therefore, we find in his writings such unscriptural views on self-esteem as the following:

> In a real sense, the health of an entire society depends on the ease with which the individual members gain personal acceptance. *Thus, whenever the keys to self-esteem are seemingly out of reach for a large percentage of the people, as in twentieth-century America, then widespread "mental illness," neuroticism, hatred, alcoholism, drug abuse, violence, and social disorder will certainly occur . . . .*[12] [Emphasis in original.]

Hunt points out that, in this view,

> Hatred, violence, and social disorder, rather than arising out of willful rebellion and sin, are caused by a lack of self-esteem, which is somehow "out of reach" for these victims of modern life. Instead of pride and an unwillingness to repent of our sin being the great barrier between men and God we are now being told that such a message is demeaning to "our authentic personhood" and the paramount need is to build up everyone's self-esteem.[13]

Loving and Improving the Old Man

Apparently without realizing it, Dobson and others who advocate self-love are actually directly contradicting scripture (as we saw earlier) by promoting the love of the old man (the flesh). But the Bible says we are to crucify the flesh, putting *off* the old man, *not* enhancing his life. Rather, we are to put on the new man who loves God and others without regard for himself. This new creation is self-*less*, giving himself for the sake of others. The new man is becoming like Jesus, righteous, holy, loving, self-sacrificing, obedient, a servant, humble, and meek. In his letter to the Colossian Christians, Paul puts it this way:

> . . . since you have taken off your old self with its practices and have put on the new self, which is being renewed in knowledge in the image of its Creator. . . .

> Therefore, as God's chosen people, holy and dearly loved, clothe yourselves with compassion,

kindness, humility, gentleness [meekness, KJV], and patience (Colossians 3:9–10, 12).

Nevertheless, Christians are being bombarded with practical suggestions for promoting self-love by well-known Christian authors and motivational speakers. Zig Ziglar, for example, gives the following suggestions for how to build up self-esteem so that we may become confident, assertive, effective, and successful:

> To build your self-image, make a list of your positive qualities on a card and keep it for handy reference. . . . Brag on yourself from time to time. Get in your own corner. . . .
>
> You should also set aside a few minutes each day for the sole purpose of deliberately looking yourself in the eye [in a mirror]. As you do this, repeat some positive affirmations of things you have done (use your victory list from step ten). Then repeat many of the things other people have said to you or about you that were positive. . . .
>
> There are also cases where plastic surgery can be quite helpful in building a self-image. This is especially true in cases of an unusually large or long nose, protruding ears . . . grossly oversized or undersized breasts, etc.[14]

Personal image building through positive self-talk, mirror gazing, and plastic surgery—these are the self-help techniques recommended to Christians for increasing self-esteem.

But the Bible doesn't say improve yourself through your own efforts. On the contrary, it says humble yourself and turn to God, denying yourself, and putting to death your old nature, relying on Him as the source of your ability, strength, success, and self-worth. Philippians 2:3 tells us to focus on others rather than ourselves, in humility: "Do nothing out of selfish ambition or vain conceit, but in humility consider others better than yourselves." Our attitude should be the same as that of Jesus:

> Who, being in very nature God, did not consider equality with God something to be grasped, but made himself nothing, taking the very nature of a servant, being made in human likeness and being found in appearance as a man, he humbled himself and became obedient to death—even death on a cross! (Philippians 2:6–8.)

INNER HEALING: IS IT REAL OR NEEDED?

As we have seen, some anti-charismatic Christians have written off inner healing as a totally invalid form of Christian psychology. They rightly note that *some* practitioners of inner healing emphasize visualization as a primary component of such treatment. These heretical teachers advocate that those with emotional and spiritual wounds from their early lives should imagine Jesus moving back through their memories and actually changing history to heal the inner child of the past.

But such manipulation of reality through mental activity is a form of shamanism and is therefore an ungodly practice. It tacitly says that God's power is not sufficient but that He requires the assistance of "creative visualization." It is in effect using God (i.e., Jesus) as a tool controlled by our mental processes. In the belief that one can control God in this manner, the individual puts himself in the place of God. And this is rightly identified as an abuse of Christian psychology.

Often, such practitioners base such treatment on Freudian theory, which says that our behavior is controlled by unconscious impulses, that the basis of adult personality is formed in childhood, and that adult behavior is driven by early experiences which have been repressed and buried. This view sees such dysfunctional adults as essentially helpless victims who must be cured by eliminating or somehow neutralizing the painful memories through a visualization or reprogramming process. This is also an abuse of Christian psychology.

However, as demonstrated in my own experiences mentioned earlier, all inner healing is not of this sort. Rather, it can be a work of the Holy Spirit in which the individual participates in a godly and scriptural manner. Therefore, to write off all inner healing because of some abuses is another case of hasty generalization (or guilt by association) and, of course, throwing out the baby with the bathwater. Thereby, Satan scores again, wiping out, at one stroke, an important means of spiritual healing and a valuable aid in the sanctification process.

Those who so discredit all inner healing do a great disservice to the church, robbing it of the means of freeing many people from the effects of spiritual wounds and from bondage to negative habit patterns that prevent them from receiving all that God has for them and becoming all that God wants them to be. The Holy Spirit is a gentleman, not forcing anything on anyone. Therefore, if one rejects the possibility of valid inner healing, refusing to seek it or receive it, the Holy Spirit respects his wishes and does not force it on him. This is analogous to someone refusing medical treatment for a broken leg or any debilitating disease and thereby preventing the doctor from healing him and condemning him to life as a cripple or an invalid.

Thus, to rightly understand and utilize inner healing is to exercise spiritual discernment, recognizing God's sovereignty in such matters and our role as petitioners. We are not in the driver's seat. God is. It is not by our mental power or manipulation of reality that the work is done, but by His Spirit.

The Bible says we are to become free of the past so we can move as God's agents into the future:

> Forgetting what is behind and straining toward what is ahead, I press on toward the goal to win the prize for which God has called me heavenward in Christ Jesus.
>
> All of us who are mature should take such a view of things (Philippians 3:13–15).

These verses tell me what to do but not how to do it. My own deliverance from anger and feelings of rejection (hurt pride) has been a long, slow healing process. It has required, first, putting to death, under the guidance and power of the Holy Spirit, those parts of my old nature which have been at the root of my problem. Second, it has involved the growth in my new nature of forgiveness, love, patience, and other positive qualities, again through the influence of the Holy Spirit.

This is obviously not a simple one-time act, as some critics of inner healing seem to think. They say that the cause of our problems is present moral choices (i.e., sin), and all we need to do is stop sinning. Unfortunately, it doesn't work that way.

The negative behavior patterns don't just disappear but continue to be triggered by circumstances and events. When we initially turned to Christ, our problems with self didn't just go away (as I am sure you have noticed). The Bible says we have a sin nature, which must be killed: "Put to death, therefore, whatever belongs to your earthly nature . . . rid yourselves of all such things . . . (Colossians 3:5, 8). Simultaneously, if you rely on the Holy Spirit, He will help you to be "transformed by the renewing of your mind" (Romans 12:2). This transformation does not happen overnight but is an ongoing process. This is indicated by the present continuous verb tense of the original Greek: *metamorphoo* ("be being [continuously] transformed"). It is therefore a matter of being gradually conformed to Christ's image as we grow closer in our fellowship with Him (2 Corinthians 3:18).

Thus, the teaching that all inner healing is invalid and ungodly is unscriptural and therefore another **lie** of the devil intended to prevent us from realizing the fullness that we have in Christ.

We see once again, then, that discernment is required to separate the ungodly, unscriptural aspects of Christian psychology from the godly and scriptural aspects. Unfortunately, a number of false teachings and spiritually harmful practices derived from secular psychology and the Human Potential Movement have crept into the church and the ministries of some Christian psychologists and counselors. These include the notions of personal transcendence and self-deification, the ideas that we are naturally good and the solution to our problems is found within ourselves, the practice of occult techniques derived from eastern religions (such as visualization and the mental manipulation of reality), and the promotion of self-esteem through self-effort as a substitute for sanctification through the work of the Holy Spirit. In each of these teachings and practices, the focus is on self and human will (the flesh) rather than on God and divine will (the Spirit).

On the other hand, real Christian psychology is based on true teachings and spiritually beneficial practices. These include biblical counseling based directly on scripture, therapy through prayer, and the use of psychological principles that are in harmony with the Bible. The benefits of this approach include the promotion of real self-esteem derived from Christ and real inner healing and wholesome behavior resulting from the practical application of biblical principles and the sanctifying work of the Holy Spirit.

CHAPTER TWELVE

False Charismatic Teachings

The term "charismatic" refers to those Christians who believe the supernatural gifts of the Spirit (as identified in 1 Corinthians 12) are operating today for those who are willing to accept them and who have received the baptism in the Holy Spirit as a separate experience from salvation. Unfortunately, a number of these charismatic Christians are also busily teaching false doctrines that are virtually identical with New Age beliefs. Several of these have been noted in previous chapters. Therefore, we will now look only at those which were either not covered or not sufficiently discussed earlier:

1. The Word of Faith idea that we are gods.
2. The prosperity gospel that says God wants all Christians to be rich.

3. The doctrine of experiential truth that says subjective experience is a valid basis for spiritual knowledge equal or superior to scripture.

We will examine Satan's strategies and tricks regarding each of these areas, but first we need to look at a related and extremely important long-range goal of the enemy.

Spiritual Polarization: Charismaniacs vs. Evangumbilicals

A major strategy of Satan is to divide the church by creating hostility and polarization between charismatics and anti-charismatics. Such a conflict is resulting, I believe, partly because of the undiscerning attitude of some evangelicals as expressed in two basic false doctrines:

*   Supernatural manifestations (gifts) are not for today.
*   All supernatural manifestations are demonic.

(See chapter thirteen for a discussion of these and other anti-charismatic heresies.)

These ideas are in turn dismissed or denounced by extreme charismatics as signs of spiritual inferiority and closed-mindedness. Thus, there is a lack of discernment on both sides on the part of extremists, and both sides are partially right and partially wrong. For convenience and because of their suggestive connotations, I will use the labels *Charismaniacs* and *Evangumbilicals* for these opposing groups.

Charismaniacs say anything goes. In this sense, they are "maniacal," tending to be irrational, anti-intellectual, and full of excessive zeal and excitement—often for their own sakes. (I shall call them "Maniacs" for short.) They believe whatever is "supernatural" must be of God. This is a major example of stereotyping, which leaves them open to satanic deception. It means they are swallowing everything whole without discernment regarding supernatural phenomena.

Evangumbilicals, on the other hand, declare that most, if not all, charismatic practices are unscriptural or carnal or even demonic, and, therefore, all charismatic teachings and practices are suspect. From this, it is an easy step to the opposite stereotype: saying that none of it is of God and all such supernatural phenomena is of the devil.

They are "umbilical" in the sense that they are as closely tied to the unscriptural traditions of their denominations as a fetus is to its mother via the umbilical cord. In fact, they are so locked into their narrow views that they are blind to any contradictory ideas (most notably those regarding the supernatural manifestations of the Holy Spirit)—no matter how clearly scriptural and reasonable they may be. (I shall call them "Umbilicals" for short.)

Along with these deceptions, on both sides, comes spiritual pride. (Or more likely *because* of spiritual pride, they have fallen into these deceptions.) In any case, the Maniacs feel superior because of their experience with spiritual gifts, which in turn has created excessive zeal regarding these gifts, leading to doctrinal carelessness.

Umbilicals, on the other hand, have exhibited spiritual pride based on their sense of doctrinal superiority. This has resulted, I believe, because they cling so tightly to their tradition of opposing the modern-day operation of spiritual gifts. This is, in essence, a kind of Phariseeism, which puts them in the position of opposing God, who wants to manifest His power in the church through these and other supernatural means.

In addition, Maniacs, by uncritically accepting all supernatural manifestations as from God, are promoting demonic deception and falling into a preoccupation with sensational experience rather than righteousness, holiness, and spiritual growth. All of this tends to give a bad name to the Holy Spirit among evangelicals and other non-charismatics.

At the same time, Umbilicals, by rejecting charismatic manifestations, are eliminating much of the power of the Holy Spirit at a time when the church needs it more than ever to combat the intensifying attacks of the enemy. Consequently, the church is also not receiving the strengthening it needs for ministry, spiritual warfare, or perseverance under increasing persecution.

Satan is the power behind this polarization. He attacks in the areas where he is being threatened or where the church is going in the way God wants it to go. This is why he is bringing confusion on both sides and division regarding the gifts of the Spirit. He doesn't want the church to have the power that God wants it to have.

Discernment is obviously needed by all concerned to separate what is of God and what is not. On the one hand, Maniacs need to check everything against scripture. And, on the other, Umbilicals need to be open to what God wants to do and to receive what He has for the church as a whole.

Neither side is receiving the fullness of God. And Satan is having a field day robbing the church of God's blessings.

What is needed is a movement away from the extremes toward a balanced and unified middle ground, discerning what is of God and consulting the scripture while rightly dividing the Word with great care to see what it really says about this issue.

Let's return now to the charismatic heresies enumerated earlier.

"WE ARE GODS"

We have already looked at several examples of false doctrines set forth by the Word of Faith movement: that faith is a force, that words have supernatural power (positive confession, name-it-and-claim-it, magical use of prayer), that creative visualization is necessary for effective prayer, and that we are gods. However, we need to look at a few additional important examples of scripture twisting

regarding the false teaching of self-transcendence—
that we are gods.

As noted earlier, self-transcendence is a New Age
concept that has to do with the desire to be more
personally fulfilled (i.e., to be happier, healthier,
wealthier, more gratified, more successful, more
knowledgeable, and more powerful)—all through
one's own efforts and for one's own selfish purposes.
In other words, it is the desire to be one's own deity.

Word of Faith teachers support this idea by referring to 2 Peter 1:4, which says, ". . . he has given us
his very great and precious promises, so that through
them you participate in the divine nature and escape
the corruption in the world caused by evil desires."
They state that here the apostle Peter is saying we are
"little gods." Kenneth Copeland puts it this way:

> Now Peter said by exceeding great and precious
> promises you become partakers of the divine na-
> ture. All right, are we gods? We are a class of gods!"[1]

Copeland's conclusion, however, is based on a
redefinition or false equivalency. "Participate in the
divine nature" is equated to "we are gods." But participating in the divine nature really means we receive what we need from God to grow spiritually so
that we reflect His character qualities. This meaning is shown by the context, which says that the
purpose of this participation is to enable us to escape the world's corruption caused by evil desires.
Verse 3 (which is ignored by the Word of Faith teachers) makes this meaning perfectly clear:

His divine power has given us everything we
need for life and godliness through our knowledge of him who called us by his own glory
and goodness.

This is about what God has given us so that we
may have a life of godliness. And it is about the fact
that He has called us to such a life and made this
possible through His promises. It is not about being
gods because we have the divine nature. Thus, this
case of scripture twisting is also another example of
totally ignoring the context.

It is important to note that this teaching is in essence identical to the New Age teaching that we are
gods and all we have to do is realize it. New Age teachers also twist scripture to support this lie of Satan.
Maharishi Mahesh Yogi (the founder of Transcendental Meditation), for example, has said the following:

Christ said, "Be still and know that I am God."
[Psalm 46:10] Be still and know that you are
God and when you know that you are God you
will begin to live Godhood, and living Godhood
there is no reason to suffer.[2]

Thus, the Maharishi implies that Jesus was merely
a spiritually advanced man who realized His own
godhood, and like Him we need to do the same, based
on the pantheistic idea that God is everything. However, to imply that this is the meaning of Psalm 46:10
is to completely rewrite scripture. First of all, it was
not Christ speaking, but Jehovah. And it is not a man

speaking to himself, but God speaking to man. He was *not* saying that, like Jesus, you and I are God.

This is also another excellent example of ignoring the context. In context, we see that God was saying we need to focus on Him and realize who He is, God Almighty, who does mighty works on the earth:

> Come and see the works of the Lord, the desolations he has brought on the earth. He makes war cease to the ends of the earth, he breaks the bow and shatters the spear, he burns the shields with fire. "Be still and know that I am God; I will be exalted among the nations, I will be exalted in the earth" (Psalm 46:8–10).

To subscribe to the doctrine taught by the Maharishi shows how badly confused and illogical the Word of Faith teachers are. For, if God is the Creator (as the Bible says He is) and we are His creations (as the Bible says we are), how can we be God? Is the creation the same as the Creator? Obviously not, no more than the clay is the same as the potter, the painting is the same as the artist, or the play is the same as the playwright. Indeed, the Lord Himself says, "apart from me there is no God" (Isaiah 44:6) and "Before me no god was formed, nor will there be one after me" (Isaiah 43:11).

In their confusion, these teachers distort another scripture (Mark 11:22) to prove their contention that, because we are gods, therefore we are in charge and God must do what we say. In another context, we saw that Word of Faith teachers say faith is a force, by which all things were created and, at the same time, the substance of that creation. And here, they use a similar idea to diminish and demean God Himself.

As Hanegraaff observes, to them "God is nothing but a 'faith being' and man is deemed to be sovereign. God is portrayed as a pathetic puppet at the beck and call of His creation." Thus, they make God "impotent rather than omnipotent, limited rather than infinite and omniscient."[3]

Mark 11:22 says, "Have faith in God." But, according to Copeland, Capps, Price, Hagen, and others, what it *really* says is, "Have the faith *of* God." This is based on a mistranslation. In this verse, the Greek verb tense shows that God is the object of our faith, not the user of faith.[4]

By making God the user of a force or universal principle called faith, they make Him dependent on something outside of Himself. But God doesn't need to have faith in anything. He is not dependent like man, but all-sufficient and omnipotent. Thus, they turn Him into a limited god who is governed by the very laws that He Himself created.

Word of Faith teachers, then, in their promotion of self-transcendence and self-deification, move Christians away from a dependent, personal relationship with God and toward apostasy.

THE PROSPERITY GOSPEL

A basic teaching derived from the New Age Movement, as we have seen, is the Positive Confession belief that God wants all Christians to be wealthy and have other kinds of abundant blessings without any suffering or lack. We discussed this briefly in earlier chapters, but here we will look more closely at how these teachers misuse scripture to support this false doctrine. For this purpose, and as an example, we will first look at *God, the Gold and the Glory*, a book written in the tradition of Oral Roberts and Kenneth Copeland, by Positive Confession teacher and charismaniac Larry Hutton, who publishes a free periodical called *The Force of Faith*.

Twisting Scriptures to Squeeze Out the Gold

Hutton begins by quoting numerous Bible verses, mostly from the Old Testament, showing that all the earth and its riches belong to God.[5] He then cites the wealth of King Solomon and the richness of the tabernacle, the ark of the covenant, and the priestly garments as bases for the idea that God wants to bless us all with wealth in an equally extravagant manner. Citing Exodus 28:2–3, 6, 17–20, regarding costly garments of the high priest, he says,

> Can you just imagine what would happen if a preacher dressed like this today? The media would be all over him like fleas on a dog! And unfortunately, many immature Christians would be too. But when we look at the Scriptures, it is certainly evident that God has no problem with it.[6]

Hutton's implication is that, just as God lavished the richest clothing on the high priest, so he wants to do for modern-day preachers. And any believer who doesn't agree with this is an "immature Christian."

Now, there are several logical and semantic problems here. First, there is an obvious ignoring of context. The verses in question were about Aaron, the Jewish high priest, and his successors, not about Christian preachers of today. Second, this is a gross hasty generalization. The fact that God provided costly garments for one of His ministers in ancient times does not mean that He therefore wants to do the same for all ministers in modern times. This is also a flagrant non sequitur which disregards the fact that there is no logical connection between the apparel of the Jewish high priest and that of the preachers in present-day America. Nor is there any logical reason to assume that what God did for the high priest He also wants to do for the preachers.

Hutton extends his hasty generalization and commits other non sequiturs as he continues.

God wants us to become aware of the truth that He is an extravagant God and that He is delighted and pleased when His children prosper. He is the Creator of all the wealth, and He is more than willing to share it with us when we use it for His honor and glory.[7]

Here, Hutton applies what God did for the high priest to all "His children." And the idea of extravagant clothing has become the idea that all Christians are to prosper. Now, we have false equivalency (redefinition), to say the least! A "high priest" is not the same as "His children." And "costly priestly garments" are not the same as "prosperity." Furthermore, to imply that God's giving expensive clothing to the high priest proves that "He is more than willing to share" all of His wealth with us is an incredible leap of illogic.

If I buy my son a new suit for the senior prom, it doesn't mean I am therefore going to share my total wealth with all the teenagers in the neighborhood. Similar non sequiturs and other examples of fallacious thinking are abundant throughout the rest of the book. But here are a few of the most flagrant:

1. *False equivalency (redefinition)*
    Hutton says that, when Jesus provided "a great multitude of fish" for Peter and his crew (Luke 5:4–7), it proved the Father "would make all the blessings of heaven accessible." Moreover, this shows, says Hutton, "that God, the Father, is our source of financial blessing."[8] Here the miraculous catch of fish for Peter is falsely equated to financial blessings for all Christians.
    This is also another case of ignoring the context, for, in verse 4, Jesus says, "Put out into deep water, and let down the nets for a

catch." And, in verse 10, He says, "Don't be afraid; from now on you will catch men." These verses indicate that the purpose of the miracle was two-fold: (1) to teach a lesson about stepping out in faith and obedience and (2) to tell Peter that his ministry of winning converts to Christ would be fruitful. It was *not* about receiving financial blessings. Hutton uses similar semantic manipulation in equating other miraculous acts of Jesus to the provision of financial prosperity. These include feeding the five thousand, finding a donkey for Jesus to ride, and paying taxes with the coin found in the fish's mouth.[9]

2. *Ignoring the context*

   One of the most heretical (and perhaps blasphemous) teachings in Hutton's book—the idea that Jesus died on the cross so that we could be rich—is arrived at by totally ignoring the context and thereby reducing the greatest event in human history to nothing but a means of fattening one's bank account. For this purpose, Hutton uses Romans 8:32:

   > He that spared not his own Son, but delivered him up for us all, how shall he not with him also freely *give us all things*? (KJV, emphasis added.)

   He interprets the phrase "give us all things" to mean give us material wealth, especially financial:

Because Jesus was one with the Father, He really did own all of the gold, silver and cattle upon a thousand hills, making Him the richest man that ever lived on the earth! And because the Father was His source and He was obedient to do all that the Spirit said to do, He had access to whatever He needed or wanted.

Did you know that we are one with God and that God loves us as much as He does Jesus? . . . Because of Jesus' act of redemption, *all our rights and privileges as sons of God have been restored* completely. What the first Adam lost by the fall, the second Adam, Jesus, purchased back for us! (1 Corinthians 15:45; Romans 5:17) And *all things* that belong to God and Jesus now belong to us! Furthermore, God wants us to have them! *He that spared not his own Son, but delivered him up for us all, how shall he not with him also freely give us all things?* (Rom. 8:32) Notice that God delivered Jesus up for us! Why? So that He could freely give us *all things*![10] (Bold face emphasis in the original; other emphasis added.)

The thinking here seems to be that, because God loves us as much as He loves Jesus and because Jesus could have whatever He wanted from the Father, therefore, we should have whatever we want (i.e., material wealth). This conclusion seems to be based on the idea that Jesus restored our rights and privileges as "sons of God" by His death on the cross, based on 1 Corinthians 15:45 and Romans 5:17.

There are at least three major fallacies in this argument:

1. It is a false analogy. The relationship between God the Father and Jesus the Son is not the same as that between God and His church. Jesus had access to all that belonged to God because He *was* God. But we are not God; we are His creations. Again we see that this thinking clearly implies self-deification, that we are God (the same as Jesus).

2. The scriptures used to support the conclusion that we should have whatever we want because we are sons of God (1 Corinthians 15:45 and Romans 5:17) have nothing to do with being restored as sons of God or receiving wealth. The conclusion, in both cases, therefore, is a non sequitur. First Corinthians 15:45 is about Christ (the second Adam) being "a life-giving spirit," the one who gives us spiritual or eternal life, not riches. Romans 5:17 is about "God's abundant provision of grace and of the gift of righteousness," not about "gold, silver and cattle" or other forms of material wealth.

3. The entire argument totally ignores the context of Romans 8:32 on which it is based. This verse is about the fact that God gives us

everything we need to complete the work that Jesus began on the cross. Verse 28 says that God "works for the good of those who have been called according to his purpose." And verse 29 indicates that this purpose is for us "to be conformed to the likeness of his Son." Finally, verse 34 says that "Christ Jesus . . . is at the right hand of God . . . interceding for us."

In this context, it is clear that an important, if not the main, reason for Jesus' intercession is so that God's purpose for us will be accomplished. No, Jesus did not die on the cross so that we could become rich, but so that we could have eternal life and be transformed spiritually into His likeness.

In the same passage of his book, Hutton implies that the purpose of the Holy Spirit in our lives is not sanctification and service, but to make us rich and enable us to enjoy life in this world:

> As we learn to follow the leading of the Holy Spirit and walk in our rights and privileges as children of God, we will **enjoy all that God's Creation affords**. John 15:7 puts it best: *if ye abide in me and my words abide in you, ye shall ask what ye will, and it shall be done unto you.*[11] [Emphasis in original.]

The verse quoted is used to suggest that the reason we are to abide in Christ is to get rich. This, of course, once more totally ignores the context. John 15 is a well-known chapter about the vine (Jesus) and the branches (us). It is about remaining in Him, as a branch remains in the vine, in order to bear spiritual fruit and be able to do the will of God:

> I am the vine; you are the branches. If a man remains in me and I in him he will bear much fruit. . . . This is to my Father's glory, that you bear much fruit, showing yourselves to be my disciples (John 15:5, 8).

This passage goes on to talk about receiving Christ's love, about having our joy made complete, and about obeying His command to love one another (verses 9–13). There is *nothing* in it about getting rich!

3. *Taking metaphors literally*

The final false teaching we shall look at in Hutton's book involves taking metaphorical language literally, again by ignoring the context, in order to twist scripture to support the prosperity gospel. In this case, it is 2 Corinthians 8:9 which is so misused:

> For ye know the grace of our Lord Jesus Christ, that, though he was rich, yet for your sakes he became poor, that ye through his poverty might be rich.

Hutton uses this verse to try to show that

> Jesus was rich financially while He lived
> on earth, then He became poor finan-
> cially while He hung on the cross. . .
> [and] He did it for our sakes so that we
> could become rich.

> . . . In other words, Jesus became poor
> and took our poverty on Himself so that
> we could become financially free! We
> now have the blood-bought right to walk
> free from poverty and be financially
> blessed in our lives![12]

Once more, we have the same basic argument:
that Jesus died so we could be rich. This statement not only negates the gospel—that Jesus
died to pay the penalty for our sins and thus
provide God's amazing grace for our salvation—but it also implies that financial blessing in this life is more important than spiritual
salvation for eternity. While I doubt that Hutton
really believes this, it shows the carelessness
with which the Maniacs use scripture and the
intellectual irresponsibility with which they
promote their prosperity doctrine.

The verse in question is not about literally
getting rich financially, but about gaining
spiritual riches—in this case developing a
generous spirit as an expression of sincere

love and willingness to give. The context makes this clear:

> . . . just as you excel in everything—in faith, in speech, in knowledge, in complete earnestness and in your love for us—see that you also *excel in the grace of giving.*

> I am not commanding you, but I want to test *the sincerity of your love* by comparing it with the earnestness of others. For you know the grace of our Lord Jesus Christ, that though he was rich, yet for your sakes he became poor, so that you through his poverty might become rich.

> And, here is my advice about what is best for you in this matter: Last year you were the first not only to give but also to have the desire to do so. Now finish the work *so that your eager willingness to do it may be matched by your completion of it*, according to your means (2 Corinthians 8:7–11, emphasis added).

Ironically, then, this passage is not about the right we have to *get* from God, but just the opposite—the grace we should have to *give* to others.

Thus, it is clear that, when Paul says through Jesus' poverty we might become rich, he is using the word "rich" metaphorically—to refer to spiritual qualities. However, he uses the word "poverty" to convey both a spiritual and material meaning.

For Jesus gave up all the spiritual riches of heaven—His glory, power, authority, and status as God (Philippians 2:5–8)—and became a human being, born in humble circumstances to a working class family where He grew up to follow His human father's trade as a carpenter. He therefore became, by contrast to His heavenly state, materially poor. Jesus Himself indicated this when He said,

> Foxes have holes and birds in the air have nests, but the Son of Man has no place to lay his head (Matthew 8:20).

During His years of ministry, He did not even have a place to live that He could call his own. Here, too, Hutton misuses scripture to try to "prove" that Jesus had a home during these years (e.g., Mark 9:28, 33) even though neither there nor anywhere else does the Bible ever say such a thing.

Moreover, Jesus relied on others for His support:

> Many women were there, watching from a distance. They had followed Jesus from Galilee to care for his needs (Matthew 27:55).

Thus, Hutton's contention that "Jesus was rich financially while He lived on earth"[13] is an untrue statement.

In addition, Hutton ignores numerous related scriptures which contradict his false teaching that Jesus was rich during His life and only became poor on the cross so that we could become rich. Perhaps the best example of such a related scripture is Philippians 2:5–8, mentioned above. Let's look at it more closely:

> Your attitude should be the same as that of Christ Jesus: who, being in very nature God, did not consider equality with God something to be grasped, but made himself nothing, taking on the nature of a servant, being made in human likeness. And being found in appearance as a man, he humbled himself and became obedient to death—even death on a cross!

This indicates that Jesus became "poor" *spiritually* making Himself "nothing" and practicing servanthood, humility, and obedience, and that we should do likewise. A servant is *not* the same as a rich man. And this passage does *not* say we should become rich, acquiring the prestige and status that accompanies wealth.

Rather than being rich, Paul described himself and his fellow workers in Christ as just the opposite: ". . . *poor*, yet making many rich; *having nothing*, and yet possessing everything" (2 Corinthians 6:10, emphasis added). Once again, Paul is speaking of being rich metaphorically. He is saying that, though they were materially poor, they were spiritually rich and were bringing others into that same spiritual richness. It is obvious to anyone (except, apparently, Hutton and his fellow prosperity proponents) that Paul was not talking about making others rich financially.

378 The Spiritual Discernment Guide

All of this is not to say that I believe God wants us to be poor. He may very well choose to bless us with financial wealth—if He thinks we can handle it properly and it suits *His* purpose. But what He is mainly concerned about is our spiritual wealth—being godly and content—as Paul himself had learned to be:

> . . . I have learned to be content whatever the circumstances. I know what it is to be in need, and I know what it is to have plenty. I have learned the secret of being content in any and every situation, whether well fed or hungry, whether living in plenty or in want. I can do everything through him who gives me strength (Philippians 4:11–13).

The Magic of Giving to Get

Another Maniac who energetically spreads the prosperity gospel is Robert Tilton. Following in the tradition of Oral Roberts' "seed faith" concept, he emphasizes the importance of *giving in order to get.* Tilton's main contribution to this false teaching is his extensive use of magical objects and gimmicks. By these means, his followers can supposedly be helped to obtain blessings in return for money. While other TV evangelists have used similar tactics, Tilton appears to be the master.

For example, proclaiming that "your giving opens the way for your MIRACLE according to Psalm 50:15 NIV," Tilton included a "Bank of Heaven" check in one of his form letters. He instructed the recipient to

"Obey God in a Sacrifice of Thanksgiving Offering" of ten dollars or "as close as possible to six dollars." He then instructed the addressee as follows:

> Now, please go to the Miracle Window Prayer Page that I've enclosed.
>
> #1. **Look at the Bank of Heaven check at the bottom**. Think about the largest financial blessing that ONLY God could give you. Write that amount on the check. The more money you need, the bigger the miracle can be!
>
> #2. **Open your Bible to Psalm 50:14–15**. Place your Bank of Heaven Check and your wallet or checkbook on the open Bible. Leave it there tonight only. In the morning, get the Miracle Prayer Sheet with the Bank of Heaven Check still attached along with your SACRIFICIAL THANKS OFFERING back to me.[14] [Emphasis in original.]

By performing these ritualistic actions, the hopeful letter recipients are led to believe that the check will magically activate God to perform a miracle and provide them with a financial blessing in whatever amount they designate.

Tilton uses Psalm 50:14–15 to justify the idea that God will respond in this way to their "sacrificial offering" (i.e., money sent to Robert Tilton). In reference to this scripture, Tilton says,

> "Your giving PREPARES THE WAY for your miracle. . . . the best way I know to operate in

the supernatural dimension of faith is to give a
gift to God. Your SACRIFICIAL THANKS OF-
FERING prepares the way for God to birth your
miracle.[15] [Emphasis in original.]

Here, once again, the context is ignored. Psalm
50:14–15 is not about giving in order to get. It is
about God's rebuke and correction of Israel for not
keeping the covenant they made with Him and about
His admonition to them to honor Him by keeping
their vows and calling upon Him in trouble. Then,
it says, He will deliver them:

Sacrifice thank offerings to God, fulfill your
vow to the Most High, and call upon me in
the day of trouble; I will deliver you, and you
will honor me.

To reduce this to mean *you must give money to
the church (i.e., Robert Tilton's ministry) so that God
will bless you financially* is to totally ignore the real
meaning: to honor God by sacrifice, obedience, and
dependence on Him. While deliverance "in the day
of trouble" could involve financial provision, this is
certainly not the usual meaning of "deliverance."
And the context shows that this was not the meaning intended by the psalmist.

Verse 4 says, "He summons the heavens above
and the earth, that he may judge his people." Verse
7 says, "Hear, O my people, and I will speak, O Israel, and I testify against you . . ." Verse 21 says,
"But I will rebuke you and accuse you to your face."

These verses indicate that the subject is judgment, accusation, and rebuke.

That "deliverance" does not mean "financial blessing" is made totally clear:

> He who sacrifices offerings honors me, and he prepares the way so that I may show him the *salvation* of God. [Emphasis added.]

The deliverance God is speaking of is something much greater than money. It is nothing less than individual and national *salvation*. And the purpose of sacrifice is not the crass and self-serving reward of riches. It is the honoring of God and the preparation for salvation. So Tilton not only ignores the context, but he also redefines "deliverance" to mean "financial reward" and "salvation" to mean "money."

In the other direct mail pieces from Tilton which I have seen, he uses an amazing variety of such gimmicks, including the following:

- "The Holy Ghost Glove of Goodness," a plastic glove which you are to touch to your forehead and both temples, lay on Psalm 23 overnight, and mail back to Tilton, accompanied by a "sacrificial seed" donation.
- "The Biblical Miracle Prayer Ring," a piece of bent aluminum which will deliver you from trouble if you wear it on your right hand for seven days, write the name of the person causing the trouble seven times on a piece

of brown paper sack, sleep with the form letter under your pillow (shades of the Tooth
Fairy!), return the letter, along with your
"number one prayer need," and send "your
best seed offering." If these instructions are
followed *exactly*, the result will be "seven
months of prosperity."

- "The Psalm 31:4 Bible Heart," a red plastic
  heart in a sealed envelope (I know because I
  peeked!), which will bring "a financial blessing," if you feel it through the envelope without opening it, touch it to your heart, "close
  your eyes and whisper, 'Jesus' two times,"
  "touch it to your forehead," "place it inside
  your billfold," sleep with the sealed heart and
  your wallet under your pillow (Let's hear it
  for the Tooth Fairy again!), and return the
  sealed heart wrapped in a recommended
  "seed" offering of twenty dollars. (Psalm 37:4
  says, "Delight yourself in the Lord and he will
  give you the desires of your heart," which,
  according to Tilton's letter, means *money*.)

- "The Bible Anointing Oil," a small amount
  of mineral oil in a plastic pouch, which will
  bring "a new anointing of God's power in
  your life" and great joy in the next five days
  if you write your name on a plain piece of
  brown paper, put some of the oil on your
  finger and make a cross on your forehead,
  "anoint" the piece of brown paper five times
  with some of the oil, place under your pil-

low the brown paper prayer page from Tilton's letter (on which you have written "THE GREATEST MIRACLE GOD COULD DO FOR YOU IN THE NEXT FIVE DAYS") (with compliments to the T. F.), sleep on it overnight, and return it all within twenty-four hours to Tilton with a "seed offering" of either $9, $15, or $21 (as you are led by God). [Emphasis in original.]

In another of his form letters, Tilton also promised a variety of other "earthly blessings," directing his followers to check off which of the following they wish to receive: "business breakthroughs, cars, clothes, favor with people, financial miracles, jobs, loans, tax problems solved, and vacations."[16]

Obviously, there is nothing scriptural about any of this. It is all charismaniac mumbo-jumbo, substituting magical formulas and occult objects and rituals for true prayer offered in humility and submission to God's will. And in each of these direct mail pieces, scripture is taken out of context and twisted to make it appear to support the heretical practices being recommended. In the process, seeds of apostasy are being sown in the minds and hearts of naive and gullible Christians who are being drawn away from an authentic relationship with God and a genuine reliance on the Holy Spirit, scriptural truth, and real prayer.

The New Idolatry

In the prosperity deception that Satan has planted within the church, he has not simply provided another substitute for authentic Christianity, he has also set up a new form of idolatry. The new idol being worshipped by thousands of Christians is *humanistic materialism* (or charismatic humanism) clothed in biblical terminology. As Carlson and Decker point out,

> Idolatry is not simply worshipping a stone image; idolatry is any concept of God that reduces Him to less than who He really is. There is a false religion growing in our land, and it is called "prosperity theology."

> Many Christians are being swept into this false religion by promises of financial prosperity, by claims that God always wants them healthy, wealthy, and prosperous. This "gospel message" has become idolatry by reducing God to someone who is there to give us what we want. This gospel says, "Ask not what you can do for God, but what He can do for you."

> This message is a uniquely American charismatic humanism whose emphasis is on man's desire for wealth and his power to direct the actions of God. It is the idolizing of the American value system of success, financial prosperity, and devotion to the here-and-now. It takes secular values and overlays them on Christian teachings. . . .

This whole philosophy of visualizing and claiming our "inheritance" is religious mind science. It is a counterfeit religion. It is a product of Western, materialistic mentality, a humanistic philosophy that reduces God to a servant of man, a god that man can manipulate for his own selfish gain. It is the new idolatry.[17]

In several churches I have attended, I heard the following scriptures used to support these heresies: *Malachi 3:10–11* (about tithing), *Matthew 13:8* (about sowing and reaping), and *Romans 8:16–17* (about being co-heirs with Christ). In each case scripture twisting was involved.

The Magic of Tithing
Malachi 3:10–11 says,

"Bring the whole tithe into the storehouse, that there may be *food* in my house. Test me in this," says the Lord Almighty, "and see if I will not throw open the floodgates of heaven and pour out so much blessing that you will not have room enough for it." [Emphasis added.]

Prosperity teachers take this to mean that, if we are faithful and generous in our monetary giving, then God will reward us with financial abundance. Thus, tithing becomes an automatic, and magical, means to wealth. (But notice that the *tithe* in the above verse refers to *food*, not money.) There are at least two major problems with this interpretation—our old friends, ignoring the context and redefinition.

The context of these verses is the covenant relationship between the nation of Israel and God. It is not about Christians who are to give money to the church in order to receive financial blessings. Verse 7 speaks of the breaking of the covenant by the Jews:

> "Ever since the time of your forefathers you have turned away from my decrees and have not kept them. Return to me, and I will return to you," says the Lord Almighty.

Verse 10 speaks of God pouring out His blessing from heaven on the Jews. This refers to the promised covenant blessing of Deuteronomy 28:12 and Isaiah 44:3[18]:

> The Lord will open the storehouse of his bounty to send rain on your land in season and to bless all the work of your hands.

> For I will pour water on the thirsty land, and streams on the dry ground. I will pour out my Spirit on your offspring, and my blessing on your descendants.

This is all about blessings on the land and the people to make them fruitful and *spiritually* prosperous. The opening of the floodgates of heaven is an idiom which refers, both here and elsewhere, to "abundant provisions of *food*."[19] [Emphasis added.]

This meaning is indicated clearly in Malachi 3:11–12, which say,

> "I will prevent pests from devouring your crops and the vines in your fields will not cast their fruit," says the Lord Almighty. "Then all the nations will call you blessed, for yours will be a delightful land," says the Lord Almighty.

The reference to devouring pests and casting fruit are examples of the covenant curses against which God warned the Jews, for example, in Deuteronomy 28:39–40. The words, "call you blessed" refer to the fulfillment of God's promise to Abraham. (See Genesis 12:2–3 and Isaiah 61:9.) There is no mention of money or financial blessings here. It is all about God's covenant blessings on the Jewish land and people. Thus, to apply it to modern-day Christians and say it is about a monetary reward for giving is to give it a meaning which the context does not support.

In order to arrive at such a distorted meaning, the prosperity teachers must resort to the semantic fallacy of redefinition. They take the word "blessing," which has the general meaning of favor and help (and in context the specific meanings of abundant crops and spiritual benefits), and redefine it as "money."

388   The Spiritual Discernment Guide

A Harvest of Wealth

Matthew 13:8 says,

> Still other seed fell on good soil where it pro-
> duced a crop—a hundred, sixty or thirty times
> what was sown.

Prosperity teachers combine this verse with 2 Corinthians 9:6 ("Whoever sows sparingly will reap sparingly and whoever sows generously will reap generously.") to come up with the idea that generous giving will be rewarded by a hundred, sixty, or thirty times what was given, depending on the level of generosity.

The trouble with this interpretation is that the two verses have nothing to do with each other or with monetary rewards, and the conclusion based on them is therefore a non sequitur. Matthew 13:8 is about hearing the word and understanding it (verse 23), which results in *spiritual* fruitfulness. It is not about *giving* at all. Thus, the Maniacs once again ignore the context in their use of scripture. Second Corinthians 9:6, while it deals with giving and receiving, is not about being rewarded financially or even materially. It is about receiving God's *grace* in order to be able to do *good works*, as verses 7 and 8 explain:

> Each man should give what he has decided in
> his heart to give, not reluctantly or under com-
> pulsion, for God loves a cheerful giver. And God

is able to make all *grace* abound to you, so that in all things at all times, having all you need, you will abound in every *good work*. [Emphasis added.]

Again, the context is ignored in the prosperity teacher's interpretation. In addition, the context shows that God promises to meet our *needs, not* our wants, if we are faithful in giving. (Incidentally, it also shows that tithing is not mandatory, as many charismatics as well as evangelicals teach. But that's another whole problem in scripture twisting.)

Our Materialistic "Inheritance"

Romans 8:16–17 says,

Now if we are children, then we are heirs—heirs of God and co-heirs with Christ, if we share in his sufferings in order that we may also share in his glory.

The Maniacs make much of our "inheritance" in Christ, placing on it the literal meaning of "money received by an heir to an estate." They thus confuse a metaphorical meaning with a literal one and simultaneously ignore the context. For this verse is not about inheriting money but about sharing "in his glory" as it plainly states. It is in fact about our future glory "that will be revealed in us" when we appear with Christ as "the sons of God" (verses 18 and 19).

Moreover, these verses have nothing to do with giving in order to get. They are, in fact, about undergoing suffering as a necessary element in the process of becoming sons of God. For we will only share in Christ's glory "if indeed we share in his sufferings." Thus, the verse also refutes an idea related to the prosperity doctrine—that we, as Christians, should never have to suffer and that it a sign of insufficient faith, sin in our lives, and/or spiritual inferiority if we do.

From the above examples, it is obvious that the prosperity teachers' emphasis on getting and on giving in order to receive, rather than on serving God and becoming spiritually mature, encourages greed and deal making with (not to mention magical manipulation of) God. Christianity is thereby reduced to a means of financial gain at the expense of truth and righteousness. Such carnality then leads Christians into idolatry.

But the Bible says you are to "put to death . . . whatever belongs to your earthly nature . . . [including] greed which is idolatry" (Colossians 3:5).

Such idolatry, unfortunately, is alive and well in the church. Again, I can speak from personal experience. Two friends from my past are good examples.

One was a pastor who, along with some of his elders, took advantage of a struggling printer (a Christian) by cheating him out of his printing press so they could take it for their own use. They did this by convincing him to give them the press in order to get a tax write-off and because he would have lost it through bankruptcy anyway.

This was done in the name of the Holy Spirit, claiming His leading in the matter and declaring that God wanted to bless them by providing them with the press free of charge. They gloated over this "blessing" without a thought of how they could have helped the poor printer—perhaps by actually *buying* his press from him at a fair price.

The other person, a successful professional man and elder in the church, was proud of his "astuteness" in business. I heard him bragging to a group of Christians (of which I was a part) about how he made money by overcharging clients—at times doubling what would have been a fair price—because he could get away with it. He justified this in the name of "free enterprise" and considered it a blessing from God.

Whatever happened to righteousness, honesty, fairness, integrity, compassion, and the Golden Rule that you should do unto others as you would have them do unto you?

A Magical Prayer for "Extravagant Blessings": The Jabez Teaching

Another example of what I believe may, in some cases, be this same spirit of greed is currently sweeping the church as I write. I know my views on this will be extremely controversial because it goes against a pervasive mind-set in the church. But I feel it needs to be said in the interest of removing confusion about the proper use of prayer.

This is the teaching about how to be "extravagantly blessed by God"[20] by daily repetition of the "prayer of Jabez." The author of the book by the same name, Bruce Wilkinson, attempts to justify this *magical use of prayer* by promising the prayer will increase the scope and effectiveness of one's ministry. However, these words on the back cover of his book make the basic motivation perfectly clear: '

> Are you ready to reach for the extraordinary? To ask God for the abundant blessings He longs to give you? Join Bruce Wilkinson to discover how the remarkable prayer of a little-known Bible hero can release God's favor, power, and protection. You'll see how one daily prayer can help you leave the past behind—and break through to the life you were meant to live.[21]

A tall order for one little daily prayer:

- abundant blessings
- God's favor, power, and protection
- freedom from the past
- entering into the new life God meant you to have

Here we have the abundant life (with its heavenly favor, power, protection, and freedom) plus the sanctification and fruitfulness of a new life—all rolled into a handy little capsule called "the prayer of Jabez." (Do you notice the familiar ring of the magical formulas of Robert Tilton?)

Is this really all there is to it? If so, why bother with the rest of the Bible? What more do we need?

Actually, the prayer of Jabez doesn't really deal with any of these things. Here is the prayer in its entirety:

> "Oh, that you would bless me and enlarge my territory! Let your hand be with me, and keep me from harm so that I will be free from pain" (1 Chronicles 4:10).

This says that Jabez asked God to *bless* him in a general way (not necessarily financially) and to give him ownership or control over *more territory* (presumably that of a clan in the tribe of Judah, since that is where Jabez appears in the genealogical list of 1 Chronicles). He also asked to be kept by God's hand from *harm* and *pain*. The words "Let your hand be with me" could also be taken as a general request for God's help, comparable to "Oh that you would bless me."

The rest of verse 10 says, "And God granted his request." But, other than expanded territory and freedom from harm and pain, it doesn't say *how* God blessed him.

There is nothing here about financial wealth, personal growth, expanded ministry, or miraculous events. However, these are exactly the things that Wilkinson says the prayer is about:

> If Jabez had worked on Wall Street, he might have prayed, "Lord, increase the value of my investment portfolios."
>
> Jabez wanted to be more and do more for God. . . .
>
> . . . He wanted more influence, more responsibility, and more opportunity *to make a mark for the God of Israel.*
>
> Let me tell you a guaranteed by-product of sincerely seeking His blessing: Your life will become marked by miracles.
>
> To pray for larger borders is to ask for a miracle— it's just that simple.[22] [Emphasis added.]

In each of these points, Wilkinson is begging the question because he gives no reasons or evidence to prove that this is in fact what the prayer means.

He also resorts to redefinition of the word "territory" in order to twist the scripture into supporting his interpretation:

> . . . when we're deciding what size territory God has in mind for us, we keep an equation in our hearts that adds up to something like this:
>
> > My abilities + experience + training + my personality and appearance + my past + my expectations of others = my *assigned territory.*
>
> . . . God's math would look more like this:

My willingness and weakness + God's
will and supernatural power = my expanded territory.[23] [Emphasis added.]

Here the word "territory," which literally means
a particular area of land, is made to mean "your overall capabilities, personality, attitude towards God,
and God's will and power as they apply to you."

Of course, this is also an excellent example of
taking a literal statement metaphorically. However,
the wording of the Jabez prayer is very plain and
straightforward. Except for its reference to the hand
of the Lord (a common expression in the Old Testament), there is nothing in the prayer to suggest that
it be taken any way but literally. Jabez asked God for
what he wanted: blessing, more land, help, protection from harm, and freedom from pain. If he had
wanted all the things that Wilkinson says he did, he
could have asked for them directly. When we pray,
we don't use uncommon metaphors for what we want.
We say what we mean. If I want more money, I pray
for more money—not for a general blessing and more
territory. If I want an expanded ministry, I pray for it.
If I need a miracle, I ask God for one.

In addition, in the phrase "assigned territory"
we have an instance of rewriting scripture. The word
"assigned" does not appear in the text, but, by adding it, Wilkinson gives the verse the implied meaning of "something divinely granted or mandated for
a special purpose," thereby opening it up for his
metaphorical interpretation.

In his interpretation of the phrase "keep me from evil [harm]" (KJV), Wilkinson further broadens his metaphorical interpretation to the idea of *success* or *winning*:

> . . . in this [chapter] our petition is for supernatural help to protect us from Satan's proven ability to make us come in second.

> Without doubt, success brings with it greater opportunities for failure.[24]

And this, in turn, is related to the ideas of *avoiding temptation* and *being protected from deception*:

> We make a huge spiritual leap forward, therefore, when we begin to focus less on beating temptation and more on avoiding it. . . . to pray that we will not have to fight unnecessary temptation.

> . . . That's why, like Jabez, we should pray for protection from deception . . . .[25]

(Incidentally, the statement that avoiding temptation is "a huge spiritual leap forward" is very questionable. *Why* is it such a spiritual leap to avoid temptation rather than to deal with it and to overcome it? The Bible says temptation comes to test us and testing is necessary for our spiritual growth. If we avoid the very thing that causes us to become more spiritual, how is that spiritual advancement?

Wilkinson's interpretations obviously take us far afield from the actual wording of the text. And, indeed, Wilkinson extends this broadened meaning even further to include the following:

- "to be spared dangerous misjudgments"
- "to be kept from the powerful pull of what feels right to us but is wrong"
- "freedom in the Spirit"
- "to live free from the bondage of evil"
- "to be more 'honorable' in God's eyes"
- "to be clean and fully surrendered to our Lord, to want what He wants for His world, and to step forward in His power and protection to see it happen now"
- "to ask Him for the God-sized best He has in mind for you, and to ask for it with all your heart"[26]

To say the least, these interpretations can only be arrived at by extreme redefining of the phrases "expand my territory," "keep me from harm," and "be free from pain." To find all these meanings in these three phrases, I submit, is *not* to rightly divide the Word of God.

Finally, Wilkinson cites "divine appointments" and other "miracles," as products of the power of the Jabez prayer. He says, in effect, he prayed the prayer in the morning and then later in the day such and such a miracle happened. For example, he says, "As I look back over this divine appointment, I can see the footprints of Jabez and his little prayer."[27]

However, to attribute such events specifically to the Jabez prayer itself is to use a **post hoc** argument, without proving any causal relationship between the repetition of Jabez's words and the divine appointments. In this, Wilkinson is also, once again, tacitly attributing such events to a magical formula. Indeed, he spells out this formula as follows:

1. Pray the Jabez prayer every morning, and keep a record of your daily prayer by marking off a calendar or chart you make especially for the purpose.
2. Write out the prayer and tape it in your Bible, in your day-timer, on the bathroom mirror, or some other place where you'll be reminded of your new vision.
3. Reread this little book once each week during the next month, asking God to show you important insights you may have missed.
4. Tell one other person of your commitment to your new prayer habit and ask him or her to check up on you.
5. Begin to keep a record of changes in your life, especially the divine appointments and new opportunities you can relate directly to the Jabez prayer.
6. Start praying the Jabez prayer for your family, friends, and local church.[28]

In other words, if you perform all these motivational and ritualistic actions (shades of Zig Ziglar and Robert Tilton), then the power of the little prayer will be released.

It is this magical aspect of Wilkinson's "discovery" that seems to be exciting many Christians. For example, a friend of mine, who happens to be an elder in his church, came to me full of enthusiasm about the prayer, saying it was producing amazing results and that I had to get the book and read it. He said the other elders in his church were equally excited.

Now, don't get me wrong. I don't doubt that the reported results were true. And I am not opposed to being personally blessed by God, having an enlarged ministry, being protected from deception and other evils, having miracles happen in my life, being fully surrendered to God's will, etc. These are wonderful things, and I have been praying for them for many years—and have received many blessings, increased opportunities to serve, and divine appointments, as well as a few miracles. But it all came about without the aid of the magical little prayer.

So let me suggest that maybe the results Wilkinson and his followers have experienced have come, not from the power of the Jabez prayer, but simply from the power of *prayer itself*. As Wilkinson himself says, "You will know beyond doubt that God has opened heaven's storehouses because *you prayed*.[29] [Emphasis in original.]

If the results came by praying for the various things in Wilkinson's expansive interpretation of the Jabez prayer, then, I submit, the Jabez prayer itself was not necessary, except as a jumping-off point for *real* prayer. But, if they came by simply repeating verbatim 1 Chronicles 4:10, as a kind of incantation, then they were produced by the magical use of prayer and, therefore, it was a form of shamanism and not real prayer. But I do not believe that the results would have come on this basis. (On the other hand, God is gracious and looks on the heart, so maybe He answered the prayer anyway—even though it was given in a magical manner.)

In any case, the basic point that I want to make is that many Christians seem to believe there is supernatural power in the words of the Jabez prayer. And to use it with this idea is to practice magic, to be confused about the proper use of scripture and what prayer really is, and to thereby swallow a seed of apostasy that is very similar, if not identical, to that of the prosperity teachers.

Spiritual Treasures

In all this false teaching about giving to get and praying to be magically blessed, there is an underlying preoccupation with acquiring money and other forms of material wealth. But the Bible says our focus should be on heavenly, eternal, or spiritual treasures. To turn from the false values of the prosperity gospel and apply the true values set forth in the Bible, we should be doing at least the following:

- *Renouncing greed:* Do not store up for yourselves treasures on earth where moth and rust destroy and where thieves break in and steal. But store up for yourselves treasures in heaven, where moth and rust do not destroy, and where thieves do not break in and steal. For where your treasure is, there your heart will be also (Matthew 6:19–21).

People who want to get rich fall into temptation and a trap and into many foolish and harmful desires that plunge men into ruin and destruction. For the love of money is a root of all kinds of evil. Some people, eager for money, have wandered from the faith and pierced themselves with many griefs (1 Timothy 6:9–10).

- *Practicing contentment:* But godliness with contentment is great gain. For we brought nothing into the world, and we can take nothing out of it. But if we have food and clothing, we will be content with that (1 Timothy 6:6–8).

  Keep your lives free from the love of money and be content with what you have, because God has said, "Never will I leave you; never will I forsake you" (Hebrews 13:5).

- *Having faith in God's provision:* And my God will meet all your needs according to his glorious riches in Christ Jesus (Philippians 4:19).

Notice that God's promise is to meet our *needs*, *not* our *wants*.

EXPERIENTIAL TRUTH

There is one more false teaching which has come out of the charismaniac church which is related to the idea of personal transcendence. This is the notion that subjective experience is a totally valid basis for truth and therefore should not be judged or even questioned in any way. In other words, those who teach this concept are forbidding the church to use discernment in this area.

Just receive it, they say, because faith means opening yourself up to the supernatural and accepting whatever comes. If you don't do this, they continue, it means you lack faith. Underlying this attitude is the deception that, if it's supernatural, it must be from God. It is, therefore, another prime example of swallowing everything whole.

It is also another case of redefinition because "faith" is made to mean "blind, unquestioning openness."

But the Bible says we are to "test the spirits":

> Dear friends, do not believe every spirit, but test the spirits to see whether they are from God, because many false prophets have gone out into the world (1 John 4:1).

Thus, this false doctrine is also a case of ignoring related scripture.

The defenders of supernatural experiential truth, however, say that such "openness" is scriptural. To prove this, they quote Jesus from Matthew 7:1: "Judge not, or you too will be judged."

However, here Jesus is not talking about "prophetic utterances" but about passing judgment on others in the sense of negatively evaluating them as people. That is, making a statement about their worthiness or value, for the purpose of finding fault. The context makes this clear, for Jesus goes on to say that they will suffer the same kind of personal judgment if they do this:

> "For in the same way you judge others, you will be judged, and with the measure you use, it will be measured to you.

> "Why do you look at the speck of sawdust in your brother's eye and pay no attention to the plank in your own eye?" (Matthew 7:2–3)

But the issue is not the spiritual or moral condition of the person. Rather it is the truth of the "prophecy" or "revelation" coming from a subjective supernatural experience. Thus, to cite this scripture to support "openness" to such "truth" is not only to ignore the context but also to beg the question—is such prophecy in fact the truth?

On the contrary, Jesus said we should "Stop judging by mere appearances, and make a right judgment" (John 7:24). And Paul says, "The spiritual man makes judgments about all things . . . (1 Corinthians 2:15) and ". . . it is time for judgment to begin with the family of God . . . (1 Peter 4:17).

So we see that judgment of those in the church, in the sense of discernment of good versus evil behavior and truth versus error in doctrine, is not only not forbidden but is given as a commandment. Therefore, the teachers of this false doctrine are also guilty of ignoring related scripture.

We have not only the right but also the obligation and necessity of judging false apostles, prophets, and teachers in this way. For, without such judgment (i.e., discernment), Satan has an open door to pass off demonic deception as "divine truth" in the body of Christ.

Satan Versus the Holy Spirit

We may well ask why Satan is so interested in counterfeiting genuine manifestations and revelations of the Holy Spirit. I submit that it is, first, because it provides a useful vehicle for injecting error and, second, because it brings great confusion into the church about the gifts of the Spirit. In this way he hopes to stop the church from receiving the fullness of God's power and the fruitfulness and ability to overcome which that power brings.

Satan focuses his deceptions on the things that threaten him and his plans. Therefore, he tries to get us off track especially where the supernatural is concerned. He wants us to think that Christianity is about acquiring miraculous powers in order to become wealthy, avoid suffering, or just have far out "spiritual experiences."

But Christianity is not about such things, and those who think it is are on a path away from knowing God and His will. Rather, Christianity is about becoming grown-up spiritual beings, sons and daughters of God who have a real, vital, intimate relationship with Him as our heavenly Father. Therefore, God's primary concern is not about giving us supernatural power or experiences—although He does perform miracles in our lives when necessary, and He does give us spiritual gifts to help us in our spiritual walk. But these are a means to an end, not the end itself. They are aids to His central purpose for our lives: spiritual maturity. They are not for our personal satisfaction, amazement, or entertainment.

CHAPTER THIRTEEN

False Anti-Charismatic Teachings

The term "anti-charismatics," as used in this book, refers to those in the church who believe the baptism in the Holy Spirit and the supernatural gifts of the Spirit are not for today. They reject the entire charismatic movement because it has been infiltrated by the unscriptural doctrines and bizarre behaviors described in previous chapters. Unlike the undiscerning Maniacs, they have not bought into the New Age ideas which are behind the charismatic heresies identified earlier. Indeed, their reaction against such ideas has been extreme—to the point of throwing out the genuine, godly baby with the counterfeit, demonic bathwater.

But the Bible says, "Do not put out the Spirit's fire; do not treat prophecies with contempt. Test everything. Hold on to the good. Avoid every kind of evil" (1 Thessalonians 5:19–21). The Holy Spirit is the Spirit of Christ—the same yesterday, today, and forever—part of Christ's sufficiency for us now, not something extra or unnecessary or obsolete.

In rejecting Spirit baptism and the manifestation gifts, then, Umbilicals are throwing out the supernatural power, signs, and wonders given to the church in the book of Acts. I believe, this anti-charismatic bias is based on four false doctrines:

1. Gifts of the Spirit are not for today. (Cessationism)
2. Supernatural manifestations (except healing) are of the devil. (Demonic supernaturalism)
3. Scripture is the only source of truth and discernment. (Scriptural legalism)
4. Supernatural phenomena are not real. (Ignoring the evidence)

"Gifts Not for Today" (Cessationism)

John the Baptist prophesied that Jesus would baptize *His followers* (not just the early church) "with the Holy Spirit and with fire" (Matthew 3:11). And Jesus Himself said this "promise of the Father" (KJV) would be initially fulfilled on the day of Pentecost when His followers would "receive power" to be His witnesses:

> Do not leave Jerusalem, but wait for the gift my Father promised which you have heard me speak about. For John baptized with water, but in a few days you will be baptized with the Holy Spirit.

> . . . you will receive power when the Holy Spirit comes on you; and you will be my witnesses in Jerusalem, and in all Judea and Samaria, and to the ends of the earth (Acts 1:4–5, 8).

Jesus did not say it would be only a temporary phenomenon for first century Christians or that witnessing (or the power needed for that purpose) would be limited to that time. When the original baptism in the Spirit was given (to those who had already received salvation) on the day of Pentecost (Acts 1:4–8; 2:1–4), they spoke prophetically in tongues. Therefore, a supernatural gift was the direct result of the baptism in the Holy Spirit.

Later in the book of Acts, *born-again, baptized believers* had the same experience (the baptism in the Spirit) when they were prayed for (Acts 8:14–17). Cornelius and all those present in his house received it and spoke in tongues *at the time of their conversion, prior to baptism* (Acts 10:44–46). Others in Ephesus received it *after conversion but before baptism.* They then spoke in tongues and prophesied (Acts 19:1–7). In these examples from scripture, the baptism in the Spirit was given *at conversion, after conversion, before baptism,* and *after baptism.* It was *not* received only at conversion as some Umbilicals teach or *not* only at baptism as others maintain. It was received when it was asked for in prayer or when God chose to give it.

As we noted earlier, some Umbilicals think it takes place automatically and only at conversion while others believe it ended when the last of the twelve apostles died and/or the writing of the New

Testament was completed. However, as defined by one highly respected and responsible charismatic organization,

> The baptism in the Holy Spirit is the empowering for service that takes place in the life of the christian. It can take place at the moment of faith in Christ as in the case of the first Gentile convert, Cornelius; but traditionally and experientially it follows repentance, saving faith, and baptism. . . . It enables a believer to witness to the Lord's salvation and to demonstrate one or more of the nine gifts, or manifestations of the Holy Spirit (see 1 Corinthians 12:7–10). Just as the indwelling Spirit reproduces the life of Jesus, the outpoured, or baptizing, Spirit reproduces the ministry of Jesus. . . . We receive, as it were, a drink of the Spirit when we are saved, but when we are baptized in the Spirit, it is as if that initial drink becomes an ocean that completely surrounds us."[1]

Some Christians reject most or all of the supernatural gifts either because they have been trained in that tradition or because of abuses in the charismatic church. I have heard the following kinds of reasons given for rejecting them: "I haven't experienced them. They don't happen in my church. My fellowship doesn't recognize them." The reasoning behind such responses is based on the fallacy of hasty generalization. "If it doesn't happen in my experience or my church, then it can't be valid in anybody else's." In jumping to this conclusion, they are once more throwing out the baby with the bathwater.

This tradition of Cessationism is strongly re-inforced by numerous anti-charismatic evangeli-cal writers. Bible scholar Merrill F. Unger, for example, in his book *The Baptism and Gifts of the Holy Spirit*, says, "These [prophecy, tongues, knowledge] are the special gifts of the Spirit mani-fest in the early church enabling first-century as-semblies to meet and have a preaching-teaching service before the New Testament was written and circulated among the churches."[2]

This is an instance of begging the question, for it assumes that the only valid purpose of the gifts of prophecy, tongues, and word of knowledge is to pro-vide material for preaching or teaching. As we have seen, this is not the case. The purpose of the gifts, including the three in question, is to provide "for the common good" (1 Corinthians 14:3), "so that the church may be edified," or built up (1 Corinthians 14:5, 12). Thus, such a teaching is not only an oversimplification but also a case of ignor-ing the context and related scripture.

So strong is this compulsion to follow tradition, that I have even heard pastors and others quote scrip-ture but leave out the parts which mention gifts, signs, wonders, or miracles. For example, the pastor of one church I have attended, teaching on the modern ap-plication of practices in the early church, quoted Acts 2:42–47. However, when he came to verse 43, which reads, "Everyone was filled with awe, and many won-ders and miraculous signs were done by the apostles," he skipped right over it, as though it wasn't there.

Such omissions are made, I believe, because they don't fit in with the traditional teachings in which these Christians were brought up or trained—that signs, wonders, miracles, and other supernatural manifestations ceased before the end of the First Century. This, I submit, is a case of rewriting scripture (by omission) to make it not say what they don't want it to say.

Such opposition is so intense in the Southern Baptist Convention (SBC), for example, that, it is reported, some churches are being disfellowshipped because of "neo-Pentecostalism" (i.e., receiving the baptism in the Holy Spirit, excitement, demonstrativeness in worship services, recognition of speaking in tongues, and laughing in the Spirit).[3]

Also, SBC missionaries are being dismissed for the same reasons. That is, for allowing charismatic experiences to take place in . . . church meetings. . . . Many Baptists living overseas are already charismatic. . . . But most charismatics remain "in the closet" for fear of getting fired.[4]

Others in the evangelical church are not getting hired because they speak in tongues.[5]

These reports show that God is pouring out His Spirit on Southern Baptists, but the ultra-conservative Umbilical leadership doesn't like it. They are Cessationists, believing that these things ceased in the First Century, dogmatically opposing the gifts of the Spirit, especially the supernatural ones and, above all, speaking in tongues.

My wife and I felt the effects of this cessationist spirit in the home Bible study which we were leading in an evangelical church. As mentioned earlier, God has used us on occasion in some of the manifestation gifts. In this instance, several of us in the group were counseling and praying with a young woman after the meeting. My wife was moved by the Holy Spirit to speak in tongues and I gave the interpretation. The young woman was comforted and encouraged by the message and all seemed well. However, at the next meeting, I was told in no uncertain terms by an elder speaking for the eldership that there was to be no more tongues or interpretation in our group.

It seems there had been a complaint about the incident by a group member, who was very upset by it. This edict came as a surprise to us because we had been told by the senior pastor that there was no objection to ministering in the gifts as long as it was done in a home group setting and in an orderly manner. Obviously, the pastor's openness to the gifts of the Spirit was not shared by the eldership.

Such unbelief in the practical power of the Holy Spirit is reflected in subtle ways, such as not expecting the miraculous but instead relying on human effort and expertise. For example, at one church that I have attended, the multi-million dollar building program made extensive use of secular fundraising techniques and Madison Avenue glitz, but, in the program presentations and publicity materials, there was no seeking for or mention of the power and anointing of the Holy Spirit as the source of guidance and success for the program.

This reliance on self-effort rather than Holy Spirit power, I believe, is basically the result of spiritual pride and/or misplaced faith—not only in one's anti-charismatic tradition but also in the human ability of the local staff and body of believers. For they are saying, in effect, "We don't need the supernatural gifts and power. We can do it ourselves."

The cessationist mentality also provides an excuse for looking for substitutes for the Holy Spirit. When Satan tricks Christians into denying the validity of the gifts, he also lures them into looking elsewhere for the help they need—for example, into secular psychology, positive thinking, visualization, other mind-over-matter techniques, and church growth consultants.

Finally, Cessationism implies that Satan has no real power to come against the church. For, if we don't need the gifts, some of which are given as weapons against the enemy (such as the discerning of spirits), then it must be because Satan is no real threat, or at least not one that we can't handle by ourselves.

Umbilicals support their cessationist view by citing 1 Corinthians 13:9–10:

> . . . where there are prophecies, they will cease; where there are tongues, they will be stilled; where there is knowledge, it will pass away. For we know in part and we prophesy in part, but when perfection comes, the imperfect disappears.

They interpret these verses to mean that the supernatural gifts ceased when the writing of the New Testament was completed (i.e., "when perfection comes"). However, taken in context, it becomes apparent that the cessation of the gifts mentioned here (prophecy, tongues, and word of knowledge) were to take place, not when the New Testament was completed, but when Jesus returns. This is indicated in verse 12:

> Now we see but a poor reflection as in a mirror; then we shall see face to face. Now I know in part; then I shall know fully, even as I am fully known.

This is about the return of Jesus, whom we shall see face to face. One does not see a book (the New Testament) face to face, but a person. I shall also know this person fully even as I am fully known by Him. One cannot be known by a book, but only by a person.

Furthermore, this one whom we shall see face to face, know fully, and be known by fully is described as "perfection." It will take place when "perfection comes." A book doesn't come; a person does. There is only one such perfect person who will come and know us fully, and that is Jesus. There is no mention of any writings, such as the New Testament, in this passage. But there are obvious allusions to Jesus—for anyone who is not tied into a traditional teaching so tightly that he cannot see what is plainly there.

Therefore, in this argument for Cessationism, we have an interpretation that is possible only by ignoring the context. This fact is supported by the NIV Study Bible, which says, "Verse 12 . . . seems to indicate that Paul is here speaking of Christ's second coming." In contrast to our present perception of the Lord, which is like a "poor reflection as in a mirror," we shall then be "seeing the Lord directly and clearly in heaven. . . . The Christian will know the Lord to the fullest extent possible for a finite being, similar to the way the Lord knows the Christian fully and infinitely. This will not be true until the Lord returns."[6]

Nelson's Bible Commentary adds this supporting comment: "The mirror is likely the Word of God . . ., seen dimly through our respective gifts."[7] If the mirror is the Word of God (including the New Testament) by which we *see* a reflection of the "perfect," then obviously the New Testament cannot *be* the "perfect" which is to come.

"Gifts of the Devil" (Demonic Supernaturalism)

The second major false teaching of the Umbilicals is that all supernatural manifestations are of the devil. This is a view that I believe is dangerously close to blasphemy against the Holy Spirit, for it attributes the manifestations of God the Holy Spirit to Satan. Speaking of this, Jesus said,

> "And if I drive out demons by Beelzebub, by
> whom do your people drive them out? . . . And
> so I tell you, every sin and blasphemy will be
> forgiven men, but the blasphemy against the
> Spirit will not be forgiven. Anyone who speaks
> a word against the Son of Man will be forgiven,
> but anyone who speaks against the Holy Spirit
> will not be forgiven, either in this age or in the
> age to come" (Matthew 12:27, 31–32).

Here, Jesus is talking about attributing the works of God to the devil (Beelzebub). And this is exactly what is being done by some who reject the genuine gifts of the Spirit.

The demonic supernaturalists, to my knowledge, have no proof texts to support their view. Rather, they simply argue that, since the gifts of the Spirit have ceased, then *all* present-day supernatural manifestations must be of the devil. As supporting "evidence," they assert that satanists can speak in tongues, that demons can perform psychic surgery and other forms of psychic healing, and that the antichrist will do miracles. While these assertions may have some basis in fact, they are not logical reasons for concluding that all supernatural manifestations are of the devil.

First of all, they ignore a number of related scriptures which indicate that Satan and his demons can counterfeit the genuine miracles and other supernatural phenomena which come from God. For example, 2 Thessalonians 2:9 says,

> The coming of the lawless one will be in accordance with the work of Satan displayed in all kinds of counterfeit miracles, signs and wonders, and in every sort of evil that deceives those who are perishing. [See also Matthew 24:24 and Revelation 13:13, 16:14, and 19:20.]

The fact that Satan can produce counterfeits does not prove that the real thing does not exist—any more than the printing of counterfeit money proves that real money does not exist. This is an obvious non sequitur.

Secondly, they are making an untrue statement when they say that the supernatural manifestations of the Holy Spirit have ceased. For, as we saw earlier, this is not the case, and the scriptural evidence they provide for this ignores the context and relates scriptures.

"SCRIPTURE AS THE ONLY SOURCE" (SCRIPTURAL LEGALISM)

Thirdly, the Umbilicals declare that the Bible is our *only* source of guidance, truth, and discernment. Therefore, any such revelation from the Holy Spirit is invalid and irrelevant. Another name for this is scriptural legalism. This is the idea that God can give us revelation only in the way the Umbilicals have decided He can, through the study of His Word. This false teaching puts God in a box called "The Bible." One anticharismatic writer, for example, puts it bluntly: "No new teachings or revelations are needed. . . ."[8]

Some Unbilicals use Revelation 22:18 to support this position:

> I warn everyone who hears the words of the prophecy of this book: If anyone adds anything to them, God will add to him the plagues described in this book.

However, to use this verse to deny the validity of *all* modern prophetic revelation, is obviously to completely ignore the context. The verse in question clearly applies *only* to the content of the book of Revelation and *not* to direct revelation by the Holy Spirit.

Rather, like the Bereans (Acts 17:11), we should take the Bible as a whole as the standard for judging (i.e., discerning) the truth of teachings or revelations coming from any source other than scripture.

Furthermore, God is not limited to what is in the Bible. God is omnipotent, which means He is not limited in *any* way! In the Bible, we have only what God has chosen to reveal by that means. But, if He chooses to provide additional, special revelation or instruction for particular situations through the prophetic gifts (prophecy, word of wisdom, word of knowledge, tongues and interpretation), then He is free to do so—because He is God!

"UNREALITY OF THE SUPERNATURAL"
(IGNORING THE EVIDENCE)

The fourth way Umbilicals display their opposition to the charismatic church is by ignoring the evidence. They do this primarily by denying or disregarding occurrences of divine healing and deliverance in charismatic meetings and rejecting other supernatural phenomena such as being "slain in the Spirit" (falling under the power of the Holy Spirit).

For example, there was the following case of divine healing (among others) in my family: Shortly after my wife and I were saved in a charismatic church, we invited my teenage son to a healing service. (He was living with his mother, my ex-wife.) He had been suffering from a painful back problem, and we wanted him to witness God's healing power and hopefully get healed. During the healing service, the pastor, speaking a word of knowledge under the inspiration of the Holy Spirit, pointed directly toward my son in the balcony where we were sitting. He said the Lord was going to heal someone there of a back problem. And, if that person would step out in faith and walk down to the platform, he would be healed. My son knew the word was for him and responded. Before he reached the platform, his back was completely healed.

Unfortunately, after he returned to his non-charismatic evangelical church, he forgot about the healings he had witnessed and even about his own healing. When I reminded him of it years later, he confessed that he had forgotten about it. I believe this happened because it was not socially or doctrinally acceptable in his church to talk about or acknowledge the reality of such supernatural activity. In other words, he succumbed to peer pressure and the need to conform to doctrinal tradition.

This refusal to consider the evidence seems, from what I have observed, to be less common now than it was at the time of my son's experience (the early 70's), but, among evangelicals, there is still widespread reluctance to trust God to heal, except perhaps indirectly through medical science. And the idea that an individual in a traditional evangelical fellowship can have a healing ministry is unheard of. In one such church I have attended, I never heard it mentioned even as a possibility. On the contrary, our adult Sunday school teacher (an associate pastor) told us he believed such a ministry was impossible because the Holy Spirit never gifted people that way.

Indeed, extreme charismatic ministries that feature healing (such as those of Benny Hinn and Oral Roberts) are written off by Umbilicals as totally invalid, even though thousands of documented healings take place under such ministries. Once again, we see a failure to discern what is of God and what is not, and to throw the genuine baby out with the counterfeit bathwater.

The same can be said regarding salvation and deliverance. Both of these take place frequently and genuinely in even the most extreme charismatic churches. Once again, I can cite my own experience.

My wife and I were both saved in a charismatic church in which all the manifestation gifts were flowing. My wife was delivered instantaneously from alcoholism and I from years of tobacco addiction. We saw others delivered from hard drugs and demon possession.

Finally, such supernatural phenomena as being slain in the Spirit (as well as prophetic utterances, visions, revelatory dreams, etc.) are discounted as bogus theatrics or mass hypnosis. However, both my wife and I have personally had such experiences and can testify to their authenticity. The phenomenon of being slain in the Spirit is well documented by many historical accounts going back to the revivals of John Wesley, George Whitfield, and others even earlier. Thousands of people were slain in the spirit in such meetings. In her autobiography, Nineteenth Century evangelist Maria Woodworth-Etter records how, in her revivals, the power of God could be felt for up to fifty miles around the meetings and people were slain in the Spirit in their farms, fields, homes, and city streets.[9]

Hanegraaff says all such manifestations, while possible for an omnipotent God, are "not normative."[10] That is, they are not the usual or expected experience of the majority of Christians. While this may be true in the evangelical church, it was not so in the charismatic churches which I have attended. According to the New Testament, they apparently *were* normative in the early church—as indicated, for example, in 1 Corinthians 12 and 14:

> Now to each one the manifestation of the Spirit is given for the common good (1 Corinthians 12:7).

> And in the church God has appointed first of all apostles, second prophets, third teachers, then workers of miracles, also those having gifts of healing, those able to help others, those with gifts of administration, and those speaking in different kinds of tongues (1 Corinthians 12:28).

> When you come together, everyone has a hymn, or a word of instruction, a revelation, a tongue or an interpretation (1 Corinthians 14:26).

(See also Romans 12:6; 2 Corinthians 9:9; Ephesians 4:8; and Hebrews 2:4.)

There is no time limit given for the operation of any of these gifts—supernatural or otherwise—and no indication here—or anywhere else in the Bible—that any of them became non-normative. Thus, to assume otherwise, is to ignore these and other related scriptures.

These facts raise the question, Why are they not normative in a large portion of the church today? I submit that they are not because the anti-charismatic traditions of these factions has produced a lack of belief and application of faith in the operation of the supernatural gifts, signs, and wonders—even though they are all clearly described and the gifts are strongly encouraged in scripture, as we have seen.

Through such false teachings and lack of discernment, then, anti-charismatics promote a divisive polarization within the church. "Having a form of godliness but denying its power" (2 Timothy 3:5), they are, in effect, I believe, practicing a form of Phariseeism. For the sake of their tradition, they are opposing God in what He wants to do in the lives of individual believers and the body of Christ as a whole through the baptism in the Holy Spirit and the supernatural gifts.

CHAPTER FOURTEEN

False Teachings from Humanism

In the last two chapters, we saw traces of the humanistic spirit in the Word of Faith deification of the self, in the prosperity gospel's glorification of material wealth, in the anti-charismatic emphasis on human effort and ability, and in secular psychology's promotion of personal transcendence through self-love, self-esteem, personal empowerment, actualization of human potential, and the realization of man's innate goodness. We turn now to the much more direct expressions of New Age humanism found within the church as a whole. These are primarily teachings on *tolerance, unity,* and *a diminished Christ*

TOLERANCE: LETTING IN THE WORLD

Francis Schaeffer has said this about the evangelical church's tolerance of secular, humanistic values:

> Having become the establishment, evangelicals have accommodated the world at almost every turn rather than confront evil. . . . If we do not lovingly draw lines in our churches and schools, many evangelical organizations will be lost from Christ's cause forever.[1]

This accommodationism is based on a major lie of the enemy—which many Christians have bought into—that what the world offers is better than or at least as good as what the church offers. This attitude, I believe, is identical to that of the church of Laodicea as described in the book of Revelation.

The Legacy of Laodicea: Materialism and Accommodationism

In the contemporary church, as in the church of Laodicea, there is a pervasive focus on materialism and self rather than spirituality and God. Like those in ancient Laodicea, many Christians today (especially in America) are becoming wealthy, self-sufficient, and comfortable with worldly priorities. But they are totally deluded about their true condition:

> "You say, 'I am rich; I have acquired wealth and do not realize that

you are wretched, pitiful, poor, blind, and naked (Revelation 3:17).

Therefore, God says, "I will spit you out of my
mouth" because you are only "lukewarm" Christians (Revelation 3:16); that is to say, worldly Christians heading toward apostasy.

I experienced such an attitude of accommodation
to the world in one of the churches I have attended.
One of the associate pastors described to me his idea
of a church as "a safe place" where one could get "comfortable with God." Thank God the first century Christians did not have such a lukewarm, accomodationist
attitude, or who knows how weak and ineffective the
beginnings of Christianity might have been.

Another associate pastor of the same church gave
his sermons while dressed in old tattered Levis, a
wrinkled Hawaiian flower shirt, and scuffed up hik-
ing boots—so he would look like just one of the
guys. His idea of the purpose of being a Christian
was so you could become "a cool, fun person to hang
out with." He described the church as "a cool place
to hang out with other cool people" and Jesus as a
"cool dude." So his point seemed to be that a church
is a kind of pool hall, disco, or coffee house—with
some "Christian" trimmings. He added that church
is also "a cool place where you can hang out with
God so some of Him can rub off on you."

I believe that he had only the best of reasons for
dressing and speaking as he did: to try to make his
presentation relevant and acceptable to the young,
postmodern seekers present in the congregation. But

let me ask you, which does this "sermon" sound more like, the revelations and truths of the Bible or the pagan attitudes and values of the street?

Actually, this attitude toward the church and God is a lot like that which is behind the hard rock "gospel" concerts mentioned earlier. (See chapter sixteen for a more detailed discussion of "christian" rock music.) It is an attitude, I believe, which implicitly devalues the church both as an institution and as a place of worship and also diminishes the very character of God. Surely, church is more than "a cool place to hang out" and God more than somebody (however cool) to "hang out" with.

The Bible says that the church, rather than a safe, comfortable place to hang out, is ". . . those sanctified in Christ Jesus and called to be holy . . ." (1 Corinthians 1:2). It is not a physical structure at all but, metaphorically, a spiritual structure composed of all true believers,

> . . . built on the foundation of the apostles and prophets with Christ as the chief cornerstone.

> In him the whole building is joined together and rises to become a holy temple in the Lord. And in him you too are being built together to become a dwelling in which God lives by his Spirit (Ephesians 2:20–22).

The Bible also says that God, rather than someone to hang out with so He can rub off on you, is someone whose glory filled the tabernacle (Exodus

40:34) and the temple (2 Chronicles 7:1). As described by Ezekiel, this glory was a

> brilliant light. . . . Like the appearance of a rainbow in the clouds on a rainy day, so was the radiance around him (Ezekiel 1:27–28).

God Himself appeared seated "high above" on a throne of sapphire and

> . . . from what appeared to be his waist up he looked like glowing metal, as if full of fire, and that from there down he looked like fire (Ezekiel 1:26–27).

When God appeared to Haggai, He said,

> "In a little while I will once more shake the heavens and the earth, the sea and the dry land. I will shake all nations, and the desired of all nations will come, and I will fill the house with glory. . . . (Haggai 2:7)

No, this is not somebody to hang out with who can rub off on you. This is God Almighty, Creator, Sustainer, Judge, and King of the universe!

This is someone to be worshipped and glorified and exalted. This attitude is expressed in the book of Revelation, where the worship of the twenty-four elders is described as follows;

> Whenever the living creatures give glory, honor and thanks to him who sits on the throne and who lives forever and ever, the twenty-four el-

ders fall down before him who sits on the throne, and worship him who lives for ever and ever. They lay their crowns before the throne and say:

"You are worthy, our Lord and God, to receive glory and honor and power, for you created all things, and by your will they were created and have their being (Revelation 4:9–11).

This is the image of God and the attitude toward Him that the Bible says we should have, for this is who He really is. A loving Father, yes—but also someone much, much more. A.W. Tozer puts the significance of all this very well:

Worship is pure or base as one entertains high or low thoughts of God . . . we tend, by some secret laws of the soul, to move toward our mental image of God.

. . . An inadequate view of God is actually idolatry . . . to worship anything less than what God has revealed Himself to be is idolatry.[2]

The accomodationist attitude that describes God as someone to hang out with is really an especially insidious seed of apostasy, for it leads us away from the God of the Bible and into an idolatrous and worldly view of Him. This not only demeans God, possibly to the point of blasphemy, but also cuts us off from truly knowing and worshipping Him.

Such accommodation to the world is, of course, a far cry from what the Bible says we should do. Romans 12:2 tells you to

> not conform any longer to the pattern of the world, but be transformed by the renewing of your mind. Then you will be able to test and approve what God's will is—his good, pleasing and perfect will.

To be transformed into what God wants us to be, we must stop conforming to the world and accommodating its values in our churches. *Then* we will be able to discern God's will. *Then* we will be able to grow up into the likeness and fullness of Christ. And *then* those who are truly seeking for something beyond what they find in the world will be drawn into the church. For it will offer, not just more of the same (if a little nicer), but the reality of a *new* life and a transcendent relationship with the true God of the universe.

The Gospel of Success

Another sign of tolerance for humanistic values in the church is the popularity of success/motivation seminars and teachings. As exemplified perhaps most fully in Robert Schuller's "Gospel of Success," this false doctrine is being promoted by ever-increasing numbers of Christian leaders. It is based on the New Age notions of "positive thinking," "positive mental attitude" (PMA), and self-esteem, all of which we have discussed previously. It incorporates "self-improvement psychologies for fully realizing human potential that are seen as scientific aids to successful Christian living."[3]

This idea of fully realized human potential is directly related to the Word of Faith heresy that we are gods. As Wilkerson puts it,

> This perverted gospel seeks to make gods of people. They are told "Your destiny is in the power of your mind. Whatever you can conceive is yours. Speak it into being. Create it by a positive mind set. Success, happiness, perfect health is all yours—if you will only use your mind creatively. Turn your dreams into reality by using mind power."[4]

Schuller makes the idea of self-esteem the center of his new gospel:

> Jesus knew his worth; his success fed his self-esteem . . . He suffered the cross to sanctify his self-esteem. And he bore the cross to sanctify your self-esteem.
>
> And *the cross will sanctify the ego trip!*[5] [Emphasis in the original.]

Sin and, therefore, grace and redemption have no place in Schuller's gospel. He says,

> I don't think anything has been done in the name of Christ and under the banner of Christianity that has proven more destructive to human personality and, hence, counterproductive

to the evangelism enterprise than the often crude, uncouth, and unchristian strategy of attempting to make people aware of their lost and sinful condition.[6]

Hunt characterizes this false gospel as nothing short of *sorcery*, which

is rampant in the business world and enters the church in the form of success/motivation and PMA techniques and the latest psycho-therapies baptized with Christian terminology.[7]

In his book, T*he Gospel of Good Success*, United Methodist pastor, Kirbyjon Caldwell says the purpose of salvation (which he calls "Holistic Salvation") is

to create an internal center of power in your own life . . . The first baby step toward Holistic Salvation is to realize that God wants you to be successful—blessed with a bounty of Good Success![8]

Thus, this false gospel considers salvation to be—not that of the Bible, based on faith in Jesus Christ which brings eternal life in heaven—but humanistic success as defined by the world. Not surprisingly, Caldwell has been trained in Schuller's Institute of Successful Church Leadership for sixteen years and "follows in the footsteps of Schuller and the latter's mentor Norman Vincent Peale."[9]

Easy Grace

Another major way in which the church accommodates the world is the increasingly common attitude of moral laxity and permissiveness. Sexual sin, for example, is rampant in the church, with many unmarried couples living together—sometimes justifying it by financial reasons (several of whom I know of personally). Wilkerson notes that "Multitudes of Christians today watch R-rated videos or surf the Internet indulging in pornography." And, as another example, he adds that "a lust for money—a spirit of covetousness" is common in the church.[10]

At the root of this worldly invasion is a "spirit of lawlessness" (2 Thessalonians 2:7). This has been called the doctrine of "easy grace," which says that grace is a cover for sin. "It's the idea that we can do whatever we please with no fear of consequences."[11]

Wilkerson points out that this is the same spirit that deceived Eve. Satan told her, in effect,

> "God is easy—he won't punish you for disobeying. You can eat the fruit and indulge your lust. You won't have to pay for it."[12]

A related form of tolerance for sin is the acceptance of homosexual marriages and clergy by several mainline denominations—even though homosexuality is specifically condemned in scripture. For example, Romans 1:24–27 says that because of idolatry, God gave pagan people over to "sexual impurity" and "shameful lusts":

Even their women exchanged natural relations for unnatural ones. In the same way the men also abandoned natural relations with women and were inflamed with lust for one another. Men committed indecent acts with other men, and received in themselves the due penalty for their perversion.

And 1 Corinthians 6:9–10 declares that those who commit such acts, along with those involved in other forms of wickedness, will be excluded from God's kingdom:

Do you not know that the wicked will not inherit the kingdom of God. Do not be deceived: Neither the sexually immoral nor idolaters nor adulterers nor male prostitutes nor homosexual offenders nor thieves nor the greedy nor drunkards nor slanderers nor swindlers will inherit the kingdom of God.

This concept of easy grace is sometimes justified by such scriptures as Galatians 5:1, "It is for freedom that Christ has set us free," and Romans 5:20, "The law was added so that the trespass might increase. But where sin increased, grace increased all the more. . . ."

Such misuse of scripture is easily refuted. In both these verses, the context is ignored.

The context of Galatians 5:1 is the contrast between the Old Covenant and the New Covenant represented by Hagar and Sarah respectively (Galatians 4:21–31). The Old Covenant is characterized as *slavery* and the New Covenant as *freedom*. Verse 31 makes the point clear: "Therefore, brothers, we are not children of the slave woman, but of the free woman." Paul is addressing the Judaizers who wanted "to be under the Law" (Galatians 4:21).

The second part of Galatians 5:1 reiterates this idea: "Stand firm, then, and do not let yourselves be burdened again by a yoke of slavery." Therefore, the verse in question is not about the idea that grace covers all our sins and therefore we are "free" to sin. It is about not returning to the bondage of the Old Covenant.

Furthermore, the freedom which is spoken of is not the freedom *to* sin but the freedom *from* sin which we have in Christ. It is the freedom not to be controlled by the sinful nature but to be able to serve and love one another. Verse 13 states this explicitly:

> You, my brothers were called to be free. But do not use your freedom to indulge the sinful nature; rather serve one another in love.

Likewise, Romans 5:20 is not about easy grace, which overlooks sin, but about the real grace of God which enables us to live righteously without sin. Verses 17–19 make this clear:

> For if, by the trespass of the one man, death reigned through that one man, how much more will those who receive *God's abundant provision of grace and the gift of righteousness* reign in life through the one man Jesus Christ.

Consequently, just as the result of one trespass was condemnation for all men, so also the result of one act of righteousness was justification that brings life for all men. For just as through the disobedience of the one man the many were made sinners, so also through the obedience of the one man *many will be made righteous.* [Emphasis added.]

Again, the idea that grace does not give us the freedom to sin is made explicit:

What shall we say, then? Shall we go on sinning so that grace may increase? By no means! We died to sin; how can we live in it any longer? (Romans 6:1–20)

Wilkerson lays out the spiritual results of the easy grace heresy:

1. The heart becomes hardened by the deceitfulness of sin.
2. Satan works on the hardened heart to justify itself, so that it's relieved from fear of penalty.
3. When God sees there is no possibility that this heart will receive and obey truth, He turns the person over to satanic delusion.
4. The believer becomes blinded by the lie that says there are no wages for sin and no judgment day, and that he can get away with his lustful pleasure.
5. The believer falls prey to doctrines of demons, thinking evil is good and good is evil.

6. He (in the end times context) eventually drifts so far from Christ and the truth, he becomes blinded to who the antichrist is—and ends up worshipping and serving him as a god.
7. On judgment day, God will say to such a person, "Depart from me, you worker of iniquity!"[13]

Thus, the permissive, humanistic attitude that says "a little sin is okay, so don't worry about it" is a deadly seed of apostasy that can lead ultimately to damnation. On the contrary, what is needed is a healthy fear of the Lord (together with a steadfast love for Him) that motivates us to obey Him and reject sin. Unfortunately, the church has failed in this regard. Many Christians have never heard a sermon or received any teaching on *the fear of God*. Consequently, the need for obedience, righteousness, and holiness has never taken root in their hearts. And the admonitions of Proverbs go unheeded:

> Do not be wise in your own eyes; *fear the Lord* and shun evil (Proverbs 3:7).

> *The fear of the Lord* is a fountain of life, turning a man from the snares of death (Proverbs 14:22).

> By love and faithfulness sin is atoned for. Through *the fear of the Lord* a man avoids evil (Proverbs 16:6). (Emphasis added in all of the above.)

The kind of fear referred to is not cowering terror or dread of injury or punishment, but a positive, holy, reverential awe and respect. Wilkerson explains what this means in practical terms:

> So, what exactly does it mean to walk in the fear of the Lord? It means reminding yourself of his warnings. And it means allowing the Spirit to load up conviction in your heart, bring your sins out into the open, and cast them far away from you. In doing this He's [the Holy Spirit is] laying the foundation to fulfill every one of God's covenant promises to you.
>
> Then, when the fear of God has fully laid hold of you, you'll dread the danger and consequences of sin. And you'll walk every day in this holy fear. Finally, you'll see that all along God has been mercifully at work in you, doing what He promised—delivering you from the dominion and slavery of sin.[14]

I would add, it also means totally rejecting the humanistic spirit and practice of accommodationism in our churches.

Wilkerson summarizes the issue:

> I'm convinced that without the fear of God, we cannot experience lasting deliverance from sin. Yet, in many churches the fear of the Lord has become a taboo subject. When was the last time you heard a sermon preached on the fear of God?

One reason for this is that society's permissiveness has invaded God's house. In recent years, the term "grace" has come to mean a cover for sin. As the psalmist writes, "There is no fear of God before [their] eyes" (36:1).[15]

UNITY: COMPROMISING THE TRUTH

In 2001, the Dalai Lama, the leader of Tibetan Buddhism, spoke from the pulpit of the Reformed Church in Geneva, Switzerland, where John Calvin once preached. He was welcomed by William McComish, general secretary of the World Alliance of Reformed Churches, who called him "His Holiness," and praised his "spirituality," declaring that Calvin's church was "becoming a home for a new religious centre to experience understanding between the world's major faiths."[16] This event is an example of the movement toward unity with other religions now prevalent in the church.

Among a number of Christian leaders and their followers, such misguided promotion of unity, both within and outside of the body of Christ, has become more important than the promotion of truth. Based on the New Age concept of "openness," it is a pseudo-broad-mindedness that says every viewpoint should be embraced for the sake of harmony. The problem is that, in rejecting nothing, no distinctions are made between truth and falsehood, right and wrong, good and evil, scriptural and unscriptural, or godly and ungodly.

Hunt calls this "absolute intolerance that poses as tolerance." It is found, he says,

> in the well-known aphorism, most often used in reference to religion, "We're all taking different roads to get to the same place." While that declaration sounds broad-minded to a fault, it clearly represents the ultimate in narrow-mindedness. Although "different roads" are generously tolerated, they are not allowed to lead to different places, for everyone, no matter what road they take, must go to the *same* place. So this seemingly broad-minded ideal of "all taking different roads" allows for only one destination.[17]

This humanistic heresy is based primarily on the idea, which we examined earlier, that truth is relative, depending on our individual, subjective experience. But there are also two other teachings that we need to examine here. Both involve compromising the truth in the name of tolerance for the sake of unity. These heresies from humanism are (1) *that there should be no "negative" teaching* and (2) *that all religious views are equally valid* (a.k.a. ecumenicalism).

"No Negative Teaching"

The first of these ideas says that false teaching should not be judged and doctrinal error should not be corrected because it might cause division. Rather, we must practice the "positive thinking" and "positive mental attitude" espoused, for example, by Robert Schuller. But Hunt points out how anti-scriptural this view really is:

> Schuller, who claims to deal in the same common denominators of all religions, has castigated preachers "who spew forth their angry, hate-filled sermons of fire and brimstone." Yet Jesus spoke often and firmly about hell, warning mankind without apology and in what Peale and Schuller would call "negative terms." . . . In a newspaper column . . . Schuller said, "We can tell the good religion from the bad religion by whether it is 'positive.'" He called upon "religious leaders . . . whatever their theology . . . to articulate their faith in positive terms." He then called for a "massive, united effort by leaders of *all* religions" to proclaim "the positive power . . . of *world-community-building* religious values." Antichrist could hardly say it better![18] [Emphasis added.]

Similarly, Leighton Ford has admonished,

> Preach the gospel but don't be so negative as to refuse to *endorse* or work with those who belong to a group that proclaims *a different gospel*.[19] [Emphasis added.]

To support their view that no false teachings, including other religions, should be judged, the advocates of humanistic unity cite Matthew 7:1: "Do not judge, or you too will be judged." They say that this means other religious teachings and practices should not be put to the test. However, as we saw earlier, this ignores the context and re-lated scripture. The verse in question is not about evaluating divergent *teachings or practices*, but about condemning *people*. Obviously, this twisting of scripture also involves shifting the meaning of *judging* from "condemning" to "exposing error." And, as we have seen, the Bible says in several places that we must test such teachings to see if they are true—and not accept any other gospel.

H. A. Ironside summarizes the issue beautifully:

> Objection is often raised—even by some sound in the faith—regarding exposure of error as being entirely negative and of no real edification. Of late, the hue and cry has been against any and all nega-tive teaching. But the brethren who assume this attitude forget that a large part of the New Testa-ment, both of the teaching of our blessed Lord him-self and the writings of the apostles, is made up of this very character of ministry—namely, showing the satanic origin and, therefore, the unsettling results of the propagation of erroneous systems which Peter, in his second epistle, definitely refers to as "damnable heresies."[20]

No, the Bible says unity with those who are in error is *not* more important than truth. As noted earlier, error needs to be recognized, condemned, and corrected, whether people like it or not. And the truth needs to be proclaimed regardless of what "positive thinkers" think. We should not compro-mise the truth of God's Word, but we should reject everything that substitutes for, waters down, or distorts that truth.

The Bible says, "Buy the truth and do not sell it" (Proverbs 23:23). This means that truth should be our priority and that we should not exchange (sell) it for anything else—such as "unity." And Jesus said, "But whoever lives by the truth comes into the light, so that it may be seen plainly that what he has done has been done through God (John 2:21). This verse shows that God wants His works to be seen and that this requires that we not compromise the truth but *live by it*.

Paul reinforces this idea of uncompromising adherence to the truth: "For we cannot do anything against the truth, but only for the truth" (2 Corinthians: 13:8). And, finally, John tells us that Jesus Himself is the truth, "the true light, that gives light to every man . . ." (John 1:9) and that we are to "walk in the light as he is in the light . . ." (1 John 1:7). This means we are to walk in the truth of God just as Jesus did.

Ecumenicalism and Postmodernism: "All Religious Views Are Equal"

The second of these false ideas about tolerance is the essence of ecumenicalism. It says that all religions contain the same basic truths and are therefore equally valid. However, as Hanegraaff points out,

> . . . sound reasoning tells us that all religions are not essentially the same merely because they contain some similarities [hasty generaliza-

tion]. A brief survey of a few religions quickly reveals that each has competing, mutually exclusive claims. How, for example, can someone logically square the Hindu teaching that the universe is God with the Muslim belief that Allah, the God of Islam, is distinct from the universe? Thus, religions harbor irreconcilable differences, demonstrating that they cannot possibly lead to the same God.[21]

The ecumenical view that all religions are equally valid is an expression of *postmodernism,* which rejects the idea that any universal truth or truths exist (or can be known). It says there is no objective, independent, verifiable reality. There are only the perspectives of individuals or groups. Therefore, since there are no absolutes, all viewpoints are equally valid and, therefore, all religions are equally true.

This view, which comes straight out of the New Age Movement and its call for a one-world religion, is already well established within the liberal Protestant church. Actually, the framework for such a religion is already in place. Introduced in June 1997, it is called the United Religions Organization (UR). By June 2005, this one-world "church" plans to be fully operational. Among its chief supporters are Bishop William Swing of the Episcopal Diocese of California and Episcopal Archbishop Desmond Tutu. Its purpose is "to be the religious counterpart to the United Nations" which "will nurture peace."[22]

In addition, in recent years, a number of ecumenical conferences have been sponsored by Christian leaders. For example, in 1986, Pope John Paul II, convened a conference attended by 130 religious leaders, including "Muslims, Buddhists, Hindus, pantheists, the Dalai Lama, and a host of others who reject Jesus Christ."[23] In 1993, the Parliament of World Religions was held in Chicago with

> "Buddhists, Hindus, Muslims, snake worshippers, spiritists, animists, witches, shamans, Protestants and Catholics honoring each others' religions." It was cosponsored by the Roman Catholic Archdiocese of Chicago, Chicago's Lutheran School of Theology, the Evangelical Church in America, Presbyterian Church (USA), United Church of Christ, and with an official Vatican representative present.[24]

In 1999, another meeting of the Parliament of World Religions was held in Capetown, South Africa. Archbishop Tutu, an attendee, reported that, at this meeting,

> . . . all kinds of faiths [were] represented . . . there are different ways of . . . discovering the transcendent, that God is a great deal larger than all of our faiths.[25]

In an interview with Larry King in 1999, Tutu demonstrated his ecumenical "tolerance" by supporting Mormonism as "soundly Christian and . . . expressed enthusiastic anticipation of an inevitable agreement among all religions."[26]

Robert Schuller, who was also a guest on the program, joined Tutu in this sentiment. Schuller also praised Islam and the Grand Mufti of the Mosque in Damascus, saying, "I have seldom met with a man [with] whom I felt an immediate kinship of spirit and an agreement of faith and philosophy quite like I have with the Grand Mufti of the faith."[27]

Schuller summarized the essence of the ecumenical spirit by adding, ". . . we have lost humility . . . we religious leaders [must] begin to say, 'I'm . . . not trying to convert other religious people to my viewpoint."[28]

Of course, this is exactly the opposite of what the Bible says:

> Therefore go and make disciples of all nations, baptizing them in the name of the Father and of the Son and of the Holy Spirit, and teaching them to obey everything I have commanded you (Matthew 28:19–20).

To carry out this great commission is not to exhibit a lack of humility! On the contrary, it is to show true humility by submitting to the will of God and obeying His commandment.

In promoting his ecumenical view, Schuller is also directly helping to prepare for the coming one-world religion of the antichrist. He does this in terms of "positive thinking." Hunt describes this process and its significance:

> This counterfeit broad-mindedness with its con-
> tempt for truth is carried to the masses by today's
> most popular televangelist, Robert Schuller . . .
>
> The fact that the theologies of Hinduism, Bud-
> dhism, Islam, Catholicism, and evangelicalism
> contradict one another on vital points is appar-
> ently nothing to be concerned about so long as
> each is presented "in positive terms." All reli-
> gions, Schuller seems to think, represent equally
> valid "world-community-building religious val-
> ues." Antichrist himself couldn't improve on that
> New Age double-talk![29]

Schuller also reveals his anti-biblical ecumenicalism in his support of Sir John Marks Templeton, founder of the Templeton Prize for Progress in Religion and a leading promoter of ecumenicalism among all religions. Hunt reports that Schuller put Templeton's picture on the front cover of his *Possibilities* magazine,

> and its major article was an interview with
> Templeton. In it he [Templeton] expressed his
> Unity/Religious Science/New Age beliefs: "Your
> spiritual principles attract prosperity to you.
> Material success . . . comes . . . from being in
> tune with the infinite . . . The Christ spirit dwells
> in every human being whether the person knows
> it or not . . . nothing exists except God." These
> heresies were promoted by Schuller to his vast
> audience of readers.[30]

Templeton believes in evolution, pantheism, and occultism. He rejects the scriptural God and Christ as Savior, and claims that Christianity is irrelevant. In spite of all this, he is highly acclaimed by leading evangelicals and was on the boards of Princeton Theological Seminary and the American Bible Society. Norman Vincent Peale called him, "the greatest layman of the Christian church in our time."[31]

Hunt states (without presenting direct evidence) that Templeton has also been praised by Chuck Colson, Billy Graham, and Bill Bright.[32] Since I have no reason to doubt Hunt's accuracy, I will assume he is correct. But let me make it clear that I have the greatest respect for each of these men and for their ministries. At the same time, we need to remember that they *are* men and therefore imperfect like the rest of us. I do not think these evangelical leaders believe the same things Templeton does. But I do think their reported praise of Templeton (if true) would show a lack of discernment which indirectly (and presumably inadvertently) compromises the truth of the Bible for the sake of "unity."

The fact that all three of these leaders have accepted the Templeton Prize for their contributions to "Progress in Religion" also suggests a tacit willingness to compromise, for this award promotes *all* religions as equally valid. Hunt makes the issue clear:

> Graham, Colson, and Bright should rather have rejected his prize and presented the gospel to this deluded man in an attempt to rescue him from a Christless eternity. And what of the multitudes

led astray by the acceptance of this prize and the commendation of it and Templeton?[33]

I am sorry to say that this same kind of compromise is also demonstrated in Pat Robertson's Christian Coalition. Robertson (for whom I also have the greatest respect) calls all who belong to his group "people of faith," tacitly expressing approval of their "religious values," even though they include Mormons, Moonies, and followers of other religions. He says all these people of faith must stand together because they "are under attack as never before."[34]

However, as Hunt points out,

Coalition members hold many faiths whose "religious values" . . . are totally incompatible. It is deceitful to speak of "people of faith" standing together, when to do so individual faith must be abandoned. Nor is it honest to call an organization which includes those of other religions "The *Christian* Coalition."[35] [Emphasis in original.]

The undiscerning attitude of tolerance exhibited in all of the above examples is, I believe, nothing short of what the Bible calls spiritual "adultery" (Hosea 1:2) and "a spirit of prostitution" (Hosea 4:12)—the mixing together of ungodly elements from pagan religions with the true religion of the Bible. In the Old Testament, this "adultery" and "prostitution" consisted of involvement by the ancient Israelites in Canaanite religious practices, including Baal worship, making sacrifices at "high places," and worshipping a calf image.

While the promoters of ecumenicalism may not have embraced false religions as fully as the Israelites, they are nevertheless, at least implicitly, giving them their approval and participating in their non-Christian forms of prayer. This can be seen clearly in a report by the Associated Press of a gathering for prayer attended by Protestant Christians and hosted by Pope John Paul II in 1986:

> Chants, temple bells and pagan spells echoed around the Roman Catholic shrine of Assisi yesterday, as Pope John Paul II and his 200 guests from the world's 12 main religions prayed for world peace. . . .

> The medicine man of the Crow Indians, Chief John Pretty-on-top, offered to cast out evil spirits. Many came forward, among them a young Franciscan monk.

> In a chapel down the road the head of the Zoroastrian church in Bombay prayed before a fire that symbolized his God. . . .

> The 14th Dalai Lama, exiled god-king of Tibet, headed the strong Buddhist contingent, mumbling sutras amid tinkling bells at the Basilica of St. Peter. . . .

African animists, their togas the envy of any designer, invoked the spirits of trees and plants to come to the aid of peace . . . .[36]

Also in attendance were

snake worshippers, fire worshippers, spiritists, Hindus, Muslims, . . . shamans, . . . representatives of the World Council of Churches, . . . evangelicals, . . . the YWCA and YMCA, the Mennonite World Conference, the Baptist World Alliance (which includes the Southern Baptist Conventions), the World Alliance of Reformed Churches, and the Lutheran World Federation.[37]

But the Bible has this to say about being united with followers of false religions:

Do not be yoked together with unbelievers. For what do righteousness and wickedness have in common? Or what fellowship can light have with darkness? What harmony is there between Christ and Belial? What does a believer have in common with an unbeliever? What agreement is there between the temple of God and idols? For we are the temple of the living God. As God has said: "I will live with them and walk among them, and I will be their God, and they will be my people."

"Therefore come out from them and be separate, says the Lord. Touch no unclean thing, and I will receive you" (2 Corinthians 6:14–17).

A DIMINISHED CHRIST: "JESUS WAS JUST A MAN"

The New Age idea that all religions are equally valid leads directly to the conclusions that Christianity is the invention of man and that Jesus Christ Himself was just a man. For, if Christianity is no better or truer than any other religion, then its claim that the Bible is the exclusive, divinely revealed Word of God cannot be true. And the idea that Jesus is the incarnation of the one true God must be equally false.

The denial of Christ's divinity is vitally important to Satan's plan of deception because, without any Son as Savior of the world, all kinds of substitutes become available as options. If Jesus was just another man, then His way is just another option. And, if I can do what Jesus did by my own innate abilities (at least on a psychic level), then the source of salvation becomes myself and not God. This leads into the following possible scenarios for why I don't need Jesus as the Son of God:

1. I am god.
2. God is an impersonal force which I can tap into, use, and manipulate.
3. God is everything and, therefore, I am part of God and partake of divinity.
4. God is everything and God is good; so evil and sin do not exist. Therefore, Satan and demons do not exit. (This view, of course, is a major advantage to Satan because it gives him free rein in the lives of people who are unaware that he is the enemy and the cause of many of their problems.)

5. Jesus evolved into the Christ and so can we. This involves the redefinition of "Christ" as "the *principle* of divine sonship."

The false doctrine that the Bible cannot be taken as literal truth and therefore Jesus cannot be God, is espoused by a number of liberal "christian" theologians and their followers. For example, Episcopal Bishop John Shelby Spong teaches this heresy in *Why Christianity Must Change or Die*. In this book, he also presents the following related false teachings:

- the resurrection of Christ was not a real event but a legend
- there was no empty tomb and no angels or appearances [of Jesus after His death]
- no reasonable person could believe in the literal interpretation of the Bible
- the virgin birth of a literal Bible . . . "will have to go"
- the church should actively endorse and even celebrate homosexual behavior, as well as heterosexual liaisons outside of marriage[38]

Such denial of biblical truth by humanistic seminary professors has also led directly to the "God is dead" movement and to the "social gospel," which has no spiritual message for mankind or the church, but only a religion of works.

All of the above heresies are promoted by a number of "liberal ministers of many mainline denominations and leaders of the liberal National Council of Churches."[39]

Probably the most flagrant promoters of false doctrine among these liberal "christians" are those associated with the Jesus Seminar. This is a group of scriptural revisionists who attack basic biblical doctrines. They claim to be Christians, but argue that the New Testament isn't accurate, so we cannot be sure of anything about Christ. Hunt notes rightly that for anyone with such beliefs to call himself "christian"

> is both fraud and folly. How can one be an obedient follower of someone about whom no accurate record exists of who He was, what He did or what He taught?[40]

Hunt goes on to identify some of the other heresies of the Jesus Seminar:

> If these scholars believe in a god at all, he can't do miracles. So the Red Sea couldn't possibly have opened for the Israelites to cross on dry ground; the walls of Jericho couldn't have fallen down as described by Joshua, who was there and saw it; Jesus couldn't have literally walked on water, healed the sick, raised the dead, fed 5,000 with a few loaves and fishes, died for our sins or risen from the dead (there must be another explanation for the empty tomb). Such unbelief is broadcast to the world as fact, while those who could prove the Bible to be true are rarely allowed to make their case.

> As a result, millions believe that the Bible is a
> collection of myths . . . .[41]

An example of such broadcasting of humanistic heresy in the name of Christianity was the TV special by Peter Jennings titled "The Search for Jesus" which was aired on ABC on June 26, 2000. The "biblical scholars" Jennings assembled for his broadcast were mostly members of the Jesus Seminar, including John Dominic Crossan, the co-founder of that organization.

On the broadcast, these scholars gave the impression that no intelligent person could possibly take any of the Bible literally. Rather, they presented the gospel (as Crossan put it) as "a metaphorical story, not an historical story." Crossan explained that the early Christians "would not let His [Christ's] death end His movement . . . but insisted [falsely] that God had vindicated Jesus by raising Him from the dead."[42]

Another liberal, humanistic organization which claims residence within the church is the American Bible Society. This group recently published an article in its magazine *The Record* entitled "Adam and Eve in the Garden of Truth." This article declares that the story of Adam and Eve is a myth and that "Genesis offers no hint that the narrative of Adam and Eve in the Garden of Eden was intended literally as a 'true' story . . . [but] it should be understood figuratively as a 'truth' story."[43]

In answer to this declaration, Hunt says,

> Adam is mentioned about 30 times in 10 books
> of the Bible. Nowhere is there the slightest sug-
> gestion that what is stated about him is not lit-

erally true [**ignoring related scripture**]. If death was here before Adam (through evolution, etc.) and was not the direct result of his sin and God's judgment upon it (as the Bible clearly states), then the gospel is not true. As soon as one begins to "adjust" Genesis to accommodate science (as has been done, for example, by *Christianity Today,* by Hugh Ross, a popular guest of James Dobson, and by Billy Graham, Promise Keepers, and others who accept theistic evolution), the Bible ceases to be God's authoritative Word.

That the American Bible Society should reject the literal accuracy of part of the Bible is not surprising. Sir John Marks Templeton . . ., a rank unbeliever, occultist and anti-Christian, was on its Board of Managers for 15 years. That fact may say more about the leadership of that Society than the quoted article.[44]

Since the Bible supposedly cannot be trusted and its revelations have been discredited or reduced to outmoded myths, new myths are needed, according to humanistic, liberal theologians. Therefore, as Hunt notes, new myths are being created for the church:

Prestigious symposiums, carried over radio and TV and reported in the press, explore new myths about God and Christ for modern man. . . . A new myth which everyone could accept could form the basis for a new world religion unifying the world—something Jesus did not attempt to do. He came "not to give peace on earth . . . but rather division" (Luke 12:51).

> The world however, wants a man who will bring peace and unity. Who could accomplish that but the Antichrist, as the Bible foretells? . . . These scholarly conferences and TV specials only help to prepare the world for that man of wickedness.[45]

In this chapter, we have seen that, as part of the New Age conspiracy discussed in chapter eight, the humanistic spirit has invaded Christendom and is alive and well in the church. It has promoted an undiscerning kind of tolerance that fosters accommodation of worldly values and focus on self and personal enhancement rather than on God and biblical truth. It has applied such tolerance to the idea of unity in a way that compromises truth, diminishes Christianity, and requires the acceptance of all religions as equally valid. Worst of all, I believe, it has diminished Christ by reducing Him from God the Son—the Creator, Savior, and Lord of all—to just another man who started just another religion. The overall result of all these heresies is a church that is so lukewarm it is in danger of being spit out by the God it supposedly serves.

What then is needed to turn the self-serving, apathetic Twenty-first Century Church of Laodicea back into the God-serving, vibrant First Century Church of Jerusalem? I believe it will take a new vision of radically transformed lives and miracle-working Holy Spirit power together with a new spirit of holy fear, self-sacrifice, unconditional love, genuine spiritual unity, and discernment of what is true, good, and important in God's eyes and what is not.

CHAPTER FIFTEEN

Infiltration by Eastern Religions

As we have seen in several previous chapters, eastern religions have impacted the church through a number of New Age concepts and practices, including pantheism, reincarnation, self-deification, and meditation as a means to altered states of consciousness and personal enlightenment. However, there are three other major influences from Eastern religions which are also alive and well among Christians:

Yoga (from Hinduism),
Tai Chi (from Taoism), and
Martial Arts (from both).

These topics do not directly illustrate Satan's tricks and strategies nor involve false teachings based on scripture twisting. But they are potential seeds of apostasy of which Christians need to be aware.

459

In common with the religions from which they spring, these three practices share the goals of controlling universal energy (prana or chi), developing psychic powers, and attaining personal transcendence (i.e., attaining supernormal levels of power and awareness). The concept of a universal energy or life force that can be activated in the body and controlled by special exercises and meditative techniques is found in a number of esoteric traditions. These practices have a long history in India, China, Japan, Korea, and Hawaii.[1]

The basic techniques of yoga meditation, for example, are common to most, if not all, esoteric schools (including the one to which I belonged). They teach that, by means of controlled breathing, focused attention, "creative" visualization, and other occult practices, altered states of consciousness are experienced, psychic powers are activated, and self-realization is attained. When practiced by Christians, these things may become substitutes for the gifts and transforming power of the Holy Spirit. They are therefore major seeds of apostasy which must be discerned and rejected.

YOGA: THE YOKE OF DECEPTION

Among the nine generally recognized forms of yoga, the one which is most practiced by far among Christians is hatha. This is commonly thought of as an innocent form of exercise for enhancing physical health. However, it is in fact a preparation for Eastern meditation and the more advanced forms of yoga.

The ultimate goal of *all* yoga forms is union with the cosmos or universe. The word "yoga" literally means "union" and is etymologically related to the English "yoke."

I personally know two Christians who actively practice hatha yoga, one as an instructor. Neither had any idea that there was anything un-christian about their involvement.

And when I warned them about its dangers, both seemed unwilling to discontinue its practice—because of the "health benefits" they would be giving up.

The Goal of Yoga

As indicated above, the ultimate goal of yoga is to yoke the individual spirit with the universal spirit in an ecstatic state of enlightenment called *samadhi*. What Christians who practice yoga do not realize is that this "universal spirit" is the pantheistic god of Hinduism and that this whole process and experience of "enlightenment" is a satanic deception.

Teachers of yoga call it "an effective tool of transformation"[2]; "a way to bring balance to a person's whole being: physically, mentally, emotionally, and spiritually"[3]; "a process in which you continually allow yourself to unfold . . . to experience 'being' rather than doing or having"[4]; finding "the *Atman*, which is pure consciousness" and absorption into the "Cosmic Being"[5]; and "psycho-physical well-being . . . even if you remain agnostic or skeptical towards the whole mystic concept."[6]

462   The Spiritual Discernment Guide

Transformation, balance, unfolding, well-being—these are powerful appeals to those seeking self-fulfillment. So it is not surprising if sincere but naive Christians are strongly attracted by the "benefits" of what is commonly called yoga. Actually, what most of them become involved in is merely the elementary level of a hierarchy of occult techniques.

The nine basic branches of yoga as defined by advanced yoga practitioners (more or less in ascending order) are as follows:

1. Hatha—union by bodily mastery through exercises, postures, and breath control for developing power, strength, and harmony.
2. Mantra—union by voice and sound for developing centered or focused consciousness.
3. Yantra—union by vision and form for developing expanded attention and awareness.
4. Karma—union by action and service for developing selflessness.
5. Bhakti—union by love and devotion for developing the heart (positive emotions).
6. Jnana—union by knowledge, intellect, and scholarship for developing the mind and wisdom.
7. Tantric—union by physiological disciplines and ritual for harnessing sexual energy and developing consecrated (sacred, holy, and reverential) sexuality.
8. Kundalini—union by arousal of latent nerve-force for developing psychic abilities.

9. Raja—union by meditation for developing mental mastery leading to final liberation, ecstasy, and enlightenment.

In the cult to which I belonged, we practiced a combination of various aspects of hatha, mantra, jnana, kundalini, and raja yoga; and I have listed these and the other forms above to show that yoga is much more than a harmless form of exercise. However, here we will look briefly only at hatha since it is the only kind most Christians are aware of or might be involved in.

Nevertheless, it is important to realize that involvement in any of the other forms would be an equally heretical and spiritually dangerous practice.

Hatha Yoga: Preparation for "Transformation"

As indicated above, the purpose of hatha yoga is to prepare the body and mind for meditation. It has been called "a powerful method of self-transformation" and a "preparation for all other yogas."[7] More specifically, it is a "purifying" process which prepares one ultimately for raja yoga, which is "work upon consciousness itself."[8]

The word *hatha* comes from *ha*, meaning "sun," and *tha*, meaning "moon." Thus, it involves the union and harmonizing of opposites—the active and passive forces of the cosmos. Additionally, *hath* (literally translated) means "force," "power," or "effort." Thus, it is "the yoga that develops strength and determination in order to unify the body and mind."[9]

This goal is accomplished by tapping into the higher energy supposedly latent in the body—the vital life-force called *prana*. You will recall that prana (the Hindu term) is the same as chi (the Taoist term). Accessing this energy is accomplished through the techniques of *pranayama* (breath control). Pranayama is said to prepare the mind in three successive stages: "concentration (dharana), contemplation (dhyana), and self-realization (samadhi), which are the final three stages of meditation (samyama).[10]

The significance of pranayama has been explained as follows:

> The breath represents much more than the oxygen we take into our lungs. . . . *Ayama* means extension. *Prana* has several connotations—breath, respiration, life, vitality, wind, energy, strength, spirit, and soul. By acknowledging all of these meanings, we are dealing with much more than oxygen when we "extend the breath." . . . pranayama also represents a subtle, energetic level of awareness. . . . as in asana (posture) practice, a yogi may articulate the breath to create specific results: Emphasis placed on inhalation will generally create a stimulating or energizing effect on the system; when a more passive relaxed state is desired, exhalation is usually emphasized.[11]

The effect of this practice is to bring

> . . . the systems and organs of the body into balance [which] has a profound influence on the psyche as well. This acknowledgment is based

on the mind-body premise that emotional sta-
bility and calmness of mind reflect balance
brought about in the physical body.[12]

When practiced according to its true nature, as
described above, hatha yoga is said to produce supernormal abilities, including incredible feats of
strength and control over normally automatic and
unconscious bodily functions (such as heart beat,
blood pressure, brain waves, temperature, nerve impulses, etc.). The result is the ability to withstand
extreme heat, cold, and pain, and even (according to
some authorities) to levitate, walk on water, and fly.[13]

Thus, it is clear that hatha yoga is far more than
just an innocent system of exercises and postures
for the improvement of physical health. It is, in fact,
a system of occult techniques for utilizing cosmic
energy which leads to altered states of consciousness, and, supposedly, self-transcendence, and union
with the universe—all of which are satanic delusions and all without the aid of faith in Christ, the
power of the Holy Spirit, or the grace of God.

Does this sound like something Christians
should be involved in? The answer, obviously, is a
resounding "No!" Yoga in *any* form is a substitute
for Christianity, and its practice by Christians can
be a deadly seed of apostasy.

TAI CHI: INTERNAL ALCHEMY

Tai chi is a system of external and internal exercises designed to "bring total control, harmony and

awareness to the mind and body."[14] As such, it has much in common with yoga and the same basic purposes: harmonizing mind and body, personal fulfillment, enlightenment, oneness with the universe, etc. Like yoga, it appears on the surface to be simply a system of physical exercises (in this case, slow, graceful movements) which will enhance one's health and general well-being.

Thus, Christians who become involved in tai chi probably believe they are doing something positive for themselves which does not conflict with the teachings of their faith.

However, like yoga, this system of occult techniques goes far beyond its innocent facade of healthful physical movements. It has been described as "a way to elevate the human body and spirit to the ultimate level, . . . the ultimate art of life,"[15] "internal alchemy or transformation of energy," "a mixture of Taoist and Shaolin [a Chinese esoteric school] influences," and "a growing intimacy with the workings of nature and of the universe itself."[16]

As with all such esoteric, occult systems, the principles of tai chi came to its founder in an altered state of consciousness. This person was Chang San-feng, who also founded a Taoist school. "A heavenly presence" came to him in a dream, giving him the methods of chi kung, which means "the cultivation of chi." This was a system of exercises in visualization and mental concentration, which in turn was based on the *Tao Ti Ching*, the classic treatise translated into English as *The Way and the Power.*[17] This work is also related to the *I Ching,* a book of divination designed to show how immortality can be achieved.[18] Chi kung is also said to be a religious way

> performed not merely to prolong life and bring health but to utilize chi to bring about a new form of experience, to realize an inherent potential for further development, and to assist the internal coordination necessary for this development.[19]

Tai chi, meaning "the supreme ultimate way of chi," was developed from chi kung and incorporates its principles. These principles include the following:

- The interplay of yin and yang. That is, the dark, passive, yielding force of the universe and the light, active, aggressive force.
- "Internal balancing of chi, leading to a different outlook, even moments of enlightenment."
- The relativity of truth, meaning there are no absolutes and one can therefore have no fixed position or opinion about anything.
- Submitting to change.
- Visualization.
- Internal alchemy. That is, the transformation of energy to attain greater consciousness and power.[20]

It is interesting that this notion of inner alchemy is taught not only in the Taoist school but also in some schools of yoga, Tibetan Buddhism, and Sufism. "Comparisons have also been made between the Eastern system and the schools of early European alchemy."[21] The book *In Search of the Miraculous* by P. D. Ouspensky is a modern exposition of this idea. (This is the primary textbook used in the Gurdjieff cult, which is an esoteric school, to which I belonged.)

Preparation for "Enlightenment"

Tai chi, then, is a system of exercises, the basic purpose of which is to accomplish the goals of chi kung. This means tai chi is a preparation for enlightenment because, as one of its teachers says, "it tends to leave the interfering mind and habits of a lifetime behind and introduces something more real, more immediate."[22] Or, to say it another way, the ultimate goal is becoming "one with the universe, beginning with "trying to be at one with one's own body in motion."[23]

The basic techniques involved are breath control, self-observation, conscious movements, and relaxation (the same basic techniques used in the Gurdjieff school). These techniques are said to have been derived from martial arts, such as kung fu, as well as Taoist meditation and Chinese medical knowledge.[24] By these means, you "yield yourself to the forces of the universe" and "you soon will be part of the entire universe."[25]

The result of this process is, supposedly, the transformation of chi into an internal high frequency vibration or power called "jing" that can be directed outside the body by the mind.[26] Such power is said to enable one to become like an eagle that "can swoop instantly to pluck a rabbit from the ground."[27] When you get to this level, "you will flow as the universe flows, move as the universe moves."[28] In this state, "Your mind should be centered like the placid cat—peaceful, but able to respond instantly to the scurrying mouse."[29]

These images suggest the aggressive abilities which martial arts masters are said to attain. And, indeed, there is a martial arts form of tai chi called tai chi chuan, "the supreme ultimate way of the fist," which is based on the development of jing.

Thus, once more, we find what appears to be merely a healthful form of exercise is in reality a demonically inspired system based on eastern religious ideas and occult techniques. Again, let me ask: is this something that members of the body of Christ should be involved in?

MARTIAL ARTS: DEVELOPMENT OF THE LIFE FORCE

New Age writer James Redfield has defined the connection between martial arts and eastern religions. He says we are usually cut off from a relationship with the higher levels of chi, which bring the transcendent experiences of expanded consciousness and oneness with the universe. Martial arts, he explains, are designed to awaken this relationship,[30] and they conceive these experiences in terms of cultivating a higher degree of spiritual energy and using it in the act of movement and feats of strength. Through repeated motion and attention, these practices gradually move us into a conscious letting-go of ordinary ways of concentrating and being.[31]

The purpose, of course, is to attain a state of self-transcendence in which one is stronger, faster, and better coordinated in the performance of martial arts techniques.

Ki: The Counterfeit Key

For Christians who engage in the martial arts, ki (the preferred Japanese form of *chi*), can become a substitute for God and the power of the Holy Spirit because it provides "transcendent" experiences and seemingly supernormal abilities. For example, as Redfield describes it, moments of heightened ki "Allow us to experience gravity in a new way, prying open the energy within, and when it comes in fully, we feel expanded to such a degree that our bodies begin to move into perfect posture."[32] This form of self-transcendence is basically a product of self-effort and self-dependence rather than dependence on God and His power.

Like the followers of Hinduism, Taoism, yoga, and tai chi, martial arts practitioners consider ki to be a psycho-physical energy, the "vital life force." Martial arts teachers describe it in the following ways:

- It moves like smoke or water, flowing and formless, yet having coherence and pattern. In scientific terms, it is the force behind particle-wave phenomena: at one instant, it appears as a particle of matter, at another, as a wave of energy. It is associated with basic vitality, mental and emotional health, intuition, body-mind relationships, electrical and magnetic effects, and paranormal powers.
- It is frequently associated with *breath* and *spirit*. This can be seen in the words of various languages which are related to this concept: In Latin, *spiritus* means "spirit" and "breath," both of which are still seen in the double meanings of our English words *inspire* and *expire*. The same combinations of meaning are seen in the Greek *pneuma*, the Hebrew *rauch*, the Sanskrit *prana*, and the Polynesian *mana*.
- It is the source of all movement and harmonious transformation, for example, that which changes food and air into blood and other body fluids. It is also the healing force manipulated by acupuncture as well as that which causes injury when disrupted at pressure points or vital spots.

The martial arts have long taught that ki can be developed through the conscious linking of physical movement, breathing, and focused attention.

(Again, these are the same basic techniques used in most esoteric schools.) By this means, they say, it can be generated and accumulated in the body to increase one's capacity for action and experience and to sense and affect other people and things more directly. It thereby enables martial arts students to do such extraordinary feats as breaking numerous concrete blocks with a single blow of the bare hand or defeating larger and stronger attackers with ease.[33]

Thus, it is clear that martial arts are derived directly from Eastern religion and occult practices much as yoga and tai chi are. Their practice therefore unquestionably contradicts basic Christian doctrine. Since many undiscerning Christians have accepted martial arts as legitimate and healthful activities and are practicing them on a regular basis, they are, at least potentially, another seed of apostasy. In any case, they are obviously, it seems to me, not something that any true disciple of Christ should be involved in.

The Bible indicates in many places that we are not to rely on the development and exercise of our own power and will in order to become and do all that God intends for us. Rather, we are to rely on Him as our source of transformation and accomplishment. Zechariah 4:6, for example, clearly has a specific application to Christians involved in the martial arts:

> Not by might nor by power, but by my Spirit, says the Lord Almighty.

In summary, yoga, tai chi, and martial arts all embody principles and practices from Hinduism and/or Taoism. They share many occult elements used in esoteric schools to produce altered states of consciousness, transcendent experiences, and supernormal abilities. They are substitutes for the power of the Holy Spirit and the truths of the Bible. They are, therefore, ungodly systems based on demonically inspired deceptions, designed to lure the undiscerning into satanic bondage. Their so-called benefits are in reality the result of demonic influence, and their supposed spiritual transformation is in fact spiritual captivity. For Christians, then, these practices are occult seeds of apostasy and, as such are "detestable to the Lord" (Deuteronomy 18:12).

Once again, I can speak from personal experience, for I was involved in both yoga and martial arts (judo, jiu jitsu, and karate). Each of these disciplines created in me, in one way or another, the illusions of self-mastery and personal transcendence. I escaped from the captivity of these deceptions only when I surrendered to Jesus and received His cleansing and liberating grace.

If you are involved in any of these or other practices derived from Eastern religions, you need to renounce them and discontinue them immediately. Then you need to pray to be delivered from any spiritual defilement resulting from them. Otherwise, you may find yourself suffering eternal consequences, for

. . . those who practice magic arts [i.e., occult-
ism] . . . their place is in the fiery lake of burning
sulfur . . . [But] Blessed are those who wash their
robes, that they may have the right to the tree of
life and may go through the gates into the city.
Outside are the dogs, those who practice magic
arts . . . (Revelation 21:8, 22:14–15).

CHAPTER SIXTEEN

Infiltration by Occultism– Satanism in the Church

Earlier, we said "occultism" is hidden or secret knowledge and practices related to supernatural phenomena and magical arts. While this is a good working definition, it doesn't adequately reveal the close connection between occultism and New Age philosophy. You will recall that the New Age movement is basically about personal transcendence, or realizing one's godhood. Douglas Groothius brings out this aspect of occultism in his definition of *the occult* as

> . . . any philosophy that seeks liberation from within the self by discovering the secret or hidden wisdom (gnosis); it may utilize a variety of practices: meditation, yoga, sensory deprivation, spirit-contact or others. In this sense the entire New Age movement is occult.

> But in another sense, *occult* refers to exotic spiri-
> tual beliefs and practices such as mediumship,
> divination (crystal gazing, palmistry, tarot card
> reading, astrology) and the [ungodly] miracu-
> lous in general.[1]

In previous chapters, we discussed such occult practices as channeling, visualization, magical prayer,
positive thinking and PMA (positive mental attitude)
(all modern forms of sorcery or shamanism), as well
as astrology, yoga, tai chi, and martial arts. All of
these forms of occultism are promoted by New Age
adherents. In this and the following chapters, therefore, we shall focus only on the major additional
forms of New Age occultism presently influencing
the church.

While satanism, strictly speaking, may not appear to be a New Age practice, it certainly fits in
with the devil's New Age master plan to destroy the
church. Thus, while New Agers in general might
deny any connection with or belief in satanism,
hardcore New Agers would have to agree that they
share a common goal with satanists—the destruction of Christianity. On the other hand, as we shall
see, satanists do directly promote New Age teachings and practices among Christians. We saw earlier how satanists have infiltrated the church much
as secret-agent "moles" infiltrate the government.

Elaine, the ex-satanic high priestess mentioned
previously, describes how she learned "to use demons against . . . churches and even ministers of

the gospel of Jesus Christ." While she was a member of the satanic cult, she was simultaneously a respected member of a large church where she "taught and sang and participated in all sorts of activities."[2]

According to Dr. Rebecca Brown in her book, *He Came to Set the Captives Free*, servants of Satan, as was Elaine, are members of many churches where they pose as Christians, often in high positions. There, they conduct spiritual attacks on ministers and other leaders and work in other ways to split and destroy the church.

Elaine explains how she was trained for this purpose:

> During my years in The Brotherhood I was carefully trained, and I in turn trained others, how to infiltrate and destroy the various Christian churches. Satan's goal is to make every Christian church like the church of Laodicea . . . Churches full of passive people who never bother to read or study the Bible, who "Having a form of godliness, but denying the power thereof . . ." are **not** a threat to Satan.
>
> . . . The fact that most all high ranking Satanists regularly attended Christian churches should not be a surprise to anyone. That is, anyone who takes the time to read God's word. We Christians are very clearly warned that Satan's attack will come from within the churches—especially in times of prosperity.[3] [Emphasis in original.]

For example, Jude 4 says,

478   The Spiritual Discernment Guide

> For certain men whose condemnation was writ-
> ten about long ago have secretly slipped in among
> you. They are godless men, who change the grace
> of our God into a license for immorality and deny
> Jesus Christ our only sovereign Lord.

Similarly, Paul says,

> I know that after I leave, savage wolves will
> come in among you and will not spare the
> flock. Even from your own number men will
> arise and distort the truth in order to draw
> away disciples after them. So be on your guard!
> (Acts 20:29–31)

THE STRATEGY OF DESTRUCTION

Satan's strategy for destroying the church by
the direct action of clandestine satanists is based
on an eight-part plan, which Elaine says is now
being used "successfully all over the world to destroy Christian churches"[4]:

1. Professing faith:

    Go forward and pretend to be saved.

2. Building credibility:

    Attend regularly, be helpful and in-
    volved, give generously.

3. Destroying the prayer base:

> Encourage and promote large church growth so the pastor and the elders will no longer be able to know every member personally. Discourage and prevent prayer groups, especially large-scale prayer meetings. (This can be accomplished by limiting corporate prayer to small home groups.)

4. Starting rumors:

> Destroy the credibility of the pastor and the true Christians.

5. Teaching false doctrines:

> Acquire teaching positions, make prayer a complicated procedure, teach the health and wealth gospel, teach the love doctrine (i.e., don't judge anybody, don't step on any toes).

6. Breaking up family units:

> Have separate groups for Bible study, prayer, retreats, etc., for men, women, and children.

7. Stopping all accurate teaching about Satan:

> The excuses are many. They say that any teaching about Satan gives glory to him,

> takes people's minds off of the Lord, tempts people to turn to Satan, etc.

> . . . God's Word clearly teaches much about Satan, and warns us that if we are ignorant about our enemy he will surely gain an advantage over us.

> One simple incantation by a high satanist will assign a demon to every person attending the church in which he is involved. The purpose of the demon is to stand guard and the instant anyone says anything about Satan, to beam thoughts into the person's mind that he or she should not be listening to anything about Satan.

> Beware, the very church members who complain the loudest about any teaching about Satan and his tactics, will probably turn out to be satanists themselves.

8. Directing attacks by witchcraft against key members of the church:

> "They will be afflicted with all sorts of physical illness, difficulties in concentrating, confusion, fatigue, difficulties in praying, etc."[5]

OCCULT DOORWAYS

According to Elaine, undercover satanists encourage New Age occult involvement in many ways.

The success of their efforts is seen in the fact that Christians, according to Brown, may be involved in such blatant forms of occultism as seances, occult books, Ouija boards, ESP, psychic experiences, astral projection, water witching, magic, levitation, moving objects without touching them, mediums or spiritists, martial arts, yoga, and witchcraft.[6]

More subtle forms of occult involvement include *rock music, magical objects,* and *wrong meditation.* According to Brown, any dealing with Satan, including these forms of occultism, can open a doorway in a Christian's life

> for the inflow of satanic power and/or demon infestation. . . . These doorways (created by sin) give Satan legal ground, according to God's word (the Bible), to exert his power in their lives. Christians are not protected because the opening of these doorways involves their conscious participation in sin and/or ignorance.[7]

Rock Music

This is "Satan's music," says Brown. It is, she explains, a direct doorway for demonic control:

> Like so many things, the whole movement of rock music was carefully planned and carried out by Satan and his servants from its very beginning . . . rock stars . . . have **all** agreed to serve Satan in return for money and fame. . . . these rock stars **know** exactly what they are doing. They are, step by step, teaching untold mil-

lions of young people to worship and serve Satan.[8] [Emphasis in original.]

The satanic origins and influence of secular rock music is obvious from even a hasty glance at its subject matter: illicit sex, drugs, occultism, satanism, atheism, anger, violence, horror, and death.[9] Three basic themes seem to dominate in all this: rebellion, moral decay, and anti-Christianity.

From its inception, it was a medium of rebellion, as one Christian writer observes:

Rock is far more than mere dissent; from its corrosive beginnings—Elvis Presley's defiant sexuality and the subtle leering lyrics of Jerry Lee Lewis and Bill Haley—much of rock and roll has always been about subversion, overthrow, and revolutionary change. . . . always questioning and even assaulting authority and tradition. . . . Rock music and revolutionary left-wing politics have always been closely intertwined, from the anti-Vietnam war protest era to the sundry concerts and causes popular with the present-day Left. . . . "against parents, against police, against power."[10]

The focus of much of this rebellion implies moral decay:

Rock and roll has spawned a vast subculture in which moral restraints are absent and the decadence of constant revolutionary change are relentlessly hammered home with all the power of amplified sound, light shows, and deliberately shocking modes of dress and conduct.[11]

Such immorality, of course, directly attacks traditional American and Christian values:

> . . . much of rock music encourages severing personal ties: to family, to church, to tradition. Children are incited to rebel against their parents, marriage and sexual purity are sneered at, and traditional modes of dress and conduct are deliberately contravened.[12]

Even apart from its hellish content, rock music has demonic power to intoxicate, addict, and hypnotize—in other words, to produce an altered state of consciousness in which reason, morality, and spiritual values are blunted and instinctive, animalistic energies are activated. These effects are a direct result of rock's primitive, pounding, monotonous rhythms which assault the senses:

> More than any other instrument, drums entrance, energize, and sensualize. Heavy percussion, often with no other musical accompaniment, is used worldwide, among cultures that have no contact with one another, to induce trances and states of euphoria and even possession. . . . The heavier the percussion, the greater the effect. . . . slurred notes are often used in conjunction with heavy percussion to bring about altered states. . . . shamans in India use squeeze-box drums—instruments that combine

heavy percussion with constantly changing pitch
. . . to induce oracular trances. . . . Anyone who
has ever observed the behavior of rock musi-
cians and their manic fans at a concert, or of
"ravers"—dancing literally to exhaustion under
the hypnotic influence of strobe lights and the
throbbing repetitive strains of techno-music—
has seen people transformed, and seldom for the
better, by the power of such musical forms.[13]

In view of these facts about the origin and nature of rock music, let me ask: is it really something
that we should have in our church services as a form
of worship—even with the lyrics cleaned up and
Christian vocabulary added—especially as the
"norm" for our young people? Is it *really* okay?

Magical Objects

Many Christians routinely use Christian objects,
such as crucifixes and Bibles, for protection or good
fortune. In so doing, they are, according to Elaine,
practicing magic:

. . . in just the same manner [as] amulets or
fetishes are used. This is an absolute contradiction of God's word. . . . The Lord has no
such objects! The Christian's power is **only**
through our Lord Jesus Christ and His finished
work on the cross.

Any Christian who accepts or uses such things is
directly using demons.[14] [Emphasis in original.]

Wrong Meditation

Another doorway for demon activity is the type of meditation which involves blanking out or "clearing" the mind. By thus opening the mind to "whatever comes," Christians may have "spiritual experiences." But they are experiences based on self-effort and producing an altered state of consciousness during which demons can plant messages or provide psychic visions or vibrations. It is therefore a counterfeit of godly spiritual experience and the activity of the Holy Spirit. Prior to my becoming a Christian, I had such psychic experiences resulting from wrong meditation. Based on my reading of personal testimonies and conversations with acquaintances, I believe that many Christians meditate in this way until they have a "spiritual experience" or "experience God." But, as Brown explains, this is a trap:

> Christians **do** have experiences in the spirit—visions and revelations—but these are **always** under the control of our Lord Jesus Christ and **never** controlled or initiated by the person himself. If a Christian is able to control when he has such spiritual experiences, then I would have to say to him that I would seriously doubt that his experiences came from God. Most likely they came from Satan.
>
> Too many Christians think that they must "blank out" their minds so that the Holy Spirit can speak through them, or "control" them. The Bible clearly shows us that we are to **actively** cooperate with the Holy Spirit. Any time we blank out

our minds, the spirit speaking through us is most likely **not** the Holy Spirit. Multitudes of Christians are, and have been, misled because of their lack of knowledge of God's principles regarding their spirits. Many so-called prophecies given by people who blank out their minds thinking this gives control of the Holy Spirit are demonic prophecies. Too many Christians are misled in this area and accept such prophecies because the person prophesying knows facts about them or their life that they think only God could know. They forget that Satan knows every detail of our lives, the only thing he doesn't know is the thoughts and intentions of our hearts.[15] [Emphasis in original.]

Deliverance from the trap of occultism requires closing all the doorways. This is accomplished through prayer by (1) confessing all occult involvement, (2) acknowledging it as evil, (3) asking God's forgiveness, and (4) asking Him to remove it completely and close the doorways by the power of Jesus' blood.[16]

FALSE TEACHINGS ABOUT SATAN

To facilitate their promotion of such occultism, satanists use three main false teachings:

1. Christians can't have demons.
2. Spiritual warfare is unnecessary.
3. Satan should be ignored because if you talk about him you "give him glory."

"No Demons"

The idea that Christians can't have demons, which is widespread in the church, gives Satan free rein, of course, to attack without opposition. But it is simply an untrue statement. Elaine and other former satanists had to go through an extensive process of deliverance from demon infestation after they became Christians. This fact is documented in detail in Brown's book.

Elaine explains that any involvement in the occult can open a doorway for demonic influence, and this influence doesn't just go away after conversion. The doorways must be closed and *all* occult involvement must be renounced and terminated.

In addition, demons can be passed down to Christians from parents or grandparents:

> . . . the Bible states plainly that the sins of the parents will be passed down to the children even to the third and fourth generation. . . . Christians need to be aware of this. If they are aware of anyone in their family that has been involved in the occult in any way, they should ask the Lord to close that doorway of inheritance with the precious blood of Jesus both for themselves and their children.[17]

"No Spiritual Warfare"

The idea here is that spiritual warfare on our part is unnecessary because Jesus did it all on the cross. Again, this is **a lie** of Satan that gives him freedom to attack at will. In this case, the doorway to deception is complacency on the part of the luke-warm, as Brown explains:

> So many Christians today are living exceedingly comfortable lives and quite naturally they don't want their comfort disturbed. They say, "Why should we even have to fight? After all, Christ won the complete victory for us on the cross. . . . All Christians have to do is claim the victory Jesus has already won."[18]

But the Bible says the Christian walk is one of spiritual warfare against demonic forces—"against the rulers, against the authorities, against the powers of this dark world and against the spiritual forces of evil in the heavenly realms" (Ephesians 6:12). We are told, therefore, to "put on the full armor of God" so that we can stand "against the devil's schemes" (Ephesians 6:11).

Brown warns that, if you do engage in this warfare, you will experience opposition not only from Satan but from your fellow Christians:

> . . . the persecution that inevitably will come will not come in the way we think. People will not stand up and say, "We are slandering you because of your stand for Jesus." No, you will be accused of doing all sorts of wrong things that you did not do, of being too radical and of becoming unbalanced in your mind. Schizophrenia and paranoia are favorite accusations of Satan's . You will be discredited by your **fellow Christians** more than by avowed non-Christians.

Satan always deceives and lies, nothing is ever
as it seems. His most effective servants are those
who are supposedly the strongest Christians, the
regular church goers, the financially successful
and respected and revered members of your com-
munity. They are the ones who will accuse and
persecute those fighting in spiritual warfare for
Christ.[19] [Emphasis in original.]

This is exactly what the scripture says we should
expect:

For such men are false apostles, deceitful workmen, masquerading as apostles of Christ. And
no wonder, for Satan himself masquerades as an
angel of light. It is not surprising then, if *his servants* masquerade as servants of righteousness
(2 Corinthians 11:13–15, emphasis added).

"No Speaking of Satan"

This **lie** says that, if we speak about Satan, we
glorify him or give him power. This is an idea, according to Brown, that is placed in Christians' minds
either by demons or satanists in the church:

The demon shoots in the thought that "These
women should not talk about Satan because in
so doing they are giving glory to Satan." The
person assumes the thought is their own and
therefore must be true.[20]

This is a situation calling for discernment specifically in the realm of one's own thoughts.

The Bible, in fact, reveals that the enemy establishes mental strongholds of false ideas which we must demolish through divine power:

> The weapons we fight with are not the weapons of the world. On the contrary, they have divine power to demolish strongholds. We demolish arguments and every pretension that sets itself up against the knowledge of God, and we take captive every thought to make it obedient to Christ (2 Corinthians 10:4–5).

COMBATING SATANISM IN THE CHURCH

If we try to fight Satan in our own strength, we will lose the battle before it starts. Instead, we must call upon God to help us through the power of the Holy Spirit. The ensuing battle will have two primary objectives: *stopping demonic mind control* and *stopping satanists' activities*.

Controlling Your Mind

In order to stop demons from implanting destructive ideas in your mind, you must first recognize that they are not your own. They are coming from outside yourself. This means you must prepare ahead of time by asking the Holy Spirit to help you in the process. Then you will be able to watch your own thinking and discern what is godly and what is not. First, rebuke Satan; then say *no* to those thoughts that are not godly, ask God to help you stop them, and deliberately start thinking in a godly way.

Brown provides a personal experience which illustrates the process. It involved her negative attitude toward her roommate Sue:

> . . . the Holy Spirit taught me and trained me to recognize that those thoughts were from outside of me and from Satan. I began to have victory as I rebuked Satan out loud in the name of Jesus. Soon I learned that the instant that first negative or angry thought would come into my mind about Sue, I immediately out loud said, "Satan and you demons, I rebuke you in the name of Jesus! I will not accept those thoughts about Sue," and would force myself to think about some portion of scripture and recite it out loud. Then I had victory because I was then resisting Satan with the power of Jesus and my whole relationship with her improved immensely.[21]

Controlling Satanists

To stop satanists in the church, we must control their activity through prayer and then work to get them saved. Elaine cautions that it is important not to expose them because this puts them in danger from other satanists:

> The little church I was sent to destroy knew that I was a witch, but they did not publicly expose me or challenge me. If they had done so I would have been killed immediately. Instead, they loved me, controlled me so that I could not bring in destructive doctrine and prayed for me until finally I was saved.[22]

She adds that church leaders must be protected by being

> continuously upheld in prayer and interceded for by the members of the congregation. . . . every Christian [should] . . . go to the Lord in prayer and seek guidance as to how to fight such attacks within his or her own church.[23]

Besides the teachings of clandestine satanists, among the most important sources of occultism infiltrating the church are two popular books: *The Celebration of Discipline* by Richard Foster and *The Celestine Prophecy* by James Redfield. They claim to be Christian but are actually occult in much of their content. We shall look at their dangerous influence in the next two chapters.

Infiltration by Occultism— Altered States of Consciousness in the Church (*The Celebration of Discipline*)

The Celebration of Discipline by Richard Foster, first published in 1978, has become something of a classic among Christians. It contains much that is true and good. But, unfortunately, it also contains much that is false and bad. I found Foster's chapters on fasting, submission, service, and confession helpful and generally scriptural.

In contrast, other chapters contain recommendations for achieving spiritual transformation through self-effort and by inducing altered states of consciousness rather than through the power and guidance of the Holy Spirit. Essentially, these chapters promote lifting yourself up by your own spiritual bootstraps. Especially dangerous and deceptive in this regard are his discussions of *meditation, prayer,* and *worship.*

MEDITATION: DO-IT-YOURSELF MYSTICISM

Foster defines Christian meditation as "an attempt to empty the mind in order to fill it." The "filling" referred to is whatever experiences come into one's mind during or following the process of "emptying." The source of these experiences is "actual contact and communion with a spiritual sphere of existence" that Foster calls entering "into the living presence of God for ourselves." In this spiritual sphere, one may experience "a communication between the Lover and the one beloved." And one may "enter into the Holy of Holies and converse with the living God."[1]

The purpose of this mystical quest is to acquire "the inner wholeness necessary to give ourselves to God freely, and . . . the spiritual perception necessary to attack social evils."[2]

Thus, Foster sees eastern-style meditation as the means of receiving what you need to be (in his view) a good Christian.

While his description of the nature and purposes of meditation may sound commendable and even inspiringly spiritual, what we have here is basically the eastern form of meditation practiced by Hindus, Buddhists and New Agers rather than the Christian form. Of course, it is profoundly unscriptural, being based on several related false teachings: (1) that meditation is a process of emptying the mind in order to have a spiritual experience, (2) that wholeness and spiritual perception come through one's own mental effort, (3) that we enter the pres-

ence of God and communicate with Him in an altered state of consciousness, and (4) that we receive
what we need in this altered state.

Let's take these false teachings one at a time.

1. The Bible does not say that we should passively
   empty our minds during meditation. Rather, it
   says we should actively meditate on the Word
   of God (Joshua 1:8 and Psalm 1:2). It also says
   we should think about (i.e., meditate on) whatever is true, noble, lovely, admirable, excellent,
   and praiseworthy (Philippians 4:8).

2. The Bible does not say that wholeness and
   spiritual perception come through meditation. Rather, it says such transformation
   comes by the Word of God and the work of
   the Holy Spirit. (See John 17:17; Galatians
   5:22–23; 2 Corinthians 3:18, etc.)

3. The Bible does not say that we enter the Holy
   of Holies and converse with God by means of
   meditation. Rather, it says we can enter directly
   into His presence and "approach the throne of
   grace with confidence" just as the high priest
   entered directly into the Holy Place. Then, as
   we bring our petitions to Him in prayer, we
   will "receive mercy and find grace to help us in
   our time of need" (Hebrews 4:16).

4. Thus, the Bible does not say that we receive
   what we need in an altered state of consciousness. Rather, according to Philippians 4:6–
   7, we get our needs met by asking in prayer:

496 The Spiritual Discernment Guide

> Do not be anxious about anything, but in everything, by prayer and petition, with thanksgiving, present your requests to God.

The techniques which Foster recommends for getting in touch with the "inner world of the spirit" are identical to those practiced by New Age adherents: correct posture, relaxation, "centering," breath control, and visualization.

"Posture," says Foster, "is of utmost importance. The body, the mind and the spirit are inseparable." Correct posture and relaxation always go together with occult techniques for attaining altered states of consciousness, whether they be those of yoga, the Gurdjieff cult, or the New Age Movement: ". . . a consciously chosen posture of peace and relaxation will have a tendency to calm your inner turmoil," Foster assures us.[3]

Next, comes centering. The aim is "to center the attention of the body, the emotions, the mind, and the spirit upon 'the glory of God in the face of Christ'" (2 Corinthians 4:6).[4] In this focused state, one is to

> spend the remaining moments in complete silence. Do not ask for any sign. Allow the Lord to commune with your spirit, to love you. If impressions or directions come, fine: if not, fine.[5]

What Foster is advocating here is essentially the eastern mystical practice of emptying the mind in order to open it up to whatever may come. But this, as we have seen, is the opposite of what the Bible tells us to do when we meditate.

Conscious breathing (which I practiced in the cult) is another standard occult technique which Foster recommends as the next step:

> Inhale deeply, slowly tilting your head back as far as it will go. Then exhale, allowing your head slowly to come forward until your chin nearly rests on your chest. Do this for several moments, praying inwardly something like this: "Lord, I exhale my fear over my geometry exam, I inhale Your peace. I exhale my spiritual apathy, I inhale Your light and life." Then, as before, become silent outwardly and inwardly. Be attentive to the inward living Christ. If your attention wanders . . . "exhale" the matter into the arms of the Master and draw in His divine breath of peace. Then listen once again.[6]

I am sorry to say that this is very similar to a "spiritual" practice recommended by a pastor at the one of the churches I have attended. He told us in his sermon to focus on our breathing, exhaling negative emotions and thoughts and inhaling God's peace and love while affirming positive thoughts and emotions.

But there is nothing in the Bible indicating that we should follow such a practice. Rather, as we have seen, it says we should *think about* what is spiritually uplifting and *forget* about what is past (Philippians 3:13, 8–9).

Although Foster does mention the value of meditating on scripture, he does so only incidentally. Instead, his main focus is on visualization. Indeed, he says you should visualize Jesus' parables and events in His life using all of your other senses as well, so that

> . . . you can *actually* encounter the living Christ in the event, be addressed by His voice and be touched by His healing power. It can be more than an exercise of the imagination; it can be a genuine confrontation. Jesus Christ will actually come to you.[7] [Emphasis added.]

He also instructs Christians to see the Father through creative visualization:

> [This] form of meditation has as its objective to bring you into a deep inner communion with the Father where you look at Him and He looks at you. In your imagination . . . picture yourself . . . observing yourself. . . . In your imagination allow your spiritual body, shining with light, to rise out of your physical body. Look back so that you can see yourself lying in the grass and reassure your body that you will return momentarily. Imagine your spiritual self, alive and vibrant, rising up through the clouds and into the stratosphere. . . . Go deeper and deeper into outer space until there is nothing except the warm presence of the eternal Creator. Rest in His presence. Listen quietly, anticipating the unanticipated. Note carefully any instruction given.[8]

Getting Christ or the Father to come to you in this manner is not only a form of idolatry, as we have seen, it is also identical to the practices used by channellers and others to contact their spirit guides. It is thus an open invitation to demonic deception and, at least potentially, a dangerous seed of apostasy.

The result of this form of meditation, says Foster, is to "yield insights that are deeply practical." He adds, "It is wonderful when a particular meditation leads to ecstasy, but it is far more common to be given guidance in dealing with ordinary human problems."[9]

This enthusiastic approval of an occult practice reveals a profound lack of discernment on Foster's part. For there is no consideration given to the source of such spiritual experiences or who the beings really are who appear in them. Thus, what Foster is doing and recommending is to swallow whole a demonic counterfeit.

In addition, the acceptance of guidance from such a self-induced experience is profoundly unscriptural. For the Bible says true divine guidance comes from the Holy Spirit by means of prayer. Furthermore ecstasy as a goal of meditation is not only unscriptural, it is, as we have seen, identical with that of eastern religions and New Age practices.

The bottom line in all this is obtaining the gnostic goal of special supernatural experience and knowledge. This comes, says Foster, from "the True Spirit which inwardly moves upon the heart." Following such an experience, he promises, you will "return home full of new life and energy."[10] This is all about entering into an altered state of consciousness, a process which is described in essentially identical terms by New Age author James Redfield and defined by him as going "within . . . to increase our energy level."[11] (We shall examine this process in more detail in the next chapter.)

PRAYER: TUNING IN TO GOD

Foster says, "Meditation is the necessary prelude to intercession." In fact, for him, prayer is simply an extension of meditation. It is a process of getting tuned in to "God" by means of visualization: "As with meditation, the imagination is a powerful tool in the work of prayer."[12]

Again, the purpose is to become a "channel" for supernatural energy:

> One of the most critical aspects in learning to pray for others is to get in contact with God so that His life and power can be channeled through us into others.[13]

The purpose of prayer, then, for Foster, is to "channel" God's power to others. There is no concept here of *petitioning* God, either for the needs of others or of ourselves. (Remember, according to Foster, you get your needs met by *meditation*.)

To begin the "prayer" process, one uses exactly the same techniques as for meditation:

> We begin praying for others by first centering
> down and listening to the quiet thunder of the
> Lord of Hosts. . . . Attuning ourselves to divine
> breathings is spiritual work, but without it our
> praying is vain repetition.[14]

Thus, for our prayers to have *any* effect, according to Foster, we must first put ourselves in an altered state of consciousness.

But the Bible does not say we must tune in to God by putting ourselves in a special state. Rather, it says that being in a spiritually awake and active state (i.e., being "light in the Lord") is something the Holy Spirit does in us, not something we do to ourselves by special mental effort and occult techniques:

> For you were once darkness, but now *you are*
> *light in the Lord.* Live as children of light. . . .
>
> "Wake up, O sleeper, rise from the dead, and
> Christ will shine on you."
>
>   . . . *be filled with the Spirit* (Ephesians
>   5:8, 14, 18, emphasis added).
>
> For God, who said, "Let light shine out of darkness," *made his light shine in our hearts* to give
> us the light of the knowledge of the glory of God
> in the face of Christ (2 Corinthians 4:6, emphasis added).

Next, according to Foster, we must use visualization as the foundation of our prayer. He quotes

St. Teresa of Avila as an endorsement of the technique: "This was my method of prayer; as I could not make reflections with my understanding, I contrived to picture Christ within me."[15]

Foster not only recommends visualization as the basis of prayer, he also promotes it as the means to faith:

> Imagination opens the door to faith. If we can "see" in our mind's eye a shattered marriage whole or a sick person well, it is only a short step to believing that it is so. . . . I have been greatly helped in my understanding of the value of the imagination in praying for others by Agnes Sanford . . . .[16]

Thus, once more we have the magical use of prayer so highly valued by the Word of Faith teachers and their spiritual mother, Agnes Sanford. Like them, Foster is saying that visualizing what you want is a proper and necessary means of getting it from God. He illustrates the point by recounting an incident in which he "prayed" in this way for a child's baby sister:

> "Let's play a little game," I said. "Since we know that Jesus is always with us, let's imagine that He is sitting over in the chair across from us. He is waiting patiently for us to center our attention on Him. When we see Him, we start thinking more about His love than how sick Julie is. He smiles, gets up and comes over to us. Then let's both put our hands on Julie and when we do, Jesus will put His hands on top of

ours. We'll watch and imagine that the light from Jesus is flowing right into your little sister and making her well. Let's pretend that the light of Christ fights with the bad germs until they are all gone. . . ." Together we prayed in this childlike way and then thanked the Lord that what we "saw" was the way it was going to be. Now, I do not know whether this created a posthypnotic suggestion in the child or whether it was divine fiat, but I do know that the next morning Julie was perfectly well.[17]

When Foster says he doesn't know whether it was a posthypnotic suggestion or God, he is, of course, giving it away that his recommendations are not based on scripture and that his "faith" is not founded solidly in God but rather in an occult technique. Moreover, by relying on visualization for healing, Foster is tacitly saying it was the use of imagination and guided imagery that made it happen and not simply God's will.

Foster offers numerous other examples of such magical use of prayer.[18] And, in all of them, it is something one does by using the imagination to manipulate or activate the "power of Christ." This is made explicit, for example, in his instructions for how to "pray" for the emotional healing of a child:

Imagine the light of Christ flowing through your hands and healing every emotional trauma and hurt feeling your child experienced that day. Fill him or her with the peace and joy of the Lord.[19]

No, Mr. Foster, you can't do it with your mind! Only Christ can do it with His divine healing power!

Foster also reveals his confusion about the true nature of prayer in his description of "Flash Prayers":

> Flashing hard and straight prayers *at* people is a great thrill and can bring interesting results. I have tried it, *inwardly asking* the joy of the Lord and a deeper awareness of His presence to rise up within every person I meet. Sometimes people reveal no response, but other times *they turn and smile as if addressed.* In a bus or plane we can *fancy Jesus* walking down the aisles touching people on the shoulder and saying, "I love you."[20] [Emphasis added.]

First, the Bible does not say we pray *at* people. Rather, it says we pray *to* God. Furthermore, "inwardly asking" joy or awareness to rise up within a person is not really prayer at all but something more akin to *wishing* or *mental telepathy*. The fact that some people "turn and smile as if addressed" would seem to indicate the latter. If so, it is a psychic phenomenon and not an action of God. In fact, it is an activity of demons, as we saw earlier. Finally, imagining Jesus touching and speaking to people to make Him more real to them is not prayer but a case of mind over matter, putting oneself in the driver's seat—in other words, sorcery!

Clearly, Foster is badly deceived, for he believes all of these occult practices are the essence of "greater, deeper, truer prayer."[21] Thus, in the spirit of a good gnostic, he provides this special knowledge and these unorthodox techniques, presumably, to supplement what he perceives as the inadequate practice of regular Christians and the incomplete teachings of the Bible.

WORSHIP: THE EXALTATION OF SELF

According to Foster, worship is "to experience reality . . . to know, to feel the resurrected Christ . . . [to be] invaded by the Shekinah of God."[22] Notice that the focus here is all on one's self—to experience, to know, to be invaded by something supernatural. In other words, he is saying that worship is getting a special experience from God. The focus is not on God but on one's inner state.

But the Bible indicates that true worship is giving ourselves to God in praise and adoration. It is to get our focus *off ourselves* and *on to Him*. Psalm 100 says it all—that we are to come before Him with thanksgiving and praise, expressing our gladness and joy:

Shout for joy to the Lord, all the earth

Worship the Lord with gladness; come before him with joyful songs.

Know that the Lord is God.

It is he who made us, and we are his; we are his people, the sheep of his pasture.

Enter his gates with thanksgiving

> and his courts with praise; give thanks
> to him and praise his name.

For the Lord is good and his love endures forever;

> his faithfulness continues through all
> generations.

According to Foster, the purpose of worship seems to be to get God to touch us rather than for us to reach out and touch Him with our spirit. He says, ". . . we have not worshipped the Lord until Spirit [God] touches spirit [us]."[23] However, Foster's statements are confusing on this point, for he also says that God must first touch us before we can enter into worship:

> Until God touches and frees our spirit we cannot enter this realm. Singing, praying, praising all may lead to worship, but worship is more than any of them. Our spirit must be ignited by divine fire.[24]

Foster seems to be saying that we must, somehow put ourselves in a special state first, and then, in this altered state, worship becomes possible. But isn't this getting it backwards? Isn't being touched by the Holy Spirit and having our spirits ignited by His divine fire a *result of* worship rather than the necessary *condition for* worship? Having divine fire in our spirit doesn't cause (or make possible) worship, but worship may cause our spirit to be so ignited.

In speaking further of preparing oneself for worship, Foster makes it clear that it is a self-induced state brought about through mental effort and visualization. Here is the technique:

> Invite the real Presence to be manifest. Fill the room with Light.
>
> Next, lift into the Light of Christ the pastor or persons with particular responsibilities. Imagine the Shekinah of God's radiance surrounding him or her. Inwardly release them to speak the truth boldly in the power of the Lord.
>
> . . . Glance around until your eyes catch some individual who needs your intercessory work. Perhaps their shoulders are drooped, or they seem a bit sad. Lift them into the glorious, refreshing Light of His Presence. Imagine the burden tumbling from their shoulders as it did from Pilgrim's in Bunyan's allegory. Hold them as a special intention throughout the service. If only a few in any given congregation would do this, it would deepen the worship experience for all.[25]

The purpose, once again, is to have an experience. All this preparation may sound like prayer, but it really isn't. It is all mental activity and self-will: inviting, filling, lifting, imagining, releasing, holding. There is no communication with God, no petitioning, no asking for anything—only visualization and mind control.

508 The Spiritual Discernment Guide

But the Bible says we must worship, not with our minds, but with our spirits:

> God is spirit, and his worshippers must worship in spirit and in truth (John 4:24).

For Foster, even singing and praising are only part of the preparation for the "experience" of worship:

> If singing and praising can occur in a concentrated manner it serves to focus us. We become centered. Our fragmented minds and spirits flow into a unified whole. We become poised toward God.[26]

Again, this is all about generating a self-induced state in which we can have an exalted experience. And this, to Foster, is clearly the whole point. It is what happens to us, not what we offer to God, that is important:

> If worship does not change us, it has not been worship. To stand before the Holy One of eternity is to change.[27]

Yes, experiencing the presence of God changes us. But this is a byproduct, not the goal or purpose of worship. True worship is to submit oneself to God—body, soul, and spirit—to recognize His sovereignty and glory and to express that recognition and our love for Him in praise and thanksgiving. *Nelson's Commentary* concurs with this view, pointing out that the Hebrew word for *worship* means "to cause oneself to be prostrate" and applies this idea to the church:

> Following the example of the ancient people of faith, true Christian worship must express more than love for God, it must also express submission to His will.[28]

Foster's focus is wrong. His priorities are inverted. And his method is occult.

Infiltration by Occultism– New Age Gnosticism in the Church (*The Celestine Prophecy*)

James Redfield claims that his popular novel, *The Celestine Prophecy*, is a fictional depiction of the real, inner, spiritual meaning of the Bible. But it is, in fact, esoteric Christianity, a modern form of Gnosticism, which perverts Christianity and diminishes Christ, the Bible, and the church. Unfortunately, many Christians, I believe, have ignorantly accepted it as a new revelation which will give them specific, practical instructions and techniques for doing what the Bible says we should do and for becoming what the Bible says we should be.

The book's general theme is spiritual and psychic evolution. This evolution supposedly brings expanded consciousness and self-awareness, transcending past conditioning and overcoming the harmful effects of family and childhood hurts. In the process, it says, one finds his true identity, individual purpose, and the meaning of life. All this comes through getting in touch with the higher, "divine" energy within—primarily by experiencing nature in a more conscious way. The insights provided by the secret manuscript on which the book is supposedly based also reveal the exact process for "truly" being saved and becoming more spiritual.[1]

These are undoubtedly powerful appeals for immature and undiscerning Christians or unsaved seekers of spiritual reality and personal transformation. I personally know two such individuals who bought into these teachings—with disastrous results. Both were Christian men who appeared to be fairly mature in their faith. Unfortunately, they lacked the discernment to see the deception permeating Redfield's book. Regrettably, both suffered serious damage in their Christian walk, being drawn into spiritual backsliding and at least the beginning stages of apostasy. When last I heard, both had gone through painful divorces, were not attending church, and were still studying Redfield's writings.

Redfield presents his primary false teachings and his basic New Age counterfeit of Christianity in this book. He then expands and develops his themes in two other books: *The Tenth Insight* and *The Celestine Vision*. Since *The Celestine Prophecy* is the one that Christians are most likely to encounter, we will focus on that, using information from the other two for clarification, as appropriate.

In *The Tenth Insight*, Redfield, provides this statement of purpose:

> Like *The Celestine Prophecy*, this sequel is an adventure parable, an attempt to illustrate the ongoing spiritual transformation that is occurring in our time. . . . a lived portrait, of the new perceptions, feelings, and phenomena that are coming to define life as we enter the third millennium."[2]

He says the "insights" of both books clarify and correct Christianity. But what they really do is deny its truth, diminish its holiness, and declare its teachings to be inadequate. All three books, with their totally false world view, are examples of what can happen when one swallows everything whole. They are, in effect, studies in demonic redefinitions of Christian doctrine, terminology, and practice.

THE NEW GNOSTICISM

In *The Celestine Prophecy*, Redfield says the secret manuscript containing the first nine insights doesn't negate Christianity but "clarifies, the truth of the church," revealing the hidden meaning of the Bible. Moreover, this meaning can only be found by reading and understanding the manuscript. This, in turn, can only be accomplished by raising one's energy to a high enough level of vibration, where transcendent consciousness is found.[3]

But, in reality, this is simply New Age occultism in the guise of Christianity—promoting all the basic teachings of the New Age Movement and the goals of the New Age Plan. The Gnostics of the Middle Ages, according to Redfield, were Catholic monks who preserved these hidden truths in the manuscript. However, they were excommunicated by a blind and shallow church.

These insights, they said, were the real core of Christianity, which is how to be transformed spiritually.[4] Rightly understood, they taught, Christ is our model for this methodology—"what the Scriptures clearly say." The "church men" opposed these ideas because they feared they would give each individual too much power and the church would thereby lose control.[5]

The secret knowledge of these Gnostic monks was acquired through altered states of consciousness in which memories of past lives were experienced. Thus, they had supposedly received the "truth" from a higher source, but the church had rejected it. Therefore, the church, according to Redfield, is the enemy of truth and knowledge. And the conflict between the church and the Gnostics was (and is) essentially a struggle between blind, unenlightened faith and true, experiential knowledge.[6] All of this, of course, is totally unscriptural, for the Bible says exactly the opposite.

The purposes of *The Celestine Prophecy*, then, can be summarized as follows:

- To discredit and replace Christianity.

- To show how to tap into the higher energy of the universe.
- To help you discover who you are and what your purpose is through occult methods.
- To transform society by means of an evolving consciousness and spiritual unfolding.
- To reveal the next stage of human evolution and to help us "realize the truth of the evolutionary process."[7]

More specifically, Redfield spells out the purposes of the nine insights (those presented in *The Celestine Prophecy*) as follows:

> I was alert to the mysterious way my life evolved, as revealed by the First Insight. I knew that the whole culture was sensing this mystery again as well, and was in the process of constructing a new world view, as pointed out by the Second. The Third and Fourth had showed me that the universe was in reality a vast system of energy and that human conflict was a shortage of and a manipulation for this energy.

> The Fifth Insight revealed that we could end this conflict by receiving an inpouring of this energy from a higher source. . . . The Sixth, that we could clear our old repeated dramas and find our true selves, was also permanently etched in my mind. And the Seventh had set in motion the evolution of these true selves; through question, intuition of what to do, and answer. Staying in this magic flow was truly the secret of happiness.

> And the Eighth, knowing how to relate in a new
> way to others, bringing out in them the very best,
> was the key to keeping the mystery operating
> and the answers coming.

> . . . What was left, I knew was the Ninth, which
> revealed where our evolution was taking us.[8]

(The "repeated dramas"—also called "control dramas"—mentioned above are strategies "for controlling others adopted in early childhood" and for getting energy from other people.[9])

Again, all these high-sounding purposes and seemingly noble goals are in reality, as we shall see, nothing but New Age occultism masquerading as Christianity. And they are all achieved—not by having a personal, saving relationship with Jesus Christ, living according to Christian principles, or being enabled by the Holy Spirit—but by entering altered states of consciousness in order to induce higher energy levels and better vibes.

THEISTIC EVOLUTION PLUS REINCARNATION: THE NEW OCCULT WORLD VIEW

Redfield sees evolution in its theistic form as the basis for all history and human development. It is, therefore, a new world view which is the central theme of the manuscript. Father Sanchez, a keeper of the manuscript, explains:

> "Yes, I fought against the idea of evolution as a
> replacement for God, as a way to explain the

universe without reference to God. But now I see that the truth is a synthesis of scientific and religious world views. The truth is that evolution is the way God created and is still creating.

". . . the Manuscript describes the progress of succeeding generations as an evolution of understanding, an evolution toward a higher spirituality and vibration. Each generation incorporates more energy and accumulates more truth and then passes that status on to the people of the next generation who extend it further."[10]

Father Sebastian, an orthodox Christian, opposes these revelations, of course, illustrating once again, according to Redfield, the "errors" of biblical Christianity.

Redfield also says that everything in this historical process is basically good, including Naziism, which is just a failed form of evolution (i.e., something that God—the universe—tried that didn't work out).

This form of theistic evolution says that everything began with the big bang and that we have been present since the beginning in one form of life or another, through countless cycles of reincarnation from the lowest form of life to the highest. Redfield makes his big bang view explicit when he says, ". . . the universe exploded into being."[11] Moreover, the big bang, evolution, and reincarnation all work together "guided by an overall plan."[12] We have been continually reincarnated since the beginning, each time on a higher level; therefore, reincarnation is an intrinsic part of evolution and vice versa.[13]

Included in Redfield's version of evolution is the idea of sudden leaps in the development of species (also known as "punctuated equilibrium"). In the case of human evolution, it is a process driven by human will in harmony with the "universal Will." That is, the self-effort of individuals to become more and do better causes changes in their "morphogenic field" which somehow results in the sudden appearance of new life forms.[14]

The bottom line of all these "insights" about evolution is that there is now emerging a breakthrough in the development of the human spirit. "I believe," says Redfield, "that we have finally reached a point, where the idea of a personal transcendent experience—variously called enlightenment, nirvana, satori, transcendence, and cosmic consciousness—has reached a significant level of acceptance."[15]

He summarizes the significance of this spiritual evolution, from the New Age perspective, as follows:

> We are at this moment, because of the truths millions of humans have slowly brought into the world, becoming aware of the full picture of evolution. By unconsciously following their birth visions [the knowledge of our life's purpose which we bring into each new incarnation], each generation throughout history has been serving to evolve human reality in a purposeful way, bringing us ever closer to the spiritual awareness that already exists in the Afterlife dimension. Step by step we are becoming aware that we are spiritual beings slowly evolving a spiritual reality on this planet.[16]

All the world's problems will be resolved as the evolution of human consciousness continues (e.g., crime, pollution, and environmental degradation). Christ will not return to renew the world as the Bible says, but this will happen as a result of human evolution.[17] To support the idea that society will be transformed by means of a new consciousness and spiritual unfolding, moving toward a completely spiritual culture on earth, Redfield cites Daniel 12:3–4:

> Those who are wise will shine like the brightness of the heavens, and those who lead many to righteousness like the stars for ever and ever. But you, Daniel, close up and seal the words of the scroll until the time of the end.

The wise who lead others to righteousness, according to Redfield, are those who are sufficiently evolved by the means revealed in the manuscript. And the words which have been sealed up until the time of the end, of course, are those that are now being revealed by Redfield in the Insights of the manuscript.[18]

This false teaching is another excellent example of scripture twisting involving ignoring the context. The passage in question is not about a final revelation of spiritual truth which has been kept hidden for centuries in a secret manuscript. Rather, it is, in context, about the Tribulation and the Battle of Armageddon led by the antichrist against Israel:

> The king will do as he pleases. He will exalt and
> magnify himself above every god and will say
> unheard of things against the God of gods. He
> will be successful until the time of wrath is com-
> pleted [i.e., the Tribulation], for what has been
> determined must take place. . . . At that time
> Michael, the great prince who protects your
> people, will arise. There will be a time of distress
> such as has not happened from the beginning of
> nations until then. But at that time your people—
> everyone whose name is found written in the
> book—will be delivered (Daniel 11:36, 12:1).

At that time, many will be led to salvation (led
to "righteousness") by those who understand what
is happening ("those who are wise and shine").
Then the meaning of the end times prophecies of
Daniel will be clear to "those who are wise [and]
will understand" (Daniel 12:10). Thus, metaphorically, the prophecies will be unsealed and opened,
which is to say their meaning will be made clear
by the events which take place. Therefore,
Redfield's misuse of this scripture is also a case of
taking a metaphorical statement literally.

ENERGY TRANSFORMATION: THE FUEL OF EVOLUTION

At the core of Redfield's occult version of evolution is the concept of energy transformation. In *The
Celestine Prophecy*, the universe is seen as a vast dynamic energy field. One taps into this field by psychi-
cally experiencing nature, especially in forests and on

mountain peaks. In this way, one raises his own energy level and thereby evolves his consciousness.

The techniques involved in this process are identical to those used in accumulating chi, which were discussed earlier. They are all occult, and they are all based on self-effort—how *we* do it, not how to let God do it. Essentially, this involves "seeing" energy fields which induce an altered state of consciousness. As depicted in *The Celestine Prophecy*, this produces such phenomena as precognition, psychic intuition, synchronicity (the occurrence of fortunate coincidences which guide one toward greater spiritual development), and other forms of psychic and paranormal phenomena.

Specifically, here's how one brings about such results: ". . . first of all, we can go within and try to increase our own energy level by focusing on love, lightness, and connecting with the environment." This is an activity "that expands our inner opening to the divine."[19] Such altered states are the means of obtaining "transcendent information," including that pertaining to past lives.

In this "going within" to receive messages from a "higher source,"[20] there is a complete lack of discernment because everything one experiences is swallowed whole. Redfield himself is a perfect example of the result. He has been totally deceived, accepting every kind of blasphemous, heretical, ungodly teaching as absolute truth with no inkling that they are all the doctrines of demons.

In addition to the occult techniques described above, a number of others are recommended in *The*

Celestine Prophecy: visualization, conscious breathing, positive thinking, interpreting dreams as guides to life, sending energy to others as a means of gaining more for oneself, and controlling matter and events by one's thoughts (e.g., improving plant growth by mental concentration). The latter is a good example of how New Agers utilize ecology as a spiritual practice which is actually a form of sorcery.

In *The Tenth Insight*, Redfield presents even more forms of occultism, including high energy locations (power centers in nature, which are gateways into the "afterlife"), past life recall (reincarnation), animal guides, spirit guides, sensing presences, travel by psychic projection (astral projection), spiritism (seeing souls in the afterlife and having other afterlife experiences), seeing "guardian angels," influencing the future, increasing chi through body sensing, mental healing, precognition, mental imaging to influence reality, channeling ("encounters with souls in the afterlife"[21]), and Native American shamanism and vision quests. Much of this, of course, is pure sorcery.

In *The Celestine Vision*, he adds yoga, tai chi, and martial arts as examples of energy transformation for spiritual evolution and as recommended techniques for the practice of "real Christianity."

To provide scriptural support for such practices, Redfield cites Matthew 18:20: "For where two or three come together in my name, there am I with them." This scripture, he says, is speaking of the "systematic increase in everyone's energy."[22] This means that "there am I with them" refers to the "divine energy" of the universe. And "come together in my name" means the spiritually advanced have gathered to help each other raise their energy levels.

This is another case of totally ignoring the context, for, according to *Nelson's Commentary*, this and the passage preceding it refers specifically to church discipline:

> It is a promise for guidance for the two or three who confront, and it is a promise for the church to claim wisdom and restoration for the erring brother. . . . the promise of Christ to be in their midst in the carrying through of the process of discipline . . . .[23]

I believe this verse also speaks of the power available in praying together, for verse 19 says, ". . . if two of you on earth agree about anything you ask for, it will be done for you by my Father in heaven." It is obviously not about obtaining energy through occult practices in a group setting. It is about Christ's presence among His people when they pray together in His name. Redfield, therefore, begs the question, Why is it about getting energy? Instead of providing evidence or reasons for this conclusion, he just states it as a fact.

COUNTERFEIT CHRISTIANITY: THE RELATIVITY OF TRUTH

Redfield bases his perversion of biblical truth on the idea that truth is relative. Subjective experience is his criterion for truth. One of the characters in *The Celestine Prophecy* illustrates this concept when he says, ". . . my truth is to help people discover who they really are. . . . My truth is helping others grasp this [sixth] insight."[24]

This concept is developed in *The Celestine Vision*. There, truth is said to be "consensus building,"[25] and it is something which changes from moment to moment:

> What particular truth, unique to myself and my experience can I now go out and convey to others about how one can live life more fully and spiritually?

> . . . The essential point, in my opinion, is that we understand what our truth is at the current moment and be ready to express it with courage, whenever appropriate.[26]

ECUMENICALISM: ALL RELIGIONS ARE EQUAL (EXCEPT CHRISTIANITY AND JUDAISM)

The idea that all religions are basically the same and therefore equally valid is a dominant theme in *The Celestine Prophecy*. This is seen in the explanation of the ninth insight (the central character is speaking):

> All religion, it says, is about human kind finding relationship to one higher source. And all religions speak of a perception of God within, a perception that fills us, making us more than

we were. Religions become corrupted when leaders are assigned to explain God's will to the
people instead of showing them how to find their
direction within themselves.[27]

This says, in effect, that pastors and teachers
("leaders assigned to explain God's will") have corrupted Christianity. Rather, its truth, like all truth,
is to be found by looking within ourselves—*not*
through the Bible or godly teaching or prayer or the
leading of the Holy Spirit.

All religions, says Redfield, are about the same
thing: one God who is not a person but a force. And
in this regard, eastern religions are superior to Christianity and Judaism because the impersonal eastern
version of God as the universe (or universal energy)
is more accurate.[28]

Redfield predicts (we must assume, unknowingly) the total ecumenism of the antichrist's one-
world religion when he says that all religions will
be synthesized into a "global spirituality," which will
be realized when they are all represented at the
temple in Jerusalem:

We could see clearly that these dialogues [com-
paring various religions] would result in the rebuilding of a grand temple in Jerusalem, jointly
occupied by all the major religions—Jewish,
Christian, Islamic, Eastern, even the de facto
religion of secular idealism . . . .[29]

This all-inclusive religion (the "true" Christianity) will supposedly result from divine "synchronicity" fulfilling the divine purpose:

> Synchronicity [meaning, you will recall, coincidences leading to spiritual evolution], as well as the overall new spiritual awareness that we're building, is merely a consciousness of the way the divine operates in our lives. All major religions—Hindu, Buddhist, Jewish, Christian, Islamic, as well as many shamanic traditions, share the notion of being responsive to the will of God. To put it differently, all are concerned with our growth toward unity with a Godhead or coming into communion with the creative force behind the human condition. Our new awareness of synchronicity is just the perception or experience of our connection with this divine force.[30]

Again, Redfield attempts to provide biblical support for his false teaching—in this case, that all religions teach the same thing. As an example, he takes the scripture about *sowing and reaping* and interprets it to mean *karma*, saying this concept is common to all religions. As his authorities for this interpretation, he cites Norman Vincent Peale and Napoleon Hill.[31]

This astonishing example of scripture twisting, once more involves ignoring the context and begging the question. Here is what the verse in question, Galatians 6:7, actually says: "Do not be deceived: God cannot be mocked. A man reaps what he sows."

This is not about receiving the results in the next incarnation for what you do in this one. There is no indication of reincarnation here. Rather, it is about receiving the results in this world and the next, of how one lives—sinfully or godly. The succeeding verses make this clear:

> The one who sows to please his sinful nature, from that nature will reap destruction; the one who sows to please the Spirit, from the Spirit will reap eternal life. Let us not become weary in doing good, for at the proper time we will reap a harvest if we do not give up (Galatians 6:8–9).

The question begged is, Why should this be interpreted as referring to karma, the so-called law of cause and effect governing one's reincarnations? Again, no reasons or evidence are given. It is simply stated as a fact.

DIMINISHING CHRISTIANITY: "IT'S NOT WHAT YOU THINK IT IS"

The Celestine Prophecy not only says that Christianity is no better than any other religion and is, in fact, less accurate and complete, but it also says Jesus was only a man, the Bible is not true, and the church is an obstacle to God's will. These ideas are introduced or indicated in *The Celestine Prophecy* and developed more fully in *The Tenth Insight* and *The Celestine Vision*.

Jesus, "the Yogi"

According to the manuscript, Jesus was just an evolved man, one who had received sufficient higher energy[32] to find His way by looking within Himself.[33] He was, in fact, says Redfield, a yogi master—a "special adept." And the Christian church is ignorant of who and what Jesus really was because He explained His evolved ability as "the mark of a deity." Furthermore, Jesus didn't really perform any true miracles. They were just what happens when one raises his vibrations.[34]

Father Sanchez explains Jesus this way:

> "The Manuscript says that sometimes in history one individual would grasp the exact way of connecting with God's source of energy and direction and would thus become a lasting example that this connection is possible." Sanchez looked at me. "Isn't that what Jesus really did? Didn't he increase his energy and vibration until he was light enough to [walk on water]?[35]

The Bible: "Myth, Metaphor, and Misinformation"

According to Redfield, the Old Testament is mostly "mythology," which is used to depict the idea of one God. This idea, he says, was clarified and completed by eastern religions, which correctly teach that we are all part of God, who is a "creative force."[36] In addition, he sees Adam and Eve and their fall from grace and Satan and his fall from heaven as only metaphors.[37] Moreover, the Bible is all wrong about divine judgment "by a vengeful God." According to Redfield, we judge ourselves "by a divine consciousness of which we are a part."[38]

Finally, he declares that biblical prophecy has no validity. The Rapture, Tribulation, Antichrist, and second coming of Jesus are all nonsense. The Rapture, for example, is at best a purely symbolic portrayal of spiritual evolution. That is, when we become fully spiritual, we disappear to those who are on a lower level of energy/vibration/consciousness. "Do you think these end-times scholars are correct?" one of Redfield's characters asks.

> He shook his head. "I don't think so. The only prophecy that's being played out in this world is man's greed and corruption. Some dictator might rise up and take over, but it will be because he saw a way to take advantage of the chaos.
>
> ". . . If someone comes along that proposes a way to save us, to straighten things out, asking that we surrender some civil liberties, I have no doubt that we'll do it."[39]

The Church: "The Enemy of Truth"

As already indicated, Redfield characterizes church doctrine as a faulty picture of reality which the insights complete and clarify. It is "a simple world of good and evil defined by churchmen," which is to say, by the church. The church thereby rendered Christianity "pompous and meaningless ritual" and thus became the enemy of the truth.[40]

The Spiritual Discernment Guide

While there may be some truth in the charge of "pompous and meaningless ritual," this is a case of gross oversimplification. Redfield attributes all of these faults to the ignorance and errors of Roman Catholic clerics in the Middle Ages. Thus, his definition of "the church" obviously does not include all Christians and does not encompass all Christian doctrine and practice.

The insights supposedly complete, clarify, and correct the doctrines of the church primarily by means of redefinitions (which, incidentally, contain many occult elements). In his three books, Redfield redefines a great many Christian terms, but here we will discuss only those which occur in *The Celestine Prophecy*:

- **God**—The universe (i.e., the god of pantheism). In *The Celestine Prophecy*, Redfield does not mention God directly but speaks of the universe in terms that suggest God, e.g., it is the source of all that we need for continued evolution. Elsewhere, he says God is "a force, a consciousness . . . a divine energy"; the "creative process lying at the heart of the universe"; a "divine energy" inside us; and "the larger aspect of our being.[41]
- **Jesus Christ**—An evolved man (as noted earlier) who fully received the universe's energy.
- **Salvation**—Spiritual evolution. The manuscript supposedly gives the exact process of becoming saved (i.e., becoming more

evolved spiritually). Father Sanchez says, "What does accepting the teachings and winning salvation really mean? What is the process through which this happens? Doesn't the Manuscript show us the exact process of becoming more spiritual, connected, saved—the way it actually feels?"[42]

- **Sanctification (spiritual transformation)**—Receiving "God's" energy. Father Sanchez explains:

> "Isn't the story of the scriptures a story of people learning to receive God's energy and will within? Isn't that what the early prophets led the people to do in the Old Testament? And isn't that receptivity to God's energy within what culminated in the life of a carpenter's son, to the extent that we say God, himself, descended to Earth?
>
> "Isn't the story of the New Testament," he continued, "the story of a group of people being filled with some kind of energy that transformed them? Didn't Jesus, himself, say that what he did, we could do also, and more? We've never really taken that idea seriously, not until now. We're only now grasping what Jesus was talking about, where he was leading us. The Manuscript clarifies what he meant! How to do it!"[43]

This is another case of reinterpreting scripture to fit New Age philosophy—and of diminishing Christ into an evolved man in the process. Thus, the idea that He was God incarnate becomes just a figure of speech (taking a literal statement metaphorically). And once more, the scripture is twisted by ignoring the context and begging the question. The question is: Did Jesus in fact say or mean that what He did was evolve by receiving energy that transformed Him?

As we know, the Bible says no such thing. Rather, Jesus made it clear that He was God, equal with the Father, saying, "I and the Father are one" (John 10:38). And, far from becoming Christ by an occult process of spiritual evolution, He was the eternal Son of God who became incarnated as a man, having been sent to earth by the Father (John 6:44).

- **Love**—The giving and receiving of energy; or a result of being connected to the energy of the universe. Redfield also says love is an inner state involving a certain feeling that can be induced through mental concentration.[44]

- **Millennial kingdom**—Evolved humanity. That is, it will be the ideal society resulting from conscious evolution, where there is no need for money and all of humanity's physical needs are met. Thus, it is a counterfeit based on the Star Trek pattern of an advanced society.

- **The Rapture**—Attaining heaven by increased energy and spiritual evolution. Essentially, this means reaching the afterlife level while

still on earth, which is the ultimate purpose
of life on earth:

> The Ninth Insight . . . says that as we hu-
> mans continue to increase our vibration,
> an amazing thing will begin to happen.
> Whole groups of people, once they reach
> a certain level, will suddenly become in-
> visible to those who are still vibrating at a
> lower level. It will appear to the people on
> this lower level that the others just disap-
> peared, but the group themselves will feel
> as though they are still right here—only
> they will feel lighter. . . .
>
> When humans begin to raise their vibra-
> tions to a level where others cannot see
> them, . . . it will signal that we are cross-
> ing the barrier between this life and the
> other world from which we came and to
> which we go after death. This conscious
> crossing over is the path shown by the
> Christ. He opened up to the energy un-
> til he was so light he could walk on wa-
> ter. He transcended death right here on
> earth, and was the first to cross over, to
> expand the physical world into the spiri-
> tual. His life demonstrated how to do
> this, and if we connect with the same
> source we can head that same way, step
> by step. At some point everyone will vi-
> brate highly enough so that we can walk
> into heaven, in our same form. . . .

> The Insight says . . . that most individuals will reach this level of vibration during the third millennium, and in groups consisting of the people with whom they are most connected. But some cultures in history have already achieved the vibration. According to the Ninth Insight, the Mayans crossed over together."

> . . . Whenever we doubt our own path, or lose sight of the process, we just remember what we are evolving toward, what the process of living is all about. Reaching heaven on Earth is why we are here. And now we know how it can be done . . . how it will be done.[45]

This explanation of the Rapture, of course, has absolutely no basis in scripture. On the contrary, it is a total rewriting of scripture to make it fit New Age philosophy. Therefore, once more it involves begging the question and ignoring the context. The question to be answered: Why should the Rapture be so defined and described when there is nothing in the Bible to suggest such a meaning? Rather, the relevant scriptures directly contradict Redfield's assertions. Here is how the Bible describes the Rapture:

> For the Lord himself will come down from heaven, with a loud command, with the voice of the archangel, and with the trumpet call of God, and the dead in Christ will rise first. After that, we who are still alive and are left will be caught

> up together with them in the clouds to meet the
> Lord in the air. And so we will be with the Lord
> forever (1 Thessalonians 4:16–17).

> We will not all sleep, but we will be changed—
> in a flash, in the twinkling of an eye, at the last
> trumpet. For the trumpet will sound, the dead
> will be raised imperishable, and we will be
> changed. For the perishable must clothe itself
> with the imperishable, and the mortal with im-
> mortality (1 Corinthians 15:52–53).

There is nothing here about working to achieve higher vibrations, remaining on earth following transformation, consciously crossing over, walking into heaven on our own, this process having happened to various people at various times in history, or this being our ultimate purpose in living. Rather, it will be instantaneous and caused by the direct action of the Lord. It will involve rising in the air to meet Christ and being taken by Him into heaven.

Two basic questions arise from Redfield's extended treatment of the Rapture: Why does he devote so much space to it? And why does he give it such a central place in his new revelation of the "real meaning" of Christianity? I believe it is because Satan knows that when it takes place, it will prove once and for all the truth of scripture to the world, and he wants to prevent this from happening. Therefore, he deludes people like Redfield into believing his counterfeit version.

Thus, not only will these people be deprived of knowing the truth, but those unfortunate Christians who buy into the deception will also be prevented from being included in the Rapture. For, as we saw earlier, Jesus is coming for those who are expecting Him and are prepared for Him.

In *The Tenth Insight*, Redfield also provides New Age redefinitions of repentance, the new heaven and new earth, prayer, the Holy Spirit, hell, evil, and faith. In *The Celestine Vision*, he adds communion, the kingdom of God, being born again, tithing, man, sin, the glorified body, and the devil.

Other false teachings, in addition to those found in *The Celestine Prophecy*, are also presented in Redfield's other books. In *The Tenth Insight*, I counted eleven of these, and in *The Celestine Vision,* nine.

In the former, he adds the following, which are even more directly anti-Christian than those in *The Celestine Prophecy*:

> Eastern religions, occultism, and mysticism are superior to orthodox Christianity.

> All religions will be combined into a one-world religion.

> Satan and demons don't exist.

> There is no evil because everything is from God (or a part of God).

> There is no sin because people are naturally good.

Science is the ultimate source of truth regarding
the material universe. (Redfield believes in many
of the same things that Hugh Ross does.)

Science is also superior to the church as a source
of truth regarding the inner psychological and spiritual world (i.e., the world of the soul and the spirit).

God exists inside ourselves as divine energy
which we can tap into.

All supernatural phenomena are true and
good; therefore, we should be open to all such
phenomena.

What we call "bad" people (e.g., criminals and
terrorists) are really just victims of their environment. They have no moral responsibility for
their behavior.

The church is opposed to science and its truth.

In *The Celestine Vision*, Redfield adds these explicitly anti-Christian teachings:

Adam, Eve, and Satan are metaphors and mythology.

The church doesn't help man find spiritual reality.

The church is an obstacle to spiritual development, truth, knowledge, and experience.

The Bible gives a false idea of heaven, hell, and death.

The church does not provide instruction on how to experience actual spiritual reality.

The church is based on religious mythology.

The church understands neither what is involved in the death process nor the true nature of the afterlife.

Contrary to scripture, the traditional roles of father and mother are unreal stereotypes.

Contrary to scripture, everything is and will continue to get better and better—all by means of raising people's energy levels.

"SATAN IS ONLY A FIGURE OF SPEECH"

Before leaving the works of James Redfield, we need to look at one final example of scripture twisting which is foundational to Satan's strategy for promoting apostasy. This is Redfield's audacious **lie** that Satan doesn't exist.

In *The Celestine Prophecy*, this is a lie of omission, for nowhere in the Manuscript is there any mention of the devil or his demons. What the Bible has to say about them is simply ignored. The assumption is, apparently, that there is no point in discussing something which is only a biblical metaphor. As noted earlier, this is perhaps Satan's cleverest deception, for it permits him to operate with complete freedom among those who do not believe he is real.

In *The Tenth Insight*, Redfield makes this false teaching explicit:

"What about the many references in sacred texts
and scriptures to Satan?"

"This idea is a metaphor, a symbolic way of
warning people to look to the divine for security, not to their sometimes tragic ego urges and
habits. Blaming an outside force for everything
bad was perhaps important at a certain stage in
human development. But now it obscures the
truth, because blaming our behavior on forces
outside ourselves is a way of avoiding responsibility. And we tend to use the idea of Satan to
project that some people are inherently evil so
we can dehumanize the ones we disagree with
and write them off. It is time now to understand the true nature of human evil in a more
sophisticated way and then to deal with it."[46]

Thus, anyone who believes in the devil is self-
justifying, irresponsible, and unsophisticated.

This illustrates beautifully the cleverness of
Satan's arguing against his own existence by citing
examples of how people use him to excuse themselves. By saying "The devil made me do it," they
avoid responsibility for their own behavior. While
it is true that some are indeed guilty in this way, it
doesn't prove Satan doesn't exist. It is, in fact, a non
sequitur. It is just as logical as saying that the effects
of spiritual wounding in childhood are not real because some people use them as an excuse for immoral or unlawful behavior.

It is also a hasty generalization because the fact
that some people blame Satan falsely, thereby fall-

ing into sin, doesn't mean that he is *never* the cause. And, of course, it is a classic example of taking a literal statement metaphorically.

The scripture says that Satan does literally exist and that he tempts and deceives people in order to lead them into sin. For example:

> At once the Spirit sent him [Jesus] into the desert, and he was in the desert forty days, being tempted by Satan (Mark 1:12–13).

> Then Peter said, "Ananias, how is it that Satan has so filled your heart that you have lied to the Holy Spirit and have kept for yourself some of the money you received for the land?" (Acts 5:3)

In neither of these verses is there any indication that the statements are not to be taken literally. They are both straightforward narratives about actual events in the lives of real people. Thus, Redfield ignores the context of such verses and likewise is guilty of ignoring related scriptures.

We see in *The Celestine Prophecy*, then, (as well as in Redfield's other books) that what is presented as the real, inner meaning of Christianity is in fact just the opposite. It denies the truth of the gospel, diminishes Christ, contradicts scripture, discredits the church, and accuses Christianity of being obsolete, misguided, and a hindrance to spiritual progress. It substitutes self-effort and occult techniques for the sanctifying work of the Holy Spirit and replaces the true, almighty God of creation with a pantheistic counterfeit—an all-pervading energy which works by the "natural" (and therefore blind, amoral, and random) process of evolution.

Let me ask you one final time: Is this the sort of teaching that Christians should be following, looking into, or even toying with?

James Redfield is a false teacher and false prophet, for he teaches heresy and he prophesies a world where everyone can become like Jesus through self-effort and higher vibrations. But the Bible says that false teachers have inflated egos and no real understanding:

> If anyone teaches false doctrines and does not agree to the sound instruction of our Lord Jesus Christ and to godly teaching, he is conceited and understands nothing (1 Timothy 6:3–4).

Moreover, they will receive what they deserve; that is, eternal damnation (2 Corinthians 11:15): "Because they introduce destructive heresies, even denying the sovereign Lord who bought them," they will bring "swift destruction on themselves" (2 Peter 2:1). Likewise, Jesus said the false prophets will be "cut down and thrown into the fire" like "a bad tree that cannot bear good fruit" (Matthew 7:18–19).

In the Old Testament, Jehovah has this to say about them:

> "As for the prophets
>   who lead my people astray,
> The sun will set for the prophets,
>   and the day will go dark for them.
> The seers will be ashamed

and the diviners disgraced.
They will all cover their faces
because there is no answer from God."
(Micah 3:5–7)

Occultism in the church, then, is a powerful seed of apostasy—whether it is satanism; misguided forms of meditation, prayer, or worship; or a New Age counterfeit of Christianity. The Bible contains strong warnings for all who practice such things:

I will destroy your witchcraft
and you will no longer cast spells.
I will destroy your carved images
and your sacred stones from among you;
you will no longer bow down
to the work of your hands.
I will uproot from among you your
Asherah poles
and demolish your cities.
I will take vengeance in anger and wrath
upon the nations that have not obeyed
me. (Micah 5:12–15)

CHAPTER NINETEEN

Conclusion (Some Final Reccomendations And Reminders)

We have seen the many ways in which Satan uses New Age teachings and practices to pervert the truth in order to deceive the body of Christ and divert them from the faith. He appeals to the desires of our sinful nature with unholy enticements of power, wealth, status, happiness, and health. He would have us believe that God, the Bible, and the church are not sufficient to meet our spiritual needs.

In their place, he offers substitutes, counterfeits, and twisted scriptures, using lies, faulty logic, and misleading semantics. He tries to make us believe science and subjective experience are better sources of truth than the Bible. He tells us to swallow everything whole because demons have no real power—or don't exist at all (take your pick), and, therefore, *anything* supernatural must be of God. Simultaneously, he tells us to throw out the baby with the bathwater because there are no *real* supernatural manifestations of Holy Spirit power—or they are demonic delusions (take your pick). He teaches false doctrines based on New Age philosophy, evolution, psychology, humanism, eastern religion, and occultism.

By means of these deceptions, he robs the church of much of the power and help it needs, including that of supernatural gifts, inner healing, natural medicine, authentic Christian psychology, sanctified self-esteem, godly suffering, real faith, genuine prayer, the authority of scripture, and the protection of discernment.

In view of the manifold ways in which Satan obscures and distorts the truth in order to delude, defraud, and destroy the church, then, what should we be doing?

The Bible has many answers to this question. It says, for example, that we should

- **Become mature so we can use discernment**

    We have much to say about this, but it is hard to explain because you are slow to learn. In fact, though by this time you ought to be teachers, you need someone to teach you the elementary truths of God's word all over again. You need milk, not solid food! Anyone who lives on milk, being still an infant, is not acquainted with the teachings about righteousness. But solid food is for the mature, who by constant use have trained themselves to distinguish good from evil (Hebrews 5:11–14).

My son, preserve sound judgment and discernment; do not let them out of your sight; they will be life for you, an ornament to grace your neck. Then you will go on your way in safety, and your foot will not stumble; when you lie down, your sleep will be sweet. Have no fear of sudden disaster or of the ruin that overtakes the wicked, for the Lord will be your confidence and will keep your foot from being snared (Proverbs 3:21–26).

- **Do what the Lord requires**

  He has showed you, O man, what is good.

  And what does the Lord require of you?

  To act justly and to love mercy and to walk humbly with your God (Micah 6:8).

- **Seek the kingdom of God and not things**

  "So do not worry, saying, 'What shall we eat?' or 'What shall we drink?' or 'What shall we wear?' For the pagans run after all these things, and your heavenly Father knows that you need them. But seek first his kingdom and his righteousness, and all these things will be given to you as well (Matthew 6:31–34).

- **Love the truth in order to overcome Satan's deceptions**

  > The coming of the lawless one will be in accordance with the work of Satan displayed in all kinds of counterfeit miracles, signs and wonders, and in every sort of evil that deceives those who are perishing. They perish because they refused to love the truth and so be saved. For this reason God sends them a powerful delusion so that they will believe the lie and so that all will be condemned who have not believed the truth but delighted in wickedness (2 Thessalonians 2:9–12).

  Wilkerson adds this timely warning:

  > I want to say this to you above all else: the antichrist is going to come on the scene as the greatest prosperity preacher in all of history. And the devil is already picking halfhearted believers to be initiated into his cult. Soon there will be no more restraints on our society, and Christians will be more vulnerable than ever to demonic seductions . . .

  > If you're rejecting the warnings of the restraining Holy Ghost—if you're disobeying God time after time, without any heart-grief—then you're being recruited for the cult of Antichrist. The devil is silently initiating you into his

mystery of iniquity. And when the promising, miracle-working antichrist comes
along, you'll be swept up in his lies and
given over to a delusion![1]

• Be ready always to speak and hear the truth

... be prepared in season and out of season; correct, rebuke and encourage—
with great patience and careful
instruction. For the time will come when
men will not put up with sound doctrine.
Instead, to suit their own desires, they will
gather around them a great number of
teachers to say what their itching ears
want to hear. They will turn their ears
away from the truth and turn aside to
myths (2 Timothy 4:2–4).

• Rely on the Holy Scripture as the primary source of truth and the guide for right living

The law of the Lord is perfect, reviving
the soul.

The statutes of the Lord are trustwor-
thy, making wise the simple.

The precepts of the Lord are right, giving joy to the heart.

The commands of the Lord are radiant,
giving light to the eyes.

The fear of the Lord is pure, enduring forever.

The ordinances of the Lord are sure and altogether righteous.

They are more precious than gold, than much pure gold; they are sweeter than honey, than honey from the comb.

By them is your servant warned; in keeping them there is great reward (Psalm 19:7–11).

- **Focus on the things of God**

  Set your minds on things above, not on earthly things. For you died, and your life is now hidden with Christ in God. When Christ, who is your life, appears, then you also will appear with him in glory (Colossians 3:2–4).

- **Remember that Christ has prayed for our protection and sanctification**

  "My prayer is not that you take them out of the world but that you protect them from the evil one. They are not of the world, even as I am not of it. Sanctify them by the truth; your word is truth" (John 17:15–17).

- **Believe in the sufficiency of Christ**

  He is the image of the invisible God, the
  firstborn over all creation. For by him all
  things were created; things in heaven and
  on earth, visible and invisible, whether
  thrones or powers or rulers or authorities;
  all things were created by him and for him.
  He is before all things, and in him all things
  hold together. And he is the head of the
  body, the church; he is the beginning and
  the firstborn from among the dead, so that
  in everything he might have the supremacy. For God was pleased to have all
  his fullness dwell in him, and through him
  to reconcile to himself all things, whether
  things on earth or things in heaven, by
  making peace through his blood, shed on
  the cross (Colossians 1:15–20).

  My purpose is that they may be encouraged in heart and united in love, so that
  they may have the full riches of complete
  understanding in order that they may
  know the mystery of God, namely, Christ,
  in whom are hidden all the treasures of
  wisdom and knowledge. I tell you this so
  that no one may deceive you by fine-
  sounding arguments (Colossians 2:2–4).

- **Be sure not to turn away from God to worship idols**

  > You yourselves know how we lived in Egypt and how we passed through the countries on the way here. You saw among them their detestable images and idols of wood and stone, of silver and gold. Make sure there is no man or woman, clan or tribe among you today whose heart turns away from the Lord our God to go and worship the gods of those nations; make sure there is no root among you that produces such bitter poison (Deuteronomy 29:16–18).

  > How long, O men, will you turn my glory into shame?

  > How long will you love delusions and seek false gods? (Psalm 4:2)

- **Choose life and not death**

  > See, I set before you today life and prosperity, death and destruction. For I command you today to love the Lord your God, to walk in his ways, and to keep his commands, decrees and laws; then you will live and increase, and the Lord your God will bless you in the land you are entering to possess.

  > But if your heart turns away and you are not obedient, and if you are drawn away

to bow down to other gods and worship them, I declare to you this day that you will certainly be destroyed. You will not live long in the land you are crossing the Jordan to enter and possess.

This day I call heaven and earth as witnesses against you that I have set before you life and death, blessings and curses. Now choose life, so that you and your children may live and that you may love the Lord your God, listen to his voice, and hold fast to him. For the Lord is your life, and he will give you many years in the land he swore to give to your fathers, Abraham, Isaac and Jacob (Deuteronomy 30:15–20).

- **Take Caleb as a role model**

Then Caleb silenced the people before Moses and said, "We should go up and take possession of the land, for we can certainly do it" (Numbers 13:23).

". . . not one of them will ever see the land I promised on oath to their forefathers. No one who has treated me with contempt will ever see it. But because my servant Caleb has a different spirit and follows me wholeheartedly, I will bring him into the land he went to, and his descendants will inherit it" (Numbers 14:23–24).

I believe Caleb is our role model for resisting apostasy and the story of Israel's entry into the promised land is a picture (type) representing our growth into spiritual maturity and our realization of the fullness we have in Christ. As God brings us to this "promised land" of the spirit, His "manna" (provision) may seem monotonous and distasteful to our old, sinful nature. Therefore, we must keep our eyes on the goal (growing up in our new, spiritual nature) and continue to walk in the Spirit and not in the flesh. Then, we will not look for substitutes or desire to return to the old, familiar ways but will appreciate the "manna" for what it is—God's spiritual food that sustains us on our spiritual journey.

The other side of this story is the bad report of the undiscerning spies whom Moses sent ahead into the promised land. The Israelites (except for Caleb and Joshua, who used discernment) were deceived by the false assessment and so refused to enter. This, I believe, is a type of apostasy in the church today. Likewise, the wandering of the tribes in the desert signifies the penalty for the undiscerning who fall away. They will be barred from the promised land of spiritual fulfillment and eternal life.

Finally, let me give you one more analogy about the undiscerning in the church who are caught in deception and are falling away from the faith. They are like the unsuspecting passengers on the Titanic. They are complacent, self-satisfied, and oblivious to the danger. They are focused on getting blessed and being comfortable.

They are running out of time, drawing ever closer to the unseen iceberg of apostasy. Soon it will be too late, and then they will sink in a catastrophic turmoil of deception and confusion. Can they correct their course? Can they avoid spiritual disaster?

I believe they can, though many, I am grieved to say, will continue on their fatal course and be trapped in the icy waters of spiritual add-ons, substitutes, and counterfeits. The alarm is being sounded and those who take heed and see the danger will not be destroyed in this way by Satan's New Age strategies. I pray that it may be so for you.

It is to help you to avoid such a fate that I have written this book. So I pray also that you will apply the concepts presented herein. By way of encouragement, I leave you this parting reminder of what to do:

When you hear an unusual interpretation of scripture, an idea that differs from orthodox doctrine, or a new teaching, first, pray that the Holy Spirit will give you insight, understanding, and the gift of discerning of spirits. Then, question what you hear.

- Does it involve logical fallacies or semantic manipulations or does it contradict scripture?

- Does it appeal to any of the five basic temptations that may become seeds of apostasy—power, wealth, status, happiness, or health?

- Does it offer substitutes for or counterfeits of prayer, the Bible, or God?

- Could it diminish your faith or weaken your belief in the Bible?

- Does it lead you away from God? (See appendices A and B for more specific checklists of these reminders.)

If the answer to any of these questions is yes, then you need to ask one more: Is it totally false and bad, or are there some aspects that are true and good?

By responding in this way, you will have applied the principles of spiritual discernment. You will have kept yourself from swallowing everything whole or throwing out the baby with the bathwater. And, most importantly, you will have been faithful and obedient in heeding the warning of our Lord: "Watch out that no one deceives you."

And this is my prayer: that your love may abound more and more in knowledge and depth of insight, *so that you may be able to discern what is best* and may be pure and blameless until the day of Christ, filled with the fruit of righteousness that comes through Jesus Christ—to the glory and praise of God (Philippians 1:9–11, emphasis added).

APPENDICES

Checklist of Logical Fallacies and Semantic Manipulations

1. **Lies (Untrue Statements)**
2. **Logical Fallacies**
   Begging the question
   Hasty generalization
   Non sequitur
   Argument by popularity
   Appeal to authority
   False cause (post hoc ergo propter hoc [after this therefore because of this])
   Either, or
   False analogy
   Over simplification
3. **Semantic Manipulations**
   Stereotyping
   Redefining
   Ignoring the context

Ignoring related scripture
Rewriting scripture
Mistranslation
Slanting
Shifting terms
Shifting meaning
Taking metaphors literally
Taking literal statements metaphorically

Discernment Questions

Basic List

1. Is it relevant?
2. Is it true?
3. Is it accurate?
4. Is it logical?
5. Does it agree with the Bible?
6. Are any valid reasons or evidence given?
7. Does it misuse or manipulate language (semantics)?
8. Does it lead you closer to God or farther away?
9. Does it leave out any important considerations?
10. Does it exalt Jesus as God the Son, or does it diminish Him?
11. Does it appeal to any of the five basic temptations that may become seeds of apostasy—power, wealth, status, happiness, or health?

12. Does it offer substitutes for or counterfeits of prayer, the Bible, or God?
13. Could it diminish your faith or weaken your belief in Scripture?
14. Does it bear bad spiritual fruit?
15. Does it violate common sense?
16. Does it throw out the baby with the bathwater?
17. Does it swallow everything whole?
18. Who wins?

BASIC CATEGORIES (WITH RELATED CONSIDERATIONS)

1. Does it contradict the Bible
   Does it agree with the Bible?
2. Does it have any negative spiritual consequences?
   Does it lead you closer to God or farther away?
   Does it exalt Jesus as God the Son, or does it diminish Him?
   Does it appeal to any of the five basic temptations that may become seeds of apostasy— power wealth, status, happiness, or health?
   Does it offer substitutes for or counterfeits of prayer, the Bible, or God?
   Does it bear good spiritual fruit?
   Who wins?
3. Is it inaccurate or untrue?
   Is it true?
   Is it accurate?
   Does it violate common sense?

4. Is it illogical?

Is it logical? (non sequitur, false cause, evading the issue, false analogy)

Does it provide evidence or valid reasons? (begging the question, argument by popularity, appeal to authority)

Does it leave out any important considerations? (over simplification, ignoring the context, ignoring related scripture, either-or)

Does it throw out the baby with the bathwater? (hasty generalization, guilt by association)

Does it swallow everything whole? (stereotyping, hasty generalization)

5. Does it misuse language?

Does it manipulate semantics? (stereotyping, redefinition, ignoring the context, ignoring related scripture, rewriting scripture, mistranslation, slanting, shifting terms, shifting the meaning, taking metaphors literally, taking literal statements metaphorically)

Evolution Versus Creation— Which Model Fits the Facts?

To see which model best fits the facts of the real world as we know it, we can take two basic approaches:

1. Identify the predictions which can be made based on each model about how the world should be if each were true and then compare these predictions with the observable evidence.
2. Look at the actual scientific evidence for each model.

PREDICTIONS OF THE TWO MODELS

To see which model best fits the observed facts— or to put it another way, which has the most actual evidence to support it—we must first look at the basic predictions each makes about the world. Then we must ask ourselves: Is this predicted condition what is actually found in the real world? Let's take these predictions one at a time.

- *Prediction 1—Transitional Forms*
  Evolution Model: Since evolution involves the slow transformation of one life form into another, there should be many transitional forms in the fossil record and also among the plants and animals presently living on the earth.
  Found in the real world? No.
  Creation Model: Since God created the species "according to their various kinds," there should be no transitional forms, but only distinct, separate kinds.
  Found in the real world? Yes.
- *Prediction 2—New Species (Kinds)*
  Evolution Model: New species should appear in the fossil record as the result of a given sequence of transitional forms and these new species should then in turn give rise to new transitional forms and additional species.
  Found in the real world? No.
  Creation Model: Since all species were created in the beginning, no new species should be appearing, but adaptation within species should appear as the result of varying environmental conditions.
  Found in the real world? Yes.

- *Prediction 3—Increasing Order*
  Evolution Model: Increasing order and complexity should be appearing and present life forms should be evolving.
  Found in the real world? No.
  Creation Model: No increasing order or complexity should be found and present life forms should not be evolving.
  Found in the real world? Yes.
- *Prediction 4—Spontaneous Life*
  Evolution Model: Life should arise spontaneously from matter and energy.
  Found in the real world? No.
  Creation Model: Life should not arise spontaneously but be passed on only by living organisms.
  Found in the real world? Yes.
- *Prediction 5—Survival Value*
  Evolution Model: All characteristics of living things should have survival value since survival of the fittest is the basic law of evolution.
  Found in the real world? No.
  Creation Model: Some characteristics of living things should not have survival value since God created them with many "unnecessary" attributes, such as beauty, self-sacrifice, self-denial, playfulness, humor, musical and other talents, etc.
  Found in the real world? Yes.

- *Prediction 6—Adapted Forms*
  Evolution Model: There should be relatively few forms adapted to a given environment since only the fittest survive.
  Found in the real world? No.
  Creation Model There may be many forms adapted to a given environment since many suitable forms were created by God.
  Found in the real world? Yes.
- *Prediction 7—Explosions and Random Accidents*
  Evolution Model: There should be evidence that explosions and random accidents sometimes produce order since evolution is based on the big bang and the premise that disorder precedes order.
  Found in the real world? No.
  Creation Model: Explosions and random accidents should always produce disorder since a basic law of nature, which God built into His creation, is that order precedes disorder (the second law of thermodynamics, discussed later).
  Found in the real world? Yes.
- *Prediction 8—Available Energy*
  Evolution Model: Available energy in the universe should be increasing to account for increasing complexity and organization.
  Found in the real world? No.
  Creation Model: Available energy should be decreasing since all available energy was created in the beginning and all activity has been

expending this energy ever since (first and second laws of thermodynamics, discussed later).
Found in the real world? Yes.

- *Prediction 9—Design or Purpose*
  Evolution Model: No particular design or purpose should be apparent in any living thing since everything has come into existence by pure random chance.
  Found in the real world? No
  Creation Model: Design and purpose should be apparent in all living things.
  Found in the real world? Yes.

- *Prediction 10—Human Artifacts*
  Evolution Model: Artifacts of human beings should be found that are very old (perhaps millions of years) since evolutionary change is a very long, slow process.
  Found in the real world? No.
  Creation Model: Artifacts of human beings should be found that are very young (only thousands of years) since the universe was created relatively recently.
  Found in the real world? Yes.

- *Prediction 11—Origin of Life*
  Evolution Model: There should be some evidence that life originated by purely natural means (spontaneous generation).
  Found in the real world? No.
  Creation Model: There should be no evidence that life originated by purely natural means.
  Found in the real world? Yes.

- *Prediction 12—Mutations*
  Evolution Model: Evidence should be found that mutations sometimes produce improvements.
  Found in the real world? No.
  Creation Model No evidence should be found that mutations produce improvements, but rather we should find that they always produce defects.
  Found in the real world? Yes.
- *Prediction 13—The Cosmos*
  Evolution Model: A well-organized cosmos (galaxies, solar systems, and planets) should not exist since the universe began with the big bang, and an explosion does not produce order but chaos.
  Found in the real world? No.
  Creation Model: A well-ordered cosmos should exist since a Creative Intelligence designed it.
  Found in the real world? Yes.
- *Prediction 14—Moral Principles*
  Evolution Model: Such moral phenomena as human ethics and compassion should not exist since all things are the products of blind, purposeless, amoral chance.
  Found in the real world? No.
  Creation Model: Moral principles (i.e., the knowledge of right and wrong) should exist since the universe is the creation of a morally good, loving God, and man, as a being created in His image, should naturally possess such qualities or at least the recognition

of and capacity for them. (If we were, in fact, the product of purely natural processes operating according to blind, amoral chance, then there would be no such things as ethics or compassion because this amoral process would provide no basis for these values. Also, there would be no basis for medical treatment or humanitarian activities because preserving and extending all human life would contradict the principle of the survival of the fittest. Instead, it would promote the survival of the weak, sickly, and defective—the opposite of what evolutionary theory says has been taking place. Thus, by eliminating the weak, Hitler was aiding the evolutionary process and therefore doing a "good" thing. How this could be thought of as a good thing in an amoral universe is another question.)

Found in the real world? Yes.

Incidentally, the latter point—that human morality exists—is a fundamental argument for the existence of God and of the non-existence of atheistic evolution. C.S. Lewis, for example, utilizes this argument in *Mere Christianity* for his brilliant defense of the Christian faith (incredibly, in spite of his belief in evolution, which is set forth in the same book; see chapter nine).

In that book, Lewis shows that all people recognize, on some level, the existence of the principle of right and wrong, which he calls the Law of Morality or the Law of Human Nature:

> . . . the Law of Human Nature tells you what hu-
> man beings ought to do and do not. . . . there is
> something above and beyond the ordinary facts of
> men's behaviour, and yet quite definitely real—a
> real law, which none of us made, but which we
> find pressing in on us. . . . I find that I do not exist
> on my own, that I am under a law: that somebody
> or something wants me to behave in a certain way.
>
> . . . a Something which is directing the universe,
> and which appears in me as a law urging me to
> do right and making me feel responsible and
> uncomfortable when I do wrong. . . . It is after
> you have realised that there is a real Moral Law
> and a Power behind the law, and that you have
> broken that law and put yourself wrong with that
> Power—it is after all this, and not a moment
> sooner, that Christianity begins to talk.[1]

Perhaps there are other predictions that could
be made from these two models, but I believe these
suffice to make the point. Obviously, creationism
fits the observable facts better than evolution does.
In fact, when rightly understood, I believe the evidence shows that evolution fits *none* of the observable facts, and creationism fits *all* of them. Why, then,
do non-christian scientists—who presumably are
interested in ascertaining truth—continue to ignore
the obvious facts and persist in believing in a theory
which has no basis in reality?

It seems obvious to me that the reason for this is
that they have been deluded into believing that the
God of the Bible does not exist and so there was never

a Creator who made all things in the beginning. Therefore, they must find some other explanation, and Satan supplied one early on in history (see chapter nine)
with the theory that more complex things have somehow evolved from less complex things. It is no less a
theory today than it was in ancient Babylon, but
modern refinements have given it the aura of "scientific truth," and therefore the humanistic educational
establishment—and along with it, sadly, the undiscerning in the church—now see it, not as unproven,
unbiblical theory but as absolute fact.

DISCERNING THE LIE OF EVOLUTION (SCIEN-
TIFIC REASONS THAT EVOLUTION IS FALSE)

Now, let's look at the second way of determining which model best fits the facts: the actual scientific evidence. We have seen how the evolution
model fails in its predictions of observable reality. It
also fails to fit the findings of science itself.

As noted earlier, evolutionists interpret scientific
data in terms of their presuppositions. They do not
base their conclusions on actual observation. Therefore, in spite of all their scientific window dressing,
these conclusions are not scientific at all but are, in
fact, faith-based. Because of this failure to follow scientific methods, the resulting theory contradicts a
number of scientific facts and principles.

Most important among these are

- the first and second laws of thermodynamics,

- the lack of reliable evidence for and the faulty logic of geological dating,
- the statistical impossibility of increased organization resulting from random chance, and
- the contradiction of the principle of Occam's Razor.

The First and Second Laws of Thermodynamics

Foremost among the scientific facts that contradict evolution are the law of conservation of energy and the law of entropy, also known as the first and second laws of thermodynamics.

The first law says essentially that nothing is now being created through the input of new energy (i.e., no new forms are appearing, or evolving) but that all energy is being preserved in one form or another. In other words, matter is interchangeable with energy, but the total amount of matter/energy in the universe always remains the same. Therefore, all things must have been brought into existence in the beginning, and that creative process is no longer operating.

The second law says that everything is moving toward a state of disorganization and inactivity (i.e., entropy). As *Webster's New World Dictionary* puts it, "entropy always increases and available energy diminishes in a closed system, as the universe."[2] In other words, entropy is what causes everything to slow down and fall apart.

Thus, to summarize, all processes in the universe are basically those of conservation of energy and disintegration of matter, *not* addition of energy and integration of matter as would be necessary for evolution to take place. Therefore, according to the basic laws of physics, evolution is impossible.

Geological Dating

The dating of fossils found in the geological strata of the earth's crust is the fundamental "evidence" that evolutionists use to support their theory that "higher" forms of life developed from "lower" forms. They argue that the less complex forms are found in lower strata and that the lower strata are older than the higher strata. They conclude, therefore, that the "lower" forms of life must be older than the "higher" forms and, therefore, that the latter must have evolved from the former. There are two basic fallacies in this reasoning: (1) the premises are false and (2) the logic consists of circular reasoning (a form of non sequitur) which begs the question.

FALSE PREMISES

It is not true that less complex fossil forms are always found in lower strata, and it is not true that a lower strata is necessarily older than a higher one. Actually, most, if not all, layers of strata could very well be the same age, for the world-wide Flood could have formed them at the same time. Moreover, strata are not always found in the same order, and, therefore, which ones are necessarily lower ("older") and which are necessarily higher ("younger") cannot be known.

Evolutionists maintain, however, that

> the fossils are always found in the same order, no matter in what part of the world they are discovered, and always the order is from simple to complex. Rocks buried lowest have the simpler fossils and those nearer the surface have the more complex fossils. The "geologic" column is the same everywhere.[3]

But, as the eminent scientist and Christian, Henry M. Morris, shows,

> . . . this is simply not so. . . . There are great numbers of exceptions and contradictions to this generalization. As a matter of fact, the geologic column really exists only in the minds of the historical geologists since it has been built up by superposition of deposits from various parts of the world.[4]

In other words, the geologic column doesn't really exist anywhere as the geologists have formulated it. *All* strata of the geologic column are *never* present at any one place. If it were, the resulting pile (based on the greatest thickness of each stratum) would be more than 100 miles high. Instead, geologists correlate various beds of strata at various sites by using fossil dating, identification of rock types, and other means, to build up an imaginary geological "column," which they then declare to be the established order of strata for all geologic ages.[5]

However, Morris notes that, on the contrary,

> . . . literally any rock system in the entire geologic column may be found lying directly on the basement complex and . . . any combination of rock systems may be found above it at any given location. . . . any series of rock systems may be found above the bottom, and there need be no difference in appearance, except for the fossils they contain. . . . it is common to find supposedly "ancient" rock formations resting in essential conformity on supposedly "young" formations. This is exactly contrary to the requirements of evolution, which would necessitate that the older rocks should be at the bottom.[6]

CIRCULAR REASONING

Geological dating is based on the circular argument that *rocks are dated by fossils and fossils are dated by rocks*. This, in turn, is based on three primary assumptions, each of which is an example of begging the question:

1. Lower rocks are older than higher rocks.
2. Simpler fossils are older than more complex fossils.
3. Complex forms evolved from simpler forms.

Here are the questions that are begged:

First, are lower rocks really older than higher ones?

Second, are simpler fossils really older than more complex ones?

Third, did complex forms really evolve from simpler ones?

No proof is given for any of these assumptions, which are used in an argument that goes something like this:

> We know that lower strata are older because they contain simpler fossils. We know that simpler fossils are older because they evolved earlier. We know they evolved earlier because they are found in lower strata. We know that lower strata are older because they contain simpler fossils. Etc.

The supposed ages of rocks (millions of years within/between each strata) are in turn determined by the type of fossils they contain. Here the reasoning goes like this:

> Simpler fossils are millions of years older than more complex fossils because these long periods of time are required for evolutionary changes to take place. Since simpler fossils are found in lower strata, these strata must be millions of years older than higher strata.

> How do we know that evolution requires millions of years (i.e., what physical evidence do we have that this is true)? We know it because simpler fossils are found in lower strata and lower strata must be millions of years older than higher strata because it takes that long for higher forms to evolve.

Therefore, fossils are dated by rocks and rocks are dated by fossils.

Every one of the statements involved in this tangle of circular argument is an example of begging the question. That is, no real evidence is given that any of them is true. Rather, it is a series of interlocking assumptions, each of which is based on a previous assumption and each of which is assumed to be true simply because it is asserted to be true. The total series of unproven assumptions goes something like this:

Assumption One: Millions of years are required for the evolutionary transformation of one fossil form (species/kind) into another.

Assumption Two: Simple forms are less evolved than complex forms.

Assumption Three: Simpler forms are older than complex forms.

Assumption Four: Simpler forms are found in older strata of rock.

Assumption Five: Lower strata are older than higher strata.

Assumption Six: Lower strata must be much older because they contain simpler forms.

Assumption Seven: Evolution must be true because simpler forms appear in lower strata.

There is no actual scientific evidence here that complex forms evolved from simpler forms, that millions of years are required, or that lower strata is much older than higher strata. These ideas, which are stated as facts, are really only the presuppositions of those making the statements. Morris succinctly summarizes the issue:

. . . at least two important questions must be satisfactorily answered before it can legitimately be concluded that the theory of evolution is the best explanation for the fossil record. One question is : "Are the ages of the rocks determinable independently of the theory of evolution which is supposed to be deduced from their fossil contents?" The other is: "Is the theory of evolution the *only* theory which can satisfactorily explain the fossil data?" Both of these questions must be answered in the affirmative if we should be expected to accept the fossils as real *proof* of evolution. But, as a matter of fact, both questions must really be answered in the negative.[7]

Statistical Impossibility and Intelligent Design (Irreducible Complexity)

Perhaps the most damning evidence against the theory of evolution is the simple fact that it is statistically impossible and therefore the life forms that exist must have been created by an intelligent designer. The fact of intelligent design is apparent in the irreducible complexity of interlocking systems present in all life forms. This truth is proven by the following scientific facts (among many others):

- The synchronization process required for the functioning of biological organisms is far too complex to have happened by chance.
- The genetic coding of DNA is far too complex to have happened by random, natural processes.

- Enzymes (components of cells) are much too complex to have occurred by chance.
- The probability of all the elements of a single protein molecule (required for organic life) coming together by chance is far too small.
- The development of millions of distinct species purely by chance is far too complex.
- The universe is not old enough for life to have developed by random processes.

Let's examine each of these in a little more detail.

THE SYNCHRONIZATION PROCESS

Evolution cannot account for the incredibly complex synchronization process needed for any one of many aspects of organized life. Let's take three examples: the egg, the eye, and human speech. Each of these requires all of its basic components to be in place in order to function. That is, its complex structure cannot be reduced to simpler components without destroying it. It involves irreducible complexity.

THE EGG

The formation of a bird's egg is an amazingly complex process. First, the calcium needed for the egg shell must be extracted from the bird's bones. Then it must be formed into a covering of exactly the right size, shape, and thickness to permit the egg to be laid, to protect the chick, and to allow the chick to hatch. This process not only provides the protective covering but also the source of calcium needed by the embryo and the membrane through which it breathes.

Just as evolution cannot account for this process, neither can it account for the astoundingly complex process required to produce a living embryo from a fertilized egg. Hanegraaff notes that a fertilized human egg, for example, "is among the most organized, complex structures in the universe. . . . A single fertilized egg (zygote), the size of a pinhead, contains chemical instructions that would fill more than 500,000 printed pages."[8]

THE EYE

For the eye to work, an incredibly complex number of integrated systems must first be in place. For example, the eye socket with its musculature must be present along with the eyelids, tear ducts, corneal lens system, retina, optic nerve, and the visual brain center. Here are some of the details of these interlocking systems:

> [The eye consists] of a ball with a lens on one side and a light-sensitive retina made up of rods and cones inside the other. The lens itself has a sturdy protective covering called a cornea and sits over an iris designed to protect the eye from excessive light. The eye contains a fantastic watery substance that is replaced every four hours, while tear glands continuously flush the outside clean. In addition, an eyelid sweeps secretions over the cornea to keep it moist, and eyelashes protect it from dust.
>
> It is one thing to stretch credulity by suggesting that the complexities of the eye evolved by chance; it is quite another to surmise that the

eye could have evolved in concert with the myriad other coordinated functions. As a case in point, extraordinarily tuned muscles surround the eye for precision mobility and shape the lens for the function of focus.

Additionally, consider the fact that as you read this document, a vast number of impulses are traveling from your eyes through millions of nerve fibers that transmit information to a complex computing center in the brain called the visual cortex. Linking the visual information from the eyes to motor centers in the brain is crucial in coordinating a vast number of bodily functions that are axiomatic to the very process of daily living. Without the coordinated development of the eye and the brain in a synergistic fashion, the isolated developments themselves become meaningless and counterproductive.[9]

THE SPEECH CHAIN

A similar synchronization of systems had to first be in place for the human speech process to work. When I was doing graduate work for my degree in applied linguistics, we studied the human "speech chain," as it is called. In some ways it is even more complex than the process of human vision. If we add the neural and cerebral functions required to learn and use a language, the complexities become even more staggering.

Here, in extremely abbreviated form, are the basic parts of the speech chain, which must **all** be in

place and fully functioning before speech communication can take place:

FOR SPEECH PRODUCTION AND TRANSMISSION
  1. The lungs and breathing system
  2. The vocal cords
  3. The mouth, tongue, lips, and nasal passages
  4. The brain centers of the speaker which form
     ideas and encode them according to a pho-
     netic system of meaningful sounds (pho-
     nemes), which are in turn organized into
     phoneme combinations (morphemes),
     which are in turn combined into a grammati-
     cal code of morpheme combinations
     (words), and word combinations (sen-
     tences), all of which are assigned specific
     meanings according to semantic principles.

FOR SPEECH RECEPTION AND COMPREHENSION
  5. The outer ear, including the outer antenna
     (which picks up speech vibrations transmit-
     ted through the air and sends them to the
     eardrum) and the eardrum itself (which
     converts the sonic vibrations into mechani-
     cal movement).
  6. The inner ear, where the movements of the
     eardrum activate complex mechanical and
     neural processes which in turn send elec-
     tronic impulses to the brain.
  7. The brain center of the hearer which dis-
     criminates between various frequency bands
     in order to recognize them as discrete pho-

nemes and then decode the grammatical and semantic codes into which these had been previously arranged by the speaker.

All of the elements in the speech chain are, in fact, fantastically more complex than this gross oversimplification would suggest. Yet we are asked by the evolutionists to believe that all of these elements developed and were synchronized simultaneously *by accident* so that human utterance could take place and eventually speech communication could develop! I don't know what the statistical probability is of all of this happening by accidental mutations or other processes operating by random chance. But I'm confident that it is so improbable that the earth is not nearly old enough to have allowed sufficient time for it to have happened. In other words, it is impossible. Or, as mathematician Emil Borel puts it, speaking of the laws of probability, "events whose probabilities are extremely small never occur."[10] Scientists generally agree that any event with a probability of less than 1 in 10^{50} is impossible.

DNA CODING

The genetic coding of DNA is even more complex than the speech chain, for it controls the development of the speech chain as well as all the other innumerable systems and characteristics of the human body. According to genetics experts Radman and Wagner, "The set of genetic instructions for humans is roughly three billion letters long."[11] This is far too complex to have been produced by chance. In fact, evolutionist scientists, according to researcher and author Luther Sutherland, "are stating that *new natural laws* will need to be discovered to explain how the high degree of order and specificity of even a single cell [which contains our DNA strands] could be generated by random natural processes."[12] In other words, *there are no known scientific laws which could account for the evolutionary development of DNA.* This one fact clearly shows that evolution is a concept which has been developed independently from real scientific principles and in fact has no scientific basis whatsoever.

ENZYMES

Even the complexity of enzymes, which are protein-like components of cells essential to life, are far too complex to have developed by chance. On this basis, the late Fred Hoyle and N. Chandra Wickramasinghe (both well-known and highly regarded scientists) have concluded that

> . . . life cannot have had a random beginning. . . . The trouble is that there are about two thousand enzymes, and the chance of obtaining them all in a random trial is only one part in . . . $10^{40,000}$ [the figure 1 with 40,000 zeros after it], an outrageously small probability that could not be faced even if the whole universe consisted of organic soup. . . . For life to have originated on the Earth, it would be necessary that quite explicit instructions should have been provided for its assembly.[13]

This means that, for the first enzymes to have formed, instructions in the DNA code would already have had to exist, and for DNA—which is much more complex than an enzyme—to have developed by evolution is impossible.

THE PROTEIN MOLECULE

The same conditions that apply to enzymes also apply to proteins, but here the numbers are even more staggering. Protein molecules are the basic building blocks of living organisms. They would have had to exist before the first living organisms could have emerged, according to evolutionary theory. As molecular biologist James F. Coppedge explains, ". . . postulating a primordial sea with every single component necessary, and speeding up the rate of bonding a trillion times":

> The probability of a single protein molecule being arranged by chance is 1 in 10^{161}, using all atoms on earth and allowing all the time since the world began. . . . *For a minimum set of the required 239 protein molecules for the smallest theoretical life, the probability is 1 in $10^{119,879}$.* It would take $10^{119,841}$ years on the average to get a set of such proteins. *That is $10^{119,831}$ times the assumed age of the earth* and is a figure with 119,831 zeros.[14] [Emphasis added.]

DISTINCT SPECIES

Mathematician and researcher I. L. Cohen has determined the statistical impossibility that evolution could have produced all the species of life on earth:

> Mathematically speaking, based on probability concepts, there is no possibility that evolution was the mechanism that created the approximately 6,000,000 species of plants and animals we recognize today.[15]

Hoyle originated the well-known analogy which illustrates this impossibility. He said that to suppose the first cell originated by chance is like believing "a tornado sweeping through a junk yard might assemble a Boeing 747 from the materials therein." According to Taylor, many, and perhaps most, researchers who study the origins of life now agree with Hoyle: "Life could not have originated by chance or by any known natural processes."[16]

AGE OF THE UNIVERSE

In the approximately eighteen billion years that evolutionists claim the universe has existed, there has not been enough time for evolution to have produced life. The odds that life could have been formed by natural processes has been calculated by Hoyle and Wickramasinghe. They estimate that

> there is less than 1 chance in $10^{40,000}$ that life could have originated by random trials. . . . even if nature could somehow have produced trillions of genetic code combinations every second for 30 billion years, the probabilities against producing the simplest one-celled ani-

mal by trial and error would still be inconceiv-
ably immense.[17]

Occam's Razor

In order to counter all such negative evidence
as that listed above, evolutionists must continually come up with modifications and additional
assumptions to bolster their theory. In doing this,
they are violating a long standing principle used
by scientists in judging the validity of a theory.
This is called Occam's Razor, a rule which says
that the simplest explanation is the best and that
one should avoid the unnecessary multiplication
of hypotheses to explain any phenomenon. But
this is exactly what evolutionists do. Morris provides the following example:

> In order to account for [the] numerous excep-
> tions to the supposed universal order of evolu-
> tionary development as revealed in the
> fossiliferous rocks, theory has to be piled on top
> of theory. Thus, the missing ages indicated by a
> disconformity are explained by a supposed re-
> gional uplift followed by a horizontal thrust fault
> followed by a period of erosion. And so forth.

> . . . It becomes obvious that the theory of evo-
> lution does not really provide a very simple and
> satisfactory framework for the correlation of the
> data of paleontology. . . . There are so many
> problems involved that subsidiary theories con-
> tinually have to be appended to it in order to
> explain the exceptions and contradictions.[18]

588	The Spiritual Discernment Guide

Another example of the addition of subsidiary theories is one called "punctuated equilibrium." This was invented to supposedly account for the synchronization of systems required for such functions as human sight and speech. We were taught this modification in graduate school to put to rest questions about how speech synchronization was possible by means of evolution. Punctuated equilibrium states that evolution is not necessarily always a gradual process of transformation based on natural selection and survival of the fittest. Rather, for some reason as yet not understood, sudden leaps in evolution occasionally take place (when a species is under conditions of unusual stress) in which entire integrated systems suddenly appear, thereby permitting amazingly rapid advances in the evolutionary process.

Rather than recognizing and admitting the obvious impossibility of such things, diehard evolutionists, in defiance of the Occam's Razor principle, invent unproven, unexplained adjustments to their theory to avoid the unthinkable—that they are wrong and therefore that there must have been a Creator!

Other Scientific Reasons That Evolution Is Not True

In addition to the important reasons given above, there are many other scientific proofs that evolution is a lie. Among them are the following, which are given here for your consideration but which we do not have space to examine in detail:

- Transitional forms would have a survival *disadvantage*.
- Mutations do *not* produce improvement.
- Natural selection does *not* produce new species.
- The fossil record shows *only* distinct forms. *No* truly transitional forms have ever been found.
- Forms thought to be extinct have been found to exist and have not evolved.
- There is *no* evidence that evolution is taking place at the present time.

SUGGESTED READING LIST

Ankerberg, John, and John Weldon. *Darwin's Leap of Faith*. Harvest House, 1998.

Ashton, John F., Ph.D., ed. *In Six Days: Why Fifty Scientists Choose to Believe in Creation*. Master Books, 2000.

Brown, Walt. *In the Beginning: Compelling Evidence for Creation and the Flood*. 6th ed. Center for Scientific Creation, 1995.

Coppedge, James F. *Evolution: Possible or Impossible?* Probability Research In Molecular Biology, 1993.

Dembski, William A. *Intelligent Design: The Conflict Between Science and Theology*. InterVarsity Press, 1999.

Gish, Duane T. *Evolution: The Fossils Still Say No!* Institute for Creation Research, 1995.

Ham, Ken. *The Lie: Evolution. Genesis—The Key to Defending Your Faith*. Master Books, 1987.

Hanegraaff, Hank. *The FACE That Demonstrates the Farce of Evolution*. Word Publishing, 1998.

Huse, Scott M. *The Collapse of Evolution*, 2d ed. Baker Books, 1993.

Johnson, Phillip E. *Darwin on Trial*. InterVarsity Press, 1995.

Morris, Henry M. *Biblical Cosmology and Modern Science*. Craig Press, 1970.

_____. *Biblical Creationism: What Each Book of the Bible Teaches About Creation and the Flood*. Master Books, 2000.

_____. *Creation and the Modern Christian*. Master Books, 1995.

_____. *Scientific Creationism*. Public School ed. San Diego: C.L.P. Publishers, 1981.

_____. *The Twilight of Evolution*. Baker Book House, 1963.

Taylor, Paul S. *The Illustrated Origins Answer Book*. 4th ed. Eden Productions, 1993.

White, Dr. Joe and Dr. Nicholas Connellis. *Darwin's Demise: Why Evolution Can't Take The Heat*. Master Books, 2001.

Notes

INTRODUCTION:
THE THREAT OF SPIRITUAL DECEPTION

1. Walter Martin, *The New Age Cult* (Bethany House, 1989), p. 47.
2. Ibid., p. 48.
3. Ibid., p. 49.
4. Ibid., pp. 49–50.
5. Ibid., p. 50.
6. Ibid., p. 51.
7. Ibid., pp. 51–52.
8. David Wilkerson, *The Times Square Church Pulpit Series,* May 31, 1999, accompanying letter.
9. Ibid., p. 1.
10. Ibid., pp. 1–2.

11. Dave Hunt and T. A. McMahon, *The Seduction of Christianity: Spiritual Discernment in the Last Days* (Harvest House, 1985), p. 94.
12. Quoted in David Jeremiah, *Invasion of Other Gods* (Word Publishing, 1995), pp. 173–175.
13. Ibid., p. 173.
14. Ibid., p. 175.
15. Hunt, *Seduction*, p. 114.
16. Selwyn Hughes and Thomas Kinkade, *Every Day Light: Daily Inspirations* (Broadman and Holman, 1988), p. 23.
17. Rebecca Brown, M. D . . *He Came to Set the Captives Free* (Whitaker House, 1992), p. 31.
18. Douglas Groothius, *Unmasking the New Age* (InterVarsity Press, 1986), p. 34.
19. Ibid., p. 35.
20. NIV *Study Bible* (Zondervan, 1985), p. 808.
21. Martin, *Cult*, p. 108.
22. Hal Lindsay, *Planet Earth—2000 A. D : Will Mankind Survive?* (Western Front, 1996), pp. 37–38.

CHAPTER ONE:
SEED ONE—THE TEMPTATION OF POWER

1. Hunt, *Seduction*, back cover.
2. C. S. Lewis, *The Screwtape Letters* (Macmillan, 1961), pp. 115–116.
3. Hunt, *Seduction*, p. 211.
4. Ibid., p. 211–212.
5. Ibid., p. 212.

6. Ibid., p. 213.
7. John and Paula Sandford, *Healing the Wounded Spirit* (Victory House, 1985), pp. 294–295. The Sandfords have received negative criticism because of their former association with Agnes Sanford, who engaged in some mind science teachings (and who is probably the "teacher of healing" whom they refer to above). However, I have read the Sandfords' works carefully and found nothing unscriptural in them. In fact, their teaching appears to me to be soundly scriptural, and my wife and I have applied it in our own lives with beneficial results. Their negative press, I believe, is another instance of throwing out the baby with the bathwater, in this case, based on guilt by association.
8. Shirley Ann Miller, *Temperamysticism* (Starburst, 1991), pp. 56–59.
9. Ibid., pp. 56, 60–61, 62.
10. Ibid., pp. 58–62.
11. Peter and Paul Lalonde, *2000 A. D.: Are You Ready?* (Thomas Nelson, 1997), pp. 67–68.
12. Quoted in Hal Lindsay, *Planet Earth—2000 A. D.*, p. 41.
13. Lalonde, *2000 A. D.*, p. 52.
14. Ibid., p. 53.
15. Ibid., p. 61.
16. Hunt, *Seduction*, pp. 215–216.
17. Gary Demar and Peter Leithard, *The Reduction of Christianity* (Dominion Press, 1988), pp. xx, xxv.

18. Ibid., p. xxviii.

CHAPTER TWO:
SEED TWO—THE TEMPTATION OF WEALTH

1. Hunt, *Seduction,* pp. 150–151.
2. Quoted in ibid., pp. 156–157.
3. Ibid., p. 157.
4. Ibid., p. 20.

CHAPTER THREE:
SEED THREE—THE TEMPTATION OF STATUS

1. John Hagee, *Day of Deception* (Thomas Nelson, 1997), p. 220.

CHAPTER FOUR:
SEED FOUR—THE TEMPTATION OF HAPPINESS

1. Peter and Patti Lalonde, *The Edge of Time* (Harvest House, 1997), pp. 104–106.
2. Dave Hunt, *Occult Invasion* (Harvest House, 1998), pp. 102–104.
3. Lindsay, *Planet Earth,* p. 40.
4. Mikhail Gorbachev, *The Search for a New Beginning: Developing a New Civilization* (Harper, 1995), pp. 64–65.
5. Quoted in Lalonde, *The Edge*, pp. 108–111.

CHAPTER FIVE:
SEED FIVE—THE TEMPTATION OF HEALTH (HO-LISTIC MEDICINE)

1. John Ankerberg and John Weldon, *The Facts on Holistic Health and the New Medicine* (Harvest House, 1992), p. 6.
2. Ibid., p. 7.
3. James Strohecker, ed., *Alternative Medicine: The Definitive Guide* (Future Medicine Publishing, 1994), pp. 261, 450–459.
4. Alma E. Guinness, ed., *Family Guide to Natural Medicine* (The Reader's Digest Assoc., 1993), p. 237.
5. Ankerberg and Weldon, *Holistic Health*, pp. 46–47.
6. Ibid., p. 26.
7. Ibid.
8. Ibid., p. 28.
9. Ibid.
10. Ibid.
11. Ibid., p. 14.
12. Ibid., p. 13.
13. Ibid., p. 44
14. Ibid., p. 35.
15. Ibid., p. 43.
16. Ibid.
17. Ibid., p. 17.
18. Ibid.
19. Ibid., p. 24.

20. Ibid., pp. 3–4. These holistic systems are all described in this informative booklet.

CHAPTER SIX:
GOD'S PLAN

1. John Hagee, *Day of Deception*, pp. 222–223.

CHAPTER SEVEN:
SATAN'S STRATEGIES AND TRICKS

1. Quoted in Hank Hanegraaff, *Christianity in Crisis* (Harvest House, 1997), p. 65.
2. Ibid., p. 66.
3. Ibid., pp. 66, 67.
4. George Ricker Berry, Ph. D., *The Interlinear Literal Translation of the Greek New Testament* (Zondervan, 1958), p. 577.
5. W. E. Vine, *Expository Dictionary of New Testament Words* (Fleming H. Revel Co., 1940), p. 225.
6. Ibid., p. 71.
7. Hanegraaff, *Christianity*, p. 69.
8. Ibid., pp. 61–62.
9. Hunt, *Seduction*, p. 222.
10. M. Scott Peck, *The Road Less Traveled* (Simon and Schuster, 1978), pp. 269–270.
11. Hunt, *Seduction*, pp. 222–223.
12. "Touched by an Angel," CBS, May 21, 2000.
13. Hunt, *Seduction*, p. 177.
14. Ibid., p. 179.
15. Ibid., p. 180.

16. Ibid., pp. 83–84.
17. Ibid., pp. 82–83.
18. Ibid., p. 84.
19. Ibid.
20. *Webster's New World Dictionary of the American Language* (William Collins Publishers, 1979), p. 417.
21. Quoted in Hanegraaff, *Christianity*, p. 85.
22. Hunt, *Seduction,* p. 201.
23. Ibid.
24. Quoted in Hanegraaff, *Christianity,* p. 98.
25. Ibid.
26. Ibid., pp. 99–101.
27. Walter Martin, *The New Age Cult* (Bethany House, 1988), p. 87.
28. Vine, *Expository*, p. 41.
29. Martin, *Cult*, pp. 89–90.
30. James Strong, *Strong's Exhaustive Concordance: Compact Edition* (Guardian Press, 1994), item 2377, p. 38.
31. Ibid., item 6544, p. 97.
32. Earl D. Radmacher, Th. D., ed., et al, *Nelson's New Illustrated Bible Commentary* (Thomas Nelson Publishers, 1999), p. 776.
33. Quoted in Hanegraaff, *Christianity*, p. 170.
34. Ibid., p. 171.
35. Bill Volkman, *The Wink of Faith: Living "As Gods" Without Denying Our Humanity* (Union Life, 1983), p. 85.
36. NIV, pp. 873–874, study notes on Psalm 82: 1 and 82:6.

CHAPTER EIGHT:
THE NEW AGE, ANTI-CHRISTIAN CONSPIRACY

1. John Ankerberg and John Weldon, *Facts on the New Age Movement* (Harvest House, 1988), p. 220.
2. Ibid., p. 7.
3. Ibid.
4. Walter Martin, *The New Age Cult* (Bethany House, 1988), p. 18.
5. Ibid., pp. 130–131.
6. Dave Hunt and T. A. McMahon, *America: The Sorcerer's New Apprentice* (Harvest House, 1988), p. 11.
7. Bernard Ward, *Think Yourself Well* (Globe Communications Corp., 1995), front cover.
8. Ibid., p. 7.
9. Ibid., p. 22.
10. Ibid., p. 7.
11. Ibid., pp. 7–8.
12. Johanna Michaelson, *The Beautiful Side of Evil* (Harvest House, 1982), p. 75.
13. Martin, *Cult*, p. 21.
14. Texe Marrs, *Dark Secrets of the New Age* (Crossway Books, 1987), p. 12.
15. Ibid., pp. 16–17.
16. Martin, *Cult*, p. 132.
17. Marrs, *Dark Secrets*, p. 206.
18. Ibid., pp. 217–224.
19. Ankerberg and Weldon, *New Age*, pp. 24–25.
20. Ibid.

21. *Webster's New World Dictionary*, p. 1063.
22. Marrs, *Dark Secrets*, p. 206.
23. Ibid.
24. Ibid., p. 207.
25. Ibid., pp. 207–209.
26. Quoted in ibid., pp. 208–209.
27. Ibid., pp. 207, 210–211.
28. LaVedi Laffery and Bud Hollowell, *The Eternal Dance,* (n.p., n.d.), p. 172. Quoted in Marrs, p. 207.
29. John G. Bennet, *The Masters of Wisdom* (England: Turnstone Press, Ltd., 1980), p. 74. Quoted in Marrs, p. 211. The Gospel of Mark was missing in this passage as quoted.
30. Marrs, *Dark Secrets*, p. 158.
31. Ibid., pp. 204–205.
32. Ibid., p. 94.
33. Hunt, *America*, p. 287.
34. David Spangler, *Revelation: The Birth of a New Age,* (The Lorian Press, 1976), pp. 163, 164.
35. Ibid., p. 61.
36. Martin, *Cult*, p. 41.
37. Spangler, *Revelation*, p. 39.
38. John Randolph Price, *The Planetary Commission* (Quartus Books, 1984), pp. 163–164.
39. Brad Steiger, *Gods of Aquarius* (New York, 1976), p. 222.
40. Marrs, *Dark Secrets*, p. 20.
41. Ibid., p. 170. The quotations are from Vera Alder, *When Humanity Comes of Age* (Samuel Weiser, 1974), pp. 20–24.

42. Quoted in Marrs, *Dark Secrets,* p. 38.
43. Ibid.
44. Ibid., pp. 39–40.
45. Oliver North and Thomas Jacobson, "A lame duck's shameful deed in the dark of night," *The Washington Times Weekly Edition*, January 15–21, 2001.
46. "Bush to 'unsign' treaty creating international criminal tribunal," *Arizona Daily Star,* May 5, 2002, p. A9.

CHAPTER NINE:
THE MASTER NEW AGE DELUSION—HOW EVOLUTION UNDERMINES THE CHRISTIAN FAITH

1. Henry M. Morris, *The Twilight of Evolution* (Baker Book House, 1963), p. 75.
2. Ibid., p. 76.
3. Hank Hanegraaff, *The Face That Demonstrates the Farce of Evolution* (Word Publishing, 1988), pp. 102–103.
4. Dave Hunt, *The Berean Call*, May 2001, p. 3.
5. C. S. Lewis, *Mere Christianity* (Fontana Books, 1952), p. 62.
6. Ibid., p. 60.
7. Hugh Ross, *The Fingerprint of God* (Whitaker House, 1989), p. 185.
8. Ibid., p. 107, footnote.
9. Ibid., p. 163, footnote.
10. Paul S. Taylor, *The Illustrated Origins Answer Book* (Eden Productions, 1991), p. 49.

11. Henry M. Morris, Ph. D., ed., *Scientific Creationism*, (Creation Life Publishers, 1947), p. 247.
12. Ibid., pp. 243–244.
13. Ibid., p. 244.
14. Quoted in Morris, *Twilight*, p. 24.
15. Ibid., p. 5.
16. Ibid., pp. 5–6.
17. Ibid., pp. 20–21.
18. Ibid.
19. Taylor, *Origins*, p. 24.
20. James Strong, *Strong's Exhaustive Concordance: Compact Edition* (Guardian Press, 1994), item 4327, p. 65.
21. Morris, *Scientific*, p. 217.
22. Duane T. Gish, *Evolution The Fossils Say No!* (Creation Life Publishers, 1973), p. 13.
23. Quoted in Hanegraaff, *The Face*, pp. 102–103.
24. Morris, *Scientific*, pp. 218–220.

CHAPTER TEN:
EVOLUTION AND SATAN'S TRICKS (LIES, LOGICAL FALLACIES, AND SEMANTIC MANIPULATION)

1. Gish, *Evolution*, p. 42.
2. Ibid., p. 41.
3. Henry M. Morris, *Biblical Cosmology and Modern Science* (Craig Press, 1970), p. 22.
4. Ibid., p. 58.
5. Ibid., pp. 58–59.

6. Ibid., p. 62.
7. Some of the most important of these proof texts and the errors involved are the following: (1) Genesis 1:28, mistranslation: Hebrew *male* (be filled) is translated "replenish." (2) Isaiah 24:1, ignoring the context: "The Lord maketh the earth empty" is a prophecy of judgment, not a description of a pre-Adamic cataclysm. (3) 2 Corinthians 4:6, shifting meaning: The meaning of "darkness" is shifted from spiritual darkness to physical darkness. (4) Matthew 13:35, mistranslation: The word "foundation" (Greek *katabole*) in "foundation of the world" is made to mean "casting down."
8. Morris, *Scientific,* p. 249.
9. Morris, *Biblical*, p. 67.
10. Taylor, *Origins*, p. 5.
11. Morris, *Scientific*, p. 218.
12. Ross, *Fingerprint*, p. 68.
13. Ibid., p. 57.
14. Taylor, *Origins*, p. 6.
15. Morris, *Twilight*, p. 57.
16. Ross, *Fingerprint*, p. 145.
17. Ibid., p. 152, footnote.
18. Morris, *Scientific*, p. 210.
19. Taylor, *Origins*, p. 13.
20. Ibid.
21. Quoted in ibid.
22. Ross, *Fingerprint*, p. 144.
23. Ibid., p. 141.

24. Ibid., p. 146.
25. Ibid., p. 141.
26. Ibid., p. 148.
27. Ibid., pp. 148–149.
28. Ibid., p. 159.
29. Ibid., p. 160.
30. Quoted in Taylor, *Origins*, p. 13.
31. Ibid., pp. 13–20.
32. Ibid., p. 14.
33. Ibid.
34. Ibid., pp. 14–15.
35. Ibid., p. 15.
36. Ibid.
37. Ibid., p. 17.
38. Ibid.
39. Morris, *Biblical*, p. 57.
40. Ibid.
41. Morris, *Scientific*, pp. 143–144.
42. Ibid. (See Exodus 31:17; Joshua 24:2; 2 Kings 19:2; 2 Chronicles 1:1–28; Nehemiah 9:6; Job 9:5–9, 12:15, 16:7–13, 31:33, 38:4–7, etc.; Psalms 8:3–8, 29:104, 33.6–9, 90.2, 3, 148.1–5; Proverbs 8:22–31; Matthew 19:3–6, 23:35, 24:37–42; Mark 10:2–9, 13:19; Luke 11:51, 17:26–27; John 8:44; Romans 5:12–19, etc.)
43. Morris, *Twilight*, pp. 81–83.

CHAPTER ELEVEN:
FALSE TEACHINGS FROM SECULAR PSYCHOLOGY

1. Dave Hunt and T. A. McMahon, *The Seduction of Christianity* (Harvest House, 1985), p. 90.

2. Ibid., pp. 114–120.
3. Dave Hunt, *The Berean Call*, August 1999, p. 3.
4. Hunt, *Seduction*, p. 194.
5. Ron Carlson and Ed Decker, *Fast Facts on False Teachings* (Harvest House, 1994), p. 140.
6. Hunt, *Seduction*, p. 57.
7. Ibid. The quotation is from Alan Watts, *This Is It* (n.p., n.d.), p. 90.
8. Ibid., p. 70.
9. Ibid., p. 114.
10. Ibid., p. 192.
11. Ibid., p. 193.
12. James Dobson, *Hide or Seek* (Revel, 1974), pp. 12–13.
13. Hunt, *Seduction*, p. 193.
14. Zig Ziglar, *See You at the Top* (Pelican, 1975), pp. 84, 88.

CHAPTER TWELVE:
FALSE CHARISMATIC TEACHINGS

1. Quoted in Hank Hanegraaff, *Christianity in Crisis* (Harvest House, 1997), p. 116.
2. Quoted in James W. Sire, *Scripture Twisting* (InterVarsity Press, 1980), p. 52.
3. Hanegraaff, *Christianity*, p. 87.
4. Ibid., pp. 90–91.
5. Larry Hutton, *God, The Gold and the Glory* (Harrison House, 1999), pp. 13–16.

6. Ibid., pp. 16–27.
7. Ibid.
8. Ibid., p. 32.
9. Ibid., pp. 32–34.
10. Ibid., pp. 35–36.
11. Ibid., p. 37.
12. Ibid., pp. 46–47.
13. Ibid., p. 46.
14. Form letter signed "Pastor Bob Tilton," undated, p. 1.
15. Ibid., p. 3.
16. Quoted in Agnes C. and John W. Lawless, *Drift Into Deception* (Kregel Resources, 1995), p. 80.
17. Carlson and Decker, *Fast Facts*, pp. 194–200.
18. *The NIV Study Bible* (Zondervan, 1985), p. 1428, study note.
19. Ibid.
20. Bruce Wilkinson, *The Prayer of Jabez: Breaking Through to the Blessed Life* (Multnomah Publishers, 2000), back cover.
21. Ibid.
22. Ibid., pp. 31, 10, 30, 24–25, 43.
23. Ibid., pp. 40–41.
24. Ibid., p. 63.
25. Ibid., pp. 68–69.
26. Ibid., pp. 70–71, 73, 74, 76–77, 90, 91.
27. Ibid., p. 82.
28. Ibid., pp. 86–87.
29. Ibid., p. 84.

CHAPTER THIRTEEN:
FALSE ANTI-CHARISMATIC TEACHINGS

1. "Baptism in the Holy Spirit: What Is the Baptism in the Holy Spirit?" The Christian Broadcasting Network, 1998, webpage: **http://www.cbn.org**.
2. Quoted in Lawless and Lawless, p. 146.
3. Ken Walker, "Shaking Southern Baptist Tradition," *Chrisma and Christian Life,* March 1999, p. 70.
4. Ibid., p. 71.
5. Ibid., p. 72.
6. *The NIV Study Bible*, p. 1752, study note.
7. Earl D. Radmacher, Th. D., et al, eds. *Nelson's New Illustrated Bible Commentary* (Thomas Nelson, 1999), p. 1482.
8. Mark Havelle, et al., *The Signs and Wonders Movement—Exposed* (Day One, 1997), p. 59.
9. Software Development Corporation, Internet document (Angels (Wm31.html), 1999).
10. Various broadcasts of "The Bible Answerman" program.

CHAPTER FOURTEEN:
FALSE TEACHINGS FROM HUMANISM

1. Quoted in *The Biblion Bible Expositor*, 23, no. 5.
2. Quoted in Carlson and Decker, *Fast Facts*, p. 31.

3. Dave Hunt and T. A. McMahon, *The Seduction of Christianity* (Harvest House, 1985), p. 11.

4. David Wilkerson, *A Prophecy Wall of Fire* (World Challenge, Inc., n.d.), pamphlet.

5. Robert Schuller, *Living Positively One Day at a Time* (Revel, 1981), p. 201.

6. "Religious Showmanship." *Time*, March 18, 1985, p. 70.

7. Hunt, *Seduction*, p. 16.

8. Hunt, *The Berean Call*, June 2001, p. 4.

9. Ibid.

10. Wilkerson, *Times Square Pulpit Series*, January 15, 1999, pp. 2–3.

11. Ibid., p. 2.

12. Ibid.

13. Wilkerson, *Times Square*, February 15, 1999, pp. 2–3.

14. Ibid., p. 4.

15. Wilkerson, *Times Square*, March 20, 2000, p. 2.

16. Quoted in Hunt, *The Berean Call*, May 2001, p. 1.

17. Hunt, *Occult Invasion* (Harvest House, 1998), p. 100.

18. Ibid., p. 576.

19. Ibid.

20. Quoted in Hunt, *The Berean Call*, October 2000, p. 3.

21. Hank Hanegraaff, *The Christian Research Report*, vol. 14, no. 1, February 1, 2001, p. 4.

22. Cornelia Fereira, "The one-world church emerges," *Homiletics and Pastoral Review*, vol. 99, no. 4, January 1999, pp. 6–15.

23. Tim LeHaye and Jerry Jenkins, *Are We Living in the End Times?* (Tyndale House, 1999), p. 176.

24. Hunt, *The Berean Call*, February 2000, p. 2.

25. Quoted in ibid.

26. Ibid., p. 1.

27. Quoted in ibid.

28. Quoted in ibid., p. 2.

29. Hunt, *Occult*, pp. 101–102.

30. Ibid., p. 102.

31. Quoted in ibid., p. 2.

32. Ibid., p. 104.

33. Ibid., p. 547.

34. Quoted in ibid., p. 547.

35. Ibid.

36. Quoted in ibid., p. 548.

37. Ibid.

38. Tim LeHaye and Jerry B. Jenkins, *Are We Living in the End Times?* (Tyndale House Publishers, 1999), p. 68.

39. Ibid., p. 77.

40. Hunt, *The Berean Call*, August 2000, pp. 1–2.

41. Ibid., p. 1.

42. Quoted in ibid., p. 2

43. Hunt, *The Berean Call*, May 2001, p. 3.

44. Ibid.

45. Ibid., p. 1.

CHAPTER FIFTEEN:
INFILTRATION BY EASTERN RELIGIONS

1. James Hewitt, *The Complete Yoga Book* (Schocken Books, 1977), p. 461.
2. Mara Carrico, *Yoga Journal's Yoga Basics* (Henry Holt, 1997), p. 63.
3. Ibid., p. xiii.
4. Ibid., p. 61.
5. Hewitt, *Complete Yoga*, p. 379.
6. Ibid., p. 4.
7. Carrico, *Yoga Basics*, p. 4.
8. Hewitt, *Complete Yoga*, p. 8.
9. Carrico, *Yoga Basics*, p. 4.
10. Hewitt, *Complete Yoga*, pp. 422, 425.
11. Carrico, *Yoga Basics*, p. 23.
12. Ibid., p. 22.
13. Hewitt, *Complete Yoga*, p. 493; James Redfield, *The Celestine Vision*, (Warner Books, 1997), p. 56.
14. Waysun Liao, *The Essence of T'ai Chi* (Shambhala, 1995), p. 34.
15. Ibid., pp. 13, 20.
16. Paul Compton, *The Art of Tai Chi* (Element, 1993), pp. 25, 19, 13.
17. Ibid., pp. 3, 7, 10.
18. Liao, *The Essence*, p. 19.
19. Crompton, *The Art*, p. 24.
20. Ibid., pp. 19, 8, 4, 24.
21. Ibid., p. 25.
22. Ibid., p. 19.

23. Ibid., p. 14.
24. Ibid., p. 4.
25. Liao, *The Essence,* p. 131.
26. Ibid., p. 142.
27, Ibid., p. 146.
28. Ibid., p. 60.
29. Ibid., . 147.
30. Redfield, p. 56.
31. Ibid., p. 92.
32. Ibid., p.98.
33. This discussion of ki is my own synthesis of information derived from a number of sources about the martial arts.

CHAPTER SIXTEEN:
INFILTRATION BY OCCULTISM—SATANISM IN THE CHURCH

1. Douglas R. Groothius, *Unmasking the New Age* (InterVarsity Press, 1986), pp. 159–160.
2. Rebecca Brown, M.D., *He Came to Set the Captives Free* (Whitaker House, 1992), p. 47.
3. Ibid., p. 233.
4. Ibid., p. 77.
5. Ibid., pp. 234–245.
6. Ibid., pp. 137–138.
7. Ibid., p. 136.
8. Ibid., pp. 145–146.
9. Steve Bonta, "Is It Only Rock 'n' Roll?" *The New American*, April 8, 2002, pp. 10–17.
10. Ibid., pp. 11, 13.
11. Ibid., p. 17.

12. Ibid., p. 16.
13. Steve Bonta, "Morality of Music," *The New American*, April 8, 2002, p. 20.
14. Brown, *He Came*, p. 138.
15. Ibid., pp. 170–171.
16. Ibid., p. 89.
17. Ibid., p. 158.
18. Ibid., p. 189.
19. Ibid. pp. 200–201.
20. Ibid., p. 212.
21. Ibid., pp. 212–213.
22. Ibid., p. 235.
23. Ibid., p. 245.

CHAPTER SEVENTEEN:
INFILTRATION BY OCCULTISM—ALTERED STATES OF CONSCIOUSNESS IN THE CHURCH (THE CELEBRATION OF DISCIPLINE)

1. Richard Foster, *The Celebration of Discipline* (Harper and Row, 1978), pp. 15, 17, 18, 19).
2. Ibid., p. 15.
3. Ibid., p. 21.
4. Ibid., p. 22.
5. Ibid., pp. 24–25.
6. Ibid., p. 25.
7. Ibid., pp. 25–26.
8. Ibid., p. 27.
9. Ibid., p. 17.
10. Ibid., p. 28.
11. James Redfield, *The Celestine Vision: Living the New Spiritual Awareness* (Warner Books,

1997), p. 147.
12. Foster, pp. 35, 36.
13. Ibid., p. 34.
14. Ibid.
15. Ibid., p. 36.
16. Ibid.
17. Ibid., p. 37.
18. Ibid., pp. 38 ff.
19. Ibid., p. 40.
20. Ibid.
21. Ibid, p. 40.
22. Ibid., p. 40.
23. Ibid.
24. Ibid., p. 139.
25. Ibid., p. 142.
26. Ibid., p. 147.
27. Ibid., p. 148.
28. Earl D. Radmacher, Th. D., et al, eds. *Nelson's New Illustrated Bible Commentary* Thomas Nelson Publishers, 1999), p. 260.

CHAPTER EIGHTEEN:
INFILTRATION BY OCCULTISM—
NEW AGE GNOSTICISM IN THE CHURCH
(THE CELESTINE PROPHECY)

1. James Redfield, *The Celestine Prophecy: An Adventure* (Satori Publications, 1993), p. 244.
2. James Redfield, *The Tenth Insight: Holding the Vision* (Warner Books, 1996), p. ix.
3. Redfield, *Prophecy*, p. 238.
4. Redfield, *Tenth*, p. 109.
5. Ibid., p. 110.

6. Ibid., pp. 108–109.
7. Redfield, *The Celestine Vision* (Warner Books, 1997), p. 143.
8. Redfield, *Prophecy*, pp. 238–239.
9. Redfield, *Vision,* p. 73.
10. Redfield, *Prophecy,* p. 245.
11. Redfield, *Vision*, p. 207.
12. Redfield, *Tenth*, p. 200.
13. Redfield, *Vision,* p. 209.
14. Ibid., p. 63.
15. Ibid., p. 88.
16. Ibid., p. 232.
17. Ibid., p. 222.
18. Ibid.
19. Ibid., p. 197.
20. Ibid., p. 199.
21. Redfield, *Tenth*, p. 147.
22. Redfield, *Vision*, p. 147.
23. *Nelson's*, p. 1174.
24. Redfield, *Prophecy*, p. 248.
25. Redfield, *Vision*, pp. 30–31.
26. Ibid., p. 121.
27. Redfield, *Prophecy*, p. 248.
28. Redfield, *Tenth*, p. 119.
29. Ibid., p. 211.
30. Redfield, *Vision,* pp. 26–27.
31. Ibid., p. 174.
32. Redfield, *Prophecy*, p. 248.
33. Redfield, *Tenth*, p. 245.
34. Ibid., p. 196.
35. Redfield, *Prophecy*, p. 248.

36. Redfield, *Vision*, p. 212.
37. Ibid., p. 196.
38. Ibid., p. 192.
39. Redfield, *Tenth*, p. 51.
40. Ibid., p. 202.
41. Ibid., pp. 120, 38, 96.
42. Redfield, *Prophecy*, p. 244.
43. Ibid., p. 245.
44. Redfield, *Tenth*, p. 175.
45. Ibid., pp. 250–252.
46. Ibid., p. 146.

CHAPTER NINETEEN:
CONCLUSION (SOME FINAL RECOMMENDATIONS AND REMINDERS)

1. *Times Square Church Pulpit Series*, 2–15–99, p. 4.

APPENDIX C:
EVOLUTION VERSUS CREATION—WHICH MODEL FITS THE FACTS?

1. C. S. Lewis, *Mere Christianity* (Fontana Books, 1952), pp. 26, 29, 32–33, 37.
2. *Webster's New World Dictionary of the American Language* (William Collins, 1979), p. 468.
3. Henry M. Morris, *The Twilight of Evolution* (Baker Book House, 1963), p. 52.
4. Ibid.

5. Information taken from the *Encyclopedia Britannica*, quoted in ibid.
6. Ibid., p. 53.
7. Ibid., p. 50.
8. Hank Hanegraaff, *The Face That Demonstrates the Farce of Evolution* (Word Publishing, 1998), pp. 66–67.
9. Ibid., pp. 62–63.
10. Quoted in Paul S. Taylor, *The Illustrated Origins Answer Book* (Eden Productions, 1991), p. 76.
11. Quoted in ibid.
12. Quoted in ibid.
13. Quoted in ibid., p. 77.
14. James F. Coppedge, *Evolution: Possible or Impossible?* (Probability Research In Molecular Biology, 1993), pp. 110, 114.
15. Quoted in Taylor, *Origins*, p. 24.
16. Quoted in ibid.
17. Ibid., pp. 23–24.
18. Morris, *Twilight*, pp. 54–55.

Index

To order additional copies of

the Spiritual
Discernment
Guide

Have your credit card ready and call:

1-877-421-READ (7323)

or please visit our web site at
www.pleasantword.com

Also available at: www.amazon.com

Printed in the United States
21961LVS00001B/1-21